At Whom Are We Laughing?

At Whom Are We Laughing?:
Humor in Romance Language Literatures

Edited by

Zenia Sacks DaSilva and Gregory M. Pell

CAMBRIDGE
SCHOLARS

PUBLISHING

At Whom Are We Laughing?: Humor in Romance Language Literatures,
Edited by Zenia Sacks DaSilva and Gregory M. Pell

This book first published 2013

Cambridge Scholars Publishing

12 Back Chapman Street, Newcastle upon Tyne, NE6 2XX, UK

British Library Cataloguing in Publication Data
A catalogue record for this book is available from the British Library

ISBN (10): 1-4438-4797-6, ISBN (13): 978-1-4438-4797-1

TABLE OF CONTENTS

Part III. Ah, Women! Oh, Women!

Part IV. The Enigmatic Wit of a World Renewed

V. Laughingstock

VI. Subtle, Seditious and Surreal

VII. I Laugh Only When It Hurts

VIII. What´s So Funny About Modern Times?

FOREWORD

At whom are we laughing? Several years ago the Hofstra University Cultural Center in Hempstead, New York, sponsored a multi-national gathering of scholars to explore this question, with specific focus on humor across the centuries in the literatures of Italy, France, Romania, and the Iberian peninsula with all its diaspora. During the three days and evenings of our discussions we were privileged to witness some seventy presentations, to view exhibits of art and to enjoy theatrical productions of comedic pieces from different times and places. From that conference arose the selected essays we now offer for your pleasure: 31 papers of varied thrust, some panoramic, some analytic, others purely interpretative, on divers and provocative aspects of humor that are little known to the general reader. They are divided here into eight sections: farce, social satire, the comic sense of the Renaissance, the female *persona*, stereotypes and other objects of derision, humor of the surreal, humor born of pain, and humor of modern day. Please note that we have made no attempt to order them chronologically, to group the themes by locale, or to interconnect the pieces except in the sense that they all reflect our universal need for laughter. Our goal has been only to present to you the articles we found most interesting and accessible and we trust that you will approve of our choices.

We would like to express our most heartfelt and sincere appreciation to President Stuart Rabinowitz and Provost Herman A. Berliner of Hofstra University, to Natalie Datlof, director, and Alexej Ugrinski of the Hofstra University Cultural Center, to Carol Koulikourdi and the editorial staff of Cambridge Scholars, and to you, who have just joined us in this venture.

And now, to read.

ZSD/ GMP

INTRODUCTION

Comedy is simply a funny way of being serious...
—Peter Ustinov

They say that laughter is a purely human phenomenon, so exclusively ours that we brook no intruders—except, of course, for the laughing hyena, the laughing jackass (officially known as the kookaburra bird of Australia), laughing *gas,* laughing *matters*, or the perennial laughing *stock.* But what is humor, that funny thing so varied in its colors and tones, so encompassing in its themes, so different from time to time and place to place? We know that its name came from way back then, when the world was still flat and the "humors" that controlled our temperaments could easily get out of whack. And when they did, our behavior became bizarre, unexpected, excessive. We were "out of order", we were unlike any other, and that was what made us laughable—as in the old Japanese joke about the field of flowers in which all the flowers were alike, except for one that was not.

Laughter. How can it be so innocent?

> When the voices of children are heard on the green,
> And laughing is heard on the hill,
> My heart is at rest within my breast
> And everything else is still. (William Blake)[1]

So ethereal?: "Humor is a prelude to faith, and laughter is the beginning of prayer." (Reinhold Niebuhr)[2] . . . And how can it be so cruel?: "I quickly laugh at everything, for fear of having to cry" (Pierre de Beaumarchais).[3] "And if I laugh at any mortal thing,/ 'Tis that I may not weep (Lord George Byron).[4]

---

[1] "Nurse's song," in *Songs of Innocence and Experience*. Whitefish (Montana): Kessinger Press, 2010: 19.
[2] "Discerning the Signs of the Times," in *The Essential Reinhold Niebuhr: Selected Essays and Addresses*. Robert McAfee Brown, ed. New Haven (CT): Yale University Press, 1987: 49.
[3] *Le Barbier de Seville*, 1775, Act I, Scene ii.
[4] *Don Juan*, 1821. Canto IV, stanza 4.

Aristotle said that tragedy portrays us as better than we are and humor portrays us as worse. Still (they say he said) we laugh, for humans are the only animals capable of laughter. To which the late French philosopher Henri Bergson retorted, somewhat belatedly, that humans are the only animals that are capable of being laughed at. Laughter, he says, is not a sign of happiness. It is in fact an absence of all sentiment and "the comic demands ... a momentary anesthesia of the heart."[5]

Innocent? Ethereal? Cruel? ... Enough! Voltaire would have long cut us off summarily: "A man who looks for metaphysical reasons in laughter is not funny,"[6] baldly ignoring Rabelais' (posthumous) response: Come now, François-Marie, you know "It is better to write about laughter than about tears."[7] And so, with Rabelais' approval, we *shall*.

Laughter. The ancients indulged in it heartily. Homer's *Iliad* tells us that uncontrollable laughter arose among the gods. It isn't clear whether they intended to share this gift with their terrestrial godlings, yet early Greece reveled in the broad, impudent comedy of Aristophanes and its theatre abounded in the mythical, the fantastic and the burlesque. As time wound toward the Common Era, comedic Greek poets such as Menander crafted plays that struck at the human dilemma, mimicking our mishaps and pitfalls, while others delighted their eager populace with slapstick and farce. The Romans took their comedies unabashedly from the Greeks (which, if you will pardon an anachronism, was par for the course). They added to the timeworn plots their own Latinized contexts and popular tongue, and the comedic mask took its place alongside the tragic in the theaters of Rome. "Comedy today!"

Gaius Valerius Catullus had chided "There is nothing more silly than a silly laugh"?,[8] and in principle, the Romans constrained their laughter into two categories—laughter that was acceptable and laughter that was not. The first was that of the free citizen—a subdued laughter, witty and refined. The second was a coarse laughter, suitable for only foreign

---

[5] Henri Bergson, *Laughter: An Essay on the Meaning of the Comic.* L. Brereton Cloudesely and F. Rothwell, trans. Rockville (MD): Arc Manor, 2008:11.

[6] Voltaire was the nom de plume of François-Marie Arouet (1794-1777) This quotation is cited in Jacques LeGoff , "La risa en la Edad Media", *Una historia cultural del humor. J. Bremmer and H. Roodenburg, eds. Madrid, Sequitur 1999, 41-54*

[7] François Rabelais, *Gargantua.* Paris: Editions Garnier Frères, 1962: 4.

[8] Gaius Valerius Catullus (87 BCE – ca. 64 BCE, *Carmina* I, l. 16

laborers and slaves.[9] In practice, however, it was hardly limited to those marginal souls, and the comedies of Plautus and Terence, the satires of Horace and Juvenal, and Apuleius' picaresque *Metamorphoses* (later called *The Golden Ass*) caused many a raucous implosion within Rome's genteel halls.

But laughter was not for everyone. In fact, it was frowned upon by some early Christians because there was no evidence in Scriptures that Jesus ever laughed. St. Clement I urged that Christian men alone be allowed to smile; Christian women and children were not to indulge at all. The Pythagoreans feared that excessive laughter could be dangerous for one's health. France's 13th-century King Louis IX, the only temporal monarch ever to be sainted, was reported never to have laughed on Fridays.[10] And the Council of Trent (1545-1563) decreed that writers must teach a moral lesson at the same time that their works sought to entertain. So no idle laughing! Even Miguel de Cervantes, whose one-act playlets reveled in lusty characters and situations, would adhere to this admonition in his *Twelve Exemplary Novels* and avowed its dictum in his master work as well.

Despite the naysayers, humor would out, and with all its vagaries intact. Often vulgar, defiant, satirical or obscene, it pervaded the carnivals and popular festivals that wrested the weary from their daily toil and soil. It invaded the holy day performances of the guilds and religious fraternities to the point that they were moved from the porticos of the cathedrals to the public square, only to be removed once again by outraged prelates or kings. And it turned a world topsy-turvy as the lesser souls burlesqued their superiors in the fetterless Feast of Fools.[11] Much of their humor was physical, though not ill-intentioned, and much of it was cruel. People delighted in the pummeling of the Devil in their "sacred" scenarios; they hooted at the un-pretty and deformed, and found it good fun to torment an unsuspecting animal if one happened to come along. Meanwhile, within the confines of castle and palace, buffoons and jesters, many of them dwarfs (some of them spies), lightened the spirits of their gorging masters with humor from clever to rambunctious to downright

---

[9] See Ana Menéndez Collera´s article, "Sources of Humor and Laughter in *Don Quixote*" in *Don Quixote: The First 500 Years.* Ed. Zenia Sacks DaSilva.. Universidad de San Marcos, Peru, 2009.

[10] Ibid. re: early Christians, St. Clement, the Pythagoreans and Louis IX.

[11] The medieval Feast of Fools, whose origins go back to the pre-Christian Saturnalia, was an annual festival celebrated in many parts of Europe at the New Year. Ruled by a "Lord of Misrule," its wanton irreverence and excesses were finally curbed by the Church in the early 16th century.

gross. Take, for example (if you're a bit squeamish, you may want to skip this) the German picaresque tale of *Tyll Eulenspiegel*, in which a jester eats his own turd. Curiously, jesters could also play the role of the wise fool who dared to speak the truth as he saw it, and some of them actually rose to positions of influence as semi-comical, semi-serious counselors to the mighty.

The Ship of Fools (1490), a sardonic representation of the Feast. (Hieronymous Bosch; Paris, Louvre)

As for the icons of literature, neither Chaucer nor Boccaccio nor Rabelais eschewed the salacious scenario, nor Cervantes the humor of blow upon blow. In Spain, elite Golden Age poets assaulted each other with satirical daggers,[12] while polite society made sport of the hunched back and red hair of the playwright Alarcon.[13] An accredited 18th century Aristotelian scholar named Alonso Pinciano declaimed that comedy was entertaining "because you get the chance to see on stage the death of people who don't deserve to live," namely scoundrels, shrews, cuckolds, and nasty old men and women.[14] All this, and we have yet to mention the

---

[12] Francisco de Quevedo y Villegas (1580-1645) and Luis de Argote y Góngora, (1561-1627) were two of the finest poets of the Spanish Baroque, both elegantly poetic in their artistic verses and devastatingly acerbic in their wit.

[13] Juan Ruiz de Alarcón (1581? – 1639), one of Spain's quadrumvirate of major Golden Age dramatists.

[14] *Philosophia Antigua Poética.* Vol. III. Alfredo Carballo Picazo, Ed. Madrid; CSIC, 1973

likes of Fielding, Swift, Larra, Mesonero Romanos, Twain, and....
Voltaire? "A man who looks for metaphysical reasons in laughter..."
You're right, François-Marie. But ere we finish, may we quote you once
more, or twice?

No, humor is not always funny. Then what is it that makes us laugh?
Here are some of its cues:

Surprise—the sudden twist that jars our expectations: Voltaire quipping
"Behind every successful man is a surprised mother-in-law," "The
superfluous is a very necessary thing" or "Anything that is too stupid to be
spoken is sung."[15] Will Rogers observing "Good judgment comes from
experience, and a lot of that comes from bad judgment."[16] Ramón Gómez
de la Serna intuiting "Rain makes us sad because it reminds us of when we
were fish."[17] A medieval Spanish archpriest waxing in praise of small
women, body (and soul?), only to conclude: "The wise man says that if
something is bad, / take the very least of it you can; / so if it's a woman for
whom you clamor, / the smaller she is, so much the better [badder?]."[18]
Surprise—the act of assuming the familiar and suddenly encountering a
brand new truth.

Exaggeration—distortion to the point of the absurd; the caricature, not the
photo. "His nose was so long that one day in midstream, when he lost the
oar of his boat, he just ..." (you can surmise the rest). This droplet is from
the well of popular Mexican humor.[19] By some coincidence, the Spanish
poet Francisco de Quevedo also displayed a certain fascination with noses
as he tells of a man attached to one so large, "'twas a bearded swordfish,
an oar of a ship, a pyramid of Egypt, an elephant upside down."[20] Cervantes
draws a more complete paradigm of beauty in his *Don Quixote:* her
"bluish-purplish lips so long and thin that if lips could be spun, they'd
make a whole skein of yarn," the pockmarks on her face so deep that

---

[15] Voltaire, *Le mondain*

[16] Quotations given here without reference to specific works are derived from
multiple internet sources such as www.brainyquotes.com, *et al.* Some of the quips were
oral comments and do not appear in literary contexts.

[17] *Greguerías Selección 1910-1960*, 8th ed. Madrid: Espasa Calpe, S.A., 1972

[18] Juan Ruiz, Arcipreste de Hita (1283?-1350?), *El libro de buen amor*. My
translation.

[19] Cited in *Antología del saber popular*. Monograph 2. Atzlán Publications.
Chicano Studies Center, UCLA, 1971

[20] Francisco de Quevedo y Villegas, "*A una nariz*". My translation.

"there lay buried the souls of her lovers," her smile so bereft of teeth, her nails so long and gnarled, her dainty frame so stooped that her head touched her knees, but if she were able to stand erect, 'twould rub against the ceiling…"[21] Heartless, yes, but so far beyond the pale that what could be mean-spirited becomes genuinely amusing.

Incongruity—disproportion, singularity. The infant talking about his investments; the little girl with the voice of a man (plus infinite variations); the clown with shoes too big and clothes too small; an enormous woman with a miniscule husband; a caveman using modern appliances; an aging small-town *hidalgo* imagining himself as the knight Don Quixote; his illiterate squire imagining himself as a governor, maybe even a king . . . but his wife as a queen? No, at most a countess, and may God help her even then!

Sur-reality, super-reality—step after step beyond the possible; animals that talk (from Indo-European tales and medieval French fables to the TV of today); people suspended in midair (Chagall knew many like that); a man chasing a fly till they both walk on the ceiling; watches that melt time into infinity[22]; portraits that mesh the seen and unseen[23]; a rare, priceless fish that swims in the pattern of dollar signs[24]; and more subtly, Cervantes disputing the authenticity of a chapter he himself is in the process of writing![25]

Hyper-reality—the opposite of sur-reality, moments of life that didn't seem funny at the time and now are hilarious in the recounting; a foray so deft into our shared experiences that we are uncomfortable, embarrassed. So we laugh instead of crying, trusting that the jabs were not intended to hurt. Voltaire recalls one of those moments and concludes wryly: "Never argue at the dinner table, for the one who is not hungry always gets the best of the argument." The Mexican Ricardo Garibay captures many of those moments in his narrative-free stories, whose only plot is the conversation of people who sound just like us, who really could be ourselves, and whose humor is not far from a sob.[26]

---

[21] *Don Quixote,* Part II, Ch. 47. My translation.
[22] Salvador Dalí, "The Persistence of Memory," 1931.
[23] Pablo Picasso, "The Weeping Woman", "Dora Maar," et al.
[24] Ramón Gómez de la Serna (1891-1963), "El pez único."
[25] *Don Quixote*, Part II, Ch, 5.
[26] Ricardo Garibay (1923 -1999, *Diálogos mexicanos*. Mexico. DF: Mortiz. 1975

Irony—the turn of thought that ends with a wince. Montaigne musing: "Nothing is so firmly believed as what is least known."[27] Beaumarchais assuring: "If you are mediocre and you grovel, you shall be successful."[28] Voltaire thrusting: "Murderers are punished unless they kill in large numbers and to the sound of trumpets." Mariano José de Larra walking the empty streets of Madrid on All Soul's Day: "Here is the National Treasury, the grave of our economy; the Ministry of Justice, tomb of our democracy . . . and to think that people go outside this city to visit the cemetery!"[29] Augusto Monterroso recalling a distant land where "black sheep" were regularly put to death, so that future generations of sculptors could enjoy placing their revered figures in the park.[30] Samuel Beckett summed it up in his own way: "Nothing is funnier than unhappiness."[31] Larra would have agreed.

Mockery—Tales of the fool, the innocent, the foreigner, the rube. Jibes at the stammerer, the lisper, the exception to the rule. They're condescending, classist, racist, and they can be mean; but we laugh because we are the "in-group" and it's our right because we're "superior." Every nation is well stocked with its laughing stock, often but not always its minorities, and the stereotypes are fairly unanimous, no matter what the century or locale. Spain had its Perogrullo, France its La Palisse, Italy its Calandrino, Mexico its tales of the ingenuous peon or of the *gringo;* its *chicano* offspring, their Don Cacahuete.[32] Argentina had its *gallegos* (slang for

---

[27] Michel de Montaigne (1533-1592), *Essays, Bk. 1*, 32

[28] *Le Mariage de Figaro*, 1784: Act III, Scene iii.

[29] Mariano José de Larra (1808-1836), "Día de difuntos de 1836" *Artículos de costumbres.* Larra committed suicide at the age of twenty-eight shortly, after completing this article.

[30] Augusto Monterroso (1921-2003), "La vaca negra*". Obras completas y otros cuentos* . My translation.

[31] Samuel Beckett (1906-1989), *Endgame, 1958*

[32] Perogrullo is a fictional character sprung from the popular wit of 16th century Spain. He is the emblem of one who says the obvious, but fills it with puns and double entendres. The term "una perogrullada" is still used today for such manners of speech. Strangely enough, a French equivalent of Perogrullo is "La Palisse", whose name may have been taken from a fairly distinguished historical figure who died in 1525 and was never associated with any kind of confused platitudes or humorous sayings. Calandrino, who also seems to have stemmed from an actual personage, perhaps even a doctor, appears first in Boccaccio's *Decameron* as a simpleton and the foil of many a mean-spirited hoax. In later years his name has been used generically to refer to a fool. On the other side of the ocean, Don Cacahuete (literally, Mr. Peanut) and a certain "Quevedo" are similar figures who

"Spaniards"), and in at least one major instance made even its gaucho the object of a poetic parody.[33]   Suddenly the proverbial folk-hero becomes funny as he watches an opera in Buenos Aires' posh Teatro Colon—funny because his language, his garb, his rough-hewn references to the pampa are completely out of context—and we're all so much "smarter" than he until we find ourselves in the rough-hewn jibes of the gauchos.

Plays on words, turns of phrase—artful puns that carve words into facets. Cocteau protesting that "Mirrors should reflect a little before throwing out images."[34] Voltaire regretting that "Common sense is not so common"[35] and Oscar Wilde, that "Immanuel doesn't pun; he Kant." Abe Lincoln lamenting: "If I were two-faced, would I be wearing this one?" Mark Twain asserting that "Age is an issue of mind over matter. If you don't mind it, it doesn't matter;" and that "Wagner's music is really much better than it sounds." … Artful phrases that spawn a playful portrait. For Gómez de la Serna "The dust is filled with old and forgotten sneezes."[36] For Molière "(He is) a wonderful talker, who has the art of telling you nothing in a great harangue."[37] For Cervantes, "[In the good old Golden Age] a maiden could spend her entire life alone in the woods, never sleeping under a roof, and still be as whole as "the mother who bore her."[38] (Clearly, one cannot praise her too highly!) …   Here is humor wrapped in a game of insinuation, double edged, open-ended, and more often than not, seditious.

Defiance—the clash between the accepted and the forbidden, the subtle to not-so-subtle insult, the vulgar word, the cream pie in the face of authority. And satire is its weapon—political, social, literary, *ad hominem*, *ad …* whoever stands in the line of its fire. "A fool and his money are soon

---

appear in the storehouse of popular *chicano / Mexican* lore. Some of their witticisms and anecdotes can be found in *Antología del saber popular*, op cit.
[33] Estanislao del Campo (1834-1880), *El Fausto*. To this day Argentinians enjoy their jokes about the simpleton "gallegos"—literally "Galicians," but extended to all Spaniards.
[34] Jean Cocteau (1889-1963), *Des Beaux Art*
[35] *Dictionnaire Philosophique, 1764.*
[36] Ramón Gómez de la Serna, *Greguerías.*
[37] Molière (pseudonym for Jean Baptiste Poquelin, 1622-1673) *Le Misanthrope, Act II, v. My translation.*
[38] *Don Quixote,* I, Ch. 9. My paraphrase. This quip is not an accidental slip-up in place of the usual "as when her mother bore her". In fact, Cervantes uses it again in I, 26.

elected." [39]   "Now and then an innocent man is sent to the legislature." [40] "The best form of government is a benevolent tyranny tempered with an occasional assassination."[41] ... Satire. Erasmus chose it to slash certain icons and practices; Aretino to broadside politics and the curia.[42] Rabelais to shake the walls of sophistry and *politesse*; Cervantes to demolish the books of chivalry; Quevedo to revile corruption and sham; Molière to twit his fellow bourgeoisie; Swift to expose our human failings; Mesonero Romanos to ridicule the budding romantics[43]; Twain to lampoon a world of absurdities; Monterroso to meld into a single essence animal, myth and a hapless humanity. Dario Fo might well have been right when he said that "Comedy makes the subversion of the existing state of affairs possible."[44] After all, is laughter not "mankind's greatest blessing—our only really effective weapon, against which there is no defense"?[45]

These are some of the prompts of laughter, whatever its decibels, whichever its shades. Still the questions remain: At whom are we really

---

[39] Will Rogers. Cited in multiple internet sources.

[40] Frank McKinney , "Kin Hubbard" (1868-1930). Bartlett's *Familiar Quotations*. Justin Kaplan, ed. Little Brown: Boston, Toronto, London. 1992

[41] Voltaire has another version of this quip in which he inserts "democracy" instead of "a benevolent tyranny".

[42] Pietro Aretino (1492-1556), known as the "Scourge of Princes," earned his first notoriety with the publication of "The Last Will and Testament of the Elephant Hanno" a scathing satire of the rule of Pope Leo X and his entourage. Knighted by both Pope Clement VII and Julius III, he produced a collection of caustically humorous writings on the politics of his time, a comical parody of Castiglione's *Courtier,* and a startling number of pornographic stories and plays.

[43] Ramón de Mesonero Romanos (1803-1882). In this abridged sample from his essay on "Romanticism and the Romantics", Mesonero gives the cast of characters of the "emblematic-sublime anonymous, synonymous, foreboding and spasmodic" play that his romanticized nephew has composed. Here is a partial list of the personages: "A woman–all women, the whole woman; a husband (all husbands); a savage (the lover); the Doge of Venice; The Archduchess of Austria; a spy; a courtier; an executioner; a pharmacist; the Triple Alliance; a chorus of Carmelite nuns; a man from the town; a town of men; a ghost that speaks; another ghost that grabs; four undertakers; musicians and dancers, and troupes of gypsies, witches, priests," *et al.* The satire builds from there as Mesonero describes every aspect of his nephew's romantic epiphany and the extremes of his "art".

[44]Dario Fo (1926—), Italian playwright, satirist, theater director, performer and composer, won the Nobel Prize for Literature in 1997. One of his most acclaimed plays is *Death of an Anarchist.*

[45] Mark Twain, cited in http://www.brainyquotes.com and other internet sources. *My paraphrase.*

laughing? And how does that laughter change as we traverse moment and place? Is it different within the parameters of romance languages or does language yield to a fundamental, universal human nature? It is time to begin our explorations.

Zenia Sacks DaSilva

PART I.

'TWAS ALL A FARCE

FROM THE ROMANCE LANDS:
FARCE AS LIFE-BLOOD OF THE THEATRE

JESSICA MILNER DAVIS

Despite the fact that farce is by tradition a lowly dramatic genre, its paradoxical nature justifies more detailed examination. It appears to be the simplest form of comedy, but is in fact a very challenging one to bring off successfully—both in terms of writing and performance. In order to identify what farce truly is (and is not), it helps to focus on differences between the pure genre at its most basic and other styles or modes of comedy such as satire, romantic comedy, 'black' or gallows humour and absurdism. (Although the latter is sometimes described as 'metaphysical' or 'intellectual' farce, it is certainly more than pure farce, reflecting the complex psychological realities of modern life.) Comedy is of course the larger term that embraces these and many other styles or comic flavours. As a unique style of comedy, farce does not consist merely of pratfalls and slapstick—although sometimes it is barely more than that—but these physical jokes are always one of its important components. It is a non-critical style of comedy, played at a pace that allows the audience to eschew reflection on either the physicality or the morality of the jokes played out before it on the stage.

Thus, satire has no part in pure farce, since farce simply stops being farcical when critical reflection is invited from the audience—although satire often makes use of farcical techniques for its own purposes. As suggested above, the same quality differentiates farce from gallows humour and absurdism, even if—like satire—those genres choose to employ some farcical devices. At the opposite end of the comic spectrum, farce is essentially unromantic: too much sympathy for any one of its characters would entail an exemption from serving their turn as a comic butt. Nevertheless, there are many successful combinations of farce with romantic comedy, where farce transmutes into a more empathetic form of comedy so as to arrive at a happy conclusion, for example to the travails of lovers. In this case, the 'pure farce' sections of a play will have a line of demarcation recognizable to the actors that runs between them and other 'farce plus romance' sections. Usually the farce will serve either as comic relief, or as a prelude to a more sentimental conclusion. For practical purposes, this chapter focuses on pure farce as a recognizable and specific comic genre.

Origins of the farce

The genre can be traced back to the style of knockabout comedy recorded as popular in the ancient Greek region of Doria. Although this seems to have been despised by the classical dramatists of the Graeco-Roman theatres, stereotypes of gluttons from the Dorian city of Megara and of uppity slaves and scheming parasites can be traced in both fragments of text and surviving plays. The records imply a connection with a laughter-producing, knockabout type of fun traditional to the area that made no claims to any literary merit. For example, as a prize-winning dramatist, Aristophanes ironically took care to assure his audience that he would not stoop to using such low 'slapstick à la Megara' (Prologue to The Wasps [Dickinson 171]), while including plenty of them in fact. Already in the classical world it seems, the characters and business of what would later be known as farce were placed on the lowest rung in the hierarchy of dramatic genres. With few exceptions, they have stayed there since.

Although the age-old tradition of skilled itinerant troupes of mimes and minstrels continued after the collapse of empire both East and West, such professions were disreputable and no doubt precarious. While the wanderers' repertoire probably included short farcical sketches, they left no texts from which we can infer the true style or nature of their performances—although a late thirteenth century Flemish piece, *Le Garçon et l'aveugle*,[1] may be one such. When formal drama using written texts was eventually reborn in Europe, it emerged first from a process of elaboration of ritual within the medieval Church resulting in communal religious drama, and later from neo-classical influences, resulting in drama for the elite. However, as religious performances became more secularized—even if still largely devotional in purpose—and as aristocratic pastimes became more widespread, it seems likely that for both a degree of rapprochement and interchange with surviving professional traditions took

---

[1] Usually dated c.1280, see William Tydeman, ed., The Medieval European Stage, 500-1550, Cambridge, Cambridge University Press, 2001, p. 330. For the text, see Mario Roques, ed., Le Garçon et l'aveugle: Jeu du XIIIe siècle, Les Classiques Français du Moyen Âge No. 5, Paris, H. Champion, 1911. English translation in Medieval French Plays, edited and translated by Richard Axton and John Stevens, Oxford: Basil Blackwell, 1971.

place. After all, the justification for the spread of religious drama was the teaching of the Gospel of Good News; and even within the formality of Church ritual there was room for invention. Early biblical texts chanted in Latin resulted in tropes that included realistic material such as the chant of soldiers guarding the Tomb through a long and dreary night, or detailed words for Mary's lament at the foot of the Cross (Sticca 127). Later, some non-biblical dialogue of this kind was composed in the vernacular, and not merely chanted but enacted, creating a range of dramatic opportunities for impersonation of the all-too-human characters involved. Expanding religious drama, allied with popular folk customs and increasing sophistication of courtly entertainments must have created a demand for specialized performers.

By late mediaeval times, comedy in general and its subordinate specialized form, farce, had both acquired new names and local habitations. For comedy, this came principally from a new awareness of classical five-act Roman comedy which was both presented and imitated in school-exercises and courtly productions. In French-speaking lands, however, a new home-grown type of short comedy called *farce/farse* also became widespread. Its name was synonymous with comic structures and performances dedicated to the production of laughter and clearly differentiated from other more serious dramatic styles, including the learned comedy. It was principally from French Romance culture that this term and the concept it identifies entered the Anglo-Saxon world.

Nevertheless, parallel specialization in type of performance and naming also occurred in other European nations: for example, the 14th-century Dutch *abele spelen* or courtly romances each included a matching *sotternie* or farce as comic relief; German pre-Lenten plays at Shrovetide, farces like those of Hans Sachs (1494-1576), were known as *Fastnachtspiele*. In Italian city-states and on the Iberian peninsula the French term *farce* was mirrored in contemporary usage of *farsa*. Not that these lands were unimportant: during the later Renaissance, the style and traditional plots of farce were enriched by the inspiration of the travelling Italian *commedia dell-arte* troupes. It is thus true to say that the naming and the valuing of this genre as a member of the wider family of comedy (albeit not one sanctioned by classical writ) is one of the many gifts from Romance lands to world theatre.

The structure and spirit of farce

The comic spirit of farce delights in taboo-violation, but avoids implied moral comment or social criticism and prefers to debar empathy for its victims. This combination is vital for farce to succeed. The more respectable its victims, and the more successfully it avoids moral implications flowing from their victimization, the funnier farce will be. Its guiding rule is to tread the fine line between offence and entertainment. As distinct from those of high comedy of manners and romantic comedy, farce-plots tend to be short. They are not peopled by complex, sympathetic characters, but by simplified comic types. Farce's comic style favours direct, visual and physical jokes over pyrotechnics of verbal wit and it declares open season for aggression, animal high spirits, self-indulgence and rudeness of all kinds (producing lurid obscenity and swearing on occasion and when appropriate to character). But in contrast to satire and black humour, which can be equally licentious and violent, the humour of farce is essentially conservative: it has little reforming zeal—or even despair—about the ways of the world and of humankind. At the end of its comic upheavals, it tends to restore conventional authority, or at least to save authority's face for it.

Wide reading of farce-texts serves to identify four recurring structures, apparently fundamental to the genre. Since any one may combine with another or with several, there is a fifth category of "combination- plots." Briefly, these structures are (Davis 6-8)[2]:

1.   Humiliation or Deception Farces in which unpleasant victims are exposed to their fate, without opportunity for retaliation. These farces are unidirectional in their joking and their plots include special justifications for the pleasure taken in the sufferings of others.

2.   Reversal Farces in which the tables are turned on the original rebel or joker, allowing the victim retaliation in return. Often there are further switches of direction, in order to prolong the mirth and ensure the conventional "proper" outcome.

3.   Equilibrium or Quarrel Farces where the plot focuses upon a narrow kind of perpetual-motion, in which two opposing forces wrestle each other—literally or metaphorically—in a tug-of-war without resolution, remaining in permanent balance.

4.   Snowball Farces in which all the characters are equally caught up as victims in a whirlwind of escalating sound and fury. Often these plots are driven by an elaborate series of misunderstandings and errors, giving rise to many "crossed lines" between the different parties (Bergson 1910). The power of nature, of inanimate objects, tools and machines, in dominating mere humans is frequently the source of the joke.

---

[2] This section and others are quoted by kind permission of the publisher.

5.   Combination Farces, principally combining types 2 and 4 above (but other possibilities exist).

This typology not only helps clarify the differences between farce and more literary comic forms but also shows how quickly farce can shade into other styles of humour. The key is equipoise, or preserving a careful balance between on the one hand, a revolt against order and propriety and on the other, a kind of *Realpolitik* which ultimately restores the social conventions under attack. The precarious balance is endangered by the intrusion of either sentiment (leading to romance) or moral purpose (leading to satire). Precluding such outbursts of empathy and serious cognition is how farce 'gets away' with its humorous social outrages and avoids invoking either formal censorship or personal constraint on the part of the audience. Historical cases in which a so-called 'farce' actually provoked formal censorship in fact proved highly useful in defining the boundaries of the genre, as I shall discuss below. This combination of aggressive, physical joking with permissive licence is just as paradoxical as the fact that farce is not (at least on the live stage) particularly fantastic or unrealistic.

Function and etymology of farce

Being by nature short and often episodic in structure, farce often serves the adjunct role noted above of serving as 'stuffing' or comic relief in a theatrical bill. This functional role supports the traditional derivation of its name from the Latin *farcire*, 'to stuff' and the word 'farce' remains current in both French and English as perhaps a rather old-fashioned name for a stuffing in meat and other foods. Accepting this for the moment (although an alternative view is addressed below), the first connection of 'farce' with drama seems to have come by absorption of the verb-form into ecclesiastical usage.[3]   In the period between the 9th and 12th centuries CE, the Latin liturgy of the Church underwent a process of musical and verbal enrichment by the addition of tropes, or embellishing phrases already referred to. When these phrases and their musical accompaniment were inserted into parts of the Mass, such as the Kyrie and the Sanctus, they were often called *farsae* or *farsurae*. The term was also used for the reading of Lessons and particularly Epistles which had been 'farced' in this way. By the beginning of the 12th century in French and Italian abbeys and cathedrals, these *farsurae* were often composed in the vernacular as a

---

[3] For greater detail, see Davis, op. cit., 2003, pp.74-83.

gloss on the meaning of the Latin passages being chanted to the congregation from the scriptures set for a particular day. *Épitres farcies* ('farced epistles') were used, for example, on the Feast of Saint Stephen First Martyr and on Christmas Day, presumably with the aim of helping the people to understand the events lying behind the story of the first Christian martyr and the birth of the Saviour.

This 'farced' material was not, of course, farcical and there is no evidence that the term *farsae* was used in reference to what may have become individual playlets. It seems likely, nevertheless, that the process of 'farcing' did acquire some connection with entertainment, or what we might now call 'audience appeal'. Among other feasts at which *épitres farcies* (farced epistles) were prescribed was the Feast of Fools (also known as the Feast of the Ass). In France this developed into a celebration which—justly or unjustly—sparked a series of official complaints at the turn of the 13th century about its celebration.[4] Despite this, the Feast persisted and continued to spread until the first half of the 15th century when a sustained series of attacks were made, invoking secular as well as religious authorities, after which it struggled to continue within the church. Records from the cathedral-schools of Beauvais and Sens give some idea of the extraordinary nature of this serious but Saturnalian feast, which took place on the Feast of the Circumcision (1 January) as the culmination of Christmas revels. From the Feast of Stephen (26 December) onwards, in ecclesiastical communities, various ranks of the clergy were permitted their special day of indulgence; on the Feast of the Holy Innocents (28 December) a Boy Bishop from the choristers might be elected to rule over the festivities. The Feast of the Circumcision was the day of the despised sub-deacons, who embodied disruption of the established order. At Beauvais, an ass was escorted in procession up the nave of the cathedral by canons bearing wine while the parodic Prose of the Ass was sung; the censing at Mass was done with black puddings and sausages; the celebrant was instructed to bray three times to conclude the service, while the congregation responded similarly. While it was an opportunity to celebrate freedom from normal discipline and to mock any sober souls who resisted this topsy-turvy reign by the 'fools', or devotees of the ass, it was also a serious act of worship, with elaborate music and scriptural precedent in the Magnificat sung by Mary at the Annunciation: "Thou hast put down the mighty from their seat / And hast exalted the humble and meek."

---

[4] According to Max Harris, these can be traced to Pope Innocent III (1198-1216) or his representatives in France, see Max Harris, *Sacred Folly: A New History of the Feast of Fools*, Ithaca NY: Cornell University Press, 2011, p. 92.

In a parallel secular celebration, however, fool societies emerged—
compagnies des fous or *sociétés joyeuses* as Petit de Julleville memorably
termed them (192-261)—with activities that did involve masking as well
as mimicry, and from which we derive the traditional fool's costume with
asses' ears (never worn in ecclesiastical rites). These seem to have
accompanied the gradual expansion of community involvement in the
organization and acting of the religious drama, which by the end of the
14th century, was largely in the hands of dedicated lay societies. In
England, these were often the trade-guilds which presented play-cycles
over several days, for example at the Feast of Corpus Christi. In Italy and
Spain, they included the charitable associations known respectively as
confraternite and *cofradías*.

It was in France, however, that specialized *confrèries* (fraternities)
were formed, intended to honour particular saints by dramatizing their
lives and miracles. In Paris, the more general *Confrèrie de la Passion* was
granted a monopoly in 1402 to perform all religious drama within the city.
Early 15th-century texts show that by then a typical French religious
play—a *mystère* (mystery) or a *vie de sain* (saint's life)—might well
include a comic episode explicitly intended as comic relief and often
referred to as a *farsse* or *farce*. A manuscript from the Bibliotèque Ste.
Geneviève comprises a series of plays (possibly associated with the
Confrèrie) about the saint's wondrous miracles. One is headed, "Miracles
de plusieurs malades / En farses pour estre main fades ("Miracles about
sick people / In farcical mode to be less dull").[5] It is interesting to note the
case of a *Mystère de St Eloi* (*Mystery of Saint Eloi*) played at Dijon in
1447, which was the subject of a law suit. Here court records affirm that:
"in the middle of the said mystery there was a certain farce, put in so that
it would excite the people to laughter" (qtd in Petit de Julleville, 330).[6]
Significantly, the complaint brought before the court was that the audience
had been excited to laughter against the King and the Dauphin by political
references in this *farse*.

---

[5] *Mystères inédits du 15e siècle*, ed. Achille Jubinal. Tom. 1, Paris: Techéner,
1837, p. 281. (My translation.) Despite the plural, there is only one farce-episode
in an otherwise serious play, its purpose made brutally clear by a further
introduction: "Cy après sont autres miracles de madame sainte Geneviève. Sachiez
que chascun emporte plusiers personnages de plusiers malades pour cause di
brieté, et a parmy farsses entées, a fin que le jeu soit mains fades et plus plaisans."
[6] My translation. See also, William Tydeman, *op. cit.,* p. 331.

For the amusement of his king, the fool blows air into an animal as if playing a bagpipe. (Miniature, Petrus Giberti, France, Early 15th Century; courtesy of British Library's Catalogue of Illuniated Manuscripts: http://www.bl.uk)

Fool Carrying a Stick before the King. (Miniature, Mildmay Master, S. Netherlands, circa 1460-1470; courtesy of British Library's Catalogue of Manuscripts: http://www.bl.uk)

Farce as distinct genre

Perhaps it was problems of this kind that brought about—at least in France—a clear, generic distinction between the *farce* and another comic form played by many *sociétés joyeuses*, the *sottie*, as two different kinds of comic performance. The *sottie* was an allegorical satire, particularly associated with the activities of the French law clerks, educated young men whose guilds, known as the Basoche, enjoyed a certain amount of economic and political independence. In a *sottie*, the actors, dressed as *sots* in parti-coloured costumes with cap and bells, set out to demonstrate the truth of the motto, *stultorum numerus est infinitus* (the number of fools is infinite).[7] The biting political satire of unmasking the *sot* behind every type of public and private figure provided the dramatic climax for each *sottie*. Inevitably, such satire was likely to provoke official reaction in the form of punishment of the actors and retaliation against their guild; fool societies were eventually suppressed in the mid-sixteenth century. The *farce*, on the other hand, embodied a more tolerant attitude towards man's stupidity. Restricting itself to a more generalized kind of comic mimicry, it proved a more long-lasting vehicle for lively fun.[8]

French farce then was understood to be an independent, short, fast-paced play designed purely to get people laughing. That these *farces* remained popular after the demise of the *sociétés joyeuses* is shown by the very large number that passed into print during the course of the sixteenth century. Popular in their own right, they had earlier been a drawcard for elaborate communal productions of religious drama. In 1496 at Seurre, for example, when it rained, the audience gathered for the out-of-doors show was persuaded to stay and wait until the weather cleared up by being offered a *farce* (Tydeman 331). By this time, such *farces* had expanded their social function to other festive events: Petit de Julleville records that late 15th century farce performers at weddings were paid in the same way as musicians (330-333). Surely such comic roles must have required and attracted the talents of actors who were increasingly professional. For the earliest embryonic acting-troupes in France, farce and comedy thus formed

---

[7] For studies, see Émile Picot, *La Sottie en France,* Nogent-sur-Rotrou, Daupeley-Gouverneur, 1878, and his collection of edited texts, *Receuil général des sotties*, Société des Anciens Textes Français. Paris, Firmin Didot, 3 vols, 1902-12. A more recent study is Heather Arden, *Fool's plays: A study of satire in the "sottie,"* Cambridge: Cambridge University Press, 1980.

[8] Play-titles very occasionally used both terms: for instance "Les sobres sots…Farce Moralle et Joyeuse," a Shrovetide play given at Rouen in 1536 (see Picot, Vol. III, No. 21 for the text).

an important part of their livelihood, and it was, as Gustave Lanson famously pointed out (129-153), in this school that Molière and his colleagues subsequently were trained.

Commedia erudita, farsa and the development of the commedia dell'arte

In both France and Italy, courtly patrons enjoyed low-brow jesting and farce and often retained a professional farceur or jester. [9] But they also aspired to a more refined, literary comedy which would observe the neo-classical rules of structure and decorum and was known in Italy as the *commedia erudita* ('learned comedy'). *Farsa* was therefore a term, not necessarily for low comedy, but for a loose genre, neither tragedy nor comedy nor pastoral, which could be easy-going precisely because it lacked classical antecedents. The dramatist Giovan-Maria Cecchi enthusiastically lauded this newly-acknowledged genre in the prologue to *La Romanesca* (*The Roman Girl*, 1585), using the conventional literary image of his work as his mistress to convey his views (Kennard 179):

> The *Farsa* is a new third species between tragedy and comedy. It enjoys the liberties of both, and shuns their limitations . . . It is not restricted to certain motives; for it accepts all subjects—grave and gay, profane and sacred, urbane and rude, sad and pleasant. It does not care for time or place . . . In a word, this modern mistress of the stage is the most amusing, the most convenient, the sweetest, prettiest, country-lass that can be found upon our earth.

Probably a rather similar and loose understanding of the term was current in Spain at this time, unlike the precise meaning of the French term.[10] Before the establishment of the term *comedia* to mean a play in the 17th century, it seems that *farsa* was simply one of several words for a dramatic performance. Thus *auto sacramental* ('sacred play') and *farsa sacramental* could be interchangeable terms and *farsa* did not necessarily indicate a comic approach. Perhaps it also connoted a "mixing" of styles or structures.

The "free-and-easy" rubric certainly suited the professional acrobats and jesters who offered themselves for hire by city authorities, academies

---

[9] For records of a bequest by Charles VI (d. 1422) of France to a court *farseur*, see Tydeman, pp. 329-30. This is in fact the earliest documented use of the term.

[10] I have not been able to document this satisfactorily.

and noble households in Italian city-states in the early 16th century. Unlike the members of literary academies (amateur playwrights and actors composing and performing their *commedie erudite*), the skills of the professional *comici* ('comedians') lay in improvisation, not in following literary rules of composition. These were of course the creators of the *commedia dell'arte* ('the comedy of the skill' or 'of the art'; hence, 'the professional comedy'). For their plots, the *comici* drew indiscriminately from literary and classical comedy, from *novelle* and romances, from traditional village pastimes, and upon their own skills in acrobatics and mimicry.[11] As the fame of their acting grew, their particular style of comedy became known throughout Europe. Historical studies have shown that from the end of the sixteenth century onwards, troupes of *comici* paid regular visits to Spain, Vienna, Paris and London, perhaps elsewhere. In 1680, a permanent company was established by royal decree at the Hôtel de Bourgogne in Paris. Comédie Italienne and Italian actors were still performing at the Opéra Comique in the late eighteenth century (cf. Attinger).

Commedia dell'arte performances famously depended upon each actor memorizing a *scenario* (or outline) and, in co-ordination with colleagues, developing his or her improvisations.[12] Since the characters of the *commedia* were fixed in personality type, each actor was also governed by the expectations associated with his or her role, although social positioning might vary from play to play. There was an established repertoire to be created and memorized for each actor's traditional character or 'mask', although it could be developed to suit a personality: this included dialogues, typical behaviour, pieces of business, or 'lazzi', standard jokes, or 'burle', set speeches, orations and acrobatic turns. According to their talents, individual actors would add their own inventions, so that the characters of the *commedia* were partly archetypal, partly original and fantastic creations. There were impotent old fathers, such as Pantalone the miser and the learned il Signor Dottore from Bologna, oldest of free university cities; languishing ladies, whether wives or daughters; buxom servant girls; smooth and potent lovers; braggart captains (often Spanish or Gascon); and pairs of clownish servants, who between them could provide enough wit to concoct a plot and enough stupidity to confuse it. Most roles were played using individualized masks or half-masks so that the

---

[11] See Kenneth Richards and Laura Richards, *The Commedia dell'arte: A Documentary History*.
[12] Having largely died out in the legitimate theatre by the 20th century, the skill has been painstakingly researched and recreated by theatre troupes such as that of Dario Fo and Francesca Rame in Italy.

acting was highly stylized. This set a premium on signaling to an audience—as caricature does in a comic strip—that favorite characters X and Y were back again.

Given these characteristics, the plots of the *commedia dell'arte* naturally tended to broad comedy and trickery rather than to complex psychological drama. However, like those of the earlier *farsa*, they were not restricted to pure farce and in later periods particularly, romance, scenic spectacle and topical satire were important parts of the *commedia dell'arte*'s phenomenal popularity. However, buffoonery and intrigue were staple ingredients in the mix, demanding from the audience detached laughter or perhaps feelings of distant and magical romance rather than close empathy and deep insight into the human psyche. The actors' skill lay in presenting the audience with an extraordinary visual combination of mental rigidity and acrobatic elasticity. It was (and is) an elaborate dramatization of the most fundamental of all practical jokes, the fact that the human spirit is trapped within and must express itself through, a physical body. Perhaps because of this, the name of the *commedia* is sometimes regarded as synonymous with farce and its re-birth in the twentieth century has certainly helped revivals of old classical comedies as well as creating new varieties of farcical comedy such as the political farces of Dario Fo.[13]

Farce in England

In England, although farce was not known by that name in the 16th century, in practice it was familiar to both audiences and actors. Broad comedy and clowning had always been part of mediaeval and Tudor drama, and early Tudor comedians such as Richard Tarleton and Will Kempe, who composed and performed their own jests and comic stories, were leading members of the first permanent acting companies whose members' names were recorded. In fact, the Elizabethan stage developed its own form of 'comic stuffing'—the stage-jig, a mimed dance with dialogue which was sung to popular tunes. Jigs, whether performed independently or as part of a larger bill, took audiences by storm, not just in England, but also in Germany and Scandinavia. Visiting English companies toured with great success towards the turn of the sixteenth

---

[13] For example, *Morte accidentale di un anarchico* (*Accidental Death of an Anarchist*, 1970), or more recently (2008-9), his spoof impersonation of former Italian President, Silvio Berlusconi, using the burlesque style of speech called 'grammelot': www.youtube.com/watch?v=D1Tfqgh187Q.

century when English theatres were shut temporarily by the plague—later more permanently closed by the Puritan regime (1642-1660). The continental term, farce, had nevertheless made its mark by 1611 when Randle Cotgrave compiled and printed an English/French educational dictionary in which he described a *farce* as "a (fond [i.e., foolish] and dissolute) Play, Comedie, or Enterlude; also, the Iyg at the end of the Enterlude, wherein some pretie knauerie is enacted" (Cotgrave).

In fact, the strength and popularity of this comic tradition helped to sustain its actors in the face of Lord Protector Cromwell's efforts to destroy the theatre as an institution. Such illegal performances as could take place during the Commonwealth period consisted chiefly of very short farces known as 'drolls'. These were played in haste at fairgrounds and in theatres that were supposed to be closed. Texts of independent jigs and comic scenes abbreviated from popular Elizabethan and Jacobean plays[14] illustrate the importance of farce to the repertoire during this period until the reopening of the theatres in 1660.

The restoration of the crown in 1660 brought French influence to bear upon the fashionable world, including the English stage—a natural development, given the sanctuary across the Channel so long provided to the Stuarts. Newly-opened London theatres were quick to include 'farces' regularly in their bills. The word as well as the kind of comedy it denoted was regarded as innately foreign—part French, part Italian (reflecting the impact of the *commedia dell'arte*). Like other foreign commodities, farce was novel, chic, amusing, probably decadent, and certainly daring. Some dramatists, such as Nahum Tate (never quite part of the literary establishment despite his later appointment as Poet Laureate in 1692), welcomed this newly-named genre for its flexibility and popular appeal. But the arbiters of taste—despising fickle popular applause—condemned it. John Dryden must have spoken for many aspiring literary dramatists when, in the Preface to his play *An Evening's Love* (1671), he deplored the fact that "as the Artist is often unsuccessful, while the Mountebank succeeds; so Farces more commonly take the people than comedies" (Dryden. *The Conquest...*). But he was pleased to follow in the well-worn footsteps of Aristophanes by making use of it from time to time in spite of deploring its economic success.

Whatever the opinions of Dryden and other critics, public taste then as now was not to be denied. Plays were called farces whether native or French in inspiration and they established themselves firmly in the British

---

[14] Examples are collected in *The Wits, Or, Sport upon Sport : A selection of drolls and farces,* ed. Francis Kirkman, Cornell Studies in English, Ithaca NY: Cornell University Press, 1932.

repertoire. In fact, such was the success of the 'new' genre, that its name became synonymous with pure hilarity. Dryden's most popular comedy, *The Feign'd Innocence, or, Sir Martin Marr-All* (1667), written in association with the Duke of Newcastle, made full use of farce and the diarist Pepys described its success in the following terms: "It is the most entire piece of mirth, a complete farce from one end to the other, that certainly ever was writ. I never laughed so in all my life. I laughed till my head [ached] all the evening and night with the laughing; and at very good wit therein, not fooling. The house full" (Mac Afee 202).

Farce, stuffing and deception: an etymological puzzle

Although the generic evolution of farce as a form of comedy is clear, its etymology is open to more than one interpretation. As noted above, the traditional derivation of '*la farce*' as a dramatic genre follows the word's apparent links with the Fr. verb *farser*, 'to stuff, or pad'. Many scholars hold to this view.[15] However, in 1984 Bernadette Rey-Flaud published her study paying close attention to the language of the old French medieval play-texts and showing that they frequently use the verb *farcer* in the sense of 'to deceive or trick'—a meaning still present in the modern French expression *farces et attrapes*, 'novelties and practical jokes (or japes)'. Accordingly, she proposed this alternative sense (*farce* as 'trickery' or 'deception') as the primary one, relating the theatrical term more closely to the French noun *fart* (or *fard,* meaning cosmetic) than to *farcer*. The derivation depends on a past stage of confusion between the French verb *farder* ('to paint, disguise, and thus deceive', derived from *farwida* with a conjectured Frankish origin[16]) and the Fr. verb *farsir* (like *farser*, derived from Lat. *farcire*, 'to stuff'), resulting in *farser,* with offshoots of *farse/farce* (in the theatrical sense) and *farseur/farceur* (meaning a joker). Independently, Rey-Flaud argues, the Latin *farcire* gave rise to the terms *farce,* used in the culinary sense to mean stuffing, and *its* offshoot *farceur* (meaning a pastrycook or confectioner). Since the farce-genre relies inherently on deception and trickery, she prefers the 'disguise' derivation to the 'stuffing' one (Rey-Flaud 155-170).

---

[15] For instance, Thierry V. Boucquet, trans. and ed., *Six Medieval French Farces*, Lewiston NY and Lampeter, Wales: Edwin Meller, 1999. My argument in this section closely follows that previously published in J. Milner Davis, op. cit, 50-1 and 171-3

[16] The conjectured Frankish verb is **farwjan* ('to dye'), from which derives the modern French *fard*, 'make-up' or 'cosmetics'.

The argument from farce's connections with trickery and deception is attractive and compelling, but it does little to account for the 12th century word-links with ecclesiastical practice and usage that seemingly lead to the role of farce as comic stuffing/relief. Indeed, this function is relegated by the line of derivation to the status of a mere happy coincidence. Rather than jettisoning the traditional derivation in its entirety, it might be more productive to focus on the co-existence of both senses and both origins, the stuffing AND the trickery. One might then hypothesize that it is precisely this verbal ambiguity—that served to imbue the French genre-term with its undoubted vigour, allowing it to connote a new and delightful phenomenon across so many cultures.

Whatever the solution of the derivational puzzle, it is certainly the gift of a long-lived type of comedy named farce from the Romance lands to the rest of the world. Down the ages in the history of theatre, farce has proved its staying-power and its appeal has persisted despite critical disdain for its lack of seriousness. Farce can take a rightful place not only in literary and dramatic studies, but also in the realm of humour studies. The enquiries of social psychologists and brain researchers in that field may one day contribute a better understanding of why the genre is so good at eliciting gales of laughter and why, given the right conditions, we love to laugh at the deception and misfortunes of others—providing no lasting damage is done in the process.

Works Cited

Arden, Heather. *Fool's plays: A study of satire in the "sottie."* Cambridge: Cambridge University Press, 1980.

Aristophanes. *Plays.* Trans. P. Dickinson, Oxford and London: Oxford University Press, 3. Vols, 1970.

Attinger, Gustave. L'Esprit de la commedia dell'arte dans le théatre français. Paris: Librairie Théatrale, 1950.

Axton, Richard and John Stevens (ed. and trans.). *Medieval French Plays.* Oxford: Basil Blackwell, 1971.

Boucquet, Thierry V. (trans. and ed.). *Six Medieval French Farces.* Lewiston, N.Y. and Lampeter, Wales: Edwin Meller, 1999.

Cotgrave, Randle. *A Dictionary of the French and English Tongues.* London: Adam Islip, 1611.

Davis, Jessica Milner. *Farce.* Rev. Ed., Piscataway, NJ: Transaction, 2003.

Dryden, John. *The Conquest of Granada.* London: Henry Herringman, printed by T. N. [Thomas Newcomb], 1671.

Fo, Dario. *Dario Fo gramelot su Silvio Berlusconi.*

<www.youtube.com/watch?v=D1Tfqgh187Q (accessed 1 April 2013)>.

Harris, Max. *Sacred Folly: A New History of the Feast of Fools.* Ithaca NY: Cornell University Press, 2011.

Jubinal, Achille, éd. Mystères inédits du quinzième siècle. Tom. 1. Paris: Téchener, 1837.

Kennard, J. S. (ed. and trans.). *The Italian Theatre*, 3 Vols. New York: Rudge, 1932.

Kirkman, Francis (ed.). The wits. Or, Sport upon sport: a selection of drolls and farces, Cornell Studies in English. Ithaca, NY: Cornell University Press, 1932.

Lanson, Gustave. "Molière e la farce." *Révue de Paris,* 1901: 129-153.

MacAfee, Helen (ed.). *Pepys on the Restoration Stage.* New Haven CT: Yale University Press, 1916.

Petit de Julleville, Louis. *Les Comédiens en France au Moyen-âge,* Paris: Cerf, 1885.

—. Répertoire du théâtre comique en France au Moyen-âge, Paris, Cerf, 1886.

Picot, Émile. *La Sottie en France,* Nogent-sur-Rotrou: Daupeley-Gouverneur, 1878.

—. *Receuil general des sotties*, Paris: Firmin Didot, 3 Vols. 1902-1912.

Rey-Flaud, Bernadette. La Farce, ou la machine à rire: Théorie d'un genre dramatique, 1420-1550. Geneva: Droz, 1984.

Richards, Kenneth and Laura Richards. *The Commedia dell'arte: A Documentary History*. Oxford and New York: Basil Blackwell, 1990.

Roques, Mario, ed. *Le Garçon et l'aveugle: jeu du XIIIe siècle*. Les Classiques Français du Moyen Âge No. 5, Paris: H. Champion, 1911.

Sticca, Sandro. *The "Planctus Mariae" in the Dramatic Tradition of the Middle Ages*. Trans. Joseph R. Berrigan. Athens GA: University of Georgia Press, 1988.

Tydeman,William, ed. *The Medieval European Stage, 500-1550.* Cambridge: Cambridge University Press, 2001.

FRENCH COMIC HEROES

JOHN PARKIN

The title of this paper derives from the work of one unsung champion of humour studies, namely Robert Torrance, whose book *The Comic Hero* mapped out one of the best strategies I have ever read for the reading of a certain type of comic figure. That figure is the one who generates humour by deliberately flouting convention, refusing standard values, rejecting the accepted morality and, most importantly, is celebrated for doing so.

The character's history is both deep and rich, having a profound importance in primitive folklore, where the trickster or joker can even be a kind of minor deity (Douglas 108), and a crucial role in Attic Old Comedy. Witness Aristophanes' process of characterisation in plays like *The Birds* or *The Wasps* (the latter being for Torrance "a calculated insult to the audience's intelligence" [50]). At the same time he comes through into our own lifetime via characters such as Sergeant Bilko or Bart Simpson, and to use a key example from Torrance, Randall McMurphy, hero of Kesey's *One Flew over the Cuckoo's Nest*. Turning to France, one can cite the famous and much loved comedian, broadcaster and comic actor Coluche who, in deliberate mockery of the electoral system, once came close to running for the French presidency.[1]

Such characters fit perfectly into a category of humour, which on my own initiative I have termed knavish parody[2]: parody in that the relevant individual creates a travesty of life whereby, for the purposes of the joke, one pretends, say, to take Coluche seriously as a politician; knavish, in that the man behind the clownish mask knows exactly what he is doing in subverting the relevant system. Bart Simpson is fully aware that he is a naughty boy; Bilko realised but did not care that he was the opposite of a responsible army sergeant; Coluche invited one to reject the entire political structure as a joke, somewhat in the spirit of the weekly journal *Charlie*

---

[1] This was for the 1981 poll when Mitterrand defeated the incumbent Valéry Giscard d'Estaing. Coluche pulled out once it proved unlikely that he would achieve the necessary signed support of 500 French dignitaries.

[2] Cf. Parkin (Conclusion) where I used the terms devilish and satanic to describe the knavish archetype.

Hebdo with whose journalists he was in close sympathy and which introduced one pre-election number in 1971 with the front-page admonition: "Votez con, vous n'avez pas le choix" ("Vote for the sap; there's no alternative.").

A considerable emotional effort may be required for one to indulge such provocative clownery, which perhaps derives more from a male than a female conspectus. For if relatively few lady comic heroes spring to mind, particularly in the French tradition, this may be because the knave's role and one's appreciation of that role require that one reject some part of one's responsible personality—a gesture that men might find more congenial than women. Yet the psychological effects of such a response could well have deep benefits. Why else would the trickster figure have gained such importance in tribal rituals, or would the famed court jesters of, say, Louis XII and Francis I, have become heroes in their own time?[3] It is arguable that until they had been inverted by the resident fool, official procedures remained incomplete within the court that sustained him. Moreover, one of the first French heroes whom Torrance presents for consideration had an influence that was comparably profound in that he even brought a change to the French lexicon. I refer to Reynard the Fox, whose fame was such that the traditional word for the animal (*goupil*) was displaced by his own originally proper name (hence *renard*).

The Reynard legends form a deliberate spoof of that genre of epic, which, through the heroic tradition of the *chansons de geste*, has proved one of the most enduring monuments to French medieval culture. With his appalling roguery that involves rape, theft, lying, the deliberate betrayal of friends and the defiling of religious ritual, Reynard stands head and shoulders above the figure of Odysseus, whom in some ways he resembles. For Torrance, therefore, the final scene of one of his adventures is archetypal: in order to avoid execution for his multiple crimes, Reynard swears repentance and vows to undertake a pilgrimage, only to violently repudiate that promise in full hearing of his king, once he is clear of the court. Given that his recantation also involves the polluting of the cross itself, this is, as Torrance puts it, "his ne plus ultra of audacity and rebellion" (108), and, as ever is the case with black humour, one is challenged to respond, if one dare.

This famous example typifies the rogue figure, but he is present in various medieval traditions, spawning the many scapegrace protagonists of the *fabliaux*, including most obviously the randy priest, plus tricksters like

---

[3] The jester Triboulet served both kings, q.v. Welsford, 147-8. The name was an alias to be used by both Rabelais and Victor Hugo for characters of their own invention.

Til Eulenspiegel and Robin Goodfellow who amuse by gulling and guying the public at large and in particular all figures of authority. An interesting cousin of theirs is François Villon, about whom a puckish legend was created on the basis of his own quite limited but very powerful poetic *œuvre*, that legend lasting from the period of his lifetime through to modernity and its romantic refashioning as *The Vagabond King*. However, a more signal example comes in the Renaissance proper and the work of François Rabelais.[4]

Torrance handles Rabelais only sketchily, and probably underestimated that author's satiric power, which follows particularly in the wake of his intellectual hero Erasmus. However, even Erasmus was not without his penchant for unconventional humour—witness his *Praise of Folly*—whilst Rabelais' great originality lay in juxtaposing his humanistic attacks on Medieval learning and religiosity with the spirit of knavish parody as encapsulated in his most original clown figure, Panurge. It is through a preposterous piece of nonsense that this figure gains entry into the heart and household of his lord, Pantagruel, whom he meets one day and for the first time outside Paris (where the young giant is completing his studies) and completely confounds him by speaking incomprehensibly in a series of languages, some of them invented, while seeking simultaneously to convey (or, to conceal?) the fact that he is desperately poor and starving.

Notwithstanding such outrageous insolence, Pantagruel warms to him immediately and vows that the man will never again leave his company, which proves in effect to be the case. Despite some appalling crimes (at one point he cold-bloodedly murders an entire shipload of merchants simply because they were bargaining too high a price for their sheep) and some pathetic weaknesses (during a storm on the same journey, he proves to be an abject coward, utterly unable to help the crew's efforts), Pantagruel never dilutes the love he bears for this man who is yet his moral antithesis. The giant may at times reprove him and pass significant moral judgments upon him, but Rabelais is clearly very proud of having invented a comic hero of such amazing richness and glamour,[5] and he

---

[4] Rabelais used the Villon figure himself in one of his more outrageous tales (*Pantagruel and Gargantua*, Book 4, chapter 13). However the *Le Recueil des Repues franches de Maistre François Villon et de ses compagnons* (The Collection of Buckshee Meals of François Villon and his Cronies) comprises a set of stories largely dedicated to his deceitful and thieving exploits, and originating long before Rabelais took him up.

[5] Just like Villon, Panurge was given an extended role in other writers' works, e.g. the *Navigations de Panurge* of 1538.

hopes that we can share an indulgence that the Pantagruelians consistently afford him. For the narrator, Alcofribas Nasier, he is "the best guy alive," a compliment uttered perhaps in the secret wish that he too could be no less deliberately and unwaveringly foolish.[6]

"Le malade imaginaire" (Illustration from Molière's eponymous work by Honoré Daumier, 1860-1862; Philadelphia Museum of Art)

As the dominant French literary tastes became more elevated in the 17th century, so the exuberance and excesses of the Renaissance tended to be replaced by a more regular satiric programme by which moral and cultural standards were not so much defied as reinforced. Nevertheless, a parallel trend of libertine humour did survive in poets like Théophile de Viau or novelists like Pierre Scarron, and we can see some echoes of the comic knaves of yesteryear even in the works of Molière, a playwright in many ways subject to, and conscious of, the need for *bienséances*—that is, those standards of seemliness that he might well have found constraining.

---

[6] The phrase, which comes in Rabelais' *Pantagruel* chapter 16, is borrowed directly from his contemporary Clément Marot, whose persona proves to be a similarly mischievous scapegrace.

Thus, to view his *L'Avare* (*The Miser*) as a moral tale denouncing meanness, or *Le Malade Imaginaire* (*The Imaginary Invalid*) as a satire on hypochondria, is at once legitimate but also very limiting. Quite apart from the fact that neither comic hero is, in fact, cured of his obsession during these plays (in their final scenes, the miser Harpagon is left clutching his treasure chest, and Argan, dupe of the medics, simply becomes one himself), one can legitimately ask if one would really want this to happen. Does the monomaniac not possess a certain fascination of his own, dependent on the simplicity with which he lives his life in a time-warp of fanatically repeated sacrifices to his own obsession? Perhaps so, but in this connection he is not a comic hero, at least to the extent that he is oblivious of the way in which he is distorting normal values by, in the case of *Tartuffe*, making his admiration for a religious fanatic the focus of his entire life.

Interestingly, the relevant protagonist, Orgon, breaks the pattern I have outlined, by in fact losing his fixation with the religious hypocrite who had deceived him. But what of Tartuffe himself? Congratulations again to this figure for having changed the nature of the French lexicon: like *renard*, *Tartuffe* is now a common noun synonymous with hypocrite, and that in more than one language. However, the man concerned is far more easily cast as the comic villain, booed and hissed from the popular stage, than as the comic hero, who is cheered for defying all moral, legal and even religious authority (such authority in fact commands his hypocritical devotion). So, when faced with charges of impiety, Molière had cause to defend himself over *Tartuffe* by asserting in his preface that he had portrayed the man as unremittingly evil: "not one of his words nor actions fails to portray to the audience the character of a wicked man" (Molière, I.884), and a sympathetic interpretation of his role, however rich it be, would prove even harder to effect than in the case of that other social enemy, Shakespeare's Malvolio.

What Molière felt obliged to do, therefore, and in his own defence, was to reiterate the Aristotelian notion whereby the role of comedy is to correct human vices, when, by contrast, one entire function of the comic hero is to have them applauded. In this connection a far more problematic and troubling example is his own Dom Juan. Hero of a play that is much less classically crafted than *Tartuffe*, this figure brings with him all the comic appeal of the illicit seducer, an appeal founded by my reading on fertility symbolism rather than any ethical value. At the same time, Molière clearly parodies that role by making his approaches to women so farcically mechanical.

His defiance of religious values bears its own ambiguities too, as he is both generous (still giving a *louis d'or* to the beggar who refused to be bribed into uttering a profanity) and brave (helping the brother of the woman he has most recently dishonoured to fight off three armed robbers who were threatening his life). However, the play's major theme concerns that *esprit libertin* which grew through the French 17th century as a counter-morality involving a defiance, particularly, of religious beliefs and obligations. In this context Dom Juan is not only unrepentantly promiscuous but also indifferent to the threats of his nemesis, the Commandeur, whom he has murdered but whose statue, in the end, drags him off to Hell. Actually, this scene is so casually constructed that it can easily be read as a parody rather than a visitation of divine justice—an issue best left to actors and directors who remain free to exploit the choices with which Molière provides them. Much clearer are the comments that Juan makes in Act V, Scene 2, concerning his own libertine role, which he justifies on the basis of authenticity—at least his villainy has been conscious and open—though he swears at the same time to conceal it henceforth under a mask of hypocrisy, seen as the key vice of modern times: " So does a wise man adjust to the vices of his epoch" (Molière, II.81)—an interesting exercise in existentialist psychology, though hardly a genuflexion before any Christian consensus.

With the Enlightenment, to be sure, that consensus was shattered in any case, at least among those writers who have commanded most critical attention. Thus, Voltaire establishes a satiric agenda based on human rather than sacred values, though a key comic figure such as Candide lacks the outrageous side of the comic hero and belongs in a different category from Molière's Dom Juan or Rabelais' Panurge,[7] a fact that potentially derives from the unremitting command which that agenda retained within Voltaire's own career. However, the point would be much less true of his contemporary, Diderot, whose *Jacques le fataliste*[8] extends the same moral and psychological experiments that one observes in the similar master-servant dialogues operating between Dom Juan and Sganarelle, if not indeed between Pantagruel and Panurge.

Even more problematic is Diderot's other dialogue piece, *Le Neveu de Rameau* (*Rameau's Nephew*), which, like *Jacques le fataliste*, remained unpublished in his lifetime. Torrance aptly discerns how the nephew, *Lui*,

---

[7] This category I have defined elsewhere as that of naïve parody (see again Parkin, Conclusion). It is embodied centrally by Voltaire's other comic protagonist L'Ingénu.

[8] This famous anti-novel derives explicitly from Sterne and emulates his refusal (witness *Tristram Shandy*) to retain a linear narrative, maintain coherent characterisation or display narratorial omniscience.

Diderot's inadequate and servile protagonist, shares the honest self-awareness of Molière's Dom Juan, along with all the vices of the parasite, including envy and spite towards those who have achieved power and success in society. To this extent the character has been interpreted as a self-examination by Diderot of his own personality,[9] and such a psychological approach can greatly impair comic heroism as we are examining it. Once a clown figure begins to take himself seriously, the humour which he secretes comes under threat.

What I would prefer to argue is that Diderot uses this work to parody his own personality, presenting the sententious *Moi*, the Nephew's interlocutor, as a sober but in the end somewhat tedious representation of his *philosophe* identity. *Lui* expresses Diderot's unorthodox side, revealed years before in his then outrageous novel *Les Bijoux indiscrets* (*The Indiscreet Jewels*), a satire of many aspects of contemporary society conducted via the tales told by a series of talking gems, euphemism for a more personal female attribute. Here the author himself emerged as a comic hero, Desné noting how much of Panurge there was in the young Diderot (Diderot 1972, 38).

Then, committed in his middle years to the highly serious task of masterminding the *Encyclopédie*, he may have condemned *Les Bijoux* as "abominable" (1981, 9), yet still found time, in the dialogue held by some to be his masterpiece,[10] to convert the real Jean-François Rameau into a jester figure who yet revealed Diderot's own self-doubt (had he not, like *Lui*, missed his true vocation?) plus his own response to unorthodoxy. Ebullient in his miming, unashamed of his sycophancy, and frank in his indulgence of black humour, Rameau conspires with his author to reveal once more a defiance of conventional attitudes that the French, if not others, have always tended honestly or guiltily to admire.

With the bourgeoisification of values through the 19th century and the failure of Napoleon (a character arguably parodied in Balzac's Eugène de Rastignac and certainly in Stendhal's Julien Sorel),[11] it perhaps became harder to portray any kind of heroism, be it comic or serious. The solution, if such it be, is best encapsulated by Torrance in his treatment of Flaubert's

---

[9] The argument is propounded by Fabre in his critical edition of the *Neveu* (Diderot 1963: LXIII ff.). That it should be so firmly contested by others, e.g. Desné in his 1972 edition, merely underlines the rich subtleties of the text.

[10] Q.v. Desné in Diderot 1972, 86.

[11] These are the protagonists, respectively, of Balzac's *Le Père Goriot* and Stendhal's *Le Rouge et le Noir*, works which, however significant, remain only incidentally comic.

unfinished comic novel, *Bouvard et Pécuchet.* Here the author's protagonists are two thoroughly inconspicuous copy clerks who benefit from an unexpected legacy by retiring to a village in Normandy where they dedicate themselves first to farming and then, following the failure of that enterprise, to a vast range of other activities, all of them equally unsuccessful.

Nevertheless, Torrance, like others, discerns within them a degree of heroism in the fact that they never abandon their quest: "If the uncertainty in which their clownish efforts repeatedly culminate is a paramount source of their comedy, their willingness to acknowledge uncertainty and renew their interminable search is the crowning proof of their heroism" (238), though such a positive reading of the work's conclusion may beg the question. We learn from Flaubert's notes that, in the end, they purposely return to their original activity as copyists (surely chosen by him as the most uncreative of professions), which decision Torrance deems triumphant: "Their gleeful resolution is simultaneously a paean of victory" (239). Yet it could equally be seen as an admission of total failure whereby they retreat from any attempt to better themselves or the world around them and become simply those two woodlice, as their author described them, and not without admitting a degree of affection, nay even identification. For example, their attempts to brief themselves on every area of human knowledge from philosophy to childcare simply mirror Flaubert's own fanatically pursued research in the composition of this and his other books.

One simply does not know with what impression Flaubert would have left his reader had the work ever been completed, for as it stands it has been described as platitudinous and boring.[12] The point I would underline is the way in which, perhaps for want of anything to admire in established society, it focuses on the obscure individual, much as Flaubert did in his other novels, *Madame Bovary* and *L'Education sentimentale*, and this is the pattern I would like to project into more recent periods by examining in conclusion a number of modern comic heroes, beginning with the protagonist of numerous films by Jacques Tati, Monsieur Hulot.

Hulot has been subjected to a great deal of intellectual analysis, much of it highly stimulating and sociologically relevant. However, the director, an expert mime and a skilled and demanding *cinéaste*, avoided any notion of a message, allowing his comic hero to bumble through his holidays (*Les*

---

[12] Q.v. Sarraute, 85, where it is condemned as "fastidieuse" and devoid of all artistic quality.

Vacances de Monsieur Hulot), his family life (*Mon Oncle*) and his encounters with modern living (*Playtime* and *Traffic*) without ever compromising his own mysterious identity. Stripped of any background, long-term relationships, verbal self-expression (in *Les Vacances* the character never actually says anything), or even a forename, he is reduced in each film to a series of sketches where he defies conventional behaviour, efficiency or any work ethic. Totally immune to the threats of modern living and unconcerned with the pressure to succeed, Hulot is in many ways a high-priest of a more traditional French way of life, and, like the Reynard and Panurge figures before him, is destined to survive against the odds. Despatched at the end of *Mon Oncle* from the modern household that he has disrupted, he will forever return.

We can admire him as a clown, if we choose to do so. We cannot fail to admire the achievement of Tati in creating such an iconic figure, instantly recognisable in silhouette form, and whom he resolutely refused either to explain or contextualise. Readable as contaminated by the ideology of Vichy,[13] as a vehicle of anti-American satire, even as reflecting the revolutionary ardour of May, 1968,[14] Tati's work and the figure personifying it are ultimately very far from catalysing permanent change: the rebellion that Hulot embodies is (like the same May 1968?) only a temporary one, stimulating a psychological relief from normality before normality is reimposed. This is not to say that all humour is conservative; just that the comic hero stands in an alternative world of which we achieve only transitory membership.

What Hulot shares with my next comic hero, or rather heroine, may not derive from conscious imitation, but it certainly reflects common preoccupations or a lack of them. I refer to Amélie, protagonist of a single feature film, *Le Fabuleux Destin d'Amélie Poulain* (2001: dir. J.–P. Jeunet). The same trend of anti-modernity is apparent in the interior and exterior sets of the tenement building she inhabits, the street markets that she frequents, the café where she works, with its highly traditional decor and clientele, the traditional Parisian locations through which she passes (including the Canal St. Martin and Sacré Cœur),[15] and the newspaper stand where she shows no interest in the headline announcing that gift to

---

[13] His biographer, Bellos, makes the point that Tati's career during the war was not above reproach: he gave performances in Nazi Germany.

[14] Q.v. Bellos, 143, on his early (pre-Hulot) feature film *Jour de Fête*, and 270 on his "masterpiece" *Playtime*.

[15] Flaubert uses the former location in the opening chapter of *Bouvard et Pécuchet*.

the media, namely the death of Diana, Princess of Wales, concentrating instead and exclusively on her own preoccupations and plans.

These form the gist of the film, which, unlike Hulot's adventures, ends when she finds what passes for true love, a highly original twist to the traditional role of the lovable rogue. By contrast with villains such as Panurge and Rameau's nephew, Amélie has made it her vocation to do good for people, finding ingenious ways of enhancing their happiness, all of which she accomplishes with great discretion. Her behaviour has the unconventionality typical of the comic hero, but it is an unconventional form of unconventionality, except in the impish tricks that she plays on a bullying greengrocer from the neighbourhood, or on a man who deceived her into thinking, as a child, that a whole series of catastrophes were her fault: in revenge she deliberately breaks his TV connection to a football match at the moment when goals are about to be scored. So Amélie is not unremittingly saintly and, thus, too good to be true. Nor, to be sure, is Hulot, with whom she also shares an indifference to great events and issues (apart from the theme of Diana's death, scarcely anything places us in the period when the film is so precisely set), a penchant for carnival locations, an attraction towards old-fashioned technology, and most particularly, the portrayal of insignificance. Neither figure reveals an ideological position, a meaningful cultural awareness or a desire to think in terms beyond the personal.

Can we reduce Coluche, one of France's acknowledged comic heroes of the last century, to the same level? Not to the extent that he developed a serious political position based on responses to poverty both in France and abroad. Conversely, his stage acts involved jokes that were openly ethnic and racist (e.g. anti-Belgian and anti-Black); he used flagrant obscenities in his monologues, and could unashamedly scout the traditions of his own country. The French cult of the unorthodox freethinker goes back at least to Rabelais, with whom Coluche could so easily be compared, but perhaps in both cases the deliberate clowning of the comic hero sat in uneasy alliance with the reforming agendas which, as social satirists, they sought to promote.

Félicien Moutot is a far less well-known comic hero, being a humble barber visited for advice and decisions by every politician of note in Marcel Aymé's novel *Travelingue*, a work set in the France of the Popular Front but written during World War II. Given his immense power (a total contrast with the slummy backstreet shop where he receives his customers, some of them sailors from the good old Canal St. Martin), Moutot is able to head off the revolution that seriously threatened France in the thirties, to

recommend devaluation at a late-night cabinet sitting in his backroom, and
to plan the eventual defence of France in collusion with a set of generals
who he admits hate war on a conscientious basis because spilt blood gives
them nightmares!

The coiffeur appears in only two episodes of the novel,[16] but he is
capable of masterminding its most serious events. His long monologues,
drawn from the tradition of barbershop trivia, are filled with an irony that
Aymé reinforces by portraying the novelist Luc Pontdebois, a cherished
customer, as a satire of that established *intellectuel* whose role is seriously
threatened by idiotic and obscure comic heroes like Bouvard, Pécuchet
and, again Hulot. Like Tati, who admitted "I am not a cultivated person"
(Bellos, 18), Moutot displays a striking lack of education—his droning
paragraphs draw on clichés similar to those found in Flaubert's *Dictionnaire
des idées reçues*[17]—and his plan for the unemployed involves the same
celebration of leisure personified in Hulot: cinema, cards, aperitifs, three
hours per day of compulsory attendance at international football matches,
etc. And would Tati have disagreed when the man says, "the Frenchman
scoffs at your revolution. What he wants is to quietly earn his money, eat
and drink well, and be amused" (Aymé 267)?

To be sure, such statements can read as an indictment of *le Français
moyen*, since Aymé wrote his novel in full knowledge of the debacle
which was to come in 1940. However, in the same passage he makes the
more acceptable generalisation that his compatriots are born with a sense
of wit and gaiety (268), whilst in the final chapter he specifies another
consistent quality, and one that may even undermine the barber's
marvellous schemes: "Let's not forget that the Frenchman is by
temperament a rebel" (328).

Witness Villon, Rabelais, Diderot, Flaubert, Coluche, et al., and this
refusal to compromise one's own individuality in the name of any
institution or system is surely one quality that has helped the French to
perpetually regenerate their comic anti-hero in the different forms in which
we have observed him from Reynard onwards. In Aymé's spectacular
conception of a backstreet nobody who, in fact, controls the destiny of his
entire country, we see a key example of this pattern. A non-conformist
who rejects non-conformity, he respects his customers more than the

---

[16] Notwithstanding this apparently minor role, he is significant enough to have
secured for himself the title of the translated version, *The Miraculous Barber* (New
York: Harper, 1951).
[17] This is the comic text traditionally published as an appendix to *Bouvard et
Pécuchet* and which represents Flaubert's satire of received opinion, perhaps the
work which his two clerks would end their careers copying up for posterity.

government ministers who solicit his advice, rejects fame and wealth in the name of his own integrity, and despite all the nonsense coming out of his mouth, still manages to incite our bemused imagination.

Works Cited

Anon. *Le Disciple de Pantagruel (Les Navigations de Panurge)*. Paris: Nizet, 1982.

—. *Le Recueil des Repues franches de Maistre François Villon et de ses compagnons*. Geneva: Droz, 1995.

Aymé, M. *Travelingue*, in *Œuvres romanesques complètes*, vol. III. Paris: Gallimard, 2001.

—. *The Miraculous Barber*, tr. E. Sutton. New York: Harper, 1951.

Bellos, D. *Jacques Tati: His Life and Art*. London: Harvill Press, 1999.

Diderot, D. *Jacques le fataliste et son maître*. Paris: Garnier-Flammarion, 2012.

—. *Les Bijoux indiscrets*, ed. J. Rustin. Paris: Gallimard, 1981.

—. *Le Neveu de Rameau*, ed. R. Desné. Paris: Editions sociales, 1972.

—. *Le Neveu de Rameau*, ed. J. Fabre. Geneva: Droz, 1963.

Douglas, M. "Jokes," in *Implicit Meanings*. London: Routledge and Kegan Paul, 1975: 90-114.

Molière. *Œuvres complètes*. Paris: Pléiade, 1971.

Parkin, J. *Humour Theorists of the Twentieth Century*. Lampeter: Mellen, 1997.

Rabelais, F. *Pantagruel and Gargantua*. Ware: Wordsworth, 1999.

Sarraute, N. *Flaubert le précurseur*. Paris: Gallimard, 1986.

Torrance, R.M. *The Comic Hero*. London: Harvard UP, 1978.

Welsford, E. *The Fool: His Social and Literary History*. London: Faber, 1935.

THE SUBVERSION OF EMPIRE AS FARCE IN FERNÃO MENDES PINTO'S *PEREGRINAÇÃO*

STEVEN GONZAGOWSKI

Fernão Mendes Pinto's sprawling travel narrative, *Peregrinação,* literally *Pilgrimage*, and most recently translated into English by Rebecca Catz as *The Travels of Mendes Pinto,* depicts twenty-one years of harrowing adventures that the author spent as an adventurer, explorer, mercenary and merchant from the day he set sail from his native Portugal as a part of a royal fleet expedition on March 11, 1537. Returning to Portugal sometime in early 1558 a wealthy man, he settles down in obscurity to raise a family and await in vain a royal sinecure in recognition for his service to the Portuguese crown. Some forty years after the breathtaking episodes that he describes in his work, he begins to compose his memoirs, emphasizing from the beginning that his sole motivation for doing so is to "write an awkward, unpolished tale which I leave as a legacy for my children—because it is intended only for them. I want them to know all about the 21 years of difficulty and danger that I lived through in the course of which I was captured thirteen times and sold into slavery seventeen times in various parts of India, Ethiopia, Arabia Felix, China, Tartary, Macassar, Sumatra and countless other provinces of the archipelago located in the easternmost corner of Asia, the outer edge of the world (Catz 1).

Some of the flavor of the work's epic scope can be ascertained in this introductory passage, as Mendes Pinto thoroughly recounts all of these adventures, and many more, in a wealth of hyperbolic detail. The outer edge of the world to which Mendes Pinto refers is the Japanese archipelago, and scholars of East Asian history, such as Maurice Collis, British colonial administrator of Burma, and Takiko Okamuro, the translator of Mendes Pinto's work into Japanese, concur that Mendes Pinto was in fact one of the first Europeans to arrive in Japan. This agreement, however, represents one of the few bits of factual evidence that remain uncontested in the entire eight hundred page account describing the initial encounter between the Portuguese and the various peoples of a wide swath of coastal Asia extending from the Persian Gulf to the Korea Strait. Owing to a convoluted history of the manuscript's being mislaid for a time in a remote convent and the lengthy process of obtaining permission to publish it from the censorship arm of the Inquisition, the book was not published until 1614, thirty-one years after Mendes Pinto's death. It quickly became a seventeenth-century best-seller, appearing in nineteen editions in six languages within fifty years of its initial publication in Portugal. Maurice Collis has studied the early reception of the work and concluded that, "By 1700, most educated people in western Europe had read Mendes Pinto's book, and by that year, Pinto had as many readers as Cervantes, whose *Don Quijote* was published in 1605 and 1615, parts I and II" (13). Thus, Mendes Pintos' text quickly gained canonical status as the most important work describing the encounter between Europe and the Far East since Marco Polo's account of his overland voyage across Asia had been published over three centuries earlier.

Since its initial publication, most of the scholarly debate on Mendes Pintos' text has focused on the problematic status of the book as historical document, with many critics, including such notables as the work's first translator into Spanish, Francisco de Herrera Maldonado, and nineteenth century British adventurer, Sir Richard Burton, vehemently contesting its author's veracity. Is the work an actual eyewitness account, or are we dealing with a fictionalized and fantastical distortion of the underlying events, largely based on an imaginative pastiche of secondary sources? At least as early as 1620, when Herrera Maldonado prefaced his translation with a lengthy apologia denouncing the book's lack of verisimilitude, as well as its author's meandering style, Fernão Mendes Pinto has often been branded a bold-faced liar. The idea that the fantastic tales told by the author in his work could not possibly be true is emblematized in a well-known Portuguese pun on the adventurer's name: "—Fernão, mentes?—Minto!" ("Fernão, are you lying?" —"Yes, I am lying!"), as recounted on the popular website, *Vidas Lusófonas.*

Nearly four centuries of criticism have overlooked the distinction between Fernão Mendes Pinto the author and Fernão Mendes Pinto the historical personage, a situation complicated by the fact that extremely little is known about Mendes Pinto's life beyond his narrative. It was not until the late 1950's that the Portuguese literary critic António José Saraiva attempted to steer the discussion of *Peregrinação* away from the debate of factuality versus veracity and towards a consideration of literary intent. Saraiva reads the text as a diffuse and inconsistent set of parodies within the genre of picaresque fiction, pitting the idealism of the Portuguese state and empire against an unflattering material reality, which in true picaresque style slyly mocks the upper strata of society from a subaltern position. Saraiva's 1958 monograph, *Fernão Mendes Pinto ou a sátira picaresca da ideologia*, is the first scholarly attempt to understand the particular sense of humor underpinning much of Mendes Pinto's narrative.

In the 1970's and 1980's, UCLA scholar Rebecca Catz, the foremost expert on Mendes Pintos' work, examines the ways in which mistranslations and abridgments in the various European editions of the work contribute to the reception of the narrative abroad as a fanciful collection of tall tales or, at best, a highly imaginative adventure story. Such reception of the work overlooks the satirical elements that she considers tantamount to comprehending Pinto's narrative on its own terms. Catz maintains that Mendes Pinto should be read as an intricately wrought satire of the discourses that are deployed to justify Portuguese imperialism. She theorizes that Mendes Pinto's grounding in a firm moralistic position exposes the entire imperial project as corrupt, hypocritical, and downright evil. In brief, she classifies the work as a mock epic that counterbalances the officially commissioned epic of Portuguese expansion, Camoes' epic poem, *Os Lusíadas*, published in 1572, a work with which Mendes Pinto was most likely familiar as he began composing his own memoirs.

More recently, Ronald Sousa has critiqued the readings of both Saraiva and Catz, which he lumps together under the rubric of "the ironic mode of reading Mendes Pinto," on the grounds that they continue to reify the binary of truth and falsehood (16). He maintains that these readings share the assumption that "Mendes Pinto, the authorial principle, is in control of the discourse to the point of intending and effecting factuality, falsity, or irony [and that] the text is elaborated from a consistent point of view, one that 'explains' everything from that vantage point" (Ibid.). Sousa alludes to Wimsatt and Beardsley's notion of the intentional fallacy here, and his reading of *Peregrinação* dismantles the true/false binary by analyzing the narrative voice separate from the issue of authorial intent. By focusing on Mendes Pinto's multifarious roles as narrator within the text, Sousa's analysis foregrounds the relationship between the satirist and the discourse that the satirist critiques. Once such a perspective is taken into account, it becomes clearer that Mendes Pinto's work lays out an implicit critique of the Portuguese empire at its zenith, just before it rapidly descends into a lengthy twilight period that against all odds will endure for half a millennium.

The ironical/satirical readings of Pinto's work beg the questions: 'To what extent does Mendes Pinto's satire reinscribe the dogma that it proposes to critique'? and 'Does the author really challenge the prevailing discourses of Portuguese imperialism from his position within its structure by strategically deploying satire in his work'? The short answer is 'yes', although perhaps not in the way one might expect. As he does not overtly focus his satire on European attitudes and the indignities and injustices perpetrated upon the peoples of Asia resulting from them, Mendes Pinto's brand of social critique does not display a high degree of such self-reflexivity on its surface. Such a form of satire would maintain and solidify a distinction of *us-versus-them*—we, the intrepid European conquerors, versus the naïve Other; we, the valiant Christians against the infidel Muslims and so on. Etymologically, the title of his work stems from the Latin word *peregrinus*, meaning foreigner, or "from other parts," and the main theme of Mendes Pinto's narrative is the encounter of the early modern European with his Others, chiefly the non-Christian peoples of coastal Asia.   Among many other topics of historical interest, *The Travels of Mendes Pinto* is an invaluable chronicle of the spread of Islam eastward into southeast Asia to the shores of the Pacific. By revealing the belatedness of Portugal's evangelizing mission in Asia, Mendes Pinto implies that the true foreign element in his narrative is not the various cultures the Portuguese encounter; it is the Europeans in Asia who are the true foreigners. It is the dissonance between this foreignness and the European presumption that only Others can be foreign that serves as the aim of his satire.

Mendes Pinto's depiction of the Muslims, Buddhists, Confucianists, and animists that he meets is his most radically subversive gesture, as it is in his description of the cross-cultural meetings that he deploys an understated but often mordant sense of humor. His narrative does not uphold the Eurocentric notion of the Asians he encounters as radical Other and he deploys satire as a means to erase the difference between European and Other by focusing an unrelenting satirical gaze on both sides. In a real sense, he equalizes the playing field. Although the Portuguese are depicted as a greedy lot of hypocrites, so too are the Chinese and Muslim leaders who oppose them at every turn. Much of his satirical critique is placed in the mouths of Asian or Muslim characters who expose the hypocrisy of the Portuguese in a deceptively ingenuous fashion. Fittingly, some of the narrative's most scathingly satirical commentators are children wise beyond their years. For instance, one Chinese lad, who is kidnapped and impressed into service by the Portuguese after they commandeer his family's fishing boat, remonstrates bitterly that in lieu of sincere demonstrations of piety that he expects from those who profess to be paragons of faith and virtue, the Portuguese merely offer up empty and perfunctory phrases to the heavens, which he exposes as mere lip service covering up a deep-rooted sense of evil and hypocrisy. He passionately reprimands the Portuguese sailors:

> I saw you, after you had filled your bellies, praising God with upraised arms and greasy lips, acting as if you think it is enough to mumble a few words to heaven instead of paying for what you had stolen. The almighty Lord does not command us to move our lips in prayer as much as he forbids us to rob and kill, which are the two most dreadful sins, as you will find out after you die from the terrible punishment that his divine justice has in store for you. (Catz 102)

The narrator thus paints the portrait of a pagan Chinese youth, who has never heard the word "Christian," speaking as if he had memorized an official catechism. Mendes Pinto places in this youth's mouth a meta-commentary that reputes the official Portuguese narrative of imperial expansion as evangelizing mission and exposes its underlying hypocrisy. By the same token, Mendes Pinto liberally sprinkles his narrative with empty ritualistic phrase such as "God punished us for our greed," whenever disaster strikes—for instance, after he and his comrades attack a band of Chinese pirates and make off with a galleon full of booty and then promptly lose it because of a violent storm or an unforeseen counterattack. Most likely, the apparently arbitrary use of such formulaic reminders of Christianity and the placing of the critique of religion in the mouths of pagan innocents, rather than Moslem infidels, is carefully constructed by the author in an attempt to address anticipated objections of the Inquisition's censors. Nevertheless, the official Portuguese mission of Christianizing the infidels is repeatedly revealed as a secondary project to the dominant motive of greed and profit making.

Certainly, one could critique Mendes Pinto here for ventriloquizing the Other by placing such an evangelical speech in the mouth of the Chinese youth. But in the larger context of his satirical project, the effect of such ventriloquizing serves to flatten out the differences between the Chinese and the Portuguese, and it is only one of multiple examples where the author draws parallels between European and Other in which the portrait of the European comes across as the less flattering These parallels become even more daring as the narrative progresses. Their cumulative effect is a reconsideration of traditional European moral certainties as a result of Mendes Pinto's calling into question the alleged differences between the Other and the European. Who is the real heathen in such an encounter –the solemn youth or the Portuguese marauders whom he addresses?

It is difficult to point out additional examples in a brief article, particularly since the rambling style of Mendes Pinto is impossible to parse into more pithy descriptions. Thus, I will briefly mention a series of episodes that are described in the account of the first Portuguese exploration into China that further elucidate Mendes Pinto's bridging of difference between the Other and the European. A significant portion of the description of Mendes Pinto's first foray into China revolves around the memorable personage of António de Faria, a prototypical swashbuckling pirate. As he wreaks havoc by savagely pillaging coastal villages, wantonly plundering venerable tombs, and lustfully carrying off virgin brides from their wedding banquets, de Faria is a caricature of the worst of Portuguese actions in Asia. His sole motivation is to score a profit, no matter the cost in human life or collateral damage. Here, Mendes Pinto's narrative exceeds the realm of the more genteel satirical commentary so painstakingly analyzed by Rebecca Catz. It enters into a realm of the Bakthinian carnivalesque that simply cannot be contained within the carefully cultivated and politically motivated imperial discourse of spreading European civilization and religion to the heathen peoples of Asia. Rather than the deft touch of satire here, Mendes Pinto's treatment of António de Faria relies upon a broad lampoon of the worst traits of greed, lust, and cruelty of the Portuguese explorers. But applying a measure of balance to the narrative, Mendes Pinto is also quick to note that António de Faria's behavior and attitude are matched by equally cruel and vindictive Asian pirates, such as Khoja Hassam, Muslim overlord of a tiny Malaysian principality, and later by Similau, a ruthless Chinese pirate who is doggedly determined to retain supremacy over the South China Sea trade routes.

The traditional ways of reading Mendes Pinto as social satire situate his narrative squarely within the genre of the picaresque. The narrator is not just a witness, as he fully participates in the series of misdeeds that arise as this trio of henchmen and their motley crews chase each other all over the high seas and terrorize the populations of the coastal villages. Indeed, there are many commonalities with the picaresque, including the picaresque hero's crucial function of exposing society's hypocrisy and falsehoods. However, the limitation of such an interpretation is that it is grounded in an Ibero-centric view of the world, according to which the Portuguese mariners correspond to the picaresque heroes, while their opponents, the Asian pirates, remain static and in the background, never attaining the status of foils worthy of their newfound trading rivals. Mendes Pinto surpasses the picaresque genre here by granting agency and narrative space to the Moorish and Asian pirates who thus become more than stock characters. They are elevated to the level of worthy opponents, with their own rule-breaking mores that contest their own societies' systems of law and order.

Mendes Pinto's narrative style subtly equalizes the playing field between Portuguese renegades and Asian outlaws as well. One of the most striking literary devices in the work is the use of a narrative style that frequently approaches the indirect free subjective style. This form of narration serves to further blur the lines between European and non-European by destabilizing the relationship between utterances and their originators. This complex narrative voice contributes to Mendes Pinto's taboo-breaking creation of a liminal narrative space in which European and non-European meet and ultimately discover that their similarities are more pronounced than their differences. The two sides are counterbalanced by being lampooned in equal measure until, in the end, the differences between the two sides virtually collapse, especially after the Portuguese once again lose their ill-gotten gains in a shipwreck and are forced to steal and don native clothing. By 'going native,' the Portuguese become indistinguishable from their Asian counterparts, which leads to many more scenes of confusion and mayhem. The resembled intermingling of various voices into a polyphonic conversation recalls Bakhtin's theories of dialogism. Mendes Pinto's narration alternately highlights different voices and points of view that enter into an ongoing but always unresolved conversation; as a result, no hegemonic discourse dominates the narrative. All parties participating in the conversation exhibit both vile and valiant traits; no one emerges as a clear-cut hero.

At this short-lived zenith of Portuguese expansion, Mendes Pinto equates the Portuguese to the peoples with whom they come in contact by alternatively directing his subversive gaze first on one party, then on the other. The Portuguese navigators are clearly astounded by what they behold when they finally reach China—a highly centralized, prosperous, and thriving society blessed with abundant riches and natural resources. In order to allay both Portuguese admiration and fear in the face of the irrefutable power and opulence of China, the official discourse resorts to denigrating the Chinese as a misguided bunch of heathens, thereby covering up the shock-and-awe factor by disavowing the glaringly obvious accomplishments of Chinese civilization. In a recent work on Portuguese imperialism, scholar Luis Madureira has remarked that "In Portugal's initial accounts of the far eastern world, China is presented as an unfathomably vast land empire, something like the inverted reflection of Portugal's own brand of maritime mercantilism in Asia" (118). Mendes Pinto's account nicely illustrates this world view, as China becomes a sort of fun-house mirror that renders everything even more ludic and surreal for the ragged band of Portuguese marines, reduced to the status of prisoners who must rely upon the charity and sense of justice of the Chinese for survival.

Reconsidered in light of the above, Mendes Pinto's depiction of the would-be Portuguese heroes and their ever-increasing divergence from European ideals of chivalric masculinity that still held sway when the first Portuguese explorers set out to discover a sea-route to India, is much more broadly drawn than a satire that critiques the imperial project in terms of, and from the vantage point of, the European. Instead of satire, I propose that the term "farce" more closely captures the intent and the effect of this one-of-a-kind narrative, for reasons beyond its frequent and often crude episodes based on slapstick humor and the dizzying pace of its constant reversals of fortune. One basic definition of farce is "a comedy that inspires hilarity mixed with panic and cruelty in its audience through an increasingly rapid and improbable series of ludicrous confusions, physical disasters, etc." (The Literary Dictionary). All of these elements are vital to understanding *Peregrinação* as a literary work that reveals much about the society in which it was generated, including the ensuing panic once the Portuguese realize the vastness of the globe and the relative insignificance in it of their nation, and by extension, Europe. Mendes Pinto's narrative anticipates, and plays with, the potential reaction of panic among his audience, hungry for news from the recently rediscovered Orient. His technique of treating the Other as equal preempts the Portuguese from dismissing the Asians as powerless inferiors who can be cajoled, tricked, or strong-armed into submitting to the Portuguese's desire to reap profits from the spice trade.

Mendes Pinto's farcical treatment, which acknowledges the presence and power of the Other, invites his fellow countrymen to give pause before embarking blindly upon a venture fraught with dangers and worthy adversaries. As such, Mendes Pinto's farce is thematically linked to the enigmatic figure of the Old Man of Restelo in Camoes' epic to Portuguese expansionism. In Canto IV of *Os Lusíadas*, this austere figure gravely points out to the first wave of Portuguese sailors under Vasco da Gama the lunacy of a small nation attempting to sail the seven seas, casting a shadow of doubt and disapprobation upon the Portuguese imperial enterprise. However, his sincere and logical arguments that Portugal is too tiny, too thinly populated and impoverished a nation to conquer the world is ridiculed and summarily dismissed by the gung-ho crowd of mariners, who see only potential wealth and glory. The epic and the mock-epic converge at the point where the exposure of imperial greed and European impropriety is laid bare and then immediately repressed, to come back to haunt the colonizers at a later date. The Portuguese imperial project goes forward and, against all odds, the nation that initiates European overseas expansion manages to rule over a far-flung collection of territories, in a reign that lasts longer than that of any other modern Empire, until the granting of independence to the Portuguese overseas territories in the wake of the Carnation Revolution of 1974. Ironically, centuries after the exploits he describes, Mendes Pinto's exposition of the similarities between Europe and its Others is appropriated in the middle part of the twentieth century by proponents of Gilberto Freyre's *Lusotropicalismo*, who maintain that the exceptionalism of Portuguese colonialism stems from an always-already relationship of mutual love and respect between colonized and colonized Other. The coopting of the Lusotropic discourse by Portugal's Salazar dictatorship during the final decades of the Portuguese empire in a last-ditch panicked attempt to hold on to its ultramarine provinces, represents the final chapter of the imperial farce initially introduced by Mendes Pinto at the empire's onset.

Works Cited

Collis, Maurice. The Grand Peregrination, Being the Life and Adventures of Fernão Mendes Pinto. London: Faber and Faber, 1949.

The Literary Dictionary Online. 2006. 10 Mar 2008
   <<http://www.answers.com/library/Literary+Dictionary>>

Madureira, Luís. *Imaginary Geographies in Portuguese and Lusophone-African Literature: Narratives of Discovery and Empire*. Lewiston, N.Y.: E. Mellen Press, 2006.

Pinto, Fernão Mendes and Rebecca Catz. *The Travels of Mendes Pinto*. Chicago: University of Chicago Press, 1989.

Saraiva, António José. *Fernão Mendes Pinto, ou a sátira picaresca da ideologia senhorial*. Lisboa: Jornal do Fôro, 1958.

Souza, Ronald. "Cannibal, cartographer, soldier, spy: the peirai of Mendes Pinto's Peregrinação" in The *Project of Prose in Early Modern Europe and the New World. Eds. Elizabeth Fowler & Roland Greene*. Cambridge: Cambridge Univ. Press, 1997: 15-30.

"Vidas Lusófonas," last modified January 31, 2013,
   << http://www.vidaslusofonas.pt/fernao_m_pinto.htm>>

THE TRANSGRESSIVE ETHICS
OF THE TRICKSTER IN LATE MEDIEVAL
AND POST-REFORMATION FRENCH FARCE[1]

BRUCE HAYES

The theatrical tradition of late medieval French farce has often been characterized as amoral. With its vast array of rogues and tricksters, no character stands out as a moral exemplar, and roles are constantly being reversed, leading to the common adage associated with farce: "À trompeur, trompeur et demi." ("Every trickster has his match.")[2] As a manifestation of so-called popular culture (a culture far from homogeneous), this genre of theater offers fascinating insights into acceptable and unacceptable forms of conduct within a varied cultural context. In this article, I will show how late medieval farce is in fact a theatrical genre governed by certain moral and ethical considerations, considerations which are in important respects at odds with Christian morality. Furthermore, as the genre begins to be employed as a form of propaganda in post-Reformation France, the new ideological imperatives imposed on the plays leads to the reduction, if not the elimination, of the trickster character, thus circumscribing the dramatic possibilities of the plays and contributing to the near disappearance of these comic plays in late 16th-century France.

I would like to explore within the context of the changing landscape of 16th-century French comic theater the question posed by this volume's title: At whom are we laughing? Farces were written and performed with the primary intent of evoking laughter, but understanding the nature of the joke, as well as its ethical underpinnings, suggests that the humor was not innocent, and that it served other purposes beyond mere entertainment. I would also like to suggest that the trickster character, as the main

---

[1] The research for this article was supported by the University of Kansas General Research Fund allocation #2301530.
[2] *The Farce of the Gentleman and Naudet*, v. 412, vol. 1. Unless otherwise noted, all references to farces are taken from *Recueil de farces (1450-1550)*, André Tissier, ed. 12 vol. (Geneva: Droz, 1986–98).

generator of laughter in the plays, is reduced and constrained in the polemical farces of post-Reformation France and that audiences' laughter and reactions change in profound ways, as the raucous, irreverent laughter of farce is replaced by more sober and sardonic partisan laughter.

In general, 1450 to 1550 is considered the watershed era of French farce. Farce is one of many related comedic genres popular during this time, such as *sotties* and *moralités*, often presented during feast-day celebrations and carnival, but also performed in the colleges and even at court (Mazouer 18-20). Within this theatrical corpus, in French often grouped together under the somewhat misleading rubric "secular comic theater" ("théâtre profane et comique") to distinguish it from the religious mystery plays, there is little or no concern shown for respecting conventions of any specific form.[3] The plays can often be rather heterogeneous, with such cross-pollination between comedic forms as, for example, a farce which contains a *sot*, the stock character of the *sottie*.[4] Despite these generic ambiguities and the hybridity of the plays, there are pieces which can clearly be distinguished as farces. In a farce, all dialogue and action are mere pretexts for the play's ultimate aim, namely the humiliating reversal, often corporal and scatological, of the victim of the farce. This key moment is meant to be the punch line, the part of the play that evokes the greatest laughter. The plays are short (on average fewer than 500 lines) and are primarily comprised of physical comedy, with great emphasis on gesture and movement, coupled with verbal pyrotechnics ranging from explosive insults to crude seductions. In all of this, the trickster is the central character and, while neither a hero nor an anti-hero, his or her actions determine the outcome of the play.

The ethical framework governing the turbulent action of traditional farce is one that places an emphasis on maintaining one's proper place in society. Behavior viewed as deviant or excessive is punished and the humiliating reversals—the ultimate theatrical expression of the world-upside-down—serve primarily to reassert the status quo.[5] The fact that the

---

[3] What is fundamentally misleading about the terminology used for the plays is that in their original medieval context, there was no such division between secular and religious. Farces and other comic plays were performed as interludes in mystery plays to provide comic relief during religious plays that could last for several hours and even days.

[4] See, for example, *Poor John* (*Le Pauvre Jouhan*), Tissier vol. 10.

[5] This tendency towards reasserting the status quo was recast as an attack on established customs and practices in realms outside the theater during this period, most notably in the works of François Rabelais. Rabelais, who was extremely familiar with farce, exploited the mischief contained in the plays and reworked

degrading punishments in farce are predicated on a victim's overstepping prescribed norms points to the conservative side of the genre. Investigating the crimes and punishments of farce illustrates specific correlations between the two. It becomes clear that those punished in farce are always guilty of excessive behavior. Whether it is the greedy, scheming lovers punished by the woman in *The Farce of the Three Lovers of the Cross* (Tissier vol. 11) or the bourgeois couple wanting to improve their position in society by hiring a servant who dupes them in *Jeninot Who Crowned His Cat a King* (Tissier vol. 5), victims in farce invariably demonstrate some sort of exaggerated appetite, typically base appetites such as greed, gluttony, concupiscence, or the condemnable vice of pride. In farces aimed at a more educated audience, the victim is typically mocked for his or her ignorance and pretentious behavior, such as the naïve women wanting to appear educated in *The Farce of the Women Who Try to Pass Themselves off as Professors* (Cohen 113–22) and *The Farce of the Women Who Learn to Speak Latin* (Cohen 123–34) or Mimin, the hapless protagonist of *The Farce of Master Mimin the Student* (Tissier vol. 3). While the victims change (and are interchangeable to a certain degree), the butt of the joke, the person at whom the audience laughs, remains a character whose actions are somehow at odds with a prescribed code of conduct.

This code most certainly does not fit within the framework of traditional Christian morality. While its ethical underpinnings can be described as traditional, farce does not adhere to any conventional Christian ethics or morality: sex, primarily in its illicit varieties, permeates the genre, and lying and cheating are essential to a character's survival in a dramatic world populated with conmen and hucksters. In farce, naïveté is very much a punishable offense, with no pity shown towards the gullible and the credulous. In a time and place where misogynistic practices were

them in narrative format (while still preserving the plays' oral and performance qualities) to produce humiliating reversals against figures representing institutions such as the legal system, the Church, and the Sorbonne. Most importantly in the context of this article, besides Pathelin, farce's most famous *farceur*, there is not a better, more imaginative example of a trickster in the literature of this period than Pantagruel's hapless sidekick Panurge. As Rabelais's Pantagrueline Chronicles unfold, Panurge's farcical reversals eventually work against him, with the eponymous trickster debased and humiliated at the end of the *Quart Livre*, the last work Rabelais published during his lifetime. For more detailed explorations of this transformation of the trickster character from the stage to the page in the Renaissance, see Bernd Renner's *Difficile est saturam non scribere: L'Herméneutique de la satire rabelaisienne* (Geneva: Droz, 2007), especially chapter three, and my study, *Rabelais's Radical Farce: Late Medieval Comic Theater and Its Function in Rabelais* (Aldershot, UK: Ashgate, 2010).

the norm, these plays stand out because of their extraordinarily sexist portrayals. Women are almost never punished in farce, as the plays consistently portray females as far too cunning and deceptive to be caught. In marital farces, it is almost always the wife who deceives her husband. Women are depicted as insatiably lustful, except when they are not being portrayed as shrewish and overbearing. (Occasionally, such as in *The Farce of the Wash Tub* [Tissier vol. 3], they are shown as both, which might explain why this is one of the only farces in which the wife is punished.)[6] Husbands who expect their wives to be otherwise are humiliated because of either their naïveté or their excessive jealousy. In any case, each time a punishment occurs in farce, it is meant as a corrective to reestablish an equilibrium which has been disturbed by the victim's actions (or in some cases, inaction). The ethical system of farce adheres to the practice of *lex talionis*, the legal principle that prescribes retaliating in kind for crimes committed. Whether it is Naudet sleeping with the nobleman's wife after the latter slept with Naudet's wife in the *Farce of the Gentleman and Naudet* (Tissier vol. 1) or Pathelin punishing the merchant for his greed, punishments are meant as a way to right what is perceived as an imbalance. This underscores the genre's overarching insistence on balance. Despite the constantly turbulent nature of the performances, the plays are always constructed with what Jessica Milner Davis has called "a kind of technical delight in the mechanics of equilibrium" (Milner Davis 111).

In French, *farceur* can refer to both a writer and a performer of a farce. This cross-usage is emblematic of the ubiquitous and polyvalent nature of the trickster character (*farceur*) in farce. While characters such as *badins* (simpletons) and *sots* (fools) are recognizable types, both by their distinctive costumes and the specific roles they play, a trickster takes on a seemingly endless number of forms. It is possible and even common for a stock character such as the *badin* to also be a trickster, as is the case in farces such as *The Farce of the Gentleman and Naudet* (Tissier vol. 1) or *The Farce of the Simpleton for Hire* (Tissier vol. 4). Each play contains at least one trickster and one victim, but the problem with any ethical consideration of farce has to do with the punisher, not the punished. Even if it can be established that the victim of reversal is always guilty of some

---

[6] Jody Enders has explored extensively, throughout several studies, the roles of violence and torture in medieval theater. In regards to the misogyny of farce, she rightly points out the irony of such portrayals of violent and lascivious wives, which masked the reality of men's rampant domestic abuse. See, for example, her discussion of the *Farce du Goguelu* in her chapter "The Performance of Violence" in *The Medieval Theater of Cruelty* (Ithaca: Cornell UP, 1999).

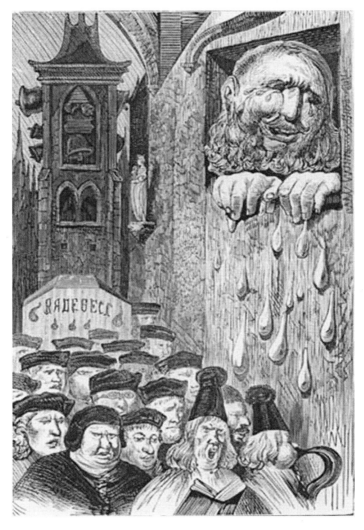

Rabelais, *Gargantua and Pantagruel*, frontispiece, 1854 edition. (Illustration by Gustave Doré, 1873; http://www.gutenberg.org)

abuse of prescribed norms, the trickster, who serves as some sort of enforcer of these rules, is also guilty of the same types of violations. All characters in farce are excessive in their appetites and desires, and although a punishment serves to put characters back in their place, it is always accomplished by a trickster who behaves in a similarly excessive manner. This moral or ethical equivalency between the punisher and the punished is the primary reason why scholars have often concluded that farce presents an amoral universe.[7]

The roles played in farce are in fact entirely interchangeable, and a trickster can quickly become the victim, a reality which supports the genre's mantra, "A trompeur, trompeur et demi." ("Every trickster has his match.") However, this reversal is almost never seen within a given farce, due to the brevity of the plays; as soon as the climax of a humiliating reversal is reached, the performance is concluded with some conciliatory dialogue or monologue. Of the rare instances where there is a doubling of tricks being played, with guilty victims being punished to reestablish equilibrium according to the ethical code of conduct of farce, the most famous example is *The Farce of Master Pathelin*.[8] In this play, the only example of a farce from this period over 1,500 lines long, the spectator is able to view directly what is merely implied in other farces, namely that the trickster is always in danger of becoming the tricked.

When Pathelin dupes the merchant through his elaborate litany of dialects, the merchant is deserving of his punishment because of his avarice and greed. However, Pathelin shares the same vice, and when a thieving shepherd comes along promising him lavish remuneration, he, like the merchant before him, takes the bait. Instead of being paid with a confounding array of dialects, the shepherd who dupes Pathelin merely mimics the bleating of a sheep ("bée"), when asked for payment. The former master of dupery is reduced to impotent protest, thus illustrating how interchangeable roles are and how polymorphous the role of trickster is. This is precisely what contributes to the vitality of the role; while the mechanics of the genre are rather straightforward and more or less predictable, the primary interest in the plays derives from the constant

---

[7] Alan Knight, in comparing farce with *moralité*, has maintained, "The crucial difference in the worlds of the two genres [...] is that the morality characters must act on the basis of an external moral standard, while farce characters have no such standard to guide their actions. [...] In the farce world there is no [...] ethical standard to which the characters are expected to conform. Cleverness is the only ethical imperative. Farce characters are occasionally punished, [...] but this is no more than personal revenge, and the wrong itself has no broader ethical status than trespass on personal property" (52–3).

[8] Another example of this is *The Gentleman and Naudet*, where the *badin* Naudet is first duped by the nobleman, who has an adulterous affair with Naudet's wife, followed by Naudet taking his revenge and sleeping with the nobleman's wife. Here and elsewhere, women are treated as property rather than as human beings.

scheming and varied strategies employed by tricksters to dupe their
victims.

On the one hand, the system of reversals in late medieval French farce
seems to suggest an overall conservative ethos which privileges the
reestablishment of order, while on the other hand, the constant mischief of
the trickster character, coupled with behaviors on stage which certainly do
not fit within a Christian moral framework, argue for a more subversive
ethos. An important element in considering the ethics of farce is the
hierarchal inversions that occur. Those who are in higher social positions
are often portrayed as greedy and willing to take advantage of any
unsuspecting individual and usually become the final victims in farce.
There exists in the plays a sort of social justice where those who have little
to lose and much to gain are usually the ones found triumphing over those
who are better off. Characters of a more privileged existence, such as the
merchant in *The Farce of Master Pathelin*, are usually portrayed as jealous
protectors of their possessions, or as greedy opportunists looking for
further gain. There are, however, limits imposed on forms of social justice.
Characters taken from the three estates, whether they are nobles, clergy, or
bourgeois, are always of a rather modest position. And while it is often
(but not always) a character of higher social position being punished in
farce,[9] it would be erroneous to assert that farce contains any form of
serious radical social critique or that the genre seeks to redress socio-
economic inequities. The ethos of farce is primarily conservative, and the
punishment of excessive behavior generally serves to reassert the status
quo, not to undermine it.

Early Ideological Uses of Farce

With the advent of the Reformation and humanist ideas in Europe and
in France, farce began to be used as a more focused ideological weapon.
This theatrical tradition is the supreme expression of the world-upside-
down, as it is precisely the humiliating reversals which occur in the plays
that define farce.[10] Late medieval farce already pokes fun at the clergy, the
legal system, and schoolmen, albeit in a rather anodyne, anonymous
fashion. But the disruptive energy of this form of theater is ripe for the

---

[9] A counter example would be *The Farce of the Pâté and the Pie* (Tissier vol. 3),
where two lowly beggars are beaten by the baker from whom they have stolen a
pie.
[10] Farce is probably the finest contemporary example of the phenomenon of the
world-upside-down explored in Mikhail Bakhtin's seminal work, *Rabelais and His
World* (Trans. Helene Iswolsky. Cambridge: MIT UP, 1968).

kinds of satirical and polemical treatment and societal critiques it was used for in Renaissance Europe. The cynical view presented in traditional farce is typically reactionary and abhors innovation and change, yet the very turbulence of the genre can be viewed as threatening and transgressive. Although rather mild, there are already examples of satirical critiques in late 15th- and early 16th-century farce, such as attacks against cowardly soldiers (*soldats fanfarons*), with particular scorn reserved for the *francs archers*, soldiers called up by Francis I during the Italian campaigns, who had a reputation for abusing peasants, pillaging, destroying property, etc.[11] More dominant in the plays is an anti-clerical attitude, which later would be exploited by reform-minded humanists and Protestants. The plays are full of lascivious monks, dissolute priests, and conmen hawking relics and indulgences. As a general rule, clerics in farce behave abominably, but there is also a resigned acceptance regarding their conduct, and while priests behaving badly may be intended to be laughable, it is hardly viewed as condemnable.

All of this changed with the influence of the Protestant Reformation in France. The anti-clerical representations in these plays became a key topic for later uses of farce and similar comedic genres, as this form of popular entertainment began to be used for very specific ideological reasons, especially in the conflict between Catholics and Protestants. The initial satirical scope of late medieval farce, lighthearted and ultimately accepting, was supplanted by bitter partisan satire and polemics which all but destroyed the playfulness and comic spirit of farce.[12]

In the post-Reformation religious and ideological debates of the sixteenth century, early authors such as Louis de Berquin, François Rabelais, and Marguerite de Navarre appropriated elements of late medieval farce into their works in order to satirize views opposed to evangelical humanism. One of the earliest examples of this type of cultural appropriation is a play performed sometime between 1526 and 1528, *The Farce of the Théologastres*,[13] whose author was likely Louis de Berquin. Accused and

---

[11] See Mazouer, *op. cit.*, 142. Examples of soldiers being ridiculed include *The Farce of the Knight and His Page* (Tissier, vol. 10) and *The Farce of the Two Freelance Archers* (Cohen 103–06).

[12] For a recent important consideration of the various types and uses of satire in the French Renaissance, see Bernd Renner's edited volume, *La Satire dans tous ses états* (Geneva: Droz, 2009). For a thoughtful study that highlights the satirical side of farce, see Sara Beam's *Laughing Matters: Farce and the Making of Absolutism in France* (Ithaca: Cornell UP, 2007).

[13] *La Farce des théologastres*. Claude Longeon, ed. (Geneva: Droz, 1989). See Antónia Szabari's recent discussion of this play in chapter two of her book, *Less*

imprisoned for heresy three times, Berquin was burned at the stake in 1529, becoming an early martyr of the Protestant cause. *The Farce of the Théologastres* has little in common with farce as I have described the genre. In this play, the would-be tricksters utterly fail to bring about the humiliating reversal which encapsulates the spirit of farce. Instead, the play resembles much more a *moralité*, replete with allegorical figures entering the stage and offering their monologues, providing the audience with a very heavy-handed moral tale centered on Protestant beliefs. Playful satire has been replaced by moralizing, polemical satire. Dramatically, the play is stilted and the characters, although ostensibly engaging in dialogue, seem instead to be taking turns offering various dogmatic observations. The characters' dialogue is laden with erudite references, which suggests that the play was intended for an educated audience. Scornful laughter is aimed at the irascible and witless behavior of the two protagonists, Fratrez and Théologastres, who represent the Catholic Church and are mocked throughout the play.

To summarize the piece, the character Faith is ill and seeking a cure. Two clerics, Fratrez and Théologastres—the latter a pun produced by conflating "theologian" with "gastric," playing on the cliché, abundant in late-medieval farce, that prelates were gluttonous—are discussing the horrors of the new Protestant heresy. They attempt to control Faith and make her follow their regime, hoping to exploit and abuse her further. The trope is a common one in Protestant polemics, portraying people as ill or infected by Catholic doctrine and in need of a cure from the New Faith.[14] Two other characters, Reason and Text (underscoring Luther's insistence on *sola scriptura*), help guide Faith away from the trap of the clerics and lead her eventually to Mercury, a figure representing Berquin. Throughout, the humor of the play, which is sardonic and heavily didactic, if not simply pedantic, centers on these two bumbling characters representing the Catholic hierarchy. These tricksters incapable of tricking are the object of the play's mocking scorn.

In this play, Fratrez and Théologastres attempt to play the role of the trickster, deceiving Faith and seeking gain from her demise. As already mentioned, the play also builds on the shopworn formula of voracious clerics, who often play the role of the trickster in traditional farce.

Rightly Said: Scandals and Readers in Sixteenth-Century France (Stanford: Stanford UP, 2010).
[14] See Jeff Persels's article on this topic, which remains the most important treatment of this topic, "The Sorbonnic Trots: Staging the Intestinal Distress of the Roman Catholic Church in French Reform Theater." *Renaissance Quarterly* 56 (2003) 1089–1111.

However, their attempts at deception are blocked and obstructed by the incessant discourse of Protestant dogma from the other characters whose humor is found in satirical quips about the excesses and abuses of the theologians. As Text remarks about his Catholic foes, "Their opinions are utter folly / Supported with a pile of stupid arguments" (vv. 144–5). Towards the end of the play, making fun of scholastic argumentation, Reason dismisses Fratrez and Théologastres' logic (and by extension the Sorbonne's disputes with Luther) as sheer gibberish. In the middle of Reason's rant, there is an intentional slip, as she confuses "lunatique" with "sorbonnique" (v. 409-10), meant to make Protestant sympathizers laugh at the Sorbonne and its perceived excesses. The earthy, excessive desires which are punished in traditional farce are here replaced with theological excess, which is critiqued and silenced. There is little that is playful in this highly circumscribed play which serves primarily as a vehicle for Protestant dogma. The edifying moral message of the play trumps all other considerations, and there remains little that is farcical or funny about this extremely sober play. The would-be tricksters are utterly inept and ineffectual. They are not able to play any tricks, verbally cordoned off by a constant stream of pious pronouncements. The notable absence of a successful trickster has the predictable result of limiting the play's comic possibilities, and the audience is reduced to an occasional smirk reserved for those who share the ideological convictions which underpin the play.

Approximately a decade later, in the capital city of Nérac in southern France, Marguerite de Navarre, along with other activities which included receiving and protecting those suspected of heresy, such as the poet Clément Marot and Jean Calvin, wrote several plays she entitled farces, all but one of which (*Most, Much, Little, Less*, the most difficult to understand and least farcical of her "farces") were not published until after her death.[15] One in particular, *The Sick Patient*, is curious for the ways that it clearly contains the key elements of a traditional farce while also containing a radical divergence from the genre, which has the effect of emptying the play of its comic potential. All of the play's characters are stock figures taken directly from the world of farce—the sick husband, his wife, the servant, and the doctor. To resume briefly, a sick husband asks his wife to fetch the doctor. She prefers folk remedies, but eventually

---

[15] *Most, Much, Little, Less* (*Trop Prou Peu et Moins*) was published in the *Suyte des marguerites de la Marguerite* (Lyon: Jean de Tournes, 1547). For a more in-depth discussion of two of Marguerite's farces, *The Sick Patient* and *The Inquisitor*, see my article, "'De rire ne me puys tenir': Marguerite de Navarre's Satirical Theater." *La Satire dans tous ses états, op. cit.*, 183–200.

accedes to his request. While she is gone, the servant tells the husband that he can be healed by having faith (echoing Luther's concept of *sola fide*). He heeds her advice, and is restored to good health just as the doctor arrives. The physician is furious that the husband has found a remedy different from his prescription; he demands payment, and leaves frustrated and uncomprehending. The evangelical tone of the play is inescapable, and the play is typically read as allegorical, with the wife's reliance on home remedies representing popular Catholic superstitions, while the pedantic doctor clearly represents the theologians of the Sorbonne.[16] The humble servant brings the good news of the New Faith and confounds the powerful.

There are obvious, important aspects which are altered in this play. The noticeably absent character in this play is the lover. In a typical farce, a lover, either the husband's, or more likely the wife's, is *de rigueur*. Marguerite's play is both aristocratic and evangelical, and therefore removes this impropriety.[17] The effect is to remove the mischief of the original form. The other character absent in the play is the trickster, the character who would be scheming to dupe the husband, the wife, or the doctor. If there is a trickster in this performance, it is the pious servant, who does in fact bring about a reversal in the play, but one that is utterly different from traditional farce. The reversal in this play is a conversion, a term that etymologically suggests a turning around or *volte face*. While the servant does poke fun at the outraged doctor in a manner that echoes the trickster character, she is such an utterly earnest character that there is little or no room for irony or playful ambiguity. The play is deeply moral, and the irreverent humor of farce is replaced by sententious piety and decorum which leaves little space for farcical comedy. However, in one of the only instances in the play of a stage direction, the text indicates, "*The Servant laughs*" (after v. 326), in response to the ranting of the perturbed

---

[16] See V.L. Saulnier's introduction to the play, *Marguerite de Navarre: théâtre profane* (Geneva: Droz, 1978) 3–13.

[17] While Marguerite's *Heptaméron* contains many examples of scatological and sexual humor that seem to contradict such an assertion, it should be kept in mind that the *Heptaméron* was published posthumously. While this play and others were also published posthumously, it is likely that they were publicly performed during Marguerite's lifetime. Any play or text made public and attached to the Queen of Navarre would need to demonstrate the piety and modesty expected from the king's beloved (and much scrutinized) sister. Moreover, as Lucien Febvre made clear in his magisterial study, *Amour sacré, amour profane* (Paris: Galimard, 1944), the distinctions we draw between the sacred and the profane are anachronistic and combining both was much more acceptable in Marguerite's time.

doctor. The humor here is both subtle and subdued, a form of laughter found in Marguerite's works that Daniel Ménager has called "mystical laughter" (135).

Crisis and Conflict

While the first half of the sixteenth century saw the continued popularity of medieval forms of comedic theater, a number of events in mid-century led to the disappearance of plays such as farce and *sottie.* Within the context of heightened religious tensions and partisan violence, the plays were often banned and the confraternities that produced them were barred from putting on plays. A symbolic moment often identified by critics is 1548, the year that the Paris parliament banned the performance of *moralités.* The following year saw the apparition of Joachim du Bellay's *Defense and Illustration of the French Language,* a polemical manifesto which laid out the aesthetic agenda of the Pléiade. In it, Du Bellay insisted on theater based on classical comedy and tragedy, restoring the "ancient dignity" that had been usurped by "farces and moralities" (II, 4, 138).

It is within such a different context, shortly after the end of the first War of Religion (Peace of Ambroise, 1563), that the *Basoche*, a Parisian legal society with a long tradition of putting on farces and other theatrical productions, staged a morality play entitled *Mars and Justice.*[18] The play follows the typical structure of a morality play, with allegorical figures commenting on the state of affairs. The views expressed are militantly Catholic, and they decry the harm done to the city and the country as a result of the unrest and conflict generated by the French Protestants and their nefarious foreign allies. (Xenophobia plays heavily in the propaganda of both Catholics and Protestants, as each side accuses the other of bringing foreigners into France.) The play's conclusion is rather curious and germane to the present study. After the various characters have completed their populist critique of the Protestants, the text switches from alexandrine versification to the lowlier octosyllabic verse, the traditional versification of farce. What follows is a stream of reminiscences by the characters, recalling a host of scabrous stories, primarily on the topic of marital infidelity. The tales the characters recount are in fact typical farces, with deceptive wives and scheming priests. It is a strange juxtaposition, but it recalls the original reputation of the *Basoche*. It is odd, after all, to

---

[18] *Deux moralités de la fin du Moyen-Âge et du temps des Guerres de Religion.* Jean-Claude Aubailly and Bruno Roy, eds. (Geneva: Droz, 1990).

have a censorious play staged by a group long known for its irreverent antics and playful spirit. This odd appendage at the end of the morality play seems to be a wistful reminder of the former spirit of the *Basoche*, now lost under the rubble of war. At the end of the play there is laughter, but it is rueful and detached, recalling rather than acting out the mirthful misbehavior of farce. The tricksters no longer seem to have a use, and instead are marginalized and silenced by the oppressive force of ideological conformity, constrained to step back from the stage and recall their former glory.

To conclude, in this overview of the trickster in farce from late 15th- to late 16th-century France, I have sought to show how the lightly satirical humor of late-medieval farce, particularly embodied in the character of the trickster, is supplanted and replaced by the much more negative and destructive partisan polemics of post-Reformation theater, as Horatian-style satire is replaced by a more sardonic Juvenalian variety. These later plays are laden with religious and doctrinal restrictions, a result of prescriptive ideologies that sought to purify and elevate such vulgar and lowly theatrical representations. Laughter is all but abolished, limited to the scornful smirks of the converted, and the modern reader is left wondering whether there is anything humorous at all about these purportedly comic pieces. This is part of the aesthetic, pedagogical, and ethical changes during the sixteenth century that Daniel Ménager defines as a change in socially acceptable behavior from laughter ("le rire") to the more circumscribed smile ("le sourire"). This simple, elegant phrasing is instructive, but slightly obscures the violence and distrust, including a growing distrust of unrestrained laughter, which contributed to this change. The creative force of mischief embodied in the trickster is deflated and constrained, doomed to oblivion were it not for the importation of the *commedia dell'arte* from Italy and the ultimate revival of farce by Molière in the latter seventeenth century.

Works Cited

Bakhtin, Mikhail, *Rabelais and His World* (Trans. Helene Iswolsky).
Cambridge: MIT UP, 1968.

Beam, Sara. *Laughing Matters: Farce and the Making of Absolutism in
France* . Ithaca: Cornell UP, 2007.

Bouhaïk-Gironès, Marie. *Les Clercs de la Basoche et le théâtre comique
(Paris, 1420-1550).* Paris: Champion, 2007.

Cohen, Gustave. *Recueil de farces françaises inédites du XVe siècle.*
Cambridge, MS: The Medieval Academy of America, 1949.

Du Bellay, Joachim. *Défense et illustration de la langue française.* Jean-
Charles Monferran, ed. Geneva: Droz, 2001.

Enders, Jody. *The Medieval Theater of Cruelty.* Ithaca: Cornell UP, 1999.

Graham, Harvey. *The Theatre of the Basoche. The Contributions of the
Law Societies to French Mediaeval Comedy.* Cambridge: Harvard UP,
1941.

Hayes, Bruce. *Rabelais's Radical Farce: Late Medieval Comic Theater
and Its Function in Rabelais.* Aldershot, UK: Ashgate, 2010.

Knight, Alan. *Aspects of Genre in Late Medieval French Drama.*
Manchester: Manchester UP, 1983

Mazouer, Charles. *Le Théâtre français de la Renaissance.* Paris:
Champion, 2002.

Ménager, Daniel. *La Renaissance et le rire.* Paris: PUF, 1995.

Milner Davis, Jessica. *Farce.* New Brunswick and London: Transaction
Publishers, 2003.

Renner, Bernd. *Difficile est saturam non scribere: L'Herméneutique de la
satire rabelaisienne.* Geneva: Droz, 2007.

—. *La Satire dans tous ses états.* Geneva: Droz, 2009.

Tissier, André, ed. *Recueil de farces (1450-1550).* 12 vol. Geneva: Droz,
1986–98.

PART II.

ABOUT MEDICS, MERCHANTS AND OTHER SUCH ROGUES

A CASE OF MEDICAL SATIRE
AS THERAPY IN COLONIAL PERU:
DIENTE DEL PARNASO
BY JUAN DEL VALLE Y CAVIEDES

PAUL W. SEAVER

Throughout the centuries, philosophers and writers have asserted that laughter has therapeutic properties. In the early Middle Ages, the *Regimen Sanitatis Salernitanum*, written by monk-physicians in Salerno, Italy, as medical advice to the King of England, recommends regular attention by three doctors: "first Doctor Quiet, Next Doctor Merry-man, and Doctor Dyet" (School of Salernum 75). ("Dyet" here refers to any regimen for eating.) Glending Olson relates in *Literature as Recreation in the Later Middle Ages* that listening to cheerful stories was customary medical advice in that period, and that Renaissance comic authors often boasted about mitigating the suffering of their readers with their funny stories. Rabelais clearly considered laughter as medicine. In the Prologue to Book 4 of *Gargantua and Pantagruel*, he writes that he is asked daily to continue his narratives since "many languishing, ill or otherwise indisposed and afflicted people have, by reading these volumes, triumphed over their worries..." and states that his only purpose is that "these pages might give some small relief to the sick and the afflicted..." (379). Cervantes also was convinced that the laughter produced by humorous stories had therapeutic qualities "because they undo the melancholy humors and reestablish a balanced temperament" (qtd. in Trueblood 79). And Juan del Valle Caviedes, colonial Spanish America's premier satirical poet (1645 - 1698), offered therapy to the afflicted through the entire body of his medical satire prescribing laughter as a way for society, specifically colonial Peru, to cure its ills both physical and social.[1]

---

[1] There is a long history of social satire, especially of doctors, in Spanish literature, and of this Caviedes was well aware. Moreover, the use of satire for social commentary and correction was commonplace in European literature of the period. Ironically, while Caviedes and others obviously recognized laughter's therapeutic potentiality, it was not until the 1970's that scientific research proved its medical

A *criollo*, Caviedes was born in Porcuna, Andalucía, near the middle of the seventeenth century. Leaving Spain as a child, he arrived in Peru around 1657. As a youth, he worked in the mining industry. He married in 1671, reared five children and probably worked as a merchant in Lima (Johnson 86-87). In 1683 he was stricken with an illness that he was convinced he would never survive and blamed his personal traumas on the treatments of the physicians who attended him. Happily, he did survive and his poems, notable for their implacable criticism of doctors and for the mordancy of their tone, attest to the impact of that experience.

In the approximately 350 poems in which Caviedes castigates most sectors of Peruvian society, by far the most frequent target of his satiric wit is the medical profession. For him, doctors are ignorant and motivated solely by greed. Unprincipled and venal, they are astute only in their skills at deception designed to conceal the reality within-- arrogance, pomposity, hypocrisy, negligence, incompetence and insensitivity. Contrary to their image, they are solely guided by the ethos of self-aggrandizement rather than by concern for patients. They abuse their power and the trust in them for financial gain and to satisfy their lust by taking advantage of women sexually. In sum, they are truly evil because they are aware of what they are doing by promoting death rather than by seeking cures. In one amusing example, one doctor sues another for having tried to scare him to death by having a priest administer the sacraments although he was not gravely ill; and when that didn't succeed, he invoked God's help and prepared a potion of poison! (360: 31-33).[2] Populating his poems with this kind of doctor, Caviedes takes perverse pleasure not only in his demeaning laughter at individuals and a profession which he condemns in a blanket denunciation but also in a black humor that sees illness, suffering, deformity and death as risible (94).

In style and theme, Caviedes, who has been called the Peruvian Quevedo,[3] owes much to the literary fashions of the period, yet he brings to his work a uniquely personal and American expression, lending local

---

value in stress reduction and in its impact on the immune system. Consult the Works Cited for a few relevant titles by Bill Fry.

[2] This and all future textual page references herein are from the 1990 edition of the *Obra completa* of Caviedes edited by Cáceres, Cisneros and Lohmann Villena. All quotes are cited and translated exactly as they appear in that text.

[3]Francisco de Quevedo y Villegas, one of the greatest writers of Spain's Golden Age, epitomizes the intricate Baroque style known as "conceptismo," with its emphasis on subtle word plays and intricate conceits. His satirical poetry and his prose *Sueños* (*Dreams*) launch many virulent attacks, much in the vein of Caviedes, on doctors as well as on other figures and occupations of his time.

color that appealed to a wide range of literate Peruvians. In *Diente del Parnaso*, his only known titled book, he develops his satire through the use of many common poetic structures of the time, and his rhetorical devices, which abound in antitheses, inversions, metaphors, paradoxes, irony, plays on words, and hyperboles, show clear evidence of Baroque influence.[4] In spite of Caviedes's ample poetic output, only three of his poems were published in his lifetime and these on topics other than medical satire (Reedy, *Satire in Colonial Spanish America,* Foreword xxii). Nonetheless, his writing was widely known in Peru through circulation of his works in manuscript form (Johnson 87). The lack of publication of his poetry until well after his death was undoubtedly due to the provocative nature of the anti-doctor animus in his poems and to moments of coarseness and bad taste which have drawn condemnation as being pornographic, scabrous and obscene.[5]

Significantly, Caviedes addresses his most satiric invectives at well-known influential and powerful public figures that he vilifies and humiliates, envisioning them as grotesque both physically and morally.[6] The power structure to which the doctors mentioned in Caviedes's poems belonged could not tolerate a public unmasking of some of its important members as either incompetent or malevolent or both. Official society certainly recognized the threat he represented and did indeed constrain publication of his works. Even one hundred years after his death, on the publication of four of his poems in the *Mercurio Peruano*, edited by the Sociedad Académica de Amantes de Lima, that body refused to publish many of his works so as to avoid potential complaints about his personal satires of well-known individuals (Reedy, *Obra completa* xi).

Most of the doctors whom Caviedes attacked poetically were historical figures known to him, including highly regarded and powerful medical authorities who taught medical theory and who ministered to important

---

[4] See Fitz, McCaw, and Torres regarding Baroque characteristics of *Diente*.... Also see Lasarte ("Algunas reflexiones…;" "Juan del Valle y Caviedes y la sombra de Quevedo") and Johnson, Echagüe, and Torres for exploration of Quevedo's possible influence on Caviedes's work.
[5] Cáceres cites the first publication of *Diente*... as dating to 1873 (30). According to the nineteenth century Peruvian writer Ricardo Palma, the lack of publication of Caviedes's poems in his lifetime was due merely to the high cost of publishing books (Cáceres 31).
[6] Johnson relates that, according to superstition, a grotesque physical appearance is indicative of "a moral and ethical flaw in a person's character…" (95). As such, then, the grotesque served as an appropriate metaphorical construct for Caviedes to describe doctors' physical characteristics.

church, social and political figures. In this group are the *rector* and *catedráticos* of the University of San Marcos, the Viceroy's personal physician, a doctor of the Inquisition, an author of medical and religious works, and members and officials of the royal tribunal that examined and licensed physicians (Ibid, xxii). In many cases, Caviedes refers to these real people not by name but by a cutting nickname founded on physical traits and peculiarities as well as on their harmful impact as physicians, and he doesn't shy away from the scatological. Caviedes chides doctors for creating the illusion of a scientific foundation for their abilities through a pompous air of authority, language that is incomprehensible to others yet contextually meaningless, the appearance of scientific knowledge, a grave demeanor with patients, and external images of their profession common to them all. The caricature includes riding a mule, wearing gloves, a large ring, certain characteristic clothing and a particular type of beard, and the continual use of aphorisms and Latin terms. Titles and degrees, wealth, political and religious connections, social standing and pretensions contribute further to their moral hypocrisy, and Caviedes offers a sarcastic formula for success as a doctor in terms very reminiscent of Quevedo's.[7]

Science, not yet a reliable basis for medical care, receives its share of cynical laughter in *Diente…* For Caviedes, it is merely a tool used by doctors for their own purposes and actually costs many lives. Since doctors are ignorant and scientific knowledge is incomplete, it is perverse in their hands as they use it to convince an ignorant public to trust them. Consequently, a public willing to accept the illusion of doctors' competence contributes to its own suffering and death.

Throughout *Diente…*, Caviedes derides Peruvian medicine on two basic fronts. First, for him doctors do not measure up to Hippocrates (460 B.C. – ca. 370 B.C.), known as the "Father of Medicine" and whom Caviedes lauds and admires, nor to their principal medical resource, Galen (ca. 130- ca. 200), whose teaching Caviedes thoroughly rejects, yet they presume to be as sage and able as their icons. Second, he alleges that their

---

[7] Regarding medical ritual for the purpose of maintaining appearances and success as a doctor, Quevedo advises the following: "If you want to be a famous doctor, the first thing you need is a fine mule, a large ring on your thumb, folded gloves, long jacket, and in summer a big silk hat; having this, although you haven't read a book, you cure and are a doctor." He then cites a series of behaviors, procedures, questions and an appropriate demeanor that are designed to deceive all present (Cortezo 74). As for advice to doctors on proper confidence-building behavior during professional visits to the homes of the sick, which is found in the *Regimen Sanitatis Salernitanum*, see Packard 18-21.

medical foundation, derived from such questionable Galenic practices as the misapplication of Hippocrates' theory of the four humors and indiscriminate use of bloodletting, is illogical, inadequate and ineffective.[8] And he concludes casting doubt on the relevance of classical medical theories to contemporary Peru "because when these learned authors wrote, times were different and men were more robust." ("Romance joquiserio a saltos" 366: 53-56).

Caviedes frames all aspects of his medical satire in terms of oppositional dualities in which things and individuals are juxtaposed as the antitheses of what the canonical vision suggests, and he embeds them in a moralizing tone of good versus evil, right versus wrong and vice versus virtue. In order that the reader not misinterpret his message, he provides a code in the *Fe de erratas* to indicate the actual signification of his poetic lexicon in terms of such dualities—for instance, "Doctor/executioner," "bloodletting/throatslashing," "medication/stabbing and "cure/certain death" (260: 2-20). Thus, if readers are attentive to the message they will not be deceived and thereby become responsible for themselves.

For Caviedes, laughter in *Diente...* fundamentally serves the purpose of personal and social therapy, a kind of antidote to fear and illusion as it works its liberating effect.[9] By deriding most segments of society, and especially ridiculing prominent figures of Lima, his poetry reflects a social conscience, a kind of public exposé which points out society's dysfunctionality and questions conventional thought. By his own statement, Caviedes feels himself compelled to be "the precise chronicler of their criminal deeds" (265: 123-124).

In the dedicatory poem to *Diente del Parnaso*, the author asserts that he recovered from his own illness by disdaining his doctor's care and laughing at them instead of taking them seriously. And in the prologue he insists that laughter contained in his poems is more curative than medical

---

[8] Galen, a second century Greek physician, established the medical value and philosophical underpinnings of humoralism five centuries after Hippocrates (Machline "Huarte's Early Modern Speculations" 77). Caviedes attacks Galen and Galenic medicine in "Al desafío que tuvo el Corcobado con un cirujano tuerto, por disputa en una junta," when Death refers to Dr. Liseras and a surgeon named el Curcuncho as the greatest of the "milicia de Galeno" (41). Avicenna (980-1037), an Arab philosopher, doctor and author, is another recipient of Caviedes's doubtful stance on science and medicine.

[9] As well as fostering a sense of liberation, Caviedes's laughter reflects the superiority theories of Plato, Aristotle and Hobbes. Following this theory, "laughter is an expression of a person's feelings of superiority over other people" (Morreall, *Taking Laughter Seriously* 4).

treatment (274-75: 113-120).[10] He continues his "treatise" by placing blame not just on doctors but first on the naïve and gullible who should not be deceived by the illusion of their medical competence. Finally, he concludes that neither pharmacists nor the "medications" they dispense are credible medical adjuncts and, therefore, just as with doctors, are to be avoided. In short, Caviedes's ridicule attacks the whole vertical structure of medicine from medical education to medical practice, from diagnosis to treatment, and from doctors to pharmacists and practitioners, as well as the credibility of its canonical social and political underpinnings.

Having freed himself through laughter from the power of doctors and the fears that standard medical interventions in Lima involve, he warns his readers with pseudo-serious logic about placing trust in doctors because they are more dangerous than the illnesses they treat. And he advises: Should you call a doctor, do the opposite of what he prescribes because doctors turn the slightest malady into a mortal illness. If they do manage to cure someone, it is only by chance, as the treatments are the same for all (270: 161-164). Within Caviedes's poems, then, there is a call for empowerment through personal responsibility. In his view, through laughter people need to rid themselves of the illusion that doctors cure, and then restore their health through laughter. Otherwise, they should just let nature take its course.

As for faith's role in healing, Caviedes cites Saint Augustine at the beginning of *Diente...* and later in "Romance joquiserio a saltos" as being anti-doctor and thus, wise and consonant with other great thinkers throughout history. Quoting from *De Civitate Dei*, he writes, "A Christian doesn't have to call doctors to cure his illnesses, for he's better off trusting in God" (259). He also cites philosophers and writers from classical Greece through the seventeenth century, as well as Alfonso X el Sabio and Philip IV of Spain, who evidenced a disdainful attitude towards doctors.[10] And in his "Romance joquiserio a saltos" he notes that Pedro Calderón de la Barca lived to ninety [actually, to eighty] without ever calling a doctor, and that Luis Vélez de Guevara was eternally grateful because a doctor he had called never crossed his door! (376: 421-428).

Throughout Caviedes's poetry there are frequent reminders that the power of Lima's doctors has corrupted society systemically. In the grim business in which doctors are involved, not only are pharmacists complicit

---

[10] Satire of doctors in Europe was commonplace at the time. Regarding satire of doctors in sixteenth-century French literature, see *The Doctor in the French Literature of the Sixteenth Century* by Nancy F. Osborne. Mary Claire Randolph examines the medical motif in English Renaissance satire in "The Medical Concept in English Renaissance Satire."

in their crimes, but other segments of society as well. Undertakers are doctors' right hand men (353: 187-189). Lawyers are part of doctors' web of deceit as they help in the conspiracy to cover up their misdeeds (376: 413-416). Even civil government succumbs to their corrosive effect. Priests cover up doctors' crimes by burying their dead, and contrary to their religious obligation, they do it for money (322: 412). In fact, the church itself is complicit because it takes money gained in the course of doctors' murderous activities.

The most frequent metaphor in Caviedes's poetry of medical satire – that of a war by doctors against society -- is presented in the frontispiece of *Diente del Parnaso* with mock-heroic bombast: "True war, medical marvels, great deeds of ignorance" (259). This is the defining struggle he portrays in many of his poems. In this war, power is in the hands of the ruling class. Doctors are seen as the foot soldiers of Death and the people of Lima as innocent victims lacking any way to protect themselves other than by avoiding doctors or disobeying their instructions. As weapons, doctors use their complete arsenal of treatments and medical apparatuses.

Now if doctors are so dangerous to society, of what good are they? Caviedes suggests several darkly ironic uses for their "skills." For one thing, they are the "justicia secreta / de Dios" for, as he refers to an assertion of Juvenal, they are executioners that God put on earth (371: 250-256). Thus, through contemporary medical treatments, society can save time and money in dealing with thieves. Caviedes advises giving them syrups, plasters and bloodletting of the ankle, syringes and cold drinks, and infusions made from medicinal plants (179). So effective is this approach that justice will soon be served: "within four days of these treatments the thief will have paid for his crime, since with this prescription he'll have given back all that he took" (386: 305-308). Also, in a poem full of bitterness at the loss of a cousin due to a doctor, Caviedes, on a note of black humor, facetiously advises that his "cures" should be exclusively of a social nature. He should "cure" only married women and mothers-in-law because "their husbands and sons-in-law will say what a good job [they've] done!" (318: 11-12).

Extending the war metaphor, Caviedes suggests to the Duke of Palata that as a benefit to society he should send all the pharmacists, barbers, quacks and charlatans of Lima off to fight the English pirates who were menacing Peruvian coastal waters, and he names twelve real people in particular. As Johnson notes, here Caviedes ridicules both military men and doctors as heroic figures. Metaphorically, doctors are portrayed as warships. In this way, Spain comes out victorious and without cost since doctors will each kill several of the enemy daily with their treatments.

Ironically, however, while ridding Peru of one pest with another, a more dangerous one remains both to individuals and to society.

Curiously, even as Caviedes reimages Lima society in mortal conflict with the medical profession, doctors are not portrayed as allies of one another, although their actions are mutually supportive. In this regard, there are numerous references to jealousies and animosities between doctors. For instance, in one episode two physicians do battle "in knightly fashion" to determine how to put a patient out of his misery. This leads to further comic effect as Death intercedes so as not to lose "ten thousand killings just to allow two" (289: 52). For their common "good" as soldiers for Death, Death urges them to renew their friendship.[11]

While humor is frequently employed by writers to lower the image of power and authority of those accorded higher social standing, Caviedes goes farther than most. Rather than merely leveling their image to that of "lesser" social beings, he often reduces it to a non-human status. He magnifies and grotesquely distorts their flaws and vulnerabilities, presenting doctors not just as quacks but as repugnant and ugly. With insidious word play he hurls insulting epithets, as for instance in the case of the mulatto Pedro de Utrilla, the "Puppy" (as a way to distinguish him from his father of the same name), whom he derides both for his bi-racial background and for his moral and ethical lapses inherent in his predatory behavior (292: 9-36). He compounds his attacks on several doctors repeatedly by demeaning them for their physical defects, his most acerbic comments being leveled at a certain Dr. Liseras, a humpback. Ugly and misshapen, he serves as a metaphor for the grotesque nature of medicine in Lima. By comparing Dr. Liseras and others to various animals regarded as primitive, possessing no human intelligence and esthetically unattractive, Caviedes animalizes them, leaving them completely dehumanized and without a soul.

In "Querella de los pepinos" ("The Cucumber Dispute"), Caviedes takes dehumanizing ridicule one step further in an attack on doctors' stupidity as exemplified by one Dr. Machuca. This poem is based on a law issued by the viceroy, the duke of Palata, at the recommendation of Machuca and supposedly based on medical science, prohibiting the indigenous population from eating cucumbers because they are poisonous

---

[11] From "A un desafío que tuvo el dicho corcovado con otro cirujano tuerto sobre salir discordes de una junta."

to them.[12] Since Machuca believes that to be so, he endeavors to have the seed from this "poisonous" fruit destroyed. For Caviedes, however, cucumbers are a natural food meant to be eaten by humans. And so, in a pseudo-judicial brief against the supposed scientific foundation of Machuca's findings, Caviedes satirizes his methods and conclusions while parodying his "authoritative" discourse (Johnson 98). Logically, Caviedes maintains, if quince, which is cold and dry, is poisonous to Indians, as was observed, then cucumbers, which are warm and moist, should be an antidote to it.[13] Following the illogical argument on which the decree is based, Caviedes hyperbolically extends the concept of dangerous foods to other fruits, then to meat, bread, cheese and wine, leaving nothing left to eat. As the whole idea makes no sense to him, Caviedes concludes that the only fruit that is dangerous is the pear, since Machuca has a pear-shaped beard, a common signifier of a doctor. He further posits that more people die from pear-shaped beards than from cucumbers (312-313).

Caviedes also reimages Lima's doctors through "vegetablization" and "fruitification" by connecting their physical features and character with various fruits and vegetables. Dr. Liseras, the hunchback, is a type of cucumber; Ramírez, a pumpkin with shoes, glasses, gloves and rings; Avendaño, a sweet potato for his light red color; and Bermejo and don Lorenzo, "the Indian," are yuccas. Antonio García, because he is old and "ripe," is visualized falling off his mule just as a ripe fig falls from a tree. Pedro de Utrilla the elder, who is bald and black, is an eggplant, and his son is a radish. Doña Elvira, the only female charlatan, is a papaya, and her son Elviro a melon of a type connoting someone dull and insipid or lazy. Ironically, Caviedes concludes that they are all "killer fruits" whose seed should be destroyed in service to the community and His Majesty. Even more, he suggests an edict directing that Dr. Melchor Vásquez, to whom he refers contemptuously as Pico de Oro, and several practitioners (those who worked in surgery and medicine under a master), be burned at the stake, the latter because they are the seed of wicked doctors (312-316).

To conclude, the frontispiece to *Diente del Parnaso* clearly outlines Caviedes's poetic objective as a comprehensive attack on the ignorance

---

[12] Reedy notes that the duke was given the nickname of Viceroy of Cucumbers and that still in Peru today the cucumber is referred to as a "mataserrano" ("killer of mountain dwellers"). (*Obra completa* xxii).

[13] Here Caviedes satirizes Galen's belief that different foods affect one's humoral balance. To that end, foods that promoted one humor were to be countered when in excess by foods that had opposite properties ("The Four Humors Philosophy and its Influence on the Renaissance").

and lethality of doctors in 17th-century Lima. He frames his poetic voice in terms of laughter as social therapy through medical satire and places it in the context of colonial Lima's social ills and moral dilemmas. Set in the metaphor of a war between the whole medical establishment of contemporary Lima and the public, Caviedes's poetry sets out to destroy the credibility of doctors by a complete subversion/inversion of their established image, delegitimizing through laughter their power and authority. Concomitantly, he derides the whole power elite of Lima, both civil and religious, that is corrupted by the medical establishment. In Caviedes's judgment, the doctors of Lima are not to be trusted since their medical abilities are illusions. As a result, rather than serve society, they are part of the problem. Rather than fight disease, they promote it, and in so doing, contribute to a diseased society.

Caviedes's laughter functions as an attack on the hegemonic discourse of the whole medical establishment. Doctors are members of the power elite who not only take advantage of patients for their personal gain, but also consciously work to cause them suffering and death. Like others in positions of power, they use their authority and position to maintain their prerogatives. In that context, he challenges the foundation and functionality of viceregal Lima society itself, a "new world" he does not seem to like very much. As personal and social therapy, he sees laughter as a means by which both individuals and society can tend to their own ills and bring about psychological, behavioral and institutional changes. Laughter is a liberator from the fear which doctors use to maintain their power. Thus, Caviedes turns the canonical vision of society upside down, delegitimizing it as its moral and ethical underpinnings have become corrupted.

Works Cited

Cáceres, María Leticia. *La personalidad y obra de Don Juan del Valle y Caviedes*. Arequipa: El Sol, 1975.

Cortezo, Carlos María. "Discurso del Excmo. Sr. D. Carlos María Cortezo." *Discursos leídos ante la Real Academia Española en la recepción pública del Excmo. Sr. D. Carlos María Cortezo el día 9 de junio de 1918*. Madrid: Imprenta del Sucesor de Enrique Teodoro. 5-94; 111-121.

Echagüe, Juan Pablo. "Un Quevedo limeño del siglo xvii: Caviedes, el enemigo de los médicos." *Figuras de América*. Buenos Aires: n. p., 1943. 21-32.

Fitz, Earl E. "Gregorio de Matos and Juan del Valle y Caviedes: Two Baroque Poets in Colonial Portuguese and Spanish America." *Inti: Revista de cultura hispánica* 1.5 (1977): 134-150.

"The Four Humors Philosophy and Its Influence on the Renaissance." N.p. n.d.Web. 23 Nov. 2010.
<http://merkspages.com/HWCIV/exemplars/four_humors_philos>.

Fry, William F. "Laughter: Is It the Best Medicine?" *Stanford M.D.* 10 (1971): 16-20.

—. "Mirth and Oxygen Saturation of Peripheral Blood." *Psychotherapy and Psychosomatics* 19 (1971): 76-84.

—. "The Physiologic Effects of Humor, Mirth, and Laughter." *Journal of the American Medical Association* 267.13 (1992): 1857-1858.

Johnson, Julie Greer. *Satire in Colonial Spanish America: Turning the New World Upside Down.* Austin: U of Texas P, 1993.

Lasarte, Pedro. "Algunas reflexiones en torno a una relación literaria: Juan del Valle y Caviedes y Francisco de Quevedo." *La formación de la cultura virreinal. El siglo XVII.* Vol. 2. Ed. Karl Kohut and Sonia V. Rose. Madrid: Iberoamericana, 2004: 135-149.

—. "Juan del Valle y Caviedes y la sombra de Quevedo." *Actas del XIV Congreso de la Asociación de Hispanistas. Literatura hispano-americana.* Vol. 4. 16-21 July 2001. Ed. Isías Lerner, Robert Nival, Alejandro Alonso. Newark, DE: Juan de la Cuesta, 2004: 323-329.

Machline, Vera Cecilia. "The Contribution of Laurent Joubert's *Traité du Ris* to Sixteenth-Century Physiology of Laughter." *Reading the Book of Nature: The Other Side of the Scientific Revolution.* Ed. Allen G. Debus and Michael T. Walton. Kirksville, Mo.: Sixteenth Century Publishers, 1998: 251-264.

—. "Huarte's Early Modern Speculations about Melancholy and Laughter." *Essays on Luso-Hispanic Humor.* Ed. Paul W. Seaver. Lewiston, NY: Edwin Mellen P, 2004: 77-92.

McCaw, R. John. "Playing Doctor: Satire, Laughter and Spiritual Transformation in Valle y Caviedes's *Diente del Parnaso*." *Calíope. Journal of the Society for Renaissance and Baroque Hispanic Poetry* 3.2 (1997): 86-96.

Morreall, John. *Taking Laughter Seriously.* Albany: SU of NY P, 1983.

—. Ed. *The Philosophy of Laughter and Humor.* Albany: SU of NY P, 1987.

Olson, Glending. *Literature as Recreation in the Later Middle Ages.* Ithaca: Cornell University Press. 1986.

Osborne, Nancy F. *The Doctor in the French Literature of the Sixteenth Century.* Morningside Heights, NY: King's Crown P, 1946.

Packard, Francis R. "History of the School of Salernum." Int. *Regimen Sanitatis Salernitanum*. By the School of Salernum. Trans. Sir John Harington. 1920. New York: Augustus M. Kelly, 1970: 7-52.

Rabelais, François. *Gargantua and Pantagruel*. Trans. Burton Raffel. New York: Norton, 1990.

Randolph, Mary Claire. "The Medical Concept in English Renaissance Satiric Theory." *Modern Essays in Criticism*. Ed. Robert Paulson. Englewood Cliffs: Prentice-Hall, 1971: 135-170.

Reedy, Daniel R., ed. *Obra Completa*. By Juan del Valle y Caviedes. Caracas: Biblioteca Ayacucho, 1984.

—. *Satire in Colonial Spanish America*. Foreword by Julie Greer Johnson. Austin: U of Texas P, 1993: ix-xii.

School of Salernum. *Regimen Sanitatis Salernitanum*. Trans. Sir John Harington. 1920. New York: Augustus M. Kelly, 1970.

Torres, Daniel. *El palimpsesto del calco aparente: una poética del Barroco de Indias*. New York: Lang, 1993.

Trueblood, Alan S. "La risa en el Quijote y la risa de Don Quijote." *Letter and Spirit in Hispanic Writers, Renaissance to Civil War: Selected Essays*. London: Tamesis Books, 1986: 65-82.

Valle y Caviedes, Juan del. *Obra completa*. Eds. María Leticia Cáceres, Luis Jaime Cisneros and Guillermo Lohmann Villena. Lima: Biblioteca Clásicos del Perú, 1990.

PICARESQUE HUMOR IN *DON QUIXOTE*

ROBERT S. STONE

While *Don Quixote* is not a picaresque novel, it is fair to say that it would not exist without either its forebear *Lazarillo de Tormes* (1554) or its contemporary *Guzmán de Alfarache* (1599). *Guzmán* was a bestseller published only five years prior to part I of *Don Quixote*, and Cervantes could not have been ignorant of this economic truth. Indeed, the way in which Cervantes folds picaresque phenomena into his narrative goes a long way towards explaining the first modern novel's early popularity with a wide audience.[1] This essay will examine a few nods to the picaresque in part I of the *Quixote*, particularly the manner in which the novel "bares pretense"—an essentially picaresque strategy—even as it "bears witness" to the world it encounters, in the manner of testimonial narratives. If *Lazarillo* is the Ur-text for the Spanish picaresque tradition, then the *Naufragios* of Cabeza de Vaca fulfills that role for the testimonial. Not coincidentally, these first-person narratives appear in the same decade. The former is apparently intended to provoke laughter in the audience, and the latter to sway opinion by empathetic means (Stone 15-46). Causes such as those championed in testimonials are, however, frequently well served by humor meted out in regular doses, opening readers' minds to unconventional thoughts and keeping them coming back for more. This is where Cervantes shines, as evidenced by his *entremeses* (the one-act plays never performed in his lifetime), a few of his *Novelas ejemplares*, and of course by the *Quixote* itself.

By citation and situation, the novel is rife with allusions to its picaresque parentage, beginning with the first sentence of the prologue to part I, where Cervantes hopes that his book will be a "child of understanding" ("hijo del entendimiento") and then refers to his protagonists as his stepchildren, which is to say, as progeny of debatable legitimacy, like a *pícaro*. We only learn later that the "true" father of

---

[1] Claudio Guillén traced the publication history of *Lazarillo* and found that its popularity dwindled in the half century after its initial publication, until the appearance of *Guzmán de Alfarache*, when it went through nine editions in four years, many of these printed by the publisher of *Guzmán* (135-138).

these characters is the Moorish author Cide Hamete Benengeli—literary blood is never pure, and Cervantes seems anxious for the reader to acknowledge this in years just prior to the final expulsion of the Moors from Spain. Ironic ancestry is taken up again in the dedicatory poems (*elogios*) between the prologue and the prose text. Following sonnets that parody Amadís and other knights of yore, Don Quixote's horse Rocinante speaks (!), claiming to be a great grandson of Babieca, the storied steed of El Cid. The horse then notes that his eating habits are quite like those of Lazarillo, who staved off starvation by outsmarting his masters, often earning a beating in the bargain. In this truncated verse, where the reader must provide the final syllable of each line, Cervantes comically juxtaposes the popular prose genres of his day, the chivalric and picaresque, as he engages the reader to fill the gaps in the poem.[2] Even before the novel proper begins, then, it invites the reader to poke fun at supposed superiors in the literary canon who have become part of national myth.

The famous opening line of the novel places uncertain geography alongside questionable lineage: "En un lugar de la Mancha, de cuyo nombre no quiero acordarme…" ("Somewhere in La Mancha, in a place whose name I do not care to remember…").[3] Cervantes's deliberate vagueness on the matter of where Don Quixote lived reminds us of the foundling in the *novela ejemplar* "El Licenciado Vidriera" who will not name his parents until he can honor their name (Stone 75-94). Moreover, the imperfect recall of the authorial "I" in this first line may be taken as yet another nod in the direction of the picaresque genre's often unreliable narrator. In the same paragraph is a discussion of whether Don Quixote's surname is really Quijada, Quesana or Quejana. Taken together, such gambits make it abundantly clear that the *Quixote* is not to be just a pseudo-serious chivalric novel—nor is it simply to be a picaresque novel wherein we might question the credibility or morality of a narrator. This is a new mixed breed, a multi-voiced text that invites us to consider the make-up of an entire society and speculate upon the direction in which it might be headed (Bakhtin 165). No *pícaro* ever says with the conviction of Don Quixote, "Yo sé quien soy" ("I know who I am") (I, 5)—the reader must decide just who or what that is. The primacy of this idea that an individual is not simply born into a life, but must become someone in spite

---

[2] Of the eleven dedicatory poems, three are of the truncated variety, including one about an enchantress.

[3] All quotations in Spanish are taken from Martín de Riquer's edition, Juventud: Barcelona, 1968, and all English translations are from Edith Grossman's edition, New York: HarperCollins, 2005.

of birthright, is ultimately confirmed by Don Quixote's epitaph, where the hidalgo is said to have been "el espantajo y el coco del mundo," a scarecrow whose role has been to shake up the reader. In a final glance back at the novel's origins, *coco* (bogeyman) is what Lazarillo's illegitimate little brother called his mother's Moorish lover, because the strange man's dusky skin filled him with fear of the Other/father, someone in whom he fails to recognize himself, just as Spain is officially in denial about its own Moorish heritage.

Humor is thus present in the *Quixote* not simply for its own sake, but as a conscious narrative strategy that makes a complex text more accessible as it steers itself away from high literacy towards a more orally attuned mass audience. In parallel fashion, the hidalgo from La Mancha, a talking book himself, edifies his squire, Sancho Panza. If the *Quixote* is read from Sancho's perspective, the novel becomes a classic *Bildungsroman* nearly two centuries before Goethe, which is to say that the education of a character occurs along with the cultivation of a readership.

This process is perhaps essentialized in Don Quixote's comment to his squire:

> Paréceme, Sancho, que no hay refrán que no sea verdadero, porque todos son sentencias sacadas de la mesma experiencia, madre de las ciencias todas, especialmente aquel que dice: 'Donde una puerta se cierra, otra se abre'. (I, 21)

> It seems to me, Sancho, that there is no proverb that is not true, because all of them are judgments based on experience, the mother of all knowledge, in particular the one that says: 'One door closes and another opens'.[4]

This same proverb is also found in *Lazarillo*, when the *pícaro's* source of meager nourishment, his *paraíso panal* (literally his "breadly paradise") has been made less accessible by the priest, and he must find some other inventive way to get at it—he abandons the notion of imitating a mouse for the more satisfying, if risky, emulation of a snake. By inventing useful

---

[4] The resourcefulness implied by the *refrán* also resonates in *Guzmán de Alfarache*'s interpolated tale of Ozmín and Daraja, the tragic Moorish lovers of Granada, where we find "De la necesidad nace el consejo," roughly "desperate times call for desperate measures" (Stone 47-74).

fictions, by following Lazarillo's example, the marginalized may raise themselves up.

Initially, the two overriding genres of chivalric and picaresque novel may seem to be at odds with each other in the *Quixote*. When he ventures out into the world the first time, without Sancho, the hidalgo "Quijano" is duped by a social inferior and laughed at by prostitutes at an inn for his high-falutin speech. But then one of these ladies helps him to sup through his visor and participates in his knighting ceremony, showing the compassion that is central to reading the world and the text feelingly. Moreover, the innkeeper whom Don Quixote takes for a nobleman is an imaginative middleman who, in advance of Sancho, can direct Quijano's fantasy and adapt to its absurdity. He devises a long straw to solve the problem of drinking through a helmet, which is another direct allusion to Lazarillo, who uses the same technique to sneak wine from his blind master. The *Quixote* suggests that a peaceful compromise is possible between competing genres, as well as among members of different social classes.

Most critics cite the episode of the galley slaves (I, 22) as the foremost intrusion of the picaresque in the *Quixote*. But we can see that the genre is already present at the inn, where it is represented by the innkeeper, a man who has, it is clearly implied, lifted himself up from petty criminality to become a small property owner. In colluding with Don Quixote's fantasy that the inn is a castle, the innkeeper indulges, in the manner of many a *pícaro*, his dream of becoming a gentleman. On the other hand, it is this man, a rogue himself, who not only dubs Don Quixote a knight errant, but also introduces him to post-feudal economic reality, suggesting pointedly that in the future it would be unwise for the knight to travel without cash, and that a squire might be just the person to carry such funds in order to bridge, as it were, the gap between fiction and reality. The exchange of knowledge among social classes has begun: the knight's chivalry has a civilizing effect on the owner and workers at the inn, and he benefits from their practical knowledge.[5]

---

[5] Two muleteers staying at the inn are the only victims of Quixote's wrath as he stands vigil in preparation for his dubbing. These drovers (*arrieros*) are known typically to have been members of the *morisco* sector of society, converts from Islam who remained in Spain for over a century after the fall of Granada in 1492. Cervantes appears to be keenly aware of their imminent expulsion, which culminated as he was preparing the second part of *Don Quixote* for its publication in 1615. See my article "Moorish *Quixote*: Reframing the Novel" in the journal *Cervantes* (Spring 2013).

Don Quixote (Honoré Daumier, 1870; Neue Pinakothek, Munich, Germany)

Throughout this first episode, the derisive laughter of these onlookers is mitigated by a certain admiration for the absurd knight's courage and cleverness, an acknowledgement of the ideals he represents. They value his worth and his knowledge over his pitiful appearance and, in the end, Don Quixote acknowledges the prostitutes' assistance by addressing them as fine ladies. Cervantes is thus by no means arguing exclusively against chivalric fiction—it may benefit others, so that they may catch glimpses of their better selves, above and beyond the merely financial. It is evident that even before Sancho appears on the scene, the idea of upward mobility is on Cervantes' mind.

In literary terms, the innkeeper and the prostitutes are examples of characters whose fate is sealed in advance for the experienced theatergoer or reader. They are recognizable types, as is Don Quixote, who is similarly circumscribed and pre-determined by chivalric romance. Sancho, on the other hand, will be an entirely original figure, a prototype of a new kind of Spaniard. He is the first true peasant with knightly values to appear in Romance literature, the first who has no prescription in Spain, and so he must either have one written for him or, preferably, write one himself, in the manner of a picaresque hero. The focus on Sancho in what follows will unfortunately ignore minor characters such as conniving servants, criminals, students, suitors, innkeepers and *moriscos* who may also spring from the picaresque patchwork. The opportunistic ruses of the student Sansón Carrasco, the love-struck Basilio and the exiled Moor Ricote are particularly intriguing. But Sancho, after Don Quixote's largely unsuccessful first sally, is in a unique position to observe and frequently interact with these characters and incorporate them into his ken, and thus to cope with the aristocrats who will try to make a fool of him in part II of the novel (Stone 95-131). He is not a *pícaro* but he may, like the reader, learn much from them.

It is central to Sancho's new literary role that he is ignorant of print culture, and Cervantes carefully writes the gap between oral and literary types of reality into the book, as he confronts Sancho with a number of increasingly complex experiences. When Don Quixote returns home from the first sally, having ventured out into a world beneath his social station, he finds himself among those who are anxious to restore him to his rightful place as a quiet member of the local gentry. They want to excise him, in effect, from the picaresque reality that does not appear in the knightly tales. In their zeal, the barber and curate wall up Don Quixote's library, placing the blame on an evil wizard. Acting as self-appointed censors and inquisitors, these men attempt to control literature brutally, not in the creative manner previously indicated by the innkeeper. Still, just as Sancho's materialist role as a money-bearer and, more significantly, as a provider of food, is forecast by the innkeeper, so Don Quixote's penchant to blame mishaps on sorcery is unwittingly reinforced by these friends.

It is plausible that Don Quixote would never have left home again had he not lost his library: he may simply have retired to his rooms. But the books' sudden disappearance fires his imagination once more, a consequence that the barber and curate did not consider. The world is mad and in collusion with the madman, as the purported authority of printed books allows for the imposition of restrictive and mediated fictions on the quotidian. Enchantment, after all, takes fate out of the hands of normal men. Perversely, then, Don Quixote thrusts himself again into the world as a talking book to which illiterates such as Sancho will be exposed. The stories he carries with him and envisions may be interpreted to help explain or revitalize lived experience. Ultimately, however, the knight provides exemplarity but fails to translate literary experience into real-world applications for his own benefit—that task is left to Sancho, and to the reader.

Into this enchanted, insane world, then, enters Sancho, who is described as a good man—if that title can be given to someone who is poor—"but without much in the way of brains" ("de muy poca sal en la mollera") (I, 7). At this early stage, even the narrator doubts Sancho's suitability as a squire, he himself employing a saying about salt shakers to describe the character who will be pouring out proverbs at every opportunity, much to the consternation of his master. Sancho will be a different kind of talking book who will refute in this same coin the claim that he is witless. The first lesson he learns from his newly knighted master is that he may aspire to much more than the peasant life, "because it might happen that one day he might have an adventure that would gain him, in the blink of an eye, an ínsula, and he would make him its governor" ("porque tal vez le podía suceder aventura que le ganase, en quítame alla esas pajas, alguna ínsula y le dejase a él por gobernador della") (Ibid.). Don Quixote is bound by the written code of chivalry that informs his every move, but Sancho bends and eventually rewrites this code in the course of their adventures, chipping away at the armor of knightly protocols and adapting them to his self-spoken identity as a garrulous, cowardly but essentially upright man, rewriting it to suit his own circumstances in historical Spain. He overcomes the narrator's early misgivings, his literary imprint upon birth.

After the famous early encounter with the windmills (I, 8), Sancho's first new claim on the chivalric tradition is the right to complain of his ills, which Don Quixote allows, since it is nowhere forbidden in the literature. The master does, however, admonish the squire never to take up arms in defense of the knight until such time as Sancho himself is duly dubbed, and Sancho is only too willing to accept this condition. The old words, then, are tested time and again against current reality, their meanings rewritten, gradually transforming the chivalric script without destroying it utterly, for as a moral code it still has considerable worth.

Cervantes of course does not limit himself to a recreation of the picaresque and chivalric literature; he constantly introduces absurdity into the wider literary landscape that includes all manner of verse and prose genres popular in his day. Such is the case, for instance, when the affected bucolic lifestyle of would-be characters in a pastoral drama is shunned by Sancho, who was once an actual goatherd himself. This rejection is instantly followed by the confrontation with two flocks of sheep that Don Quixote takes to be two great armies (I, 18). Reality confirms fiction and vice versa. In the aftermath of the knight's defeat by the shepherds of the two armies, he explains to Sancho how easily enchanters make us see what they want. Then the knight errant's curative balsam—an artifact of chivalry—is brought up literally in an incident reminiscent of *Lazarillo*. Don Quixote and Sancho vomit prolifically on each other (as Lazarillo threw up on his blind master), and Sancho is driven to distraction because he cannot find anything to clean up with:

> "Sancho went to his donkey to find something in his saddlebags with which to clean himself and heal his master, and when he did not see the saddlebags, he almost lost his mind. He cursed his fate again and resolved in his heart to leave his master and return home, even if he lost his wages for the time he had worked, along with his hopes for the governorship of the promised ínsula" (I, 18).

Within this eventful chapter is compressed all that has passed between master and squire up to this point in the narrative: a quasi-picaresque equivalence as wanderers of their native land (Bakhtin 243-244); a fragile economic interdependence as evinced by the lost saddlebag; and a shared desire for better times. In an inversion of Don Quixote's madness, Sancho is on the verge of giving up the dream of a governorship. He is comforted by the knight, who asserts that deeds are the currency of human value and promises a brighter future, saying "that a man is not worth more than any other if he does not do more than any other." Yet Don Quixote is also still at pains to maintain a certain social distance from his squire, whom he says should not suffer as a result of the misfortunes that befall a knight.[6]

---

[6] Here is the entire passage in the original: "Acudió Sancho a su asno para sacar de las alforjas con qué limpiarse y con qué curar a su amo, y como no los halló, estuvo a punto de perder el juicio. Maldíjose de nuevo y propuso en su corazón de

By the end of the chapter, however, it is the squire who consoles the master for the bloody loss of his teeth. The compassion of the low born, first glimpsed in this novel at the inn, and in picaresque literature when Lazarillo pitied an impoverished nobleman who could only pretend to be well-fed, is a newly secularized measure of worth that will lift Sancho above the common mass, both spiritually and materially. Sancho and Don Quixote are the world and the word meeting each other halfway and being read into each other's context, with benefits for both. Cervantes sustains the potential wisdom of old books, not rejecting but rewriting them in accord with picaresque literature. He turns the tradition to new and almost revolutionary didactic ends.

The novel's most obvious nod to the picaresque is found, of course, in the encounter with Ginés de Pasamonte (I, 22), alias Ginesillo de Parapilla, a name with echoes of that other galley slave, Guzmán de Alfarache. After Don Quixote and Sancho release Ginés and the other prisoners from their chains, the real-life *pícaro*'s ingratitude is such that he divests knight and squire of all their clothing and beats Don Quixote silly with his own *baciyelmo*, a neologism that combines the Spanish words for basin and helmet, for the object is in fact both of these things, depending on who uses it: a barber or a crazed knight. This drubbing is a kind of revenge of the real, i.e., the picaresque world, upon the chivalric ideal. Sancho's pragmatic response is to recommend a hasty retreat and, very much like a picaresque narrator in his own right, he finds the rhetoric to rationalize his somewhat less-than-honorable survival instinct.

It is significant that following this trouncing, Sancho, mounted on his ass, leads the way for the first time. No longer is the route to be chosen by the whim of the old hack Rocinante. Perhaps this is why Cervantes, when

---

dejar a su amo y volverse a su tierra, aunque perdiese el salario de lo servido y las esperanzas del gobierno de la prometida ínsula.

Levantóse en esto don Quijote, y, puesta la mano izquierda en la boca porque no se le acabasen los dientes, asió con la otra las riendas de Rocinante, que nunca se había movido de junto a su amo—tal era de leal y bien acondicionado—y fuese adonde su escudero estaba, de pechos sobre su asno, con la mano en la mejilla, en guisa de hombre pensativo además. Y viéndole don Quijote de aquella manera, con muestras de tanta tristeza, dijo:

Sábete, Sancho, que no es un hombre más que otro si no hace más que otro. Todas estas borrascas que nos suceden son señales de que presto ha de serenar el tiempo y han de suceder bien las cosas; porque no es posible que el mal ni el bien sean durables, y de aquí se sigue que, habiendo durado mucho el mal, el bien está ya cerca. Así que no debes congojarte por las desgracias que a mí me suceden, pues a ti no te cabe parte de ellas."

he had to explain the odd disappearance of the ass in the novel's second edition, has Ginés returning in the night to steal it. It is as if Ginesillo, the self-proclaimed *pícaro*, were the negative of Sancho, seeking to cancel out the squire's compassion and humane wisdom with mere calculation. This would appear to be the sentiment behind the words found in the prologue to part II: "la honra puédela tener el pobre, pero no el vicioso: la pobreza puede anublar a la nobleza, pero no escurecerla del todo." ("A poor man may have honor, but not a villain; need may cloud nobility, but not hide it completely.") Don Quixote declares that he *knows* who he is, but Sancho, in the course of the novel, *becomes* who he is, a new type of Spaniard. Sancho's life story will remain a work in progress beyond the final pages of the book, where readers are left to wonder what he will do with the ethical and material inheritance left to him by his master. He who never ceases to learn survives, and there is the distinct feeling that Sancho's story (like the meta-fictional autobiography of Ginés de Pasamonte) is far from over.

Works Cited

Alemán, Mateo. *Aventuras y vida de Guzmán de Alfarache*. Ed. Benito Brancaforte. Madrid: Akal, 1996.

Anonymous. *La vida de Lazarillo de Tormes y de sus fortunas y adversidades*. Ed. R.O. Jones. Manchester: Manchester UP, 1963.

Bakhtin, Mikhail M. The Dialogic Imagination: Four Essays. Trans. Michael Holquist and Caryl Emerson. Austin: U Texas P, 1981.

Cervantes, Miguel. *Don Quijote de la Mancha*. Ed. Martín de Riquer. Barcelona: Juventud, 1968.

—. *Don Quixote*. Trans. Edith Grossman. New York: HarperCollins, 2005.

—. *Novelas ejemplares*. Ed. Julio Rodríguez-Luis. Madrid: Taurus, 1983.

Guillén, Claudio. "Toward a Definition of the Picaresque." *Literature as System*. Princeton: Princeton UP, 1971.

Stone, Robert. *Picaresque Continuities: Transformations of Genre from the Golden Age to the Goethezeit*. New Orleans: UP of the South, 1998.

ESTEBANILLO GONZÁLEZ AND THE COMIC ART OF THE BUFFOON

MANUEL GALOFARO

The Life and Deeds of Estebanillo González, Man of Good Humor, published in Antwerp in 1646, is an excellent example of the humor typical of the genre and times in which it was written. This quasi-autobiographical novel is endowed with a profusion of elements that make it entertaining and amusing. Perhaps it may seem from our present perspective that the writer's wit was faulty, but we must interpret it within the buffoons' tradition and Estebanillo's own living context; for humor is governed by time and place and may be difficult to assess outside of its cultural frame.

Here is the story of a man who begins as a rogue and ends his days as a professional buffoon wandering about the courts of Europe.[1] Estebanillo belongs to a cruel society in which he must reduce his existence to a continuum of burlesque performances in order to entertain an elite, who hopefully will reward him in return (Bjornson 438). In effect, his novel becomes the record of the services he rendered in the hopes of securing for himself a comfortable retirement. Estebanillo produces a subjective account from his own experience and perspective, not as a mere chronicler, but playing with the fine line between fiction and reality, instilling the work with a certain degree of verisimilitude[2] and large doses

---

[1] *La vida y hechos de Estebanillo González, hombre de buen humor*, was first printed in 1646 in Antwerp and is the last Spanish picaresque novel. It narrates the story of a 17th Century rogue who roams through Europe during the Thirty Years War using his wits and tricks to survive. Eventually he earns a reputation that makes him a professional entertainer in the European courts and becomes Ottavio Piccolomini's official buffoon. It is not clear whether the author, narrator and main character are the same person or not. Cf. Ángel Valbuena Prat, *La Novela Picaresca Española*, 6th ed. (Madrid: Aguilar, 1968), Carreira and Cid (1990, xiii and civ), et al.

[2] For more about the confluence of the buffoon's fiction and verisimilitude, see Valbuena Prat (1968, 76 and 1719) and Carreira and Cid's introduction to their edition of *Estebanillo González* (cxxxvii-cxxxviii).

of humor (Roncero 1996, 281-296).

In general, the humor in *Estebanillo* is physical and pursues the guffaw, often by introducing events filled with cruelty, overindulgence, violence, humiliation and pain, and diverging thus from the Aristotelian concept of *eutrapelia* and the fine humor advocated (but not always followed) in courtly quarters. The acrimony inherent in this kind of humor is not surprising. In the words of Roncero: "the buffoon was completely aware of the degradation of the values that underlay the social structure. The corrosive, bitter humor, a result of the mockery, punishment and social despise that his occupation entails, is in Estebanillo a sample of the deep skepticism and distrust toward those who surround him" (1993, 420).

From the very beginning of the novel, in the title itself, Estebanillo is introduced to us as a "man of good humor." But, what is meant by "good humor" in this case? It is an allusion to Estebanillo's pragmatism, a mechanism that helps him survive and endure his existence, dealing with the daily woes and sharpening his wit to benefit himself (Stamm 485). However, this concept of "good humor" goes beyond helping the buffoon bear the misery in his own life. He must entertain and amuse his audience with his adventures, and in order to do that he must be an excellent narrator and an accomplished comedian (Roncero 2004, 250). That "good humor" is the foundation for his subsistence; it is the essential tool of his trade.[3]

As numerous critics have demonstrated, lineage is often the object of mockery in the picaresque novel. Estebanillo mocks the possibility that his own lineage stems from medieval nobility, saying: "I only know that my name is Estebanillo González; such a product of my actions that, if through the thread you can unravel the spool, through them you will unravel my noble lineage" (*Estebanillo*, 1:31).[4] Since Estebanillo's actions are typical of a buffoon, his "noble" lineage is a parody that ridicules the pretension-obsession of blood purity. Through self-mockery, Estebanillo is also laughing at all those who boast about their ancestry and create noble ancestors to ennoble themselves. Unlike other rogues, Estebanillo never attempts to escape his tainted origin, because he is a buffoon. The scorn he

---

[3] See Juan Bautista Avalle-Arce, "El nacimiento de Estebanillo González," *Nueva Revista de Filología Hispánica* 34, no. 2 (1985-86): 532, and also Nicholas Spadaccini, "Estebanillo González and the Nature of Picaresque 'Lives'," *Comparative Literature* 30, no. 3 (Summer, 1978): 216. Both critics point out that Estebanillo's systematic intention of making people laugh constitutes a difference when compared to preceding rogues.

[4] All translations are mine.

endures is manifested publicly, before the court, before the reader and, in sum, before the eyes of society. This behavior falls under the concept of the *indignitas hominis* and within a more generalized criticism toward all the elements that the buffoon deems corrupted and in plain decadence, in an era infused with the ideology of the lineage (Roncero 1989, 234-235).

The contrast between Estebanillo and the figures of respectability appears to enhance the latter and diminish the former. However, we must not forget the subsidiary role of the buffoon as social critic, a tradition inherited from Greco-Roman times and celebrated in the Horatian concepts of *ridentem dicere verum*—to tell the truth through laughter— and *prodesse et delectare*—to educate and please (Roncero 2001; 152, 156). Within the art of buffoonery there is also room for criticism of war, the abuse of power, vanity, arrogance, and the attitude of those that "have been nothing and find themselves on a pedestal," abusing their privileges (*Estebanillo*, 2:187-188). For example, in *Estebanillo* there is an attack on arrogant servants "who never tire of licking [their masters'] plates, and in the hope of reaping some personal profit or endless glory, display more vanity than their masters …" (2:244-245).

Estebanillo is often reminded of his proper place. As Nina Cox Davis points out, the identity of Estebanillo as a buffoon entails a number of public humiliations, but at the same time places him next to the powerful. However, since he cannot share their hierarchical level, each time he tries to equate himself with any of them and enjoy their privileges, he suffers the painful consequences (52-53). Estebanillo realizes where he belongs, but this does not stop him from employing his pragmatic philosophy: "considering that I was already fit as a man of humor and as a model of an entertaining gentleman, I said to myself: 'My pleasure is my honor and let people laugh at me as long as I am comfortable; because it does not matter that my father's name is bread if I am starving'" (*Estebanillo*, 2:50).

Estebanillo never forgets that his best weapon is humor, "because there is no law or reason that forces to be serious those who have the necessity of serving and giving pleasure in order not to starve to death" (2:244). He takes pride in his cunning wit and praises his occupation: "I could read, write and count … which has served me to continue the art that I profess; because I can assure you, certified by an honest rogue, that this is no occupation for the foolish" (1:41). Obviously, the expression "honest rogue" is a paradox, and it is here where we find the finest humor. Estebanillo delivers a eulogy on the art of buffoonery and the dual role of its practitioners as entertainers and at times even as advisers to the powerful, with license to show them through laughter their own flaws and their subject's feelings. He may be a buffoon, but he is also a sage. To be

The Ferrarese Court Jester, Gonella, known for exerting influence on his master, Duke Borso d'Este. (Jean Fouquet, 1445; Kunsthistorisches Museum, Vienna)

sure, many such as Estebanillo served in the courts of popes, noblemen and kings and among them were some who did have their master's ear.

It is indeed amusing to see the ease with which Estebanillo recounts his adventures and his sharp wit—since his early school days—to deceive people: "I had so confused the teachers with lies and the pupils with tricks that everyone referred to me as the Spanish Judas. I used to buy rosemary powder and mix it with wild barley and, placing them into small folded pieces of paper, I was selling them for one 'real'[5] to the novice students, pretending that they were cashew powder and that, by inhaling them through their noses, they would have a happy memory." (1:41).

By mocking other people and being mocked or deceived by others, Estebanillo improves his skills. On one occasion he is tricked and robbed when he tries to buy a ram, an incident celebrated with laughter by his colleagues. We can perceive a tinge of pessimism and lack of confidence in human nature as he concludes "not only do men trick other men, but they teach animals how to trick them" (1:82). In another episode (reminiscent of the one in *Lazarillo de Tormes*[6] in which the blind man smashes Lázaro's head against the stone bull, taking away his innocence) Estebanillo comes to a harsh realization when he is told: "Mister Estebanillo, you have been living a lie … [Y]ou are in all things and everything another Lazarillo de Tormes" (1:93).

Another typical ingredient of the genre is the physical violence received or administered by the buffoon. For example, Estebanillo is threatened with being castrated, a punishment that he is told "very quickly and with little pain will leave him like a country horse, tamed and not at all bucking" (2:80). At first, Estebanillo thinks it is just a joke, but later he admits his fear, although he will present it to his audience in a humorous manner: "I fainted, considering myself a neighbor from Capadocia" (Ibid).[7] With understandable terror, the buffoon asks his master for mercy: "I begged him, kneeling down and with my eyes like two tear fountains, to have pity on my youth, and not to take away from me assets so essential to it; that when old age sets in, he could then execute on me such a rigorous sentence … that it was to go against all the laws of Nature, turning a

---

[5] The 'real' was a coin used in Spain since the XIV century. At the end of its existence as currency in use it had a value equivalent to approximately a quarter of an American cent.

[6] *Lazarillo de Tormes* (1554) was the first Spanish picaresque novel. See Kevin Larsen's interesting article in this volume.

[7] Capadocia is a region of Anatolia; it is in present day Turkey. Because it resembles the word "capado" (castrated), Estebanillo makes a joke of it.

chicken into a gelding" (2:82).

It must be pointed out that Estebanillo never abandons his jocular tone even when narrating his misfortunes: "he left me completely locked up and in a secure place that prevented me from fleeing, telling me as a farewell that another day the tailor would come, and he would lighten my weight and accomplish what my master had ordered" (Ibid).[8] Ever the buffoon, he recurs to all his wit to make us laugh, often employing semantic games such as: "I told him that for playing the 'capadillo' [gelding] I was being placed in a 'caponera' [chicken-coop]" (2:87).[9] Estebanillo describes with such equanimity and detail these many incidents of violent humiliation that Roncero López, remarking on the indignities inflicted on buffoon characters in the picaresque novel, calls him "the character that suffers the most humiliations and yet recounts them with the most joy" (2001; 159, 165).

Animalization is another very productive comic device in this type of literature. While it elicits laughter, it also presents a dehumanized view of society and of the world. Estebanillo appears animalized as a donkey, pig, horse, bird, ram, chicken, gelded chicken, deer, snail, etc. On one hand, the comparison between Estebanillo and animals with a shell symbolizes his cowardice and his ability to retreat and evade the situation; on the other hand, the comparison between him and animals with antlers, horns or antennas relates to his condition as a cuckold. We can see it, for example, when he is asked to wear the antlers of a deer and is paraded on a horse through the streets of Brussels (*Estebanillo…*, 2:75). Coupled with the humiliation, Estebanillo also receives physical pain from the apples that the public throws at him. The whole scene is enjoyed by the nobleman, who rewards Estebanillo for providing such good entertainment and even has his portrait made (2:78).

We also find in this novel parodies of courtly love, often accompanied by animalization of the lovers. In one episode, Estebanillo's courting of a woman includes a lexicon associated with courtly love, but used ironically. The lovers undergo animalization. The parody is embellished with love verses that Estebanillo exchanges with his lover. In these verses both lovers ridicule each other, and we find comic allusions to literary

---

[8] "El sastre de cortar bolsas." The term refers to a tailor who cuts bags or pockets, implying both someone who is going to castrate him by cutting his "bags" and also a thief who takes the money bags from people by cutting them off from their belts.

[9] Terms like "capadillo" and "caponera" are used here with double meaning. "El capadillo" is a card game and "caponera" is the place where the chicken were kept; in the text both also allude to "capar" (to castrate).

characters as when Estebanillo says: "I sent a nice present to my lady Dulcinea, with one of my servants, [who was] the spitting image of Sancho Panza, and a love note informing her of my intentions" (2:126). There is also mockery of the Baroque literary style called culteranism.[10] During a poetry contest, one of the participants confesses to Estebanillo that "the craze during those times was to gongorize with pompous elegance, in a way that what seems like a lot was in fact nothing, and neither the author nor those curious to read it would understand it" (2:300-301).[11]

Mockery extends itself to ethnic and religious realms as well. On a certain occasion, Estebanillo locks up a Jewish man in a frozen well, leaving him to freeze to death. On another, during the Vienna carnival, Estebanillo performs some skits with four Italian Jews wearing ridiculous costumes and pretends he is pulling out a tooth from one of them. Later, in a performance before his Majesty, Estebanillo recalls: "I grabbed with my pliers one of his molars, the one that seemed to me the biggest of all, and to make Their Majesties laugh at somebody else's crying I pulled with such force that not only did I pull it out, but also a good part of his jaw [came out] with it. The Jew began to cry out loud and his comrades [began] to get furious with me, Their Majesties [began] to laugh, and the town [began] to rejoice" (2:94). When Estebanillo notices that things are starting to get ugly, he justifies his actions: "Notice all of you that the one suffering is a Jew and his comrades Hebrew, and that I have done on purpose what you have seen and not because I did not know my occupation" (Ibid). From our present perspective, this kind of "humor" is in the worst of bad taste. Within its original context, where the carnivalesque still held rein, humor was far less scrupulous and moments such as these were hardly off base.

Physical violence, overindulgence and scatology are all typical ingredients of the buffoon's trade and his carnivalesque humor. In the episodes where Estebanillo performs the role of an apprentice in a barber shop, the gruesome once again goes along with the comic. The character's *turpitudo* as a barber is part of the humoristic mechanism. Again, the double entendre is frequent. For example, when speaking about a pauper whose hair he is going to cut, Estebanillo says: "I made him sit down on an old chair reserved for and most befitting to those with little hair"

---

[10] Culteranism ('culteranismo') refers to a convoluted writing style that flourished during the Spanish Baroque. Its principal exponent was Luis de Góngora y Argote (1561-1627).

[11] Gongorize ('gongorizar') alludes to the imitation of Góngora's style.

(1:122).[12] The whole passage is narrated in a mocking tone: "Instead of a
towel, I placed on him a sifter's apron for straining bleach, and taking out
of an apprentice's box a pair of scissors like those of a cloth shearer, and a
comb discarded from a dappled gray horse, I approached my patient;
[then] saying 'in the name of God!', since it was the first sacrifice that I
was performing, I started to snip left and right" (1:122-23). The pauper is
mercilessly animalized: "I tried to shear him like a lamb right down to the
scalp ... In fact, I started to shear him like a pauper, and then I sheared him
like a ram, then I trimmed him like a furry dog" (1:23). Estebanillo tries to
convince the poor man that "it was a new trend from Poland and Croatia,
with which he would enjoy cleanliness and his bad mood would leave him
best" (Ibid). On each of these occasions, Estebanillo creates deformity: "I
started not to cut but to tear off fur from that bush-like beard, whose
thickness could be a place of wild animals... I was cutting the flesh and
not the beard ... the whole face of my 'perroquiano'[13] was like the boot of
a gouty person[14] ... I took out a big handful of spider webs[15] ... and I
proceeded to cover all the small lumps [I had] made on that craggy face,
and those that I was still giving him at each moment" (1:127-128). Despite
the disaster, the master barber cannot stop laughing when he sees the result
of Estebanillo's work: a ridiculous figure of a pauper halfway beheaded.

    Occupations are also the object of the buffoon's mockery. We find
scornful attacks on doctors, bankers, merchants, barbers, servants and even
the deteriorated condition of the military. The scorn usually melds
violence with humor, as in the episode in which Estebanillo severs a
massive chunk from the ear of a merchant's son and defends his action by
saying that the son paid for the sins of the father, that the merchant would
forgive him [for severing his son's ear], among other things, on seeing that
"the punishment that he deserved had been endured by his son" (1:135).
The comic effect is complete when Estebanillo rebukes the sliced-off ear,
scolding it for not having warned him about its presence under the hair,
and then attempts to use glue to reattach it to the lad.

---

[12] The expression "de poco pelo" conveys a double meaning, since it refers to both
people with little hair and with little money.
[13] "Perroquiano" has a double meaning here. The author makes up a new word
from the terms "perro" (dog) and "parroquiano" (client), so he is bringing together
both meanings with the intention to animalize his customer.
[14] He is comparing the face of his customer with the shoe full of holes of a person
suffering from gout. The holes were made in the shoe so the patient would feel
some relief.
[15] Spider webs were used as bandages in those times.

Estebanillo not only inflicts pain. As we have seen, he also receives pain, and the pain he receives translates into the delight of the spectator or the reader. He was warned early in his career: "[He] who enjoys the good times, must [also] enjoy the hard ones; and [he] who eats meat, must chew the bones" (1:91). To be sure, it is very common in this sort of literature to find anecdotes in which the buffoons receive beatings from their masters, from the servants, and even have to fight with others of similar condition, participating in spectacles devised to entertain the court (Roncero 2004, 248). In one episode, Estebanillo participates in a table game with the noblemen. While these bet for money, Estebanillo bets for slaps, so that along with earning money, he is also receiving his share of slaps administered by the gentlemen and their servants. At the end of the game, Estebanillo is left with his face completely swollen, amidst the noblemen's loud guffaws. He accepts his pain and humiliation as part of his job, with his habitual "good humor," just as he had accepted the simulated attempt at castration, after which he had confessed to his master: "Sir, these are the caprices of the noblemen and the pension of those of my art" (*Estebanillo*, 2:90). His trade has its benefits as well as its occupational hazards. As he is reminded by one of the servants: "Brother Esteban, the occupation of the buffoon has a bit of bread and a bit of pain, a bit of honey and a bit of bitterness, and a bit of pleasure and a bit of fear; and one must suffer to be beautiful" (2:290).

Having taken refuge in the kitchen, Estebanillo makes us laugh when he narrates his adventures, his mischievous behavior, his buffoonery, and his horrendous culinary skills. In fact, his cooking is so repulsive that we feel somewhat relieved when we realize that we have not been invited to dinner. He himself recounts: "Every day I used to make a stew that even I didn't know what to call it … [and] the pot where it was cooking had so many bits of all kinds of herbs and such a variety of meats, without discarding any animal, no matter how filthy and disgusting it was, that it was only lacking soap and wool …" (1:284).

Since it is characteristic of humankind to laugh at each other's fears, especially when they seem disproportionate, the novel also makes fun of the buffoon's cowardice. In one scene of combat, fear makes Estebanillo seek refuge under a rotting horse, where he finds another terrified soldier – clearly a jab here at the state of the military. However, at the end of the battle, now that the enemy has been completely defeated, Estebanillo brazenly vaunts his valor. Callously, he offers a surreal view of the battlefield, with an animalized description of the corpses and drawing a grotesque and tragicomic parallel between the battlefield and the kitchen, using gastronomic terminology: "I found a fishery of Swedish tuna, a slaughterhouse of young Arian bulls and a butchery of Calvin slices […] I started […] to puncture pieces of fat, to drill bellies and slash gullets […] since [actually] I am not the first one who has shown up after the storm [is over] or who has given a good stab [in]to [the body of] a dead Moor" (1:316).

In other instances, we attend absurd duels in which alcohol plays the central role. Estebanillo recounts having one of these duels with a soldier who was equally drunk: "building up my courage, I challenged him to combat, and taking off one of my shoes, I handed him a sock, [the] glove of my left foot, for I did not have one [glove] on my hands" (2:13). According to Roncero López, these duels follow a tradition of ridiculous duels that are commonplace in certain burlesque literature contemporary to *Estebanillo González* (2004, 239). Estebanillo also describes his love relations and alcohol consumption in warlike terms, and scatology is an habitual protagonist of his tales. Take, for example, the story of his *intestine* war: "I drank a bit of cider because it was quite hot out and I had been told that it was good to cool off; but as soon as I had stored it … in the cave of my belly, then it started to have a disagreement with the wine that was inside and [began] to punch each other, and I felt within me, … against my will, the battle and the combat" (*Estebanillo*, 2:347). As a consequence, Estebanillo has to travel "on foot, holding his unfastened underwear in his hands, and having to stop every twenty feet" (2:348). Again, in the episode of his skit about the sick donkey, a beer barrel simulates a urinal, from which Estebanillo, dressed up as a doctor, is ready to drink. The donkey is given an enema and he ends up violently defecating all over everyone, which amuses the public enormously. Estebanillo recounts: "His Highness was dying of laughter and his servants were dying of pleasure" (2:139).

Entertainment is the buffoon's primary goal and, to achieve it, he must surprise with exaggerated and bizarre stories, cruel jokes and hyperbolic fears. His screams and remonstrations may strike us as being ridiculous— for example, Estebanillo hears a shot of a cannon, falls from his horse, suffers a minor scratch, and screams: "Jesus, they have killed me! Confession, confession!" (2:101)—but they achieve their purpose, the amusement of his audience. Tall stories, even outright lies, are his forte. Speaking of his stay at the court of the Empress María, Estebanillo relates: "There, I told marvelous things about the battle, and lies never before seen or imagined, earning a lot more with them than I made in Yelves collecting olives" (2:209). As for his stay at the court of the Count of Oropesa, he boasts: "Many gentlemen from Navarra used to come every night … and after selling them [papal] bulls without its [even] being Lent, I used to tell them the biggest lies and tales that could ever be imagined, and in order for them not to be verified, I said that they had happened in Germany and in Poland. They used to give me [right] there very good [gifts] and gratuities, and in their homes very expensive and tasty clarets" (2:343-344). As a buffoon, Estebanillo is not supposed to behave with honor; on the contrary, his most dishonorable and shameful actions will be rewarded for the rejoice caused in his audience (Bjornson, 439). And he is already aware of this toward the end of the first book, when he says "I left … the army and, observing the conniving of the court, I recognized what a good opportunity it was and I set foot [there], returning from death to life and from poor to rich" (*Estebanillo*, 1:286-287).

In the course of the novel we notice a transition in Estebanillo's status, from the original drifter and free-lance rogue to the court's buffoon.[16] He has grown up and he has realized that he needs stability in his life, even to the detriment of his freedom. The decisive moment in his career arrives when he enters the service of the Duque of Amalfi, where he receives a costume to make him easily recognizable as a buffoon. Even though he seems to detest this garb because it symbolizes his ties to the court and to the ever-changing favor of his master, he gives in. He has to, because this is the mark of the masquerade, the emblem of buffoonery, and it draws the attention of others onto himself.

Wherever he goes, Estebanillo is recognized as a buffoon, receiving a dichotomous treatment of distinction and pain. His fame grows with each service he carries out, with each letter of recommendation and reference he receives, parading his curriculum vitae of buffoonery throughout Europe. He is obsessed with the desire to augment his fame and to establish business contacts that will buy his comic merchandise. With each bizarre story, derisive anecdote and act of self-humiliation, the buffoon increases his marketability and reputation as an object for the amusement of others (Bjornson 439). His services are highly appreciated and rewarded.

Since ancient times, laughter has been considered a healthy remedy and a balance to the stress of life. Estebanillo recounts that Piccolomini "enjoyed spending some time with whom to entertain himself, since Cesar was not always winning battles, nor Pompey [was] conquering kingdoms, nor Belisarius [was] subjecting provinces, because there are times to fight

---

[16] For more on this transition, see Idalia Cordero de Bobonis, "*La vida y hechos de Estebanillo González*: Estudio sobre su visión del mundo y actitud ante la vida," *Archivum; Revista de la Facultad de Filosofía y Letras* 15 (Oviedo: Universidad de Oviedo, 1965): 180.

and times to have fun" (*Estebanillo*, 2:45-46).[17] The buffoon has won the favor of his master and holds a license to perform his comic art. However, he must conduct himself cautiously, taking care not to offend the powerful with his jokes and mockery.

Works Cited

Bjornson, Richard. "Estebanillo González, The Clown's Other Face." *Hispania* 60 no.3 (Sept. 1977): 436-442.

Cox Davis, Nina. "The 'Pícaro' as Jester in the Spanish Picaresque." *Romance Quarterly* 36 no. 1 (Feb. 1989): 49-61.

La vida y hechos de Estebanillo González, hombre de buen humor. Edited by Antonio Carreira and Jesús Antonio Cid. 2 vols. Madrid: Cátedra, 1990.

Roncero López, Victoriano. "Degradación caricaturesca en el *Estebanillo González*: Dos ejemplos." *Annali dell'Istituto Universitario Orientale Sezione Romanza* 31 no. 1 (June), 233-44. Napoli: L'Orientale Editrice, 1989.

—. "El tema del linaje en el *Estebanillo González*: la 'indignitas hominis'." *Bulletin of Hispanic Studies* 70 no. 4 (Oct. 1989): 420.

—. "Autobiografías del Siglo XVII (Duque de Estrada, Estebanillo González): Poesía e Historia." In *Príncipe de Viana* Anejo 17 (Año 57, Separata, 1996): 281-296.

—. "El humor y la novela picaresca: primera aproximación." *Annali dell'Istituto Universitario Orientale Sezione Romanza* 43 no. 1, 152-156. Napoli: L'Orientale Editrice, 2001.

—. "El humor del *Buscón*." In *Quevedo en Manhattan: Actas del Congreso Internacional, Nueva York, noviembre, 2001*, edited by Ignacio Arellano and Victoriano Roncero, 231-253. Madrid: Visor Libros, 2004.

Stamm, James R. "The Use and Types of Humor in the Picaresque Novel." *Hispania* 42 no. 4 (Dec. 1959): 482-87.

---

[17] For more on the contrast between times of war and times of pleasure, see Carreira y Cid (*Estebanillo* 1, xxxvi-xxxvii).

MACABRE HUMOR AND MODERN PARADOX IN GRACIÁN'S COURT OF DEATH

YUN SHAO

We have always laughed at things that frighten us. Among them death is the most dreaded and thereby an infinite source of inspiration for humor. In 17th-century Spain, the world's first modern empire in decline, it is not surprising to find great wits poking fun at human mortality and its various causes and manifestations: aging, illness, poverty, and above all, violence. Macabre humor entertained the mass through popular theater and picaresque novel. It also denoted the sensibility of the intellectual elite, balancing metaphysical contemplation of the somber subject with an explosive dynamic of jesting hysteria. Baltasar Gracián presents a unique example in his allegorical prose epic *El criticón*. His comedic rendition of death transcends medieval and classical traditions and creates paradoxes of modern ambiguity.

Gracián's epic *El criticón* delineates the steps of its hero, Andrenio, on a quest for Felicity, which consists of four stages or seasons: childhood / spring, youth / summer, adulthood / autumn, and old age / winter. At the end of his journey, Andrenio arrives in Rome, where he first observes a forum of philosophers debating the definition of Felicity in the grandiose palace of the Spanish Ambassador; later at night, he is lodged in a hotel named "Mesón de la Vida" at times and "Venta del Sol" at others, which turns out to be a murderous trap for unsuspecting travelers. The hospitable hostess is in fact the Queen of Death, who presides over a court of homicidal ruffians every night in a deep dungeon under the hotel. As the court is summoned, a boisterous parade of Death's ministers leads their queen into the subterranean chamber and then they report to her about their recent slaughtering feats. Here at the Court of Death, our hero, Andrenio, witnesses both the carnage of human life in all forms and his own demise at the hand of one of Death's courtiers, Decrepitude.

In the epic convention, the descent of the hero often anticipates his re-ascent and final achievement with a revelation or prophecy that infuses the hero with inner power or serves him as guidance. Andrenio's fall into the trap of Death is also framed within such a convention. Having sought Felicity in the courtly world to no avail, the pilgrim comes to the ultimate "desengaño" or disillusionment: the revelation that life is vain and death is inescapable. While many other Baroque authors such as Quevedo and Calderón have expounded a similar theme, Gracián's representation of death seems to evoke directly earlier traditions of didactic and religious literature. The procession of the queen recalls the late medieval Dance Macabre, a choreomaniac form often utilized to teach the Ars moriendi, or simply to preach Christian doctrines. In the sixteenth century the dance has already evolved into the allegorical configuration of a courtly assembly, as evidenced in Luis de Hurtado's comedia titled *Las cortes de la muerte* (*The Parliament of Death*), which was published in 1557, about a hundred years before Gracián's narrative version of the court of death. Thus, combining epic motif with the moralistic theme of "desengaño" Gracián imagines the fall and redemption of the hero. The pilgrim plunges into the abyss of horror only to leave it behind and to be ferried over the Sea of Ink to the Island of Immortality, where he will join all those of great fame in history. In a symbolic sense, Gracián envisions an intellectual deliverance from Spain's political and economic decay: the cultural achievements are to be remembered by future generations and therefore to transcend the physical limits of the empire in time and space.

On the other hand, Gracián's rendition of the hero's descent presents a complex body of witty satires that are not to be found in a conventional epic. It rather bears a kindred spirit to the picaresque novel, a genre that is a stock parody of the epic. The setup of Andrenio's deception by the false hostess of the seemingly magnificent "Inn of Life" in fact evokes a popular burlesque theme: the roguish innkeeper scheming to take advantage of unsuspecting guests. It recurs in the picaresque novel and even expands to other narrative genres, establishing memorable examples in most successful best sellers of the sixteenth and seventeenth centuries such as *Don Quijote* and *Guzmán de Alfarache*. If the picaresque novel mocks the chivalric characters and idealized eroticism of early modern romances, Gracián's Court of Death subverts the philosophical discourse of the Renaissance, pitching the morbid underworld of hooligans against the Platonic symposium of enlightened courtiers and elite scholars, the abrasive queen against the Spanish Ambassador, a convivial patron of arts and letters.

Likewise, the theme of "desengaño" is constructed upon a metaphysical premise quite different from the ascetic view of life that dominates the moralistic literature of the Counter Reformation. Instead of defining death as the only essence of life and thereby negating life's proper value,

Baltasar Gracián, a Jesuit, incurred the disfavor of his superiors after publishing his work *El criticón* without their permission. This painting was made during his exile in Graus. (Anonymous; Parroquia de San Miguel, Graus)

Gracián's hero rather sees the true meaning of his existence in the dichotomous figure of his hostess: hospitable and treacherous, beautiful and heinous, magnificent and monstrous, rich and poor, merry and miserable. She is at once Life and Death. In other words, Andrenio's revelation is not that death overrides life but rather that humanity is a paradox, being one thing and its opposite at the same time. This view suggests a dialecticism that constantly seeks and plays contradictions instead of annihilating them by asserting one value at the expense of the other. In fact, a closer examination of Gracián's Court of Death in comparison to the medieval dance and the sixteenth-century moralistic play bestows more differences than similarities, which will further illustrate the dialecticism underlying Gracián's wit and humor.

The ceremonious entrance of the queen and her ministers singing and dancing merrily may be the most obvious similarity to the medieval dance. There is also a sense of hysteria common to both representations, suggesting comparable circumstances of social crisis[1]. However, the comic tone of the queen's pageant contrasts sharply with the somberness of the medieval dance, while the humorous and even clownish quality of the queen and her ministers bears no resemblance to the deadly serious character of the dance leader. The most conspicuous absence is the medieval dance's primary theme of the chaotic world being turned upside-down by Death, who establishes a new order of absolute justice[2]. On the contrary, the queen and her ministers are rather preoccupied with not accomplishing their duties, given the adamant resistance of the living. The incompetence of the supposedly most powerful and lethal force may be read as a ridicule of the faltering political machine of the empire, but at the same time it certainly reveals the absence of an absolute ruling value: Death can no longer undisputedly claim her dominance over the living.

The difference is more noticeable in Gracián's transformation of the conventional motif of Death's confrontation with various human types. The basic structure of Dance is a procession in which those representing various social estates are portrayed unwillingly wending their way towards Death. In *El criticón*, it is utilized to present a new theme, namely the

---

[1] Various critics, including Alan David Deyermond and Patricia F. Mikus, suggest a connection between macabre dance and frequent outbreaks of epidemics during the late Middle Ages, when hysteria manifests in both physical symptoms and psychological reactions to the rising death toll.
[2] David Hook and J.R. Williamson point out that the medieval dance "achieved a remarkable thematic and structural coherence by the systematic use of [...] the traditional topos of the *mundus inversus* at the center of which Death [is] portrayed as a 'merciless hunter' [that] spares no one, high or low, rich or poor, and thus imposing an inescapable force of unification and equalization over the society" (97).

difficulty of killing, and to serve as the frame of the queen's autobiographical speech, in which she recalls her troubled apprenticeship of earlier days to comfort her frustrated ministers. Unlike the medieval dance, the variety of human types falling victim to the queen represents neither social estates nor moral conditions. It rather introduces complaints against her justice from different perspectives. While the queen obviously illustrates the hardship of her mission with these accusations, they function less as social or moralistic criticism than as a device to contrast views and values, and to distinguish the very human desire to live. In Death's own words, man's job is to live exactly as hers is to kill. None can desert his/her duty[3]. Not without a hint of irony, Gracián lets the living voice their will to live in the form of "llanto" or lament, a medieval elegiac tradition often found in poetry and epic. They persistently attempt to reset the rules for this game of hide-and-seek, while the fearsome queen often sees herself losing the upper hand. In her own words, Death has fallen victim to an exhausting hunt in which the prey plays the hunter like a violin, tricking her again and again in a futile chase ("pegándome bravas burlas, haziéndome todos ir y venir, que no hay mejor deuda ni más mala paga") (Gracián 780).

Likewise, *El criticón* differs considerably in style and ideology from the sixteenth-century play *Las cortes de la muerte*. The *comedia* takes the form of a parliament composed of deputies from various social estates, who present their complaints and requests before Death. It resembles the medieval dance in its essence: there is an inner structure of panoramic scrutiny of society, with strong satirical intention and critical attitude; the *Ars moriendi* remains a distinctive subtext especially in Death's speeches in response to requests for her either to postpone or to advance her arrival. On the other hand, the *comedia*'s didacticism becomes even more doctrinal since it not only introduces characters personifying moral concepts such as Flesh ("Carne"), World ("Mundo"), and Satan ("Satanás"), but also preaches through the voice of the angels and the saints. Finally, Death is explicitly identified as "instrumento de Dios", who proudly and solemnly announces her impeccable justice. Further advancing the didactic theme of the medieval dance, the play presents Death as a purging power and a better order of things.[4]

---

[3] "Mas no podía dejar de hacer mi oficio: los hombres a vivir y yo a matar" (779).

[4] Several other theatrical works on death contemporary with this comedia, such as "Farsa llamada danza de la muerte" by Juan de Pedraza (1551) and "Farsa de la muerte" by Diego Sánchez de Badajoz (1554), are cast from the same mold of social criticism and doctrinal exposition. Emphasizing different aspects of the Christian doctrine on sin and salvation brings about certain variations in the

As I have shown above, Cracián's Court of Death has a very different thematic focus. Despite the similar courtly setting, the main theme in Gracián's underworld theater ("teatro soterráneo") is the hardship of the missions of the queen and her ministers. Gracián transforms the structure of the traditional procession of Death's victims and their confrontation against her into a different rhetorical device to contrast the human will to live. Although it can still be read as a moralistic reproach of human illusion ("engaño"), this modification shifts the thematic focus to Death's ineptitude in performing her duties. As a result, the serious sermonizing developed from the medieval genre to the elaborated sixteenth-century allegory is cast away. Instead, ridicule and mockery especially at the expense of the deadly queen and her ministers, have become the overtone of the morbid farce.

The idea of absolute order and homogeneity embodied in the medieval and early modern figure of Death is subverted in Gracián's portrait of the queen. Aside from being a paradoxical figure, she is a failing power, unable to govern her own ministers, who often refuse to execute her commands. She loses her composure on several occasions, disappointed by the incompetence of her ministers and frustrated by her own governmental crisis. Her court is a malfunctioning administration whose reputation for efficiency and fairness is rapidly decreasing and whose principle of delivering absolutely equal service is often violated. For Gracián, it is not Death's victory over the world but rather the decline of her prowess that actually symbolizes a general disintegration of the society. By subverting the allegorical and satirical convention, Gracián infuses his witty humor with complex ironies. Instead of celebrating a single absolute ideal as in the medieval dance or the 16th-century *comedia*, Gracián projects a rather modern vision of multiplicity of perspectives and

---

respective personifications of Death. For example, Diego Sánchez de Badajoz made Death perish together with the character of a fearless old man in order to illustrate the eternal bliss enjoyed by the virtuous. Death is confronted or annoyed by its victims in these works, but never ridiculed as in *El criticón*. Not even in the "Entremés cantado de la Muerte" by Luis Quiñones de Benavente does the figure of Death have any noticeable comic quality, which is represented as a constable hunting for hustlers and their clients. Despite the typically farcical setting of a brothel that trivializes the didactic seriousness usually associated with allegories of death, the idea of justice and power embodied in death remains the core of its dramatic structure. In short, these works seem to reflect a continuous literary and ideological tradition since the Middle Ages, which Gracián's peculiar rendering of Death's image sets out to subvert.

values, which are conflictive and subversive against the moral conventions and religious doctrines. It is in the paradoxical mode of thinking, the dialecticism of contradictions, that Gracián finds a liberating dynamism of humor.

This unique representation of Death and her court has its sources in the classical tradition of satire and its inheritance by Renaissance humanists. There is no doubt that Gracián's mastery of ridicule and mockery belongs to the same lineage as Lucian and Erasmus. The way Gracián unfolds his travelers' Roman experience through the symposium and the underworld is clearly reminiscent of Lucian's dialogue on Mennipus' search for a reliable course of life first among living philosophers and then into the realm of Hades. Gracián's farcical characterization of Death and her ministers finds its precedent in the comic portrayal of Charon and other agents of the Underworld sketched by Lucian and Erasmus. However, there is a subtle difference between Gracián and his predecessors in the manner of structuring the satirical discourse. Every joke in the dialogues on the underworld by Lucian or Erasmus is directly related to their central themes, while Gracián's caricature of Death's court does not seem to have a consistent target of criticism or a clearly defined moral criterion.[5]

First, unlike many allegorical characters in contemporary genres such as the *auto sacramental*, which amply utilizes personification of moral concepts, Death's ministers in *El criticón* mostly represent biological and social conditions, such as diseases, plagues, and other physical and mental conditions, which are by themselves neutral terms without explicit ethical connotations. Consequently, their interactions do not constitute a dramatic conflict that illustrates religious doctrines or moral principles. The queen's

---

[5] Lucian makes the tyrant a clownish figure that embodies thought and behavior that the satirist reprimands. Mennipus the Cynic appears to represent everything antithetical to the tyrant, and their interactions with Charon and his crew constitute a systematic denunciation against worldly values. At the most climactic moment, when Mennipus drives Charon out of his mind by not paying the ferry, there is an implicit assertion of the cynic way of life, which is shown to be fearless of death. By making Charon whine about huge crowds of weighty souls killed in war at one moment, and express worries about not having any of them due to human and divine efforts of peace at the next, Erasmus elaborates his criticism of the conflictive situation of Europe and laments the breakdown of human brotherhood. In short, the comicity with which Lucian and Erasmus present the interlocutors does not undermine but rather consolidates the seriousness of their intended criticism and argument. Directly inspired by Erasmus, Alfonso de Valdés also wrote a dialogue between Charon and Mercury, a satire that has an even more explicit ideology as its unifying theme.

council serves as a free-flowing structure in which satire is launched into various directions. For example, at one moment the so-called fool-killers ("matabobos") complain about not being able to accomplish their task because no one dies innocent any more and there is malice everywhere ("no se usa ya el morir de tontos, todo va a la malicia"). The punch line critically targets the moral degradation of a whole society. At the next moment, when the queen turns to War, another minister of hers, the latter confesses that only about eight thousand died every year on each side instead of twenty thousand as were reported in the Spanish and French official gazettes. Here the horror of violence is curiously alleviated or downplayed by the political gibe at the military campaigns of the empire. Thus the satirist points his lance at diverse phenomena and individuals, skipping from one to another as the Queen and her assistants carry on their conversation.

Despite the lack of a unifying theme in social satire, there is a coherent characterization of Death and her ministers. Unlike the figures in the medieval dance or the moralistic *comedia*, which embody an absolute authority and power over their victims and whose competence in executing their task is ruthlessly perfect, Gracián's Court of Death shows carnivalesque raunchiness and comic flaws. There are approximately two groups of characters, one cheerfully celebrating the assembly with singing and dancing, while the other is sadly facing scrutiny and rebuke from their queen. The transfer of power from the older generation of ministers to a new one is an original device by Gracián, and in addition each of the two groups of characters also brings new elements to the traditional allegorical themes of justice and equality.

The first group of characters is associated with food and sex, clearly alluding to an Epicurean way of life. The implicit criticism is not original, but rather echoes ideas perceptible in many of Gracián's contemporaries such as Quevedo. As in the latter's "Epístola satírica y censoria contra las costumbres presentes," a contrast of lifestyle is made between the present and the past. Glut ("Hartazgo"), one of the partying crew, explains that a new class of happy-faced assistants has replaced the former ministers of misery in the court. Therefore, observes Glut, instead of pains and worries, what kills people more effectively nowadays are hearty meals and too much love-making. The implicit criticism resonates with what Quevedo laments in his poem: the excess of comfort and lack of discipline in contemporary aristocratic lifestyle. However, instead of plainly expressing nostalgia for the good old days as Quevedo does, the character Glut passes no value judgment on either way of life What he emphasizes is the difference in the *modus operandi of* the two groups of ministers, as well as the transfer of power from the old ministers to the new-comers: fewer and fewer people have perished at the hand of Death's old murderers, while more and more killed themselves with the aid of her new assistants.

The contrast between the groups of ministers and the shift of power from one to the other in Death's court may imply a satirical social commentary on certain changes within the Spanish nobility itself during Gracián's time. As Antonio Maravall has explained, new political forces were infiltrating the monarcho-seigneurial system of the medieval society: rising bourgeoisies of commercial wealth and administrative professionals from moderate non-aristocratic origins were able to move up the social ladder and became gradually aristocratized. Many of the new ministers of Death seem to indicate traits often associated with the new upstarts: they are perceived as indulgent and ostentatious in their pursuit of material luxury and physical pleasure. As David Castillo has argued, Gracián's writings project the concept of public personae defined by individual superiority and by their knowledge and power rather than by inherited noble status. He believes that "Gracián's courtly philosophy is commensurate with the interest of public individuals belonging to the new elite" (203). It is also to be noted that Gracián's macabre humor in caricaturing such social transformation may suggest a more complex sentiment than his presumed ideological alliance with the new courtly elite.

While Glut and his colleagues are enjoying their increasing success, the old-fashioned ministers, who are mostly causes of sufferings such as war and illness, are facing a tough situation. As personified concepts, these figures seem to have an unusual touch of human sensibility, and thus differ from many other allegorical characters such as those of Pain ("Dolor") and Old Age ("Vejez") in the sixteenth-century *comedia*. The supposedly fierce and merciless agents of Death have become exhausted, preoccupied, and reluctant, and their reports to the queen often turn into complaints and excuses. As Glut has observed, these murderous companions of Death do not always have their way with the living and they can often fail to execute exactly the queen's command. When told to kill the wealthy, the ministers Rib Pain ("dolor de costado"), Urinary Blockage ("detención de orina"), and Yellow Fever ("tabardillo") simply refuse to do so, protesting that the task is too difficult. Their coyness produces great comic effect as they overturn the attribute of irresistible fierceness conventionally associated with Death. No wonder the queen herself is very much troubled by her own ministers and constantly expresses utter disappointment and irritation, reproaching Gout ("la Gota") severely for prolonging rather than terminating life quickly, and scolding Plague and Contagion for only finishing off the poor and powerless.

Yet the queen herself relents oftentimes with ambiguities and contradictions, just as her paradoxical figure suggests. At one point, she warns her vassals: "I want you to know that I'm going to crack down on my ministers who aren't performing well and send them all away "por inútiles y ociosos donde hay médicos" (776). This statement is a perfect example of Gracián's double-edged irony. One cannot easily determine what the queen means. Does she threaten to banish her lazy, useless ministers to a place where doctors can teach them how to kill people, or banish them because they're letting doctors do their job for them? The joke is also ambiguous as to its target: is it poking fun at the incompetence of her ministers in killing or the ineptitude of the doctors in curing? Probably both! What is clear is that such ambivalence is what the author intended as an underlying mechanism of creating humor. It dismantles the didacticism of traditional allegories of death and complements the play of contradictions that runs throughout the dual configuration of the Queen of Life and Death.

Another significant example of the queen's ambivalence can be found in the inconsistency of her instructions to the ministers. In her recollection of her training days, she confesses her earlier struggles to decide whom to persecute because the living would always find a reason to question her decisions. Therefore, she urges her ministers to be indiscriminate in their killing, targeting young and old, rich and poor, healthy and sick, so that they'll all be aware and be properly scared (783). The indiscriminateness of Death is a crucial trope in the medieval dance and in the sixteenth-century *comedia*, conveying the ideal of absolute justice and order and laying the foundation for the ethical principle of conscience. Gracián's queen is evidently modeled after these earlier characters and is even depicted as blind. Her preaching on fear resonates to the didactic overtone of the medieval dance and the sixteenth century *comedia*. Nevertheless, the queen changes her tune and contradicts her own decree. Upon hearing the report that her ministers have tried in vain to finish off a carefree merrymaker, she instructs her vassals to be selective with their victims and to pursue only the sick and the frail (784).

The very foundation of Death's power is in peril: the principle is being ignored and violated constantly and her place in the divine scheme of the universe becomes meaningless. In short, Death no longer rules Life as a moral agent. As one of the queen's ministers laments in tears, their efforts serve no purpose because people aren't going to change their evil ways; in fact, they may even behave worse. The ambivalence and contradictions of the queen and the ineffectiveness of her ministers all point to a caricature of the traditional allegorization of death and subvert the value system constructed by such literary didacticism. Portrayed as comic figures, Gracián's queen and her company evoke picaresque antiheroes and farcical buffoons of the Spanish baroque theater.

The conventional symbolism of death is utterly dismantled by the critical and deconstructive mentality that emerged since the Renaissance among thinkers like Erasmus. One can trace Gracián's rhetoric of paradox and parody back to *Praise of Folly* and his multiplicity of perspectives to *Don Quijote*. On the other hand, Gracián's vision of life and death in *El criticón* differs considerably from the Erasmian Christian humanism or the ideology of Counter Reformation. If the recurrent themes of decadence and death of the late sixteenth and early seventeenth century metaphysical and moralistic literature created a sense of Apocalypse and urged social and spiritual reform both within and without the Catholic Church, such trends seem to have reached the limit of their momentum in Gracián, where the promised punishment and reward are no more than empty words. It is in this trivialization of the ideological and rhetorical authority that a sense of nihilism emerges. On the other hand, it is not a complete defeatism either. Gracián suggests that if life and death do not induce social, moral, or spiritual progress, the individual can still transcend the futility of human existence through intellectual endeavor and civic success. The sea of ink, evidence of such achievement, is the only passage to the Island of Immortality and the afterlife of Fame. The ultimate irony is that the hero has set off searching for one thing (Felicity) but achieves another (Fame) instead at the end. The subversion of the epic and the heroic by macabre humor and picaresque parody is the consummation of Gracián's creation.

Finally, it is necessary to point out another artistic representation of death that bears a striking contrast and parallel to that of Gracián's. M. Romera-Navarro has long before noted that the Jesuit author's verbal caricatures often recall the comic realism of sixteenth-century Flemish paintings and that Gracián specifically praises Bosch Van Aken in the first part of *El criticón* (135). I would simply point out in Gracián's overall conception of the Court of Death some comparable motifs and images to those created by another influential Flemish artist Pieter Brueghel. In an allegorical piece known as "The Triumph of Death", Brueghel depicts the horrendous carnage of human lives by death embodied in a massive troop of skeletons. While reflecting a medieval spirit in its vision of death as the absolute equalizer of society, the contextualization of the scene is more akin to Gracián's Court of Death in its contemporaneous immediacy. The confrontation between life and death takes place as a battle over a Flemish seaport. At the foreground of the scene, a courtly banquet on the bank of a canal is under siege and throngs of captives are being herded into a gigantic coffin; far in the background, a sweeping slaughter along the coastline has just come to an end and Death's troops are cleaning up the last pieces of the remains of human civilization. Like Gracián, who evokes a familiar courtly setting and carnivalesque theatricality in his allegory, Brueghel projects his allegory in the realistic liveliness of a recognizable local landscape and urban life scene. The contrast is especially revealing of the effect of Gracián's macabre humor, for compared to the stunning horror the Flemish painter portrayed through gruesome and vivid details, the underground chamber that entraps Gracián's hero is far from being frightening, where it is the Queen of Death and her ministers who feel at a loss and even powerless. The conventional morality anchored on the fear of death is thus canceled and in its place emerges the paradox of a modern subjectivity, whose morality is only definable in terms of historicity rather than an immutable ideal or dogma.

Works Cited

Castillo, David. "Gracián and the Art of Public Representation" in *Rhetoric and Politics: Baltasar Gracián and the New World Order*, edited by Nicholas Spadaccini and Jenaro Talens. University of Minnesota Press: Minneapolis and London, 1997: 191-208.

Egginton, William. "Gracián and the Emergence of the Modern Subjectivity" in *Rhetoric and Politics: Baltasar Gracián and the New World Order*, edited by Nicholas Spadaccini and Jenaro Talens. University of Minnesota Press: Minneapolis and London, 1997: 151-69.

Deyermond, Alan David. "El ambiente social e intelectual de la danza de la muerte." *Actas del tercer congreso internacional de hispanistas*. México, 1970: 267-75.

Gracián, Baltasar. *El criticón*. Edited by Santos Alonso. Catedra: Madrid, 1990.

Hook, David, and J.R.Williamson. "'Pensaste el mundo por vos trastornar': the World Upside-down in the *Danza general de la muerte*" *Medium Aevum*, 48 (1979): 90-101.

Hurtado, Luis. "Las cortes de la muerte" (1557), *Biblioteca de autores españoles: colección de poesías cristianas, morales y divinas*. Madrid: Ed. Justo de Sancha, 1872: 2-41.

Mikus, Patricia F. "The Spanish *Danza general de la muerte* in the European Context of the Theme." *Mid-Hudson Language Studies* 1(1978): 35-50.

Pedraza, Juan de. "Farsa llamada danza de la muerte" (1551). *Biblioteca de autores españoles: autos sacramentales.* Madrid: Ed. Eduardo González Pedroso, 1865. 58: 41-46.

Quevedo, Francisco de. "Epístola satírica y censoria contra las costumbres presentes de los castellanos." *Renaissance and Baroque Poetry of Spain.* Ed. Elias L. Rivers. Waveland Press: Prospect Heights, Illinois, 1988: 268-77.

Quiñones de Benavente, Luis. "Entremés cantado de la Muerte". *Colección de entremeses, loas, bailes, jácaras y mojigangas* (t.1, vol.2). Madrid: Ed. Emilio Cotarelo y Mori, 1911: 506-591.

Romera-Navarro, M. "El humorismo y la sátira de Gracián." *Hispanic Review* 10 (1942): 2, 126-46.

Sánchez de Badajoz, Diego. "Farsa de la muerte" (Sevilla, 1554). *Recopilación en metro del bachiller Diego Sánchez de Badajoz.* Madrid: Real Academia Española, 1929: 13-20.

PART III.

AH, WOMEN! OH, WOMEN!

LAUGHING AT LEARNED WOMEN
IN THE MEDIEVAL FRENCH FARCE

LISA PERFETTI

Consider these three words: *medieval, laughter, women.* As you read these words, did you imagine medieval women laughing? Or did you imagine men laughing at women? My guess is the latter. Medieval comic literature is infamous for its misogyny, and with good reason. Leaf through the folios of a collection of medieval jokes and you will find numerous jokes about sexually insatiable, gossipy, and deceitful women. Men, on the other hand, are never targeted as a whole group, as one can find today in the humor of stand-up comediennes across the world. Yet, the conventional wisdom that medieval humor was misogynous has kept us from paying attention to the underlying debates about women's place in medieval society that often contributed to that humor and has caused us to miss the ways in which medieval literature could be enjoyed by women. A closer examination of learned ladies in the medieval farce tradition enables us to see how the rhetorical games of the farce genre reflected uncertainty surrounding not only gender roles but also the control over language as a vehicle for making claims about women's intelligence.[1]

I am going to focus on one particular debate that raged in Europe from about the fourteenth through the seventeenth centuries: can a woman be educated, and if so, to what end?[2] As with all debates that occupy people's attention, the debate about women's intelligence made its way into a large body of comic texts. I will look at a number of French farces, with a particular focus on a farce called *Les femmes qui apprennent à parler latin*

---

[1] For a detailed examination of women's laughter in the Middle Ages, see Lisa Perfetti, *Women and Laughter in Medieval Comic Literature.* Chapter 5 is devoted to the French farces.

[2] The farces I examine could be considered early modern or Renaissance since they are contemporaneous with the early development of humanism in France. However, in content and spirit, they draw on medieval literary traditions, which is why I use the term "late medieval" in much of the essay.

(*The Women Who Learn to Speak Latin*).[3] We have little information about
when this play was written or under what circumstances it was performed,
although it seems likely to have been written some time around the end of
the fifteenth century, and a reference in the text suggests it was written by
and produced for students in one of the colleges of la Montagne Sainte-
Geneviève on the left bank of Paris. We should also note that all of the
roles, even those of the women, were performed by the students.

The farce opens with a rather curious proclamation that according to a
new edict of "Le Provincial," an academic authority and professor (he is
addressed as "maistre") attached to one of the colleges of Paris, Parisian
women can now learn Latin, the language of the European university. His
incredulous assistant, Robinet, objects that if women become learned, men
will no longer be able to master them. The master insists, and Robinet sets
off to post the message around the city. He is approached by Guillemette,
who asks him what the message says. Since she can't read, he explains the
content to her, and she hurries to tell her friends (*commères*) Alison,
Barbette, and Marion about this wonder. The women excitedly decide that
their new learning will enable them to get the upper hand over their
husbands, and for that reason they must keep their lessons a secret. When
the women present themselves to the master, he asks in which of the
"facultés" they wish to study. He proposes law to Alison. In order to test
her knowledge, he proposes a theoretical case: a young squire married a
knight's daughter, but he didn't have the "baggage" required on his
wedding knight. Should the newly married woman "unmarry" the squire?
Alison shows her brilliant new knowledge by answering "ita" (yes), and
passes the next case as well, in which a woman and her lover escape being
punished for adultery.

Barbette is to study medicine. She becomes expert in potions for
invigorating lovers and making husbands sick. To Guillemette, the eldest
of the four women, the provincial proposes that she be inducted into the
Faculty of Arts as its Regent. Through her ability to manipulate arguments
with Aristotelian logic, she will be able to make it appear that husbands
are saying nothing but foolish nonsense. Finally, Marion, who is eager to
study theology, is encouraged because of her youth to study rhetoric
instead. She learns to decline several Latin verbs, all of which end up
having a sexual meaning. The master declares Guillemette a "clergesse"

---

[3] This farce is found in Gustave Cohen, ed., *Recueil de farces françaises inédites
du XVe siècle* (Cambridge: Medieval Academy of America, 1949), pp. 123-134.
The plays in the anthology were printed around 1540 but probably date from 1480-
1492, according to Cohen (p. xxi).

(lady clerk, l. 467) and the women go off together boasting proudly of their newfound fluency in Latin.

It seems pretty clear that the producers of this farce were laughing *at* women, particularly women with pretensions to become learned. The very title laughs at the idea of women learning Latin. While some French women of the nobility were literate in the fifteenth and sixteenth centuries, Latin was by and large restricted to an elite community of formally educated men. Indeed, humanist educators were concerned about the education of young boys, whose early learning of Latin would be impeded by their contact with mothers, sisters, or nurses at home, since these women would speak vernacular languages, not Latin, with the impressionable boys. More than a practical language, Latin was a marker of identity, separating private and public, masculine and feminine.[4]

Women could gain an advanced education through instruction with private tutors, and literacy among women, although limited, was not unusual. But the formal learning provided by a university was closed to them until the 1860s, when a handful of Frenchwomen finally received the baccalauréat. Given that Latin and university life were the domain of men, could women have found this farce amusing? First, it is unlikely that this play would have had women in its audience. Many other farces were performed in public squares for holidays or processions or were commissioned by royal figures to be performed at court, and women would have been included in those audiences. The heavy use of Latin in this farce, however, was unlikely to make its humor very appealing to anyone other than the restricted academic circle that wrote and performed it.[5]

---

[4] Walter J. Ong characterized Latin as a kind of "puberty rite" for medieval and Renaissance males, part of their departure from the sheltered and feminine world of the home into the public realm of masculine affairs. Concomitant with their learning of Latin was a submission to the physical rigors of learning through floggings for poor academic performance. See "Latin Language Study as a Renaissance Puberty Rite."

[5] There are no references to audience members in this farce, although there are quite a few farces that specifically address men and women in the audience. Sara Beam notes, however, that it is wrong to suppose that all plays mounted by specialized guilds such as the Basoche were not performed for the public: "These are not merely skits to amuse fellow clerks during a day off of work but events that might disturb the public peace." *Laughing Matters*, p. 48). For another example of a farce that mentions women's lack of knowledge of Latin, see *Farce des femmes qui demandent les arrérages de leurs maris (Farce of the Women who Demand Payment of Debts in Arrears from their Husbands)*, where a woman who sues her husband for divorce because he hasn't slept with her for five years doesn't want to

It could be argued, in fact, that women were not the only ones unable to appreciate the humor of this farce. Much of the play's humor is derived from the incongruity of any person outside of the elite academic world speaking Latin. The students mounting this play could just as easily have chosen uneducated men as the targets of their humor, and indeed there are a number of farces in which foolish boys or peasants are ridiculed in their attempts to speak Latin. Much of the humor in this play comes from the transfer of learned Latin expressions of law, medicine, logic, and rhetoric to a nonacademic setting. Other farces, especially those produced by the society of law clerks, the Basoche, also focus their laughter on the tortured language of jurisprudence, or what we might call "legalese." Their humor comes from the incongruity resulting when the serious discourse of their profession was applied to trivial or ridiculous matters (Harvey 86-88). [6]

However, the farce does more than mock those ignorant of academic discourse; it clearly uses misogynous stereotypes to elicit laughter. From the beginning it is clear that the women are not exactly driven by the spirit of scholarly inquiry. Guillemette's wish to become learned in logic is motivated by her desire to out-argue her husband, and she notes that women will be able to rule everywhere: The women later imagine that while they are going off to study, their husbands will have to do the shopping and take care of the children (ll. 114-116). As in much other medieval humor, this is the topsy-turvy world where women wear the pants and men do women's work. In effect, we might say that the women are pursuing their "Master's" degrees. Indeed, in another farce women are given the title of "master" by simple virtue of the years of experience they have in dominating their husbands. [7] Robinet's sarcastic voice of conventional wisdom serves to highlight the absurdity of the master's ludicrous idea to instruct women. Robinet's shorter half-lines serve as ironic cutting stabs at the master's nonsense. Robinet warns him, for example, that the throng of women being "instructed" will sound more like a tempest: (l. 159). Sure enough, the four women look childish and ridiculous, arguing over who should approach the master first (ll. 155-165).

---

plead her case in the ecclesiastical courts because they speak Latin, which she doesn't understand. Vol I of *Ancien Theatre français*.

[6] In his classic work on the subject, Harvey argues that the Basoche productions did not lampoon lawyers themselves: they either apply legalistic language to ridiculous matters (*cause grasse*) which would have amused the Basoche or other student societies, or ridicule charlatans (*Maître Pathelin*, for example).

[7] *Les Femmes qui se font passer maistresses*, XVI in the Cohen collection, pp. 113-122.

It is also important to note the play's emphasis on the women's sexuality. Before we even see the four female characters, we hear the master proclaim that his teaching is now available to "doulcinettes," "parisiennes gorgettes," "petites riglettes," and "mignonnettes" (which one could roughly translate as "little sweeties, pretty little Parisians, partygirls, and cutiepies"). He appears more like a lecherous seducer than a master in search of students. His lessons are also entirely sexual in nature. Alison's talents in jurisprudence are confined to letting women off the hook for adultery, and Barbette's medical skills are meant to make husbands weak and lovers strong. Marion's prowess in conjugating Latin is demonstrated through a series of salacious puns, as when she is asked to give the preterite of *amo, amare* and correctly answers *amavit.* When asked to define it ("Qu'esse à dire?") she answers, "La femme ama vit," ("A // The// woman loves prick." [ll. 404-405]).

This sexualization of the female characters is a reflection of the medieval literary tradition and university culture that produced the play. As Ruth Mazo Karras has noted, Latin was not only an academic and professional language: it was "a bonding ritual and a marker of identity" for male students that went hand-in-hand with the misogynous curriculum of an academic world closed to all women except washerwomen and prostitutes (192). Indeed, there is a wonderful irony in this play. Whereas medieval texts view women as the enemies of clerks (we might think of the Wife of Bath or of images of women and clerks jousting in the margins of medieval manuscripts), in this play women are admitted as masters into the very institution known for its propagation of clerical antifeminism.[8]

Yet woven within the farce's conventional satirizing of unruly women is a more sympathetic view of female learning. When Guillemette first hears the announcement, she praises the master: "It is right that he be valued highly when he behaves so honorably to ladies in this way. By God, the world will run differently and people will behave better" [ll. 59-62]). These words of praise for a defender of women would likely have evoked the longstanding debate about women, the *querelle des femmes.* This debate about women was not just about women's rights, but also about the representation of women and the proliferation of antifeminist texts that defame them.

It is worth noting that another farce directly addresses the question of how women respond to the defamation of women. In a farce called *Le*

---

[8] One has only to think of the Wife of Bath's fight with her fifth husband, the clerk Jankyn, over his pleasure at reading and reciting to her his misogynous books. On clerical antifeminism and laughter at women, see chapter 1 of Perfetti, *Women and Laughter in Medieval Comic Literature.*

Vendeur de Livres (*The Bookseller*), a traveling bookseller calls out his wares to two women (Picot and Nyrop, 140-153).[9] But when they request saints' lives and other devotional texts, he keeps countering with obscene titles like the "Farce of the women with big asses." The women angrily chastise the bookseller for his lewd offerings by continually shouting "Fie on you, shame, that's disgusting!" Furthermore, they explicitly charge the bookseller's texts with dishonoring women: "Curse him who made such a thing that dishonors women!" [ll. 138-139]. The harassment of the women by the incorrigible bookseller and their indignant response were no doubt meant to be amusing. But the women's objection to material they claim is injurious to women echoes the actual charges of defamation Christine de Pizan made against Jean de Meun's *Romance of the Rose* in the early fifteenth century; it thus participates in the wider debate in late medieval culture concerning antifeminist themes in literature and the response of women readers.[10] While both of the farces I have discussed show women as the victims of laughter, women's concerns about men's defamation of their sex nonetheless emerge prominently.

Women's education and sexuality were intricately related in the medieval and early modern periods. While many humanists encouraged women to be educated enough to read devotional texts and to oversee the education of their children, the highly educated woman was often thought to be unfeminine and even unmarriageable. Women who chose a life of the mind often lived in painful isolation in "book-lined cells" (King, 66-89).[11] Although she did manage both to marry and have a career as a writer, Christine de Pizan was given a somewhat backhanded compliment by the Chancellor of the University of Paris, who called her an "insignis

---

[9] Translations are my own.

[10] See Helen Solterer's discussion of Christine in the context of her discussion of how the fictional female respondent figure, although created by a male author, could later enable women such as Christine to articulate a response to the defamation of women. *The Master and Minerva: Disputing Women in French Medieval Culture* (Berkeley: University of California Press, 1995), especially p. 148.

[11] Margaret L. King comments of learned Renaissance women, "Male by intellect, female in body and in soul, their sexual identity was rendered ambiguous...Not quite male, not quite female, learned women belonged to a third and amorphous sex" (75). Also see Lisa Jardine, "Women Humanists: Education for What?" in *Feminism and Renaissance Studies*, ed. Lorna Hutson, (Oxford University Press, 1999), pp. 48-81. For a somewhat more upbeat assessment, see Holt N. Parker, "Women and Humanism: Nine Factors for the Woman Learning," *Viator* 35 (2004): 581-616.

femina, virilis femina" ("distinguished, manly female").[12] By the mid-seventeenth century, virulent humor at the expense of learned women is fully expressed in Molière's *Les Femmes Savantes (The Learned Ladies)*, a comedy that clearly demonstrates the notion that women who pursue advanced learning are unnatural. The matriarch, Philamente, presides over a circle of women who discuss philosophy and literature, but she neglects her household affairs and domineers over her henpecked husband. Her eldest daughter refuses marriage because it will interfere with her learning. The clear heroine of the play, Henriette, the youngest daughter, eschews such learning in favor of a normal marriage. She declares to her mother, "I'm quite happy, mother, with being stupid. And I'd rather speak plainly than torture myself to say clever things" [ll. 1058-1060]).[13] The learned women in the play are all sexually aberrant in some way whereas the only conventionally normal woman is quite content to embrace her ignorance.[14]

Christine de Pizan devoted much of her life to countering the view of women as creatures of lesser intelligence ruled by their bodily passions. In 1405 she wrote her eloquent and learned defense of women, *La Cité des Dames*. A particular focus of her defense was women's education. Early in the work she asks Lady Reason whether God has ever chosen "to honor the feminine sex with the privilege of the virtue of high understanding and great learning, and whether women ever have a clever enough mind for this. I wish very much to know this because men maintain that the mind of women can learn only a little" (de Pizan, I.27.1). Reason answers that the only reason women don't know as much as men is because they are required to stay at home and run the household. Thus while it might be accurate to say that women are less learned, it is not because of any natural inclination, but rather because of social circumstances that prescribe

---

[12] Cited in Joan M. Ferrante, "The Education of Women in the Middle Ages in Theory, Fact, and Fantasy," in *Beyond their Sex*, pp. 9-42, at p. 38. Christine, herself, in her debate with Jean de Meun's defenders, refers repeatedly to her "feminine ignorance," indicative of Christine's care not to appear presumptuous in taking on the learned men of her time. See Christine McWebb, ed., *Debating the Roman de la Rose: A Critical Anthology* (New York and London: Routledge, 2007), pp. 107-198.

[13] Molière, *Oeuvres complètes*, ed. Georges Couton (Paris: Gallimard, 1971), p. 1040. Translation is my own.

[14] Caldéron, Molière's contemporary, similarly used the debate about women for comic effect. See the article by David Román, "Spectacular Women: Sites of Gender Strife and Negotiation in Calderón's 'No hay burlas con el amor' and on the Early Modern Spanish Stage," *Theatre Journal* 43.4 (1991): 445-456. Román notes that the play's heroine, Beatriz, "contains the dual anxieties of a culture suspicious of learned women and of affected, precious speech" (449).

women's roles.   Christine later questions men's motives in denying
women's access to education. Lady Rectitude notes of men who believe it
is bad for women to be educated, "But it is very true that many foolish
men have claimed this because it displeased them that women knew more
than they did (II.36.4)." Reason thus suggests that men keep women from
being educated not because they believe women are incapable of learning,
but rather because they know full well it is in their own interests to keep
women ignorant. The male monopoly over education goes hand in hand
with stereotypes about women's natural cunning. Women were considered
irrational, but they were said to possess a certain kind of cleverness that
continually threatened to undermine men's power.

A common medieval maxim states, "Mulierum astutia decepit
sapientissimos" (Female cunning deceives even the most learned) (qtd in
Solterer 24). This maxim plays out in hundreds of comic texts of the
Middle Ages. The famous example of the *Lai d'Aristote,* where a woman
masters and humiliates the besotted Master Philosopher by riding him like
a horse, demonstrates the anxiety provoked by the threat of women's
usurping of men's monopoly over the learned tradition that ensured their
status and power.[15]   In effect, the master of this farce is another Aristotle:
led astray by his attraction to women, he betrays the dignity of male
learning and, even worse, gives women the arms they need to usurp men's
authority and power.

This notion that women are denied an education because it is
threatening to men appears in the *Femmes qui apprennent à parler latin.*
The four women not only marvel at their new knowledge but lament that it
has been deliberately and maliciously hidden from them. Barbette declares:
"We'll finally get what was meant to be ours. I don't know how it's been
hidden from us for so long" [ll. 93-94]. Alison retorts that women have
been left out so that men would be able to dominate the public realm of
discourse. Guillemette declares "Oh, the villains!" and Barbette adds
"Those wicked men!" Men are calumnied as uncouth and mean-spirited.
The women envision the ability to learn Latin not just as a means of
turning the household upside down, but as a means of punishing men as a
whole for depriving women of their access to learning. Alison concludes

---

[15] Helen Solterer, *Master and Minerva*, remarks that the *Lai* is a prime example of
how in the Middle Ages "Any intelligence ascribed to women (*astutia*) is
described *a contrario*, as a threat to men's. It rivals the trait distinguishing the
clerk" (24). She further notes that the wide circulation of the story along with other
common images of women getting the better of clerks shows that it "touched a
nerve in the medieval clergy. It provoked concern that—like these amusing
marginalia—underlies their thinking."

that the men will be "riglés," or "paid back" (l. 98). When Alison later is instructed in law, she again declares "Law! And they hid it from us and it is so fitting for women [ll. 187-88]."[16] In all of these passages there is an implicit assumption that men, rather than sincerely believing that education is unnecessary for women, are simply keeping education a secret from women so that men might maintain their status and power.

Were men in the late Middle Ages, in fact, attempting to hide the benefits of learning from women? While any direct evidence of such an intention would be difficult to find, it is clear that men profited from the exclusion of women from formal education: it was after the emergence of universities in the thirteenth century that the socioeconomic gap between men and women most increased because the highly specialized schools of law, medicine, and theology prepared men for careers in government, university teaching, the professions, or the church (Ferrante 17-18). If women could receive the same formal academic training as men, they could then gain access to political and economic power. This is precisely what Erasmus, one of the foremost humanist educators, imagines in a colloquy printed in 1524. In this dialogue, an ignorant abbot discourses with a married woman called Magdalia about the unfeminine Latin and Greek books he sees in her living room. The lady, thought to be modeled on Margaret Roper, the eldest daughter of Thomas More, refutes his nonsensical arguments point by point. She finishes by chastising the abbot for his ignorance, noting the many women across Europe who are as learned as men, and then warns, "If you're not careful, the net result will be that we'll preside in the theological schools, preach in the churches, and wear your miters" (Thompson 223). The dialogue ends with the woman declaring that she feels like laughing—at the abbot's foolishness. We have here, of course, a fictional woman's response, imagined by a male author. Erasmus, like other late medieval and early modern "advocates" for women, spoke on behalf of the need for women to be educated, but carefully avoided advocating access either to formal university education or to the professions for which this education trained urban middle-class men. A woman's education was valued primarily as a means for her moral and spiritual development and as preparation for her role as wife and mother.[17] Even Christine de Pizan, so eloquent in her defense of the same

---

[16] The idea that women view their education as a way of paying back men for wronging women would later appear in Molière's *Les femmes savantes*.

[17] See, for example, J. K. Sowards, "Erasmus and the Education of Women," *Sixteenth Century Journal* 13.4 (1982): 77-89. Another notable example of the comparatively enlightened view toward women's education is Juan Luis Vives's *The Education of A Christian Woman [De institutione feminae Christianae]*,

right of women to pursue learning as men, never argued that women should be admitted to the university.[18] Yet Magdalia's witty jibes at the abbot debunk men's claims that they are the wiser sex and demonstrate the potential for women to succeed on the same intellectual terrain. Christine, too, used her wit to joust with her clerical adversaries in the debate over the *Roman de la Rose*.[19] While neither men nor women argued that women *should* gain access to the university, by the time of our farce, the idea that women, by virtue of their intellect, *could* do this, was circulating far and wide in the intellectual circles of Europe.

To return to our farce, it is noteworthy that the women are not only ignorant of Latin, but just plain illiterate. When Guillemette asks to know the content of the message Robinet is posting, he mockingly suggests that she read it herself: "Read the words; they're written down. Do I really have to read them out loud to you?" (ll. 40-41). Robinet bluntly ridicules her illiteracy, no doubt savoring the irony that she cannot even read the proclamation that claims to make an educated woman out of her. While highly educated women like Christine de Pizan were well known in the fifteenth century, and literate noble and bourgeois women were plentiful enough in Paris, the farce authors chose as their targets completely illiterate women, perhaps because the incongruity was heightened; perhaps

---

written around 1524 and commissioned by Catherine of Aragon, Queen of England, who had learned Latin and was known for her learning. In it, Vives refutes the popular idea of his time that learned women are unchaste, giving numerous examples both from Antiquity and the contemporary period of chaste and virtuous women of learning. Indeed, his emphasis on chastity as the primary goal of women's education pervades the work. For him, the kind of learning women need is "the study of wisdom, which teaches the best and holiest way of life.

[18] While some modern feminists consider Christine a rather unimpressive exemplar of early feminism, Christine's defenders point out that she should be judged in the context of her own time and that in that context, her feminism was actually quite bold. Rosalind Brown-Grant notes, for example that she "was able to adapt the traditional premises of medieval social theory to new ends", using them to strengthen her case for women and to argue that it was in the interests of both social cohesion and natural justice that the estate of women be allotted its rightful, acknowledged, and honored place in the body politic alongside that of men. It might also be noted that Marguerite de Navarre, prolific author of the French Renaissance, had a prominent role in founding the Collège de France in 1530 (then known as the "Collège Royal.") Although, like Christine, she did not advocate entrance of women to the university, her writing was devoted to elevating the status of women and promoting their learning.

[19] See Thelma Fenster, "Did Christine Have a Sense of Humor?" Christine specifically mocks learned men who use their schooling ("escoles") to run around bragging (falsely) about women whose favors they have enjoyed.

because the farce generally represented the lower classes. But by choosing illiterate women as their students of Latin, the play authors were perhaps also refusing to engage with the reality of women who could read and write, and, perhaps, even debate with learned men.[20]

I mentioned earlier that the farce's humor relies on the incongruity resulting from the juxtaposition between the highly specialized domain of Latin and academic discourse on the one hand and the use of that discourse by outsiders on the other. Recent critical work on the farce genre has in fact argued that its humor is less interested in the subversion of social mores than it is in playing with reason or with language. One scholar, in particular, argues that the authors of farces were not focused either on blaming or on defending women. The battle of words between husband and wife was used rather to demonstrate the instability of language in a fallen world. (Lucken, 173).[21] The notion that farce humor is really about language helps to explain why many farces allow women to prevail in the end. If the laughter depends on our knowledge of specialized discourses and not on our view of women, then it does not matter whether women win or lose. Yet we need to be careful not to privilege a genderless view of farce humor. There are certainly rhetorical games at work that use misogynous conventions for other purposes, but these farces participate in gender ideology nonetheless. We must not ignore the way in which laughter reflects or reshapes the audience's attitudes toward women's intelligence.

It is also important to recognize that whereas the conventional view has been to see the medieval audience as a unified group laughing or crying in unison, dramatic productions were just as likely to foment discord and debate among playgoers.[22] While *Les Femmes qui apprennent à parler*

---

[20] Natalie Zemon Davis notes "Thus, in the first half of the sixteenth century, the wealthy and well-born woman was being encouraged to read and study by the availabiltiy to her of printed books; by the strengthening of the image of the learned lady, as the writings of Christine de Pisan and Marguerite appeared in print; and by the attitude of some fathers, who took seriously the modest educational programs for women being urged by Christian humanists like Erasmus and Juan Luis Vives. Reading and writing for women of the *menu peuple* was more likely to be ridiculous, a subject for farce" (73).

[21] See also Jody Enders who, following Harvey, argues that much of the humor of the farces written by the Basochiens depends on a knowledge of legal disputation. *Rhetoric and the Origins of Medieval Drama* (Ithaca: Cornell University Press,1992), 213.

[22] Claire Sponsler argues that whereas the conventional view is that medieval theater performances fostered collective identity and communal feeling, performances were just as likely to sow discord among competing interests in the

latin probably evoked a fairly homogenous laughter because of its
restricted performance setting, the many farces performed in public were
likely to arouse diverse reactions in its audiences, particularly along
gender lines. The satire on learned women was well established by the
time of Molière, Shakespeare, and Calderón de la Barca, authors familiar
to many readers today, but it clearly was already developing in the late
Middle Ages. The laughter was not necessarily subversive: while
numerous French farces may have been considered dangerous enough to
be suppressed by local magistrates or royal officials, farces focusing on
women largely upheld the status quo, hardly surprising given that they
were written and performed by male-dominated groups.[23] Yet in these
conservative farces we see reflections of serious debates about women's
capacity for learning and the degree of education considered appropriate
for them. Although *Les femmes qui apprennent à parler latin* does not take
seriously the idea that women could study at university, it does provide the
opportunity for men to play with, and thus contain, the anxiety that women
could some day equal men in their learning and attain the power that such
learning confers.[24]

How did the laughter at educated women change when women did gain
access to a university education? As the debate about women's intelligence
and competence shifted, how did humor respond to those shifts? This is
an issue that is still with us today in popular culture, and even in modern
university classrooms, where student expectations regarding the use of
humor by their professors differ according to gender.[25] While the idea of

audience: "The Culture of the Spectator: Conformity and Resistance to Medieval
Performances." *Theatre Journal* 44 (1992): 15-29. See also Robert Clark,
"Community versus subject in late medieval French confraternity drama and
ritual," in *Drama and Community: People and Plays in Medieval Europe*, ed. Alan
Hindley (Turnhout, Belgium: Brepols, 1999), 34-56.

[23] For a study of the subversive force of the French farce, see Sara Beam, *Laughing
Matters*.

[24] Anthropologists and psychologists often view the play-element of humor as a
way of coping with social conflicts. See Brian Sutton-Smith, *The Ambiguity of
Play* (Cambridge: Harvard University Press, 2001).

[25] While we have made considerable progress in that students do not view female
faculty as laughable (even those who can speak Latin), some research shows that
students are more likely to value a sense of humor in their male professors and to
rate female faculty members who use humor as less effective and competent. See,
for example, J. Bryant, P.W. Comisky, J.S. Crane, and D. Zillmann, "Relationship
between college teachers' use of humor in the classroom and students' evaluations
of their teachers," *Journal of Educational Psychology* 72 (1980): 511-519. Other
studies are more mixed in their conclusions, but do suggest that female faculty

women speaking Latin is no longer amusing today, the relationship between women, learning, and laughter continues to be a vexed one.

Works Cited

Beam, Sara. *Laughing Matters: Farce and the Making of Absolutism in France*. Ithaca: Cornell University Press, 2007.

Clark, Robert. "Community versus subject in late medieval French confraternity drama and ritual," in *Drama and Community: People and Plays in Medieval Europe*, ed. Alan Hindley. Turnhout, Belgium: Brepols, 1999.

Cohen, Gustave, ed. *Recueil de farces françaises inédites du XVe siècle*. Cambridge: Medieval Academy of America, 1949.

Davis, Natalie Zemon. *Society and Culture in Early Modern France*. Stanford University Press, 1975.

de Pizan, Christine. *The Book of the City of Ladies*, trans. Earl Jeffrey Richards. New York: Persea Books, 1982.

Enders, Jody. *Rhetoric and the Origins of Medieval Drama*. Ithaca: Cornell University Press,1992.

Fenster, Thelma., "Did Christine Have a Sense of Humor? The Evidence of the *Epistre au dieu d'Amours*," in *Reinterpreting Christine de Pizan*, ed. Earl Jeffrey Richards. Athens: University of Georgia Press, 1992.

Ferrante, Joan M. "The Education of Women in the Middle Ages in Theory, Fact, and Fantasy," in *Beyond Their Sex: Learned Women of the European Past*. Patricia H. Labalme, ed. New York: New York University Press, 1980.

Grant-Brown, Rosalind. "Christine de Pizan as a Defender of Women," in *Christine de Pizan: A Casebook*. Barbara K. Altmann and Deborah L. McGrady, eds. New York and London: Routledge, 2003.

Harvey, Howard Graham. *The Theatre of the Basoche; the Contribution of the Law Societies to French Mediaeval Comedy*. Cambridge: Harvard University Press, 1941.

---

continue to be concerned about being taken seriously. See, for example, Joan Gorham and Diane M. Christophel, "The Relationship of Teachers' Use of Humor in the Classroom to Immediacy and Student Learning," *Communication Education* 39 (1990): 46-62; Ron Tamborini and Dolf Zillmann, "College Students' Perception of Lecturers Using Humor," *Perceptual and Motor Skills* 52 (1981): 427-432; Katherine Van Giffen, "Influence of Professor Gender and Perceived Use of Humor on Course Evaluations" *Humor* 3 (1990): 65-73. I would like to thank Rachel Leavitt, my undergraduate research assistant, for her help with these references.

Karras, Ruth Mazo. "Sharing Wine, Women, and Song: Masculine Identity Formation in the Medieval European Universities" in *Becoming Male in the Middle Ages*. Jeffrey Jerome Cohen and Bonnie Wheeler, eds. New York: Garland Publishing, 1997.

King, Margaret L. "Book-Lined Cells: Women and Humanism in the Early Italian Renaissance," in *Beyond their Sex: Learned Women of the European Past*. Patricia H. Labalme, ed. New York and London: New York University Press, 1980.

La Farce Joyeuse à troys personnages, c'est ascavoir deulx femes et un vendeur de livres. Picot, Emile and Christophe Nyrop, eds., *Nouveau recueil de farces françaises des XVe et XVIe siècles*. Paris: Damascène Morgand and Charles Fatout, 1880.

Lucken, Christopher. "Woman's Cry: Broken Language, Marital Disputes, and the Poetics of Medieval Farce," in *Reassessing the Heroine in Medieval French Literature*. Kathy M. Krause, ed. Gainesville: University Press of Florida, 2001.

Molière. *Oeuvres complètes*. Georges Couton, ed. Paris: Gallimard, 1971.

Ong, Walter J. "Latin Language Study as a Renaissance Puberty Rite," in *Rhetoric, Romance, and Technology: Studies in the Interaction of Expression and Culture*. Ithaca and London: Cornell University Press, 1971.

Perfetti, Lisa. *Women and Laughter in Medieval Comic Literature*. Ann Arbor: University of Michigan Press, 2003

Riché, Pierre and Jacques Verger. *Des nains sur des épaules de géants: maîtres et élèves au Moyen Âge*. Paris: Tallandier, 2006.

Román, David. "'No hay burlas con el amor' and on the Early Modern Spanish Stage," *Theatre Journal* 43.4 (1991): 445-456.

Solterer, Helen. *The Master and Minerva: Disputing Women in French Medieval Culture*. Berkeley: University of California Press, 1995.

Sutton-Smith, Brian. *The Ambiguity of Play*. Cambridge: Harvard University Press, 2001).

Sponsler, Claire. "The Culture of the Spectator: Conformity and Resistance to Medieval Performances." *Theatre Journal* 44 (1992): 15-29.

Thompson, Craig R., trans. *The Colloquies of Erasmus*. Chicago: University of Chicago Press, 1965.

SEX, VIOLENCE, AND THE HOLY: ASPECTS OF HUMOR IN MEDIEVAL NARRATIVE

STEFANO MULA

In Umberto Eco's famous novel *The Name of the Rose*, the blind monk Jorge of Burgos is ready to commit any mischief in order to prevent the long-lost second book of Aristotle's *Poetics* from falling into the wrong hands. This (hypothetical) book concerned comedy, and the fact that Aristotle, the Philosopher par excellence, considered comedy as a force for good was enough to send Jorge into a killing frenzy. Our hero and sleuth, William of Baskerville, finally confronts Jorge and asks him a very simple question: "But what frightened you in this discussion of laughter? You cannot eliminate laughter by eliminating the book." To which Jorge replied: "No, to be sure. But laughter is weakness, corruption, the foolishness of our flesh. It is the peasant's entertainment, the drunkard's license; even the church in her wisdom has granted the moment of feast, carnival, fair, this diurnal pollution that releases humors and distracts from other desires and other ambitions" (576-577). Authentic quotation, or modern reconstruction of medieval thinking, these ideas on laughter and the comical expressed by Jorge represent one of the common medieval attitudes towards laughter, but certainly not the only one.

Recent times have seen increasing attention to topics such as humor, parody and laughter in the Middle Ages, and also to issues relating to the obscene.[1] This article aims at showing how three seemingly unconnected elements of medieval literature—sex, violence and the holy—combine in certain texts to produce humorous moments. My goal is not to study tales that are explicitly comic in nature, such as *fabliaux* or the short nonsense poems called *fatrasies*, but to concentrate instead on texts such as *novelle*

---

[1] See for instance: Jan M. Ziolokowski (ed.). *Obscenity, Social Control and Artistic Creation in the European Middle Ages*; Jeannine Horowitz and Sophia Menache. *L'Humour en chaire. Le rire dans l'Eglise médiévale*; Felice Moretti. *La ragione del sorriso e del riso nel Medioevo*; Martha Bayless. *Parody in the Middle Ages.*

and *exempla,* where humor is only one of the aspects of the narrative, giving special attention to stories related to Purgatory. It is not difficult to see how the topic of the Purgatory can easily be the subject of parody, but what is not often noticed is how humor is also present even in the most serious of works. Here violence is present as part of the punishment for sinners, often for sins related to excessive or deviant sexuality. The souls purged by their sufferings will then be able to move to heaven, but the scenario in many cases is encased in humor.

Pieces collected by Ernst Robert Curtius in his *European Literature and the Latin Middle Ages,* show that the attitude of the medieval period towards humor was at best inconsistent. Curtius notes how the sixth-century *Rule of Saint Benedict* set the guidelines for monks on laughter and humor: IV, 53-54: "Do not speak idly nor so as to cause mirth. Do not love boisterous laughter"; or, again: VI, 8: "We always condemn and ban all small talk and jokes; no disciple shall speak such things." [2] At the same time, however, hagiographical texts were full of passages clearly meant to instigate laughter. How else should we consider the words that Prudentius puts in Saint Lawrence's mouth when he was put on the grill to be tortured? Instead of complaining about the pain, he encourages his torturer to turn him on the other side, since one side is already cooked, and finally adds, jokingly (*ludibundus*): "Now it's cooked: eat it and see if it's tastier raw or cooked (Gurevich 181). Evidently, the medieval public expected authors to introduce comic moments into those narratives since humorous elements are found even in the burial scenes of saints. (Gurevich 181).

Is it possible to present medieval humorous texts without the putatively, or explicitly obscene? (See Caviness, 156-165) Medieval stories have frequently been bowdlerized in modern times. Medieval manuscripts, however, were frequently illuminated with seemingly inappropriate images that range from the merely comic to the frankly obscene. One only needs to refer to Michael Camille's magisterial work on images on the margin to find plenty of examples of that mix of obscene and the sacred. To take just one example, a particularly surprising miniature is spread over two folios (*Image...,* 44-45). The first part is on the bottom verso, where we find a monkey with a spear sitting on a big bird. What catches the viewer's attention, however, is the second image, which is on the bottom recto of the following folio. Here we find the figure of a naked young man with long hair and a striking resemblance to the traditional visual image of Christ, bent over and presenting his buttocks to the monkey of the facing page.

---

[2] Translation by Anthony C. Meisel and M. L. del Mastro, 1975.

This coupling of the two images seems obscene to us. The real question is whether medieval people would have found it so. The manuscript itself is a collection of Latin psalms, the famous *Rutland Psalter*, now in the British Library in London and probably composed around 1260.[3] Given the text, we can assume that the manuscript was made for a religious purpose. Did the owner of the manuscript think that the images were not obscene? What was that image doing there? The last verse placed immediately over the naked man reads: "Princes went before, joined with singers, in the midst of youths playing on timbrels" [Ps. 67:26]). Michael Camille observes that the image may possibly be a pun on the word "iuvencularum," because of the presence of the word "cul" (ass), but he does not overly stress this interpretation. More importantly, he notes the "striking resemblance to Christ"—a resemblance that, in context, borders on the blasphemous (43).

The Russian scholar Bakhtin, along with many who followed him, theorized that humor was a tool of subversion. The fact that during Carnival all hierarchy was mocked, the world was depicted upside down and during those days everything was permitted, seemed to indicate a desire for rebellion on the part of the masses. (*Rabelais*, 1-58) Other scholars have taken the opposite position: since the Carnival was permitted by the Church, all the partying and rebellion was essentially false, a simple way of letting off steam. In other words, humor and parody in medieval times had, as Howard Bloch has put it, an "essentially conservative impetus" (120).

A third position is taken by Philippe Ménard, a French scholar who has worked extensively on medieval humor in texts such as chivalric prose romances and the *fabliaux*. For Ménard, these images cannot be subversive because of the place where they are located, and he notes also that most of the time there is really no connection between the text and the image. On the other hand, neither are they conservative, but simply the expression of the artistic sensibility of the artist. In Ménard's words: "those painters give us photographs of daily life, and sometimes they draw a few comic scenes. Why? Quite simply because they wanted to enjoy themselves, and they were deeply moved by the energy of everyday life, and of the taste of the fleeting moment" (86). So what was the motivation? Rebellion? A conservative impulse? Or just the expression of an artistic bent? I will leave this question hanging for a moment, while we move our attention from image to text.

---

[3] Ms Add. 62925, from around 1260. The two pages contain Psalm 67, 8-26.

Scholarly literature on *exempla* and on the Italian *novelle* is too broad to be even summarized here even briefly. For the purpose of this article, we can define as *exempla* any short religious or edifying stories written in Latin and meant to be incorporated in sermons or retold orally among the members of a religious community (Bremond, LeGoff, *et al.*, 38). A *novella*, on the other hand, is a story written in a vernacular language by a secular author, without any explicit religious intent. One evident similarity between *exempla* and *novelle* is that they are short narrative texts, but similarities go much deeper than the surface.

Authors of secular *novelle* sometimes share their subject matter with religious *exempla*. One example among many is the story of the philosopher who, interested in the stars, falls into a well and needs to be rescued by a servant. Tubach's description of the *exemplum* (# 3750) reads: "Philosopher, star-gazing, falls. A philosopher, star-gazing, falls into a ditch and is mocked by his servant."[4] The story is not only part of *exempla* collections, but is also retold in the *Novellino*, a collection of *novelle* composed towards the end of the thirteenth century by an anonymous Tuscan author. The intended audience of this work could have been the merchant class, or, as has been recently argued, the aristocratic milieu.[5] The ultimate origin of this tale goes as far back as Plato, who in his *Theaetetus* appears to have been the first to tell this episode. In the western Middle Ages, the responsibility for the spread of this tale is Peter Damian, who retold it in one of his letters. Peter Damian's letters were later collected, the exemplary stories were excerpted, and one particular collection of such excerpts became a collection of short stories.[6] The story, though not hilariously funny, is clearly meant to elicit the sympathy and a complicit smile from the audience, be it made of monks or of merchants.

A typical feature of both the *novelle* and the *exempla* is that most of the humor can be concentrated in the final punch line. Attention to an effective delivery of a joke is evident, for instance, in the collection of *exempla* inserted in some of Gerard of Liege's sermons (ms Paris, BNF

---

[4] Frederic C. Tubach. *Index Exemplorum. A Handbook of Medieval Religious Tales.* Tubach's reference is to a collection of *exempla* of London, British Library, ms Burney 351, where at ff. 39-40 there are five tales taken from Peter Damian. The *exemplum* is present at least in two other collections now in Paris. The first one, Paris BNF, lat. 14657 is an interesting collection from the early thirteenth century, of which I am currently preparing an edition, and the second is Paris, BNF lat. 3338, from the late thirteenth century, based on BNF lat. 14657.

[5] Cf. Lucia Battaglia Ricci. "Leggere e scrivere novelle tra '200 e '300."

[6] See Stefano Mula. "Les *exempla* de Pierre Damien et leur diffusion aux XIIe et XIIIe siècles."

lat. 16843, second half of the thirteenth century),[7] where many of the stories are centered on the final *bon mot*, transmitted in French. Nico Van den Boogaard recalls one concerning a priest and his fake intransigent honesty:

> Exemplum of a certain priest of a great prince, who refused many great benefices that had been offered to him. And one day, when the prince was talking with someone and expressing wonder at the priest's behavior, his interlocutor said that he thought that the priest didn't want to accept any church [post] paying less than one hundred pounds. The prince called the priest and asked him if it was true, and the priest said that it was, and when the prince asked him why, he answered: "Because I don't want to go to hell except for a good fistful of money!" (178)

The punch line is offered in French, with an added Latin translation for those who might have missed it.

The differences between the *novelle* and the *exempla* seem to lie more in the way they were delivered than in their absolute content, or even in their worldview. Although the Latin *exempla* usually stressed Christian morals, they shared their material, their topics, and their entertainment value with the *novelle*. Religious stories are full of sexual innuendos and sometimes the difference with a secular *novella* lies simply in the greater explicitness of the secular authors. The main difference was actually in the way those stories were put into writing. For Cistercian monks of the twelfth century or preaching friars of the thirteenth century, the *exempla* collections were databases to be mined for the appropriate story to tell in a sermon to lay people or to fellow monks. The stories were meant to be delivered orally in order to share information and pleasure, not to be read silently, and the early collections were memory troves where tales were stored for preservation. On the other hand, fourteenth-century *novelle* were much more likely to be distributed in written form and read even if, as the frame of the *Decameron* clearly attests, they were supposedly presented and shared orally in the first place. The sheer number of manuscripts of *novelle* collections, compared to the often single-manuscript version of the early *exempla* collections, attests to this different means of distribution. For this reason also, the form of the *novelle* is often much more polished. Boccaccio was a conscious author and was not simply telling a story; he

---

[7] Cf. Nico H.J. Van Den Boogaard. "Exemplum de Ysengrino et Renardo." In *Autour de 1300. Etudes de philologie et de littérature médiévale.*

was telling *his* particular version of the story, in *his* own particular style. Although a medieval religious was probably more interested in the content of the story than in the style, style would certainly matter when telling or retelling the story aloud. Aside from any personal skills of the writer or the narrator, it is the distance between oral and written consumption of the texts that is responsible for most differences between *novelle* and *exempla*. When we read an *exemplum*, we should always keep in mind that something is always missing: the performance.

The Italian scholar Enrico Malato notes that Boccaccio's novelle, though still part of the medieval tradition, offer "the first open and free representation of the life of the new mercantile society that was born in Italy between the thirteenth and the fourteenth century. A life finally freed from the prejudices and the anguish of the moral constraints imposed by medieval asceticism" (I-3). To be sure, Boccaccio was straddling an emerging society, and unquestionably his *novelle* and those of the fifteenth and sixteenth century *novellieri* reflect a temper less reproving of "sinful" pleasures and more aware of noisome realities. However, to imply a strong discontinuity not only between two literary genres, but also in the passage from the Middle Ages to the Renaissance, would be hyperbolic. In many ways the *exempla* and the *novella* continued to share a commonality of purpose, of context and of style.

As we have seen, the presence of humor, violence and obscenity is not limited to stories meant for a secular audience. Titillating stories are present in many *exempla*, even if the goal is to convey a moral, i.e., Christian, message, and the temptation of the flesh is common in secular and religious tales alike. In those connected with Purgatory, religion, comedy, and violence can be found all closely connected. Tales of travel to the other-world were common well before Dante, but the first full description of Purgatory and the various tortures souls encountered there appears only with the anonymous *St. Patrick's Purgatory*, composed in the last quarter of the twelfth century.[8] In this work, a knight named Owen travels to a small Irish island and asks for entry into Purgatory while still alive. Dragged by a host of demons, Owen travels into the other world and sees with his own eyes the suffering of souls, barely escaping those punishments himself, thanks to the saving power of the name of Christ.

The theme of Purgatory quickly found place not only in narratives of travel to the Other world, but also in sermons, with preachers instilling in their flock the fear of the horrible sufferings awaiting sinners there. In

---

[8] The classic reference is of course Jacques LeGoff. *The Birth of Purgatory*. Also, Claude Carozzi. *Le Voyage de l'âme dans l'au-delà d'après la littérature latine (Ve-XIIIe siècle)*.

Boccaccio's *Decameron* III, 8, a clever abbot exploits the widespread fear of Purgatory to his own very secular advantage. Though this fear was meant as a disincentive for the sins of the flesh, among other things, the abbot shows that it could be used creatively to actually indulge in those very sins.[9]

In the novella we find a man named Ferondo, uncouth and jealous, married to a beautiful young woman. The abbot of the local monastery, reputed to be a man of holy life, lusts after her, and through a crafty and unorthodox exploitation of his role as a confessor, convinces the woman to accept his advances. To achieve his goal, the abbot drugs Ferondo, who falls deeply asleep and is believed dead by all the community. When Ferondo wakes up, he believes himself to be dead and in Purgatory, where he is told he has to expiate his most important sin, jealousy. In "Purgatory" Ferondo is beaten daily while his wife's confessor fulfills his lustful desires with Ferondo's wife, explaining to her that "this in no way diminishes [his] holiness, since holiness resides in the soul and what I am asking of you is a sin of the body" (III, 8, p.302).[10] The trick works because the abbot is able to play on the expectations and beliefs of the community. Ferondo in particular is not overly surprised to find himself dead and in a place where he is beaten up daily: he knows about Purgatory, and acknowledges that he has been very jealous. Instead, what surprises him is that he is offered some food to eat, since that is certainly something that never appears in any of the stories about Purgatory. Ferondo thought that souls had no need of food, but the "devil" (in fact another monk, friend of the abbot) convinces him otherwise:

> Then the monk brought him something to eat and drink, and when Ferondo saw this, he said: "Oh! Do the dead eat?" The monk replied: "Yes, and what I am bringing you is the food the lady who was yours brought this morning to the church requesting that Masses would be said for your soul, and it is the wish of God Almighty that you be given it here." (III, 8. p.305; translation, 223)

Boccaccio was not the first one to insert humor into the theme of Purgatory. In fact, to many manuscripts of *Saint Patrick's Purgatory* a few

[9] Carlo Delcorno has studied the relationship between *exemplum* and *novella*, with explicit reference to *Decameron* III, 8, in his article "Studi sugli «exempla» e il «Decameron.» II – Modelli esemplari in tre novelle (I 1, III 8, II 2)."
[10] English translation by Mark Musa and Peter Bondanella, New York, London: W.W. Norton & Company, 1982, p. 220.

exempla are added—one of which exploits the humoristic potential of the excessive violence present in the main narrative. In said *exemplum*, a monk who has made a vow of chastity is incessantly tormented by the devils who, without success, have already tried everything possible to make him fall into temptation. The story opens with a meeting of devils and with the leader of the group asking how the temptation is going. A little devil pops up, and announces that he has a plan, and that in fifteen years the monk will break his vow. Everything has been carefully planned and he does not need any help. At that news, the devils cheer; even in Hell you can have fun. The following day the small devil abandons a baby girl in the cemetery where the monk goes everyday to pray. The monk, being a good soul, picks up the baby and decides to adopt her. After fifteen years when the baby has become a most beautiful girl, the devil decides that it is time to act. He inspires lustful thoughts in the monk, who for the first time is ready to break his vow. In a moment of doubt, inspired by God, he decides to postpone his shameful act, and invites the girl to his cell for the following day. Change of scene, Hell again: the devils gather and their leader requests an update, to which the young devil happily says that finally everything is ready, and the monk will fall into sin tomorrow. Again, shift to the monk's cell, the following day. The monk and the girl are inside, ready to consummate their passion. But the monk abruptly goes out, picks up a knife, chops off his genitals and exclaims what can be freely translated as: "Ha! you devils thought you were going to trick me, but I tricked you!" (*Easting* 153-154).

The story could end right here, since the message is already quite clear. But instead we have another change of scene, back to Hell. The leader of the devils asks how everything had gone and the poor little devil has to meekly answer the truth: he failed. And here all hell breaks loose and all the devils jump on the one who failed, and beat him mercilessly (95). The scene is violent, quick, and has a cathartic but humorous tone. If the goal of the narrator had only been to say that faced with the strongest temptation the only resistance would be to castrate oneself, the message would probably have fallen on deaf ears (and would have been theologically problematic in any case). But the punishment and the beating of the devil conclude the story with a liberating and satisfying scene quite worthy of Quentin Tarantino.[11]

---

[11] The twelfth-century French author and translator Marie de France keeps this *exemplum* at the end of her French translation of the Purgatory, showing her understanding of its relevance for the comprehension of the Purgatory main story.

Sex, violence and the holy come together as well in a variant version of *St. Patrick's Purgatory*, written by Peter of Cornwall, soon after the original work was composed. [12] Peter, a priest, loved to collect stories, and also wrote some of his own. His retelling of the Purgatory is clearly a polished text: attention is paid to the rhythm, the sounds, the repetition of words and the structure of the story. It is more like a *novella* than an *exemplum*. One central element of the plot is based on the frustrated desire of a knight, who thinks he is making love to a beautiful girl, but who wakes up to realize that his penis is stuck in an old piece of wood, with devils all around cheerfully hammering on the wood. The knight does not seem to understand what is transpiring, and when Gulin asks him: "Would you like to get into a warm bath, to restore your broken and suffering member?" he is quick to accept with eagerness: "Libentissime!" ("Most gladly!"), only to find himself in boiling water, hotter than any fire. Offered a cold bath, he is happy to accept, but it is yet another torture, this time with water colder than any ice or snow.

Robert Easting, in the preface to his edition of Peter's story, stresses its "sadistic brutality," noting how it matches the violence found in "other mediaeval visions from St. Patrick's Purgatory and elsewhere; but unlike all the major visions at Lough Dergh, this knight's experiences were wholly demonic and punitive" (404). All this is certainly true, though the excessive violence and the description of the knight's gullibility both indicate that the story is not to be taken at face value, but as a parody. The humoristic side of the story can be easily overlooked if we read it with a preconceived notion of what a Purgatory story should be in a religious context: serious, and not humorous. And yet, Peter shows that his interest lies not only in the edifying message, but also in crafting an interesting, captivating narrative. What is also important to stress is that what was humorous for Peter of Cornwall was not the violence nor the punishment for sexuality in themselves, but the naïveté and the frustrated expectations of the knight and his audience. The story continues with other similar scenes of punishment where the basic humor comes from the same pattern of creating and destroying expectations.

While discussing the images on the margins, I left one question suspended. Did those images represent rebellion, a sign of social conservatism, or simply the free expression of the inspiration of an artist? The answer is likely "all of the above," depending on the context or

[12] The only known copy of this vision is in the manuscript now in London, Lambeth Palace Library, ms 51. The original Latin text of this vision has been edited by Robert Easting in his article "Peter of Cornwall's Account of St. Patrick's Purgatory."

purpose of the text. To better answer this question, we should not ask what was the role of laughter in medieval society, as if laughter and humor were something separated from the context where they appear. In a highly oral culture, the images on the margins and the gargoyles and the little obscene pillar capitals were all part of the narrative world, a world where the distinction between the religious and the secular was not as clear as our modern categories would have us believe. In his *Apology* to Saint Thierry, the Cistercian abbot Saint Bernard was not upset at the mere obscenity of the images he saw around the monks; he was worried that those images could distract the monks from their meditation. In his *Rule*, Saint Benedict did not ban *all* mirth, but only *immoderate* laughter. In medieval times, sexuality and humor were a normal part of everyday life, and the images on the margins, the *exempla* and the *novelle* are all representations of the ways medieval artists were depicting the variety of life, in all its details.

Works Cited

Bakhtin, Mikhail. *Rabelais and His World.* Bloomington: Indiana University Press, 1984.

Battaglia Ricci, Lucia. "Leggere e scrivere novelle tra '200 e '300." In *La novella italiana* (Atti del Convegno di Caprarola, 19-24 settembre 1988). Roma: Salerno Editrice, 1989: 629-55.

Bayless, Martha. *Parody in the Middle Ages. The Latin Tradition.* Ann Arbor: The University of Michigan Press, 1996.

Bloch, R. Howard. *The Scandal of the Fabliaux.* Chicago and London: The University of Chicago Press, 1986.

Boccaccio, Giovanni. *Decameron.* Antonio E. Quaglio (ed.), Milano, Garzanti, 1974. English translation by Mark Musa and Peter Bondanella, New York, London: W.W. Norton & Company, 1982.

Bremond,C., J. Le Goff, J.-C. Schmitt (eds.). *L'Exemplum.* Turnhout: Brepols, 1996.

Camille, Michael. *Image on the Edge: The Margins of Medieval Art.* Cambridge, MA: Harvard University Press, 1992.

Carozzi, Claude. *Le Voyage de l'âme dans l'au-delà d'après la littérature latine (Ve-XIIIe siècle).* Rome: Ecole Française, 1994.

Caviness. Madeline H.. "Obscenity and Alterity. Images that Shock and Offend Us/Them, Now/Then?" in *Obscenity. Social Control and Artistic Creation in the European Middle Ages.* Ed. by Jan M. Ziolkowski, Leiden-Boston-Köln: Brill, 1998.

Delcorno, Carlo. "Studi sugli «exempla» e il «Decameron.» II – *Modelli esemplari in tre novelle* (I 1, III 8, II 2)." *Studi sul Boccaccio* XV (1985-1986): 189-214.

Easting, Robert. (ed.). *St. Patrick's Purgatory. Two versions of Owayne Miles and the Vision of William of Stranton. Together with the long text of the Tractatus de Purgatorio Sancti Patricii.* Oxford: Oxford University Press (EETS 298), 1991.

Eco, Umberto. *The Name of the Rose.* New York: Warner Books, 1984.

Gurevich, Aron. *Medieval Popular Culture: Problems of Belief and Perception.* Cambridge: Cambridge University Press, 1988.

Horowitz, Jeannine and Sophia Menache. *L'Humour en chaire. Le rire dans l'Eglise médiévale.* Geneva: Labor et Fides, 1994.

Jenkins, T. Atkinson. *The Espurgatoire Sant Patriz of Marie de France, with a Text of the Latin Original.* Chicago, Chicago University Press, 1903.

LeGoff. Jacques. *The Birth of Purgatory.* Chicago, University of Chicago Press, 1984 (Originally *La Naissance du Purgatoire.* Paris: Gallimard, 1981).

Malato, Enrico. "La nascita della novella italiana: un'alternativa letteraria borghese alla tradizione cortese." In *La novella italiana* (Atti del Convegno di Caprarola, 19-24 settembre 1988). Roma: Salerno Editrice, 1989: 3-45.

Ménard, Philippe. "Les Illustrations marginales du *Roman d'Alexandre.*" In Herman Braet, Guido Latré and Werner Verbeke (eds.) *Risus mediaevalis. Laughter in Medieval Literature and Art.* Leuven: Leuven University Press, 2003.

Mula, Stefano. "Les *exempla* de Pierre Damien et leur diffusion aux XIIe et XIIIe siècles." In *La Tonnerre des exemples. Exempla et médiation culturelle dans l'Occident.* M.A. Polo de Beaulieu, P. Collomb, and J. Berlioz, eds., Rennes: Presses Universitaires de Rennes, 2010: 187-199.

Tubach, Frederic C., *Index Exemplorum. A Handbook of Medieval Religious Tales.* Helsinki: Academia Scientiarum Fennica, 1969.

Van Den Boogaard, Nico H.J. "Exemplum de Ysengrino et Renardo." In *Autour de 1300. Etudes de philologie et de littérature médiévale.* Sorin Alexandrescu, Fernand Drijkoningen, Willem Noomen (eds.), preface by Paul Zumthor, Amsterdam: Rodopi, 1985 (Faux Titre, 21): 175-178 [originally: *Marche Romane* 29 (1979): 175-178].

Ziolokowski, Jan M., (ed.). *Obscenity. Social Control and Artistic Creation in the European Middle Ages.* Leiden, Boston, Köln: Brill, 1998.

CASTING ABOUT:
SELF-FASHIONING AND PARODY
IN TERESA DE LA PARRA'S *IPHIGENIA*

RoseAnna Mueller

Venezuelan writer Teresa de la Parra's first novel, *Iphigenia: the Diary of a Young Lady Who Wrote because She Was Bored* (1924) created a sensation, achieved instant popularity, and won the Casa Editora Franco-Ibero-Americana prize in 1924. As she finished chapters, they appeared serialized in both Spanish and French-language literary magazines. And yet, while European readers loved de la Parra's novel and found it witty and exotic, *Iphigenia* was not critically well-received in Caracas. In fact, Venezuelan critics took the author to task, accusing her of writing a subversive novel that would damage her young female readers and give them bad ideas. Today Ana Teresa Parra Sanojo, (1889-1936), is considered one of the most distinguished Venezuelan authors of the twentieth century.

Born in Paris to a Venezuelan couple and educated in Spain, Teresa de la Parra lived and traveled throughout Europe. She returned to Caracas from Spain only to find it mired in the past. While the city had been modernized to some extent, the mores and values of its inhabitants had remained old-fashioned. The contrast between the realities of life in the Venezuelan capital and the life she had led in Spain and Paris shocked her. Like the English author Jane Austin, de la Parra wrote about polite society and its preoccupation with class, manners, and the need for young ladies to make a good match. Both authors use gentle humor to poke fun at contemporary manners, and both are not above showing their heroines as less than perfect, perceptive of the imperfections in others, but unable to see their own faults.

De la Parra's time in Caracas is recreated in *Iphigenia,* in which she exposes the hypocrisy, backwardness, *machismo* and political institutions that held women back and forced them into marriages of convenience. She broke free of other literary styles of her time and concentrated on representing her contemporary Venezuela. Modernism, which was in vogue

Photograph of Teresa de la Parra in the 1920s (photographer unknown; Archivos de la Biblioteca Nacional, Caracas, Venezuela.)

at the time, left her cold, as she explained in her letters. She wrote in a colloquial style and wanted to capture everyday Venezuelan speech.

Unlike the novelists who preceded her, de la Parra did not take her material from the past. She depicted her own world and its problems as she saw them. She showed a socio-economic group, Venezuela's *criollos,* in decline and scrambling to save themselves through profitable alliances, sacrificing the happiness of their daughters in the process. Traditions like arranged marriages and prolonged periods of mourning continued to be observed in Venezuela. She questioned these traditions and brought them to life in the pages of her novel. Humor was a rare feature in Venezuelan literature in her time, and Teresa de la Parra broke new ground by treating contemporary issues in a humorous way.

In *Cinco perspectivas críticas sobre la obra de Teresa de la Parra* Laura Febres notes that there are few books of criticism about this Venezuelan writer—notoriously few in English—and remarks that when a writer is called a humorist, it tends to put her in a superficial, frivolous, and shallow category. In truth, no other Venezuelan author had ever undertaken the act of writing so seriously, and for de la Parra writing was an act of protest. Humor and irony can be used to call attention to social issues, and *Iphigenia* succeeded in doing just that. Although she agonized over the fact that some readers did not "get" the humor in her novel, others found it side-splittingly funny, and she was especially proud that the Infanta Eulalia, the King of Spain's aunt, herself a writer, was very much amused by *Iphigenia*. The Infanta invited the author to take tea with her and told her that she had laughed so loud at some passages in the novel that once her maid came running to see what the matter was!

María Eugenia Alonso, the first person narrator of *Iphigenia*, is not a romantic heroine. She is a bored young lady, but she is not indifferent or bitter; she is always engaged with the people around her. She is not just a rebellious young woman; she is more complex than that. She is a composite of young girls de la Parra met after she returned to Caracas. She is real, and charming, and deeply moving. We first meet the effervescent heroine as an adolescent who writes to dispel her "acute crisis of boredom." She wants to recount her Parisian experiences to her best friend Cristina and share her adventures. The letter begins breathlessly, "At last I'm writing to you, dear Cristina! I don't know what you must have thought of me. When we said goodbye on the station platform in Biarritz, I remember that I, full of sorrows, sighs, and packages, told you while I hugged you, 'I'll write soon, soon, very soon'!" (8).[1] Eighty pages later, the overblown letter concludes, "Receive then, this portion of my spirit, and don't forget that here from my solitude, sunken in the silence of its 'closed orchard' it waits in turn for you to come" (89).

María Eugenia first casts herself as a heroine of her own story. The letter itself takes up the first part of the novel, which is titled "A very long letter wherein things are told as they are in novels," and she writes to her friend that her restrictive life in her grandmother's house is "like a tale of chivalry or the legend of a captive princess (9)." The letter establishes an intimate tone that invites the reader to become an accomplice. Identifying

[1] All English translations are taken from Bertie Acker's edition.

with the fiction she has been reading, she writes to Cristina that "You and I—all of us who, moving through the world, have some talents and some sorrows—are heroes and heroines in the novels of our own lives, which is nicer and a thousand times better than written novels" (10). The letter is mailed, and María Eugenia has gotten into the habit of writing daily. Having no other friend to write to, she begins a diary.

María Eugenia has returned from her Catholic education in France to Caracas and to life in a provincial city governed by the mores and values of the *criollos,* the landed gentry of Venezuela. Among the members of her family are the freethinking and alcoholic Uncle Pancho, the Francophile Mercedes Galindo, and María Eugenia's heart-throb Gabriel Olmedo, who ultimately marries a rich girl. But the young girl leads a frustrated existence confined to her grandmother's house in Caracas. She cannot speak freely or leave the house on her own. She unknowingly spent the last of her money in Paris, and her hopes of living an adventurous and independent life are dashed when she learns that her unscrupulous uncle and greedy aunt have appropriated her inheritance. She has a classical education, thanks to the convent school she attended in Spain, but she can't put her erudition to good use. During the course of the novel, she writes to relieve her boredom, to describe her hermetic world, to learn about herself, and sadly to accept her fate and enter into a marriage of convenience.

The humor in the novel begins with the chapter titles, a parody of 17th-century novels, much like the chapter titles of *Don Quixote* and the sentimental and picaresque English 18th-century novels. Chapter I of the Second Part, for example is titled, "Having now sent the interminable letter to her friend Cristina, María Eugenia Alonso resolves to write her diary. As will be seen, in this first chapter, the genteel Mercedes Galindo appears at last." Chapter II of the Second Part is called "After sailing for three days in the caravel of her own experience, María Eugenia Alonso has just made a very important discovery." Chapter V is titled "Here, María Eugenia Alonso, sitting on a large rock, confesses to the river; the river gives her advice, and she, obediently and piously, decides to follow the advice exactly."

While sailing to Caracas, María Eugenia preens in front of the mirror, poses, and casts herself as a romantic heroine with a fashionable short haircut and a trunk full of the latest fashions from Paris. She has spent the last of her inheritance purchasing this wardrobe, but she is unaware of this at the time. On board she meets a flirtatious Colombian poet who is attracted to her, and he comments on her languid pose as she rests her chin on her hands on the ship's guardrail. He showers her with flowery poetry in an attempt to seduce her, and he praises the whiteness of her hands. "'Now they look like two lilies holding a rose', my friend recited again. 'Tell me, María Eugenia, haven't your cheeks ever been jealous of your hands?' –'No', I responded. 'Everyone here lives in perfect harmony'" (20). In *The Three Columbian Lectures*, which de la Parra delivered in Bogotá in 1930, she told her audience, most of whom were fans who had read her novels, that this incident was based on a true story, and that she hoped to meet with the romantic Colombian poet someday and to reveal his name.

Humor in the novel is injected through digressions, a slow pace, circumventions, dialogue with the reader, interruptions, exclamations, reoccurrences, and instances that may seem unnecessary to the reader and take our attention away from the plot. De la Parra infuses the heroine's letter and diary entries with historical, mythological and religious references, sometimes to give her thoughts deeper meaning and at other times to satirize, mock, or call attention to events. She puns on the character's names. Gabriel is her angelic lover. Her suitor, César Leal is rich, and he is loyal to the government. At the novel's end, the heroine becomes "rendered unto César." María Eugenia finds it amusing that her cousins have double names: María Antonia, Género Eduardo, Manuel Ramón, Cecilia Margarita, and Pedro José. She claims, "I then hugged them in order, wondering if that obsession or mania for double names pertained just to my family or if it extended throughout the whole of Venezuela" (28). She herself has a double name, María the "well-born." It is this name that will be bartered for money. As she hugs her cousins she imagines a map of South America "with its shape like an elongated ham" (28). She is irritated that her cousins resemble each other and have no original thoughts, whereas her grandmother thinks María Eugenia has too many thoughts at the same time, a head full of cockroaches instead of brains, and is constantly uttering too many foolish things.

María Eugenia's speech is full of hyperbole and melodramatic rhetoric. When after a strict two-year period of mourning, she is allowed to sit at the window and display herself, she writes, "My person acquired a notable likeness to those luxury items that are exhibited at night in store windows to tempt shoppers. I am for sale!" she cries out. "Who will buy me, who will buy me?" (218). As a reflection of her classical education, her discourse assimilates, appropriates and reflects many genres, voices, and ideologies from French, English, German, Spanish, and Italian literature. There are many intertextual literary allusions, such as the Shakespearean reference to Juliet's balcony, to Dante, Cervantes, and Bécquer. In the letter to Gabriel, she casts herself as the Shulamite in the *Song of Songs*.

While the first part of the novel is funny, ironic, and satirical, the second part becomes more tragic and melancholy. At first María Eugenia ridicules the customs, thoughts and feelings of people she thinks are still living in a colonial time and mentality: her grandmother, Aunt Clara, Uncle Eduardo and the pious María Antonia. She thinks herself to be refined and educated, since living in Paris has exposed her to modern ways. She makes full use of allusion, satire, sarcasm, irony, and caricature. As readers we enjoy recognizing, understanding and appreciating her literary allusions. It involves us in the heroine's creative process as she casts about for an identity to which she can cling. Her literary references are game-like, and we are invited to play along, a device that cultivates intimacy and strengthens the connections between reader and writer.

María Eugenia tries hard to be a naughty adolescent. She scandalizes her grandmother with her outright rejection of Catholic dogma. Defending herself against her Aunt Clara and her grandmother, who consider her too outspoken and rebellious, she responds, "Do you want me to tell you what I think now, Grandmother? Do you want me to admit it? Very well! I think that morality is a farce…Yes, I had three years of philosophy in school, and the teachers who graded my homework and compositions used to fill the margins of my papers with praise" (121). She also likes to show off her own knowledge of languages. She bemoans the fact that her grandmother is always curtailing her choice of words. And when her grandmother objects to her unladylike outbursts, she exclaims "Eureka!!... Since this, although a little pretentious, was the only interjection Grandmother had left me" (105).

María Eugenia's newly-purchased Paris fashions are too immodest for her conservative relatives and seem out of place in Caracas. In any event, she should be dressing only in black in observance of her father's death. To bolster her argument concerning modesty, she paraphrases a parable from the *New Testament*: "Tell me, do lilies wear clothes, Aunt Clara? Do they dress? Do doves dress? Without dressing they preach purity and they are the symbol of chastity. If doves wore clothes, we'd be scandalized to see them fly, because they'd probably lift their dresses with the movement of their wings, and this from below would make a very indecent display" (107).

She writes to her friend after realizing that "the truth to which I refer is not humiliating, but instead is picturesque, interesting, and somewhat medieval" (7). In Paris, she buys a widow's black toque, a highly inappropriate hat for an unmarried young lady, and she is delighted when shop clerks address her as "Madame." She likes to pretend she is naughty. On her walks through Paris with her three-year-old charge, she is mistaken for his mother. Amused by this, she writes to Cristina, "If that were true, I began figuring that given Luisito Ramírez' age he would have been born when you or I were in the tenth grade. Imagine how the nuns would have been scandalized and how much fun we would have had with a little tot then. Surely we would have been forced to hide him in our desks as we used to do with boxes of candy" (15).

María Eugenia sees old texts with fresh eyes and gives them new meaning. She revises the *Song of Songs*, assuming the role of the first person narrator, re-casting gender roles and appropriating and subverting patriarchal biblical discourse. She becomes the Shulamite, which gives her a way to describe female erotic longing and sexual fantasy. "Like the Shulamite, Gabriel, I too have learned the words of the *Song,* and like her I call you constantly in my solitude and in my song to tell you, 'Gabriel, in the burning desert of your absence, you are my glorious Solomon, and I your adoring Shulamite... for the festival of love with which I await you.'" (175). But then she has second thoughts: "Probably Gabriel no longer even remembered the *Song of Songs!*" (178). She destroys the letter, after realizing that it is "wildly eccentric." She boils down the content of the letter to a poem, a sonnet she titles "Juliet's Balcony," which is a parody of Shakespeare.

Teresa de la Parra meant this sonnet to be a joke, but the poem was praised by Miguel de Unamuno. In fact, one day she came upon Unamuno as he lectured to a large audience and was surprised that he was analyzing *Iphigenia.* [2] He asked later in a letter to her why she hadn't written more poetry. She replied she had managed to write only three poems in her life, and in order to write poetry one had to be shameless and not mind baring one's soul to expose its comic side. Clearly, she did not mind putting this poem in the mouth of her hopelessly in love young heroine.

The satire in this novel acts on an intellectual level and requires readers to know what is being ridiculed. Comedy makes demands on the reader, but satire most of all. It is a way for de la Parra to point out the habits and rituals in her society that impede movement toward a better world. To this end, María Eugenia paraphrases. She makes use of literary references, cultural allusions, and uses self-reflexive parody. She is a reader of Dante, Walter Scott, and Voltaire and is proud of it. She is given to wild exaggeration and histrionics when she wants to get her way: "Oh, Grandmother, for Heaven's sake, let me go out! If I don't go out I'll

---

[2] From a letter of de la Parra to Unamuno in July, 1925. Teresa, who traveled frequently to Paris in 1924, had met the exiled Unamuno at a literary lunch a few weeks before (the actual place is unspecified) and given him a signed copy of her book.

smother, yes, I'll die, and tonight what the visitors will see will be my dead body lying in state surrounded by four candles!" (67). Her grandmother's visitors are beyond medieval, she writes her friend; they are Etruscan. Scolded for her unladylike posture, she persists, "I put my hands on my hips, a stance, no matter what Grandmother may say, highly suited for moments of indecision" (106).

Trapped in an antiquated society with its patriarchal values, she now decides that the feminists were right all along—if only she had paid attention. Now she wants to become a suffragette, but her fashion sense has gotten in the way. Instead of paying attention to a talk by Pankhurst, an early English feminist activist, the fashion-conscious María Eugenia confesses she was too focused on outward appearances:

> Once I attended a feminist lecture in Paris and I paid no attention at all to what they said. If it were today I wouldn't miss a word. But well, it was because of those feet and those shoes! Just think, Uncle Pancho, the old lady who was giving the lecture, you could see her two feet crossed, on the floor, of course, under the table they were, well you can't imagine. How coarse! Hobnailed shoes, and thick stockings, this thick, Uncle Pancho, made of cotton! (81)

She is well-versed in the teachings of the Church Fathers, and she disagrees with St. Jerome, "who apparently wrote horrors about the chic woman of his day" (18). Even her best friend and erstwhile role model comes under attack. Of the Francophile Mercedes Galindo, María Eugenia reports that "she continually sprinkled her conversation with French words that were completely unnecessary because all of them had a perfect equivalent in Castilian" (97). She, herself, however, finds it perfectly acceptable to express herself in the three languages she learned in her convent school, not to mention the occasional "Eureka!"

Two years later, the narrator has embraced her family's conservative values. María Eugenia has given up writing. Failing to live up to her own expectations, she shares her compromises with us: "I no longer paint my lips with *Rouge éclatant de Guerlain*. Instead I paint them with *Rouge vif-de Saint-Ange*, whose tone is much softer... I don't read novels whose heroines have lovers... I have learned to embroider and sew... I know three kinds of drawnwork...I say the rosary" (214). Her fashion choices are not based on the latest trends from Paris. She wears blue clothes, the colors associated with the Virgin Mary. "Aunt Clara, who has no eye for color and who is obsessed by paintings of the Immaculate Conception and the Virgin of Lourdes, is of the opinion that blue is my best color" (230).

But physical appearances are still very important to María Eugenia. Contemplating her future as a wife and mother, she ponders: "I might have a daughter, who instead of looking like me, might look like her aunts, an irreversible disaster, which would probably leave me forever inconsolable" (227).

María Eugenia is reunited at the bedside of the dying Uncle Pancho with Gabriel Olmedo, who is married but still in love with her. Gabriel asks María Eugenia, who is now engaged, to elope with him. After a bungled attempt to keep her tryst with Gabriel, she decides she has no choice but to marry Leal, casting herself as a tragic heroine and a Greek sacrificial victim. Marriage becomes the sacrifice, a choice she makes after two years of entombment in her grandmother's house, after having been exposed to two dysfunctional female role models: her maiden aunt and the unhappily married Mercedes.

Now the tone of the novel shifts as an even more dramatic María Eugenia identifies with the Greek heroine:

> As in the ancient tragedy, I am Iphigenia. We are sailing against adverse winds, and in order to save this ship of the world that, manned by I know not whom, races to sate its hatreds I know not where, it is necessary for me, branded by centuries of servitude, to yield up my docile, enslaved body as a burnt offering. (353)

She commits herself to the seven-headed monster of Society: family, honor, religion, morality, duty, conventions and principles. As she trudges to the altar the reader must decide if the old María Eugenia will see her way through this loveless match. When Leal informs her that as his wife she will not be allowed to read because reading is not an appropriate pastime for women, she wisely counters "[a]n ignorant person can become a wise one, but a wise person can never become an ignorant one" (281).

The third part of the book, soberly titled "Towards the Port of Aulis," outlines the steps the heroine takes towards her symbolic immolation as she becomes the modern Iphigenia. The title of the book itself is either a revision of the Greek myth or a tongue-in-cheek mockery of it. After all, the Venezuelan heroine, unlike her Greek namesake, traded her principles for a comfortable life.

De la Parra is not so much a funny writer as she is a witty one. When French editors wanted to shorten the length of *Iphigenia*'s, text she wrote them: "What can I cut from María Eugenia? Her dress and her hair are short already...perhaps I should remove an arm or a leg" (56)? A keen observer of her social scene, she continues to be praised by literary critics for her grace, wit and irony. Elisa Lerner, in "La desazón política en Teresa de la Parra," calls *Iphigenia* a "political novel wrapped in the cellophane of a love story" (2). As de la Parra herself remarked in her charming, self-effacing manner, the best part of the novel was "the part not written." She was a master of irony and an excellent observer of delicate social relationships. Through this novel, she offered a daring and frank analysis of women's lot in the Venezuela of her day. Her sensitive characterizations, her gift for writing dialog and conversation with natural grace and her realistic descriptions bring the reader into the world of changing values. She wrote with wit, warmth and humor about the stresses associated with a declining social class. The novel is by turns ironic and melodramatic. Indeed, the narrator's melodramatic tone is what makes it difficult for some readers to take seriously her final decision.

Iphigenia can be read as a tragic-comedy, in which María Eugenia's marriage to César Leal is seen as the tragic finale of the story. Some readers interpret the heroine's identification with her sacrificial end as a mockery, and Edna Aizenberg treats the novel as a failed *Bildungsroman,* since the heroine does not achieve self-realization. Readers waited for a sequel in which María Eugenia did not marry César Leal, after all. But while most readers sympathized with the heroine's plight, one critic, Angélica Palma, the daughter of the Peruvian writer Ricardo Palma, suggested that instead of sighing "poor María Eugenia," we should be thinking, "poor Leal." In 1986 Ivan Feo directed the film *Ifigenia* (Venezuela, 1986), based on Teresa de la Parra's novel. His solution to the ambiguous and problematic ending of the novel is to have the character who plays María Eugenia contemplate her wedding dress, disrobe, and walk off the set.

Works Cited

Febres, Laura. P*erspectivas críticas sobre la obra de Teresa de la Parra.*
    Caracas: Editorial Arte, 1984.
Feo, Ivan. *Ifigenia.* Cinemateca, Universidad Central de Venezuela, 1986.
Lerner, Elisa. "La desazón política en Teresa de la Parra"
    <<http://www.analitica.com/biblioteca/elerner/teresa.asp>>
Mueller, RoseAnna "Maria Eugenia Alonso" *Women Characters in Latin
    American Literature*
    http://www.stmarytx.edu/latinwomen/?go=ess_malo 2006
Ibieta, Gabriela, "Teresa de la Parra", Martig, Diane E. *Spanish American
    Women Writers*: *A Bio-Bibliographical Source Book. New York*:
    Greenwood Press, 1990

Parra, Teresa. *Iphigenia: The Diary of a Young Lady Who Wrote because She Was Bored.*Trans. Bertie Acker. Austin: University of Texas Press, 1993.

—. *Obra: Narrativa, Ensayos, Cartas*. Ed. Velia Bosch. Caracas: Biblioteca Ayacucho, 1991.

STAGING RIDICULE: DRAMATISTS ANA ISTARÚ AND DIANA RAZNOVICH DEBUNK GENDER PRACTICES

GISELA NORAT

In their humorous acts of resistance within an oppressive Latin American patriarchal culture, Costa Rican playwright Ana Istarú in *Baby boom en el paraíso* (*Baby Boom in Paradise*, 1995) and Argentine Diana Raznovich in *De la cintura para abajo* (*From the Waist Down*, 2004) exploit laughter in order to challenge their particular society's *status quo* concerning women's issues. In these countries, where strong adherence to a traditional division of labor makes men generally less amenable to women's autonomy, humor is critical when proposing change in relationships between the genders. If instead of enlisting comic popular theatre, Istarú and Raznovich were to articulate womens' concerns in a lecturing tone or as high drama, they would be preaching to a limited female choir. Hence, this study will analyze their use of the comic approach as a viable ruse with which to debunk gender practices that devalue women.

Nancy A. Walker points out that the humor of women's and other marginal groups intends to be "at odds with the publicly espoused values of the culture, overturning its sacred cows, pointing out the nakedness of not only the Emperor, but also the politician, the pious and the pompous" (Walker 9). She reminds us that "for women to adopt this role [of humorist] means that they must break out of the passive, subordinate position mandated for them by centuries of patriarchal tradition and take on the power accruing to those who reveal the shams, hypocrisies, and incongruities of the dominant culture (Ibid.). Especially for Latin American women, who are typically raised to model self-sacrifice in service to others and self-effacing modesty, making the shift from the traditional space of the home to the stage of the public theatre to air their protest, even under the guise of entertainment, constitutes overstepping gendered boundaries. Nevertheless, despite less than ideal market reception in their own countries,[1] *Baby Boom in Paradise* and *From the Waist Down* attempt to raise awareness of women's issues and advocate social change, a goal towards which humor, as a non-confrontational approach, can help draw a wider audience. Like the vaudeville comedy that played a role in undermining Victorian refinement, these plays provide Hispanic women a place in the theatre where, in the company of those who subordinate them, they can envision alternatives to prescribed cultural dictates that limit their lives (Kibler 61).

In the public domain of the theatre, feminist playwrights walk a "we-they" dialectic tightrope typical of minority humor (Walker 106). Humor has its codes that may be so tied to a particular group's values, experiences and identity that these playwrights must be careful not to alienate non-members, including those sitting in the audience (Walker 105-6). Istarú and Raznovich both know that, although their plays also incriminate women for participating in their subordination to men, in the Hispanic market, where men markedly surpass women in economic clout, disaffecting the male corporate sponsor, theatre owner, drama critic or ticket buyer is highly inadvisable. And so, to avoid the pitfall of male-bashing that can easily emerge from the "we-they" paradigm, they espouse what Janet Bing calls a subversive but inclusive feminist humor that "makes fun of absurd attitudes, ideas, beliefs and systems that keep females at a disadvantage" without attacking any specific group (28).

---

[1] Costa Rican playwrights as well as producers, directors, actors and theatre critics lament the media's and audience disinterest in plays about Costa Rican reality and the lack of government sponsored support for an industry that too often looks to European classics, foreign or light commercially-oriented and escapist plays for staging at home. Meanwhile. the work of dramatists, among them Istarú, who address local issues goes practically ignored by the Costa Rican media (Bonilla 81-84; Bell 876-879). Not surprisingly, *Baby Boom* won the "Premio María Teresa León para Autoras Dramáticas" in 1995, in Madrid, Spain. It was only after receiving the foreign prize and its subsequent publication in Spain in 1996 that it was staged in San José that year. The first edition of the play by Editorial Costa Rica was not published until 2001. In the case of Raznovich, the military regime forced her into exile in 1975 and during her return in 1981 the State burned down a theatre where she and other dissidents were staging one-act plays to send the dictatorship the message that "Argentina's artists had not succumbed to the government's silencing tactics" (Taylor 74). Although her own colleagues criticized her harshly for a "frivolous" approach instead of writing plays with explicit political themes, Raznovich remained committed to the use of humor as an effective instrument for subversion (Taylor 74-75).

Both Istarú and Raznovich steer clear of alienating the Other, but in very different ways. Istarú, like other "New Wave" Costa Rican authors of the 1980's—a time of economic crises and Central American revolutions —writes about Costa Rican realities instead of providing escapism and fantasies for an essentially provincial, traditional audience rooted in the soil (Bell 876; Miller 270). Her work communicates a restrained critique of the social pressure put on women to become mothers within a culture that devalues women. By contrast, Raznovich, who grew up in cosmopolitan and Eurocentric Buenos Aires,[2] is overtly radical in her use of slapstick-like exaggeration, incongruity and role reversal to debunk the myth of the Argentine *macho* whose unchecked power resonates with military regimes and violent repression (Taylor 74). Both dramatists, however, do share the overall common ground of functioning on two levels: one that presents women in popular stereotypes, and another that aims to defuse the stereotypes that define them only in terms of their relationship with men (Walker 12).

In *Baby Boom in Paradise* Istarú poses a feminist but seemingly more subtle challenge to the situation of women, reduced on the surface to little more than a description of the *status quo* (Ibid. 13). For example, the play ends with the protagonist, Ariana, giving birth, apparently her one goal during the entire performance. Disguised amid self-deprecating comments, much sarcasm and orthodox traditions, Istarú's protagonist, stereotypical in her obsession with her biological clock, manages a feminist plea for reform, camouflaged in humor as an entertaining ploy.[3]

---

[2] In the 1960s Raznovich began her career as a playwright and a cartoonist. Her "Manifesto 2000 of Feminine Humor," graphically depicted through cartoons, can be found in the volume *Holy Terrors: Latin American Women Perform* edited by Diane Taylor and Roselyn Costantino.

[3] In *The Costa Rican Women's Movement*, Ilse Abshagen Leitinger documents the strong history of Costa Rican women's feminist activities, organizations and participation in a Women's Movement. However, the Costa Rican idiosyncrasy of "not making waves" and preference for negotiation over confrontation cannot be underestimated in understanding the Costa Rican way of getting things done. Keeping the peace is a valued approach that permeates all aspects of Costa Rican life from the home to the boardroom (Leitinger, *The Costa Rican Women's Movement*, xiv). To understand both the subtle and transgressive aspects of Istaru's play, which she negotiates through humor, non Costa Ricans must keep in mind that peace is a dominant social value that guides behavior, to the extent that Ticos, as Costa Ricans refer to themselves, "will nod or say 'sí' even when they don't mean it simply to avoid conflict" and to keep from pronouncing the syllable "no" that seems rude to them (Biesanz, *The Ticos*, 7).

From the opening monologue about the difficulty of conceiving a child, Ariana addresses the audience directly as would a comedian in a stand-up routine. While her procreative angst falls within the traditional and acceptable scope of issues of concern to women, the topic subverts masculinist values by highlighting intimate female experiences such as menstruation, ovulation and birthing, but cushions it in humor. For example, she compares her offbeat cycle to that of female elephants and laments that her sparse egg production makes her the laughingstock of hens. Without sounding like an angry feminist, Ariana gets the point across that Costa Rican society considers a barren wife in the home as worthless as a non-laying hen in the chicken coop.

Artfully criticizing the fairy-tale fantasy surrounding most gender relations, Ariana confesses that for months on end she has subjected her husband to a sexual marathon on the one day her ovum leaves the ovaries making its way "audaciously" through her Fallopian tubes in search of that one prince charming of a spermatozoid. "It's a lie," Ariana tells the audience, "that you end up pregnant that way," and assures them that all statistics indicate "the only infallible way of getting pregnant is to be sixteen, a virgin, and sleep with your boyfriend" (*Baby...*12)[4]—an observation that also serves as a reminder of the high incidence of adolescent pregnancy in Costa Rica.

To convey women's fears about childbirth, Istarú exploits the incongruity between the easy delivery embedded in the stork fantasy and the reality of labor (Morreal 192-193). Ariana shares with the audience that while other women are the first to encourage motherhood, their unsolicited horror stories of Caesarean carnage, of surviving "the Vietnam of operating rooms" and of episiotomies performed with garden shears cause her womb to become "paralyzed with terror" (*Baby...*12-13). Once Ariana conceives, other mothers shower her with tales of alarming physiological changes, prelude to years of round the clock service to the child. Again, the incongruity between motherhood as a woman's ultimate desire and maternity as martyrdom is meant to amuse while representing female reality (Morreall 195).

Given that in Western culture bodily changes that occur with pregnancy traditionally have been treated as a private affair to be hushed and relegated to obscurity within marriage and even masked in shame when experienced out of wedlock, Istarú's focus on female reproductive experience should not be underestimated. Far from the "paradise" of the play's title, Ariana's expressions of fear, discomfort and pain act out a

---

[4] All translations from *Baby Boom...* are mine.

gendered resistance to invisibility, which is rarely articulated in mixed company and far less staged in the theatre.

Although by all indications Ariana is privileged as a married middle-class woman, and a working professional translator, in Costa Rican society she is lagging in status behind poor, uneducated, rural women who have produced progeny. Fertility gives a woman the upper hand, at least in a social regard. That is why, when Ariana finally becomes pregnant, she jokes: "I walked around looking down at men as those poor inferior and rudimentary creatures devoid of a uterus. I, in turn, was worth two. And ate for two. And barfed for three" (*Baby...* 25). As "bitter truths" disguised in humor, the criticism of a society that values women's procreative achievements over any other chosen endeavor becomes clearer as the play progresses (Goldstein 5): a woman becomes a real woman by birthing a child. To rattle the audience's gender expectations, Istarú contrasts Ariana's sexual aggressiveness with her husband's lackluster reaction to her chronic obsession to procreate. Realizing that her society routinely questions a wife's fertility and rarely the husband's, Ariana takes charge of getting pregnant. This role reversal, where the female appropriates the sexual initiative associated with males, inevitably elicits laughter.

Istarú injects and resists stereotypes, such as the infertile wife, to expose behaviors that devalue females (Niebylski 10). At the first news of Ariana's pregnancy, her meddling mother-in-law picks out the name for a boy, envisions him enrolling in the best private school, learning English and attending college in the United States (some of this funded with the money Ariana will save by abandoning the "silly idea" of giving birth in a state-of-the art clinic). Ariana's monologue reveals the extent of her subdued rage, a hostility that, as Niebylski points out with respect to women writers in general, "is almost always aimed at all-too-restraining or constraining familial, social, and cultural environments" (10). Since it would be improper for Ariana to vent her rage at her mother-in-law, Istarú diffuses female anger with comic relief. Wittingly playing on the French term for mother-in-law, Ariana exposes how often a "belle-mère" or "beautiful mother" camouflages herself as a spokeswoman for patriarchy and does the vile work of devaluing other women and baby girls, even within the womb.

In *Baby Boom in Paradise* the culture's privileging of males also plays out in the stereotype of the "other woman." Istarú presents a fragile female self-esteem derived from a relationship inherently based on humiliating dependence and subordination to a man. When Ariana visits a friend to use her computer, the unnamed chocolate-bingeing mistress swears that this time she is fed up with her married lover and angry enough at him to "tear his innards out with white hot tongs" (17) because he bought his wife expensive mahogany furniture. In this particularly funny scene, Ariana gobbles down bonbons in a show of female camaraderie, only to learn that her friend sold the computer: "Well . . . to help the poor guy pay for the furniture" that he bought his wife (Ibid.). Such mockery of the self-effacing woman in servitude provides a lens through which Latin American women can begin to recognize their internalized sense of inferiority and re-envision options for autonomy. Driven by the cultural directive that a woman is nothing without a man, Ariana's friend embodies the invisible mistress.

In Istarú's social critique, Ariana, married and finally pregnant, paradoxically experiences invisibility too, even though she is big enough to identify as a human "Moby Dick" when admitted to the maternity ward at the hospital (48). The soon-to-be mother feels simultaneously ignored and mistreated while her body, stripped of any semblance of modesty, is pawed, mishandled, and subjected to the scrutiny of medical professionals. With a knack for mordant observations couched in hilarity, the birthing scene that concludes *Baby Boom in Paradise* serves to raise awareness about feelings of indignity and vulnerability at a time in a woman's life that for most is veiled in much silence and isolation.

As an aspect of "performing marginality," Joanne Gilbert notes that "gynecological humor may serve as a means to address and express women's feelings of anger and victiminzation in a public context" (91). In *Baby Boom in Paradise* Istarú's humor about the frustrations of pregnancy succeeds because it does not estrange men with male bashing or make women who are not mothers feel excluded. But undeniably, her humor is feminist in its two-tier function of seemingly upholding patriarchal values—Ariana's priority in life is motherhood—and undermining them by making the audience take notice of the lengths to which women go to conceive and how they fashion their identity on a physiological function over which they have little control. The play ends with Ariana giving birth to a little girl who will be called Valentina, suggesting that she must be "valiant" in order to cope with the same indignities and frustrations as her mother. Ariana, however, is delighted that in producing a girl she complies with the socially-mandated task of motherhood while undermining the ideal of the highly-prized male offspring that her mother-in-law anticipates.

The Argentine Diana Raznovich also centers her play, *From the Waist Down*, on a married woman who is utterly frustrated over her lack of control, this time in her love life. Act I immediately establishes a humorous situation in the marriage bed where the wife, Eleonora, wearing a beautiful nightgown, sits up with the light on while her husband Antonio snores away. When her attempts to stop his snoring do not work, she switches from sighs to shrieks and the couple's "sort of duet" escalates to something "like a musical score" consisting of "two snores, a shriek, two snores, a shriek" (43-44). Raznovich accentuates the wife's displeasure by having Eleonora shriek ever more loudly as she "voraciously eats cookies," almost to the point of choking. Groggily, Antonio makes clear his lack of interest in engaging his wife. "On the verge of tears," Eleonora confesses that she is "always buying more and more expensive nightgowns" (46). The audience quickly suspects that the very expensive nightgowns, the "desperate and discordant" shrieks and the stuffing of cookies into a ravenous bodily orifice all add up to one horny woman who cannot get laid. Through humor Raznovich, like Istarú, stages female-centered experiences common in women's everyday lives, but typically not presented for public airing.

From the Waist Down relies heavily on the comic devices of "reversal of expectation and the inversion of values" that Ronald Wallace notes in his study on humor (91). By exaggerating, Raznovich manipulates her audiences' reaction to "incongruity," and she is able to provoke laughter in a work that undermines the myth of the Argentine *macho* as the norm while raising serious gender issues (Morreall, 188). In a society accustomed to portrayals of the womanizing husband and the demure or frigid wife, Argentines, and Hispanic audiences in general, will laugh at the sexual role reversal in the play. However, in keeping with a semblance of culturally appropriate conduct, *From the Waist Down* builds up to the gender role reversal gradually. For example, implied in Eleonora's habitual buying of pricey sleepwear and in her "desperate sighs" is her adherence to the modesty Hispanic culture expects of women. That is why out of sexual frustration "she paces nervously around the [bed]room like a caged lion," but she does not come out and directly ask her husband to make love to her (47). As expected of a discreet wife and decent woman, Eleonora broaches sexuality with linguistically pure, albeit contextually explicit, innuendos: "Don't you realize that nights and nights are going by and nothing? Don't you realize that nothing ever happens in this room? (*She shakes him.*) Antonio, how long do you think it has been since something happened?" (47).

The wife's doggedness in pressing for sexual satisfaction (an appropriation of maleness) culminates with the revelation that since their marriage Antonio makes love to her only once a year—on his mother's birthday! This exaggerated version of a bad love-life deals an unexpected blow to the public image of the Argentine macho's libido, scores a good laugh, and literally sets the stage for Raznovich to exploit this mama's boy as an inoffensive subject because Hispanic men are not likely to identify with the spoof. As a comic technique, the two protagonists reverse their roles simultaneously. As Eleonora becomes more aggressive in demanding sex, Antonio demonstrates more feminine qualities. At one point, when Eleonora finally shouts "I want to make love!" and quickly strips to titillate her husband, stage directions have Antonio react like a nervous virgin. "He covers his head with the pillow so that he doesn't have to look at her" and disdains her sexual provocation with the exclamation "Depraved woman!"(48). Here incongruity draws laughter because, as John Morreall notes, the scene deviates from "the way things are supposed to be," based on our expectation of gender-specific behavior (190).

Raznovich feminizes the Argentine *macho* "from the waist down" and unveils his mother as a patriarchal pawn, since the deprivation of sexual pleasure typically falls to women to enforce in the socialization of children. Symbolically, after Antonio's reproval of his wife's sexual provocation, Eleonora acts out the destruction of her self-confidence by putting her nightgown back on, and adds a "robe, a hat, a pair of boots, a scarf, and gloves" (48). To further accentuate the husband's feminine behavior, when Eleonora asks what will happen to their limited love life when his mother dies, Antonio, "in a state of emotional shock" and "clearly desperate" kneels in bed to invoke God in prayer and casts an image that suggests the suffering Madonna (47-48). In this role reversal, Antonio, acting as a caregiver and nurse, immediately telephones his mother, Paulina, and wakes her up with questions that humorously exaggerate his concern for every detail of her health. Among other things he asks: "Is your urine clear?" (52). Then switching roles between caregiver and frightened child, he makes his emotional attachment known: "I can marry again, but I will never have another mother" (54).

In this portrayal of a mama's boy, Antonio's feminine inclinations escalate to transvestite-like acting out. "I like nightgowns. They give me lusty dreams," he affirms (53). When he actually puts one on, the incongruity between his physical maleness and lack of masculine behavior entails another inversion of expectations manipulated as comic device (Wallace 94). By this point in Act I, the dialogue insinuates an abnormally close filial bond. Not only do mother and son dream the same dreams nightly, but Paulina also has the ability to defy distance and time and can appear instantly whenever Antonio beckons. This exaggerated intimacy, funny in itself, builds up to an absurd mother/son relationship that verges on incest. Drawing from Morreall's study of the reactions to incongruity, laughter provoked by this unexpected mother/son relationship may "set off negative emotions [because] we are upset by a violation of what we see as the proper [moral] order of things" (190). However, this negative reaction spurs awareness of the situation and motivates us to improve it, which is precisely the intention of the dramatist.

Raznovich further inverts the normative in family relationships. Paulina takes off her clothing and puts on a lush transparent nightgown, gets into bed with the couple and hugs her son, thus displacing Eleonora who jumps out of the matrimonial bed and attempts to hang herself with strips from a nightgown (53). As Diane Taylor points out, the theme of a woman about to commit suicide runs through all of Raznovich's work "to illustrate the social forces that drive women to self-annihilation" (74), although she chooses humor to launch her protest. With the mother-in-law at the root of all the excesses that provoke laughter in the play—invariably at the cost of much pain for the daughter-in-law—Raznovich literally undresses the mother figure as a cultural icon and reveals her as a powerful agent of female frustration and marital dysfunction.[5] As Taylor observes, Raznovich presents a "ferocious ridicule of the construction of sexual identity and practice in Argentina" (87).[6]

In another example of inversion of values, Raznovich debunks the cultural construct of the meek Virgin Mary of Catholic tradition as prototype mother. Like the repressive government of the 70's and 80's, Paulina figuratively "makes her son disappear" by emasculating him sexually, "tortures" her daughter-in-law with forced abstinence and consequently ensures a childless marriage since the couple makes love only on her birthday. Paulina, the incarnation of foolproof contraception, and at odds with the cultural veneration of motherhood, is an incongruous figure who produces a situation that is both "funny strange" and "funny

---

[5] Coincidentally, Istarú´s first play, *El vuelo de la grulla* [Flight of the Hen Crane], a one act piece published by the University of Costa Rica's theatre journal *Escenas* in 1984, is also about a dysfunctional family triangle in which a young married woman, stifled by the bond between her husband and his mother, is not able to overcome the mother-in-law's sway and ends up trapped in a marriage that squelches any dream of flight from tradition (Champagne, "Social Commitment," 74-79). In that play, however, Istarú does not use humor as a ploy for advocating social change.

[6] In a political reading of the play, the critic lucidly argues that Paulina's harmful control of her son's marriage alludes, on a broader scale, to the power the Argentine military regime in the 1970s and 1980s exerted over all aspects of family life (89).

ha-ha" (Morreall 188, 190). In her advocacy for change, Raznovich makes the mother-in-law an intentional object of negative emotion.

Patriarchy grants women who observe tradition power over other females that have yet to earn societal recognition (Paulina married and produced a son). Hence, Paulina's need for authority hinges on Eleonora. "Without you there is no scene," she tells her daughter-in-law, "You are indispensable. Stop trying to kill yourself and come to bed" (53). The degree to which Raznovich insists on presenting the controlling mother-in-law as a destructive force in her son's marriage becomes apparent when Paulina schemes to exploit the couple's sexual problems in order to benefit her own writing career: "This is definitely bestseller material. It would sell out the first day . . . The woman on the left, the husband on the right, and the mother, like a goddess, in the middle of the bed" (54).

Many married women could readily identify with this metaphor of the overbearing mother-in-law. They could also relate to Eleonora's war cry— "Enough with your mother" (57)—when she takes action to secure professional therapy for her dysfunctional marriage. In the play Raznovich suggests that marriages typically do not survive the wife's declaration of war against the mother-in-law, and moreover that patriarchy castigates women who dare to subvert the *status quo*. Eleonora ends up paying dearly for contriving to eliminate Paulina from the love triangle. She contacts Troncoso, a sexologist, to help her save the marriage, but her punishment is imminent when he shows up wearing "the uniform of the motorcycle police" and his "militarized" demeanor gives him away as an unemployed ex-torturer turned therapist (58-59).

With the introduction of Troncoso, who overtly references a traumatic military period in Argentina's recent history, Raznovich ups the ante on transgressive humor, underscoring it as "a form of power," a tool of domination (Goldstein 7). Troncoso's name derives from "tronco" or trunk, figuratively the pillar of patriarchy with its many branches and social ramifications. He immediately imparts a lesson in domination, which is the underlining credo of a patriarchal system at the root of Argentine reverence for maleness in the image of the gaucho, the *compadrito*, the military man and the household macho.[7] Combining material from the Marquis de Sade and his own paramilitary experience, Troncoso quickly teaches Antonio the mechanics of gender relations and sells him overpriced paraphernalia of "hard-core sex"—chains, a whip,

---

[7] The gaucho, a figure associated with the 19th century cattle herding in the vast *pampas* or plains of provincial Argentina, is the equivalent of the American cowboy. The *compadrito* is associated with the history of the tango and can denote the streetwise man, a petty criminal, a rascal, or even a pimp.

billy club and torture devices—what every self-respecting man needs in order to subjugate his woman. When Eleonora resists the beating that Antonio attempts to proffer with his sex toys, both husband and wife not only end up in the hospital with multiple injuries but also in the major newspapers, which feature them as hard core erotica enthusiasts. This exaggerated aggression speaks to the culture of violence that permeates an Argentine society whose popular subconscious is fed by military images at the national level and spousal hostility in the domestic sphere

Unwilling to put up with Antonio's violence, Eleonora demands a legal separation, but Paulina intervenes, urging the couple to stay together and sign a lucrative contract with an American S/M magazine for an exclusive photo feature. Paulina's peddling of Eleonora's sexual objectification means further debasing her amid the domestic violence that the couple is made to represent. Through the destructive mother-in-law Ranovich "acts out the links between capitalism, sexism and abuse" (Pramaggiore 48). Paulina's push to commercialize sadomasochism for profit eventually annihilates Eleonora, who by the end of the play has been so manipulated and brainwashed that she accepts complete abstinence in her marriage as a desirable way of life. "This is the best birthday of my life," Paulina declares at hearing that the couple no longer has sex at all. She exerts further control by telling the couple to keep it secret, for any leaks to the media would be "terribly damaging" to the career she has directed for them (72). The play concludes with a desexualized, defeated Eleonora lying to herself about her happiness and submissively accepting the castrating mother-in-law back into the marriage triangle. Despite the bleakness of the last scene, the characters use the words "happy" and "happiness" so many times to convince themselves of familial bliss that the audience is made to laugh at this final absurdity.

Significantly, as Latin Americans Istarú and Raznovich contribute to what Barreca identifies as "a tradition of women's comedy informed by and speaking to the experiences of being female in a world where that experience is devalued" (9). As Hispanic women, whose culture expects feminine discretion in all aspects of life, casting a spotlight on their lot in mixed company in the public forum of the theatre demonstrates defiance. These playwrights' humorous irreverence constitutes a revolutionary act. The plays draw on a variety of comic techniques to couch issues of female sexuality, subordination, exploitation and autonomy, all linked to their protagonists' underlying quest for self-realizing identity in a society that generally disregards their needs. Clearly, their humor entertains despite its subversive intent to undermine gender practices perpetuated on women, often by women, in the name of tradition. Both *Baby Boom in Paradise* and *From the Waist Down* incarnate a comedy theatre of "objection, defiance and absurdity" whose transgressive humor leaves no doubt as to its power to bring women's experience to the forefront, raising audience awareness of the need to re-envision the social construct of gender in Latin America.

Works Cited

Barreca, Regina. "Making Trouble: An Introduction." In *New Perspectives on Women and Comedy*. 1-11. Edited by Regina Barreca. Philadelphia: Gordon and Breach, 1992.

Bell, Carolyn V. "Special Report: Costa Rican Theatre in Transition." *Hispania*. 79 (December 1996): 876-880.

Bienz, Mavis Hiltunen, Richard Biesanz, and Karen Zubris Biesanz. *The Ticos: Culture and Social Change in Costa Rica*. Boulder: Lynne Rienner, 1999.

Bing, Janet. "Is Feminist Humor an Oxymoron?" *Women and Language*. 27 (Spring 2004): 22-33.

Bonilla, María. "Costa Rica y el derecho a soñar: Audacia teatral del siglo XX." *Latin American Theatre Review*. 34 (Fall 2000): 79-85.

Champagne, Carole A. "Social Commitment and Dramatic Discourse in Three Contemporary Costa Rican Paywrights." Diss. University of Massachusetts, 1998.

Gilbert, Joanne R. *Performing Marginality: Humor, Gender, and Cultural Critique*. Detroit, Wayne State UP, 2004.

Goldstein, Donna M. *Laughter Out of Place: Race, Class, Violence, and Sexuality in a Rio Shantytown*. Berkeley: U of California P, 2003.

Istarú, Ana. *Baby boom en el paraíso*. 2nd edition, San José: Editorial Costa Rica, 2005.

—. *El vuelo de la grulla*. *Escena* V, San José: Universidad de Costa Rica, 1984. 15-19.

Kibler, M. Alison. "Nothing Succeeds Like Excess: Lillian Shaw's Comedy and Sexuality on the Keith Vaudeville Circuit." In *Performing Gender and Comedy: Theories, Texts and Contexts*. 59-77. Edited by Shannon Hengen. Amsterdam: Gordon and Breach, 1998.

Leitinger, Ilse Abshgen. *The Costa Rican Women's Movement: A Reader*. Pittsburgh: University of Pittsburg Press, 1997.

Miller, Elaine Marnell. *Migrating Texts: Cross-Cultural Readings of Costa Rican Plays of 1990-2000*. Diss. University of Maryland, College Park, 2003.

Morreall, John. "Funny Ha-Ha, Funny Strange, and Other Reactions to Incongruity." In *The Philosophy of Laughter and Humor*. Edited by John Morreall. Albany: State U of New York P, 1987: 188-207.

Niebylski, Dianna C. *Humoring Resistance: Laughter and the Excessive Body in Contemporary Latin American Women's Fiction*. Albany: State U of New York P, 2004.

Pramaggiore, Maria. "Belly Laughs and Naked Rage: Resisting Humor in Karen Finley's Performance Art." In *New Perspectives on Women and Comedy*. Edited by Regina Barreca. Philadelphia: Gordon and Breach, 1992: 47-56.

Raznovich, Diana. *From the Waist Down*. Translated by Shanna Lorenz. In *Holy Terrors: Latin American Women Perform*. Edited by Diana Taylor and Roselyn Costantino. Durham: Duke Up, 2003. *De la cintura para abajo*. In *Dramaturgas: en la escena del mundo*. Edited by Mercedes Farriols, Nora Glickman and Diana Raznovich. Buenos Aires: Nueva Generación, 2004: 42-72.

Taylor, Diane. "What Is Diana Raznovich Laughing At?" In *Holy Terrors: Latin American Women Perform*. Edited by Diana Taylor and Roselyn Costantino. Durham: Duke UP, 2003: 73-92.

Walker, Nancy A. *A Very Serious Thing:Women's Humor and American Culture*. Minneapolis: U. of Minnesota P, 1988

Wallace, Ronald. *The Last Laugh: Form and Affirmation in the Contemporary American Comic Novell* Columbia: U. of Missouri P, 1979

PART IV.

THE ENIGMATIC WIT
OF A WORLD RENEWED

CASTIGLIONE AND CICERO: WIT AND LAUGHTER IN *THE BOOK OF THE COURTIER*

PAUL SCHULTEN

Introduction

Cicero was probably the classical author most beloved by the Renaissance humanists. One of his many admirers was Baldassare Castiglione. Cicero's *De Officiis* and *De Oratore* were two of the great bestsellers of the Cinquecento. So was Castiglione's book *Il Libro del Cortegiano* (*The Book of the Courtier*), published in 1528. Here, Castiglione describes conversations supposedly held in the ducal palace of Urbino in Italy over four evenings in March, 1507. Notwithstanding some dissenting opinions, there can be little doubt that Castiglione derived heavily and openly from Cicero's work, besides boldly plagiarizing other classical authors such as Plato, Plutarch and Livy. By the sixteenth century, *De Oratore*, written in the fifties of the first century B.C., as well as the later *De Officiis* had become the main model for the ideal of *Humanitas*. They also provided the inspiration for the countless instruction manuals that, from the sixteenth century onwards, spelled out the codes of behavior thought desirable for the higher classes of society. Castiglione's book was one of the first and most popular examples of this type of literature.

Good manners were to be displayed in all sorts of human interaction, including pleasant and amusing conversation. The point is amply illustrated in Castiglione's chapters on the humor and wit that the perfect courtier should be able to exercise (II. 42-93). Whole parts are taken almost verbatim from Cicero's well-known treatise on that subject in the second book of *De Oratore* (II, 217-289). But *The Book of the Courtier* cannot be considered merely an imitation of classical writings. In the days of Castiglione, the classics had already been well assimilated and Castiglione made use of contemporary writings as well. In fact, next to

Cicero's work, Poggio Bracciolini's *Facetiae* and Giovanni Pontano's *De Sermone* were among his favorite sources (Speroni 10).[1]

The objective of this essay is twofold: to determine what differences, if any, can be found in Castiglione's treatment of humor in comparison with Cicero—other than a few contemporary jokes; and, whether these differences can shed light on eventual disparities between Roman culture and its later Italian admirers and imitators.

The Danger of Humor

Obviously, the Renaissance practice of imitating much admired classical examples results in more resemblances than differences. Both Castiglione and Cicero start with the question of whether the competent use of humor is an art or a gift of nature, and they mention people who are more skilled in this than others. Castiglione's speaker, Federico Fregoso, considers the Florentines as the wittiest persons of his age; Julius Caesar Strabo, in the *De Oratore*, bestows this honor on the Athenians. Both speakers express the same idea that there is no need for art in the two ways one can be funny. These two ways are: maintaining a jocular tone to the end of the story that is told; and throwing in brief shafts of sudden, illuminating wit.

Skill in quick, witty repartees comes across in both treatises as a pre-eminent natural quality; the only thing one could teach himself in this respect would be to know when to let the moment slip by, if one is not able to shine in a truly witty response. This is easier said than done, for according to Cicero, who quotes the early Roman author, Ennius, it is easier to keep a flame in your mouth than a stinging repartee (*De Oratore* II, 59). It might be much wiser, however, because this second way of arousing laughter by a quick and witty response is generally more aggressive, and the first distinction between classical and Renaissance notions of humor lies in the awareness of the danger of humor, which was more acute in the Graeco-Roman world.

Cicero and his admirer, Quintilian, regularly warned their audience that it was better to lose a good joke than a good friend. This concern about the risk of giving offense seems to have been, in general, more present in the Roman mind than in the minds of the people of the Renaissance. *The Courtier* might copy the theoretical remarks of Cicero in this regard, but it is far less precise in defining those (Ibid., II, 229; Castiglione II, 50.) This is obvious, for instance, in the respective difference in views on the

---

[1] *De Sermone* was written around 1499. *Facetiae* was published in 1470.

superiority of spontaneous repartees over what Cicero depreciatingly calls "jokes brought from home," or, witticisms that were prepared before (Cicero, *De Oratore* 89). Classical discourse not only stresses the feebleness of the latter, but also points to the increased danger of their capacity for giving offense. Plutarch viewed prepared jokes as more dangerous, for they were the gratuitous results of insolence and bad character, while ordinary insults were perhaps the unintended result of anger: "We pardon and license a joke that springs simply from the immediate circumstances, but it seems like a planned insult if it is foreign to the context of the talk" (*Quaestiones Conviviales* 2. 1).

One of Castiglione's characters, Bernardo Bibbiena, repeats a joke of *De Oratore* about an uninvited guest who nevertheless stayed for dinner. The host had only one eye, so the impertinent guest said he would stay because he saw that the host had an empty place, pointing his finger to the man's empty socket (Castiglione, II, 59). True, Bibbiena considers that premeditation renders the joke weak, but he does not discuss the greater danger of offending by this kind of witticism. Plutarch, on the contrary, goes even further in his warnings against overly personal joking. According to him, fun should be made only of the manifestly non-existent shortcomings of the target of the joke, thereby throwing a spotlight on his good qualities. Greeks and Romans liked to make fun of physical defects, but tried hard to avoid it when it concerned powerful people.

The Scurra

Another interesting difference, however small, lies in the appreciation and use of the words "buffoon" ("scurra" in Latin, and "buffone" in Italian) and "mimicry." Castiglione, like Cicero, warns against foolish behavior in search of laughter, whether in words, gestures or facial expressions. Like his Roman model, he uses the Aristotelian definition of the laughable as something that is ugly or defective (Aristotle, *Poetics*, V). He seems, however, to misinterpret the Ciceronian remark that the chief object of laughter are those sayings that remark upon, and point out, something unseemly in no unseemly manner (*non turpiter*) (*De Oratore* II, 236). In Castiglione's text, these last words become a different nuance (Castiglione 46). The idea that laughter is aroused by something ugly or deficient makes it understandable that references to physical shortcomings as a form of amusement were popular in both cultures. The Athenians never stopped cracking jokes about the disproportionate head of Pericles (Plutarch, *Pericles* 8. 3-4), and rich Romans displayed their own house-fools, often a deformed individual.

According to Castiglione, too, physical defects often provide splendid material for laughter if one exploits them discreetly, but to be too savage in doing this is the work not only of a clown but of an enemy. That statement seems to repeat Cicero's argument that an orator should not let his jesting become buffoonery or mere mimicry (*De Oratore* II, 239). Roman gentlemen, however, were much more specifically aware which deformities could be the butt of jokes and which could not. Joking about a bald head was acceptable, while bad breath could not be the subject of jesting.[2] But where there are rules, there are violations and exceptions. In the only surviving joke book of Antiquity, the *Philogelos*, or *Laughter-lover*, of the late Roman Empire, out of a total of 265 jokes, no less than 12 deal with the subject of bad breath (Baldwin 106). It seems that Castiglione mainly thinks of professional jesters, while rejecting buffoons and buffoonery. The Romans, on the other hand, did use the word *scurra* even for someone like Cicero himself who, notwithstanding his tenets, could seldom resist the temptation of punning. Cato the Younger once contemptuously called him "our scurrilous consul" (Macrobius, *Saturnalia* 2. 1. 12; 2. 30). Cicero must have been heavily offended by Cato's remark because he himself had defined a *scurra* as somebody who could not refrain from inappropriate jokes and, therefore, as a non-gentleman (*De Oratore* II, 245).

Status of Humor

Such concerns did not trouble to the same extent the gentlemen-courtiers of the gatherings at Urbino. A good Renaissance courtier was expected sometimes to attend to grave matters, and other times equally to festivities and games where wit was an indispensable quality (Castiglione, II, 31). This said, being in good standing with the lord did not hurt, either. According to Castiglione, the favor of the lord alone could create the appearance of wit: in this way, any person may have been considered a success, his lack of wit notwithstanding. Conversely, the good jokes of someone who was held in contempt by his lord would fall flat, and his genuine wit would not receive its deserved acclaim (Ibid. II, 32.) These observations, issuing from the august mouth of the distinguished courtier, diplomat, and future cardinal, Federico Fregoso, reveal that the ability of making good jokes was an important, if not indispensable, means of validating a *gentiluomo*. They point to a much more positive view on the

---

[2] In the presence of the bald emperor Domitian, however, it was not wise to crack jokes about being hairless.

uses of humor than the classical authors had ever expressed. The latter will always make excuses before getting to such a light subject as joking, and, should the discussion require it, they will explicitly stress that certain jokes might be allowed at specific functions or hours of the day.

Classical writers usually apologize for indulging in humor, a defensive attitude not encountered in authors of the Renaissance. Judgments on mimicry and imitation point to the greater freedom of the Renaissance in this respect. In the Graeco-Roman world, actors' masks with contorted faces were to be used in theatres and in theatres only. Greek and Roman gentlemen would not transfer such expressions in normal life, as they were absolutely not supposed to indulge in any vehement gesticulation or making faces. Quintilian categorically forbids grimacing as in farces, putting excessive facial expressions on the same low level as ribald jokes and obscenities (Quintilian, *Institutio Oratoria* 6. 3. 25). He copied his model, Cicero, who wrote that making grimaces was far beneath the dignity of a good man (*De Oratore* II, 252). Towards the end of the Roman Empire, this principle even led to extremes in facial control, culminating in Theodosian emperors, experts in maintaining a motionless countenance.[3]

However, Cicero did provide examples of successful mimicry and imitation in speeches, but only because they were rather reserved and modest (*De Oratore* II, 242), not buffoonery or mere mimicking (Ibid. II, 239). The same restrictive remarks recur in the work of Castiglione, as he, at least theoretically, follows the general precepts discussed in *De Oratore*; he constantly recommends prudence and asks that considerable attention be given to place and time, and to the kind of people with whom we converse (Castiglione, II, 50). Still, as far as mimicry goes, he allows much more latitude, as seen in the praise bestowed on one of his courtiers, Roberto da Bari, for the latter's ability to provoke laughter by mimicry or imitation. Roberto apparently mimicked everyone and touched on people's raw spots, even in their presence. Although he did this often, he managed not to upset the victims of his imitations—another sign of lesser need for reserve (Ibid. II, 49-50).

Cicero allowed for merriment as long as it was reasonably civilized and only indulged in "during relaxation" (*De Officiis* I, 104). In such settings, the elite of the Greek and Roman societies could forget all reticence and freely enjoy games of imitation. In Rome, mimicry remained a favorite game at the imperial court. Professional entertainers often either

---

[3] On this development see P. Schulten, "To cry or not to cry: public emotions in Antiquity," *Cultural and Social History* 2 (2005): 20.

impersonated or described in a funny way guests at dinner parties, as seen in an anecdote about the emperor Vespasian offering himself as a butt of pleasantry. A hired entertainer, however, refused, saying he could only engage in an imitation of the emperor after Vespasian, who always bore a constipated facial expression, would have relieved himself (Suetonius, *Vespasian* 20). Nevertheless, in contrast with the Renaissance, Greek and Roman social standards never required a gentleman to be good at joking.

Practical Jokes

In contrast with Cicero, Castiglione's character, Bernardo Bibbiena, indicates that there are not two but three ways of making pleasantries. Besides the long and amusing narrative and the single cutting remark there is a third kind, called practical jokes ("burle," or "beffe"), which include the addition of a certain amount of action (Castiglione, II, 48; Bremmer 4). These cause a certain amicable deception regarding things that give little or no offense. Bibbiena distinguishes two kinds of practical jokes: either somebody is tricked in an adroit and amusing fashion; or, a net is spread with bait, so that the victim of the joke causes his own downfall (Castiglione, II, 85).

Notwithstanding his obligatory statement that a practical joke also should give little or no offense, the illustrations Bibbiena uses are of a somewhat different nature. One elaborate prank, for instance, that ultimately backfired on him, cruelly ridiculed and terrified the friar against whom it was directed (Ibid. II, 87). Bibbiena explicitly calls his next story exemplary as an entertaining source of practical jokes. He feigned that a friend of his wanted to commit suicide by jumping from a bridge in Lyon. French passers-by helped him to restrain the man whose denials they did not understand. Finally his friend was carried bodily into an inn, all disheveled and without his hat, pale with shame and anger (Ibid. II, 88). Surely, the butt of this prank was hardly amused, nor were the victims in the stories of Boccaccio's *Decameron*, so popular with Bibbiena, notwithstanding his rather non-committal warning that the practical jokes of a courtier should be less scurrilous (Ibid. II, 89).

Although totally absent in Cicero's treatise on oratory, practical jokes were loved by the Greeks and Romans, as well. One only has to remind oneself of the famous scene in Homer's *Iliad* where cuckold Hephaestus traps his wife, Aphrodite, and her lover, Ares, in an unbreakable golden net. Practical jokes were at the heart of many Roman comedies by Plautus and Terence, as well as in the very popular mimes of the imperial period. The notorious Roman emperor Caligula liked to burden his environment with practical jokes, mostly extremely cruel ones (Plass 66). He built himself such a reputation that even after he was murdered, people still believed he was playing a prank on them and would all of a sudden reappear. Suetonius calls him a monster, mainly because of his twisted sense of humor (*Caligula*, 48). So practical jokes existed in the Ancient world and were a popular pastime for many. Popularity, however, does not mean that practical jokes officially were endorsed among gentlemen.

Women

A final noteworthy difference between Cicero and Castiglione is obviously the role of women, both in the act of joking and as protagonists in the jokes themselves. As far as we can judge by the sources, women in the Greek and Roman world almost never participated publicly in humorous banter. Significantly, the few exceptions were mostly women with a *reputation*. In the first century B.C., Sempronia, the wife of senator Decimus Junius Brutus, was admired for her quick wit because she could hold her own in repartee. She was at the same time condemned for her unbecoming boldness (Sallust, *Bellum Catilinae* 25).Julia, the disreputable daughter of Augustus, was one of the very few women to whom were attributed various humorous, sometimes rather saucy, sayings in the *Saturnalia*, the work of the Roman author Macrobius. These were rare examples and were probably only mentioned because of their subjects' deviant behavior.

In the book of *The Courtier* the situation is totally different. Women are not only present at the discussion about wit, but actively participate.[4] Emilia Pia, one of the main protagonists in the dialogue on wit, is extolled as a model lady for her virtue, as well as for her gaiety. This is a very different perspective from the one we notice in the Ancient World. There were without any doubt many witty women then, but they were seldom praised for it, being at best reticently admired like the aforementioned Julia, or, in a more distant past, Pericles'consort, Aspasia.

Social Change

Despite Castiglione's repetition of Cicero's general reflections on humor and wit, the difference lies in the actual expression in the jokes of his main characters. The most important discrepancies relate to a lesser awareness of danger in humor and to a somewhat more positive approach

---

[4] See for instance their mocking of Gaspare Pallacino in *Il Cortegiano* II. 96.

to the subject. Certainly, it could be argued that Cicero employed keywords like *urbanitas* (civilized behavior) and its related term *comitas* (courteousness) in his own special way, and in so doing he gave them a stricter meaning than was the custom among his societal peers. If that were true, we don't have to look for eventual changes in society to explain the difference with Castiglione, for the Ciceronian code and his interpretation of decorum could have been exceptional, rather than exemplary, in the Graeco-Roman world. The gap would then be between the Ciceronian code and the norms of his society. There is, however, very little distance between the Ciceronian thoughts on humor and those of his Greek predecessors like Plato, Aristotle and the Stoics. Coming back to the Renaissance, it becomes apparent that real social change must have accounted for the shifts in the ways the elite discriminated between good and bad humor.

The divergent representations of humor produced by, or about, women must have resulted from important changes in the position and status of women. Women were allowed larger participation in public life and were generally more visible in the upper rungs of Renaissance society. The question of what kind of humor was deemed decorous or not in the two periods is much trickier. The attitude towards practical jokes is the greatest departure from the classical model. Even if Cicero himself, in private, indulged in many more daring witticisms than any courtier in the Renaissance, his view was that men ought not spend their precious time in frivolous jesting, but engage in serious pursuits (*De Officiis* I, 103). This stern position became even stricter in the teachings of the Fathers of the Church at the end of the Roman Empire in the West.[5] They considered laughter and banter a danger for the necessary discipline of religion and the holiness of the miracle. Later representatives of the Church in the sixteenth century might have censored some of Castiglione's jokes, especially those on cardinals, yet the fact remains that in *The Book of the Courtier* Castiglione allows more latitude in joking than the classical code implies (See Burke, 1996; 102).

One of the main reasons for the classical attention to appropriate behavior in joking was the fear of offending a person who could strike back, as honor and shame were still extremely important elements of the social code. Loss of status could not be tolerated and mockery could easily bring that about. Although powerful persons, like the Roman emperors Augustus and Vespasian, earned praise for their acceptance of witty

---

[5] On this see J.S. Gilhus, *Laughing Gods, Weeping Virgins. Laughter in the history of religion* (London, 1997).

remarks made against them, they were obviously not expected to tolerate overly striking insults. The emperor Marcus Aurelius, generally admired for his clemency, was censored for the fact that he let puns about the adultery of his wife go unpunished. Such a sensitive and finely tuned attitude towards humor is hardly a distinctive characteristic of the Renaissance. During the late Republic and early Empire, the Roman elites found it more and more necessary to distinguish themselves from the lower people by showing cultural refinement and civilized behavior.[6] Political and economic distinction was no longer enough in a society of a growing complexity, where even freedmen could become rich and influential.

Though the political life in the Italian cities of the fifteenth century was no less turbulent, the real reasons for less restriction towards humor must be sought in the different hierarchical structure and in the relative crudeness of court life in sixteenth-century Italy in comparison with the higher Roman society. Renaissance humanists tended to overestimate the sophistication of their social graces. A contributing factor might have been the influence of Christian codes of behavior, which might have induced some humility and clemency in the powerful. It could have lessened the fear they inspired, which is important considering that fear was one of the most important reasons for the restrained attitude towards humor in Antiquity. Taken together, these factors surely accounted for the more respectable status humor achieved throughout the Renaissance. It was a time when so many humanists, from famous authors like Desiderius Erasmus to somewhat less remembered figures, such as Juan Luis Vives and Laurent Joubert, uninhibitedly shared their (by and large) positive feelings and thoughts on the subject of humor and laughter. Vives and especially Joubert even found direct physiological and medical benefits in humor, which would have been lost on the Ancients.[7] In this respect, notwithstanding the vigorous counter-attacks of the Calvinistic age, we are still the inheritors of Castiglione's cheerful and upbeat understanding of humor.

---

[6] This seems to be one of the main themes in the *Satyricon* of Petronius. It is also reflected in the growing importance of the concept of urbanity.

[7] On this point see P. Schulten, "Physicians, humor and therapeutic laughter in the Ancient World," *Social Identities* 7 (2001): 67-75.

Works Cited

Baldwin, B. *The Philogelos or Laughter-Lover*. Amsterdam: Gieben, 1983.

Brand, C. P. "The Renaissance of Comedy: the achievement of Italian 'comedie erudite'." *The Modern Language Review* 90 (1995): 29-42.

Bremmer, Jan. "Jokes, Jokers and Jokebooks in Ancient Greek Culture," in J. Bremmer/H. Roodenburg (eds.), *A Cultural History of Humour*. Cambridge: Polity Press 1997: 11-28

Burke, P. *The Fortunes of The Courtier. The European Reception of Castiglione's Cortegiano*. Pennsylvania: Polity Press,1996.

—. *The Art of Conversation*. Ithaca: Cornell University Press,1993.

Castiglione, Baldassare. *Il libro del cortigiano*. London: Penguin, 1967.

Cicero, *De Oratore*; *De Officiis*.

Corbett, P. *The Scurra*. Edinburgh: Scottish Academic Press, 1986.

Craveri, B. *La civiltà della conversazione*. Milano: Adelphi, 2001.

Garland, R. *The Eye of the Beholder: Deformity and Disability in the Graeco-Roman World*. Ithaca: Cornell University Press,1995.

Gilhus, J.S. *Laughing Gods, Weeping Virgins. Laughter in the History of Religion*. London: Routledge, 1997.

Graf, F. "Gestures and Conventions among Roman Actors" in J. Bremmer and H. Roodenburg (eds.), *A Cultural History of Gesture*. Ithaca: Cornell U.P., 1991: 36-58

Hall, J. "Social Evasion and Aristocratic Manners in Cicero's *De Oratore*," *The American Journal of Philology* 117 (1996): 95-120.

Halliwell, S. "The Uses of Laughter in Greek Culture." *Classical Quarterly* 41 (1991): 279-296.

Macrobius. *Saturnalia.*

Morreal, J. "The Rejection of Humor in Western Thought." *Philosophy East and West* 39 (1989): 243-265.

Plass, P. *Wit and the Writing of History. The Rhetoric of Historiography in Imperial Rome*. Madison: The University of Wisconsin Press, 1988.

Plutarch, Quaestiones Conviviales.

Quintilian. *Institutio Oratoria.*

Ramage, E.S. *Urbanitas: Ancient Sophistication and Refinement*. Norman: University of Oklahoma Press,1973.

Richards, J. "Assumed simplicity and the critique of nobility: Or, how Castiglione read Cicero," *Renaissance Quarterly* 54 (2001): 460-464.

Speroni, C. *Wit and Wisdom of the Italian Renaissance*, Berkeley: The University of California Press, 1964.

Suetonius. *Caligula; Vespasian.*

'RIDENTEM DICERE VERUM':
THE ROLE OF LAUGHTER
IN THE *SATYRES CHRESTIENNES*
DE LA CUISINE PAPALE

BERND RENNER

In France, comical literature, in the widest sense, reaches one of its first and most accomplished peaks in the sixteenth century, owing to a complex mixture of medieval vernacular sources, such as farce and sotie plays, and venerated Greco-Latin models of comedy and satire (Aristophanes, Plautus, Terence, Lucilius, Persius, Horace, Juvenal, Lucian, and Martial). I would like to look at the first great polemical text of the French Wars of Religion, the *Satyres chrestiennes de la cuisine papale* (1560; *Christian Satyres of Papal Cooking*), to add the perspective of satirical laughter to the concerns of this volume—whom or what are we laughing at? Satire seems particularly appropriate in this context since of all literary endeavors it is the form that boasts the closest ties to reality, given its moral calling to cure the ills of society.[1] Satirical laughter in the Renaissance had two major models: the gentle Horatian version and Juvenal's harsher variant. Whereas the Horatian model has dominated satirical discourse since the late Middle Ages, above all thanks to reliable editions, Juvenalian *indignatio*, far closer to the tragic mode and revalorized by Justus Lipsius and Jules-César Scaliger, is becoming increasingly popular in the second half of the 16th century, as it appears better adapted to the political and religious strife that haunts the country.[2]

---

[1] Among the multitude of sources, see for example Joachim du Bellay's advice to "moderately criticize the vices of your time and omit the names of the perpetrators" (*The Defence and Illustration of the French Language*, bk. 2, ch. 4, p. 71 in *Poetry and Language in 16th-Century France*, tr. L. Willett, Toronto, 2003). This gentle Horatian model will give way to *ad hominem* satire during the Wars of Religion.

[2] For the influence of Roman satire in Renaissance France, see the work of P. Debailly, especially "Juvénal en France au XVIe et au XVII siècle," *Littératures classiques* 24 (1995), 29-47, "Le Lyrisme satirique d'Horace à la Renaissance et à

Our text marks a turning point between the two tendencies, since it is written in a transitional phase marked by mounting violence, yet still before the start of the civil war between Catholics and Protestants. In the preface, the text's pedagogical objectives are expressed in the terms of the Horatian *topos* of *ridentem dicere verum*. The anonymous author, likely Theodore of Beza, is horrified to remember his reliance on "the knowledge and conscience of ignorant and hypocritical abusers" instead of having devoted himself to reading the Holy Scriptures, "which show in broad daylight the errors and abuses of these 'papelastres.' [...] And then I thought of Horace's verse: What, says he, prevents the one who laughs from telling the truth?"[3]

The "sugared pill" of the remedy against the abuses of the Catholic Church is described in rather conventional terms and is administered under the transparent veil of culinary allegory, which is also explicitly decoded in the preface.[4] The pamphlet claiming to be at the service of "truth," the graphic description of reality nonetheless aims to shock, an approach validated by the principles of *imitatio*, proclaimed since Aristotle's *Poetics*. Though the shock value is accompanied by intended pedagogical effects, the danger of pure invective—an attitude that usually contradicts the description of "truth" and "reality" by pushing caustic laughter to its limits—is always latent in the potential gratuitous obscenity of this approach, which constitutes an integral part of *imitatio*. Beza attempts to neutralize this menace throughout the text, making the pamphlet's search for truth the chief endeavor of the *Satyres chrestiennes*.

It is hardly surprising that the alleged facetious nature of the text, which is meant to facilitate the application of the harsh satirical cure, proves problematic, as the main objective of laughter in the *Satyres chrestiennes* remains the brutal and utter destruction of the Church of Rome's "edifice of lies." Let's keep in mind that the text is published on

---

l'âge classique" in *La Satire dans tous ses états*, éd. B. Renner (Geneva, 2009), 25-48, and *La Muse indignée*, vol. 1 (Paris, 2012).

[3] All quotes from the *Satyres chrestiennes* are taken from Ch.-A. Chamay's critical edition (Geneva, 2005), here p. 5-6. All translations are mine. For Renaissance laughter, see P. Debailly, "Le rire satirique," *BHR* LVI (1994), 695-717, esp. 709 for the three main categories of laughter (plaisant; bouffon; acerbe et mordant), D. Ménager, *La Renaissance et le rire* (Paris, 1995), and M.A. Screech, R. Calder, "Some Renaissance Attitudes to Laughter" in *Humanism in France*, ed. A.H.T. Levi (Manchester, 1970), 216-28.

[4] See Y. Giraud, "Le Comique engagé des *Satyres chrestiennes de la cuisine papale*," *Studi di letteratura francese* 10 (1983), 60: "L'allégorie ici n'a pas pour fonction de voiler, mais de démasquer."

the eve of a major armed conflict and thus announces the violence of coming events through destructive laughter, a laughter that implies its own annihilation. As a consequence, the nature of the laughter is radically opposed to the more conciliatory laughter of previous Renaissance satirists, such as Clément Marot, the early Rabelais, or even the polemical texts in the early days of the Reformation. Satire has adapted to the increasingly disconcerting extra-literary circumstances that have come to dominate religious discourse. All variants of satiric laughter are henceforth meant to be entirely at the service of the overall objective, the complete demolition of the Catholic edifice, as the author announces at the end of the preface: "I await [God's] grace so that soon I may demolish it all, the kitchen and the house all told" (7). The construction of the promised new "House of God" (Ibid.) will therefore have to be postponed, for the *tabula rasa* of destructive furor must imperatively precede any project of reformation. Even if gentle Horatian laughter is presented as the model of the author's approach in this same preface, the overall tone and the multiple references to, and borrowings from, Juvenal in the main body of the text and in the marginal annotations (as early as in verse 176 of Satyre 1), clearly attest to the dominant satirical inspiration of the *Satyres chrestiennes*.

The eight "Satyres" that make up the text paint a complete picture of the "papal kitchen," progressing logically from a description of the building and the gardens (1 and 2) to the officers and utensils (3 and 4) before reaching their peak in the papal banquet and the penitential banquet (5 and 6). The text closes with the "after-dinner talk" and a series of short poems (7 and 8). These last sections constitute a return to a more farcical satire, a welcome relief after the violent attacks of the previous "satyres."[5] In accordance with this episodic structure, the laughter follows a curious trajectory. It is particularly visible in what one could call the "preamble" and the "epilogue" (preface, sat. 1, 2 and 7, 8 respectively). Despite its often farcical linguistic verve,[6] the nucleus of the text (sat. 3-6), however, is notable for its pronounced display of Juvenalian indignation which, via its frequently vulgar or obscene outspokenness, usually sacrifices satirical laughter for the pursuit of its moral objectives. These objectives in turn can only be reached by employing a "shock-value" pedagogy conveyed

---

[5] For a more detailed summary, see Y. Giraud, art. cit., and B. Renner, "Rire et satire à l'aube des guerres civiles: l'exemple des *Satyres chrestiennes de la cuisine papale*," *The Romanic Review* 101 (2010), 655-71.

[6] See Y. Giraud, art. cit., Ch.-A. Chamay's introduction to his edition, and Ch.-A. Chamay, B. Renner, "*Les Satyres chrestiennes de la cuisine papale*: Jeux et enjeux d'un texte de combat" in *La Satire dans tous ses états, op. cit.*, 267-284.

rhetorically by *ethiopoia* and *parrhesia*. The serious subject of the *Satyres chrestiennes*—to unmask "this anti-Christ, the Pope" supported by "miserably stupefied and idiotic people" (6)—is meant to justify this brutal approach. It is the only valid remedy for the universal disease of blind obedience to a corrupt institution.[7]

After the quasi-burlesque beginning of Satyre 1, which mixes medieval legends (Melusine's voluptuousness,11), pagan myths (Proserpine, a symbol of the papacy, 12, 18), and conventional imagery (a donkey symbolizes the clergy's ridiculousness, 13) to provoke the rather innocent laughter that the text seems to favor initially, the comic nature of the *Satyres chrestiennes* is quick to undergo fundamental changes. Without abandoning its bent for frequently unusual wordplay, the laughter becomes increasingly aggressive as the text progresses. The comical lists of Satyre 2 are an example of this development. The comment in the margins of the list of garden herbs explains precisely that "the priests' bawdiness and outrageousness are exposed under the names of various herbs" (26-27).

Furthermore, the lengthy comparison between Catholic saints and pagan idols, a classic attack denouncing the idolatry, materialism, and lies of the "papists", finishes in a transparent *lapsus linguae* (miraculeux/triaculeux, 35) that comically confirms Catholic clergymen as charlatans and impostors. Laughter thus becomes ambiguous as it emanates from the targets of the satire, and such ambiguity might well threaten the pedagogic mission of the text. Therefore, we are hardly surprised that the element of laughter, as aggressive and biting as it may be, is losing ground at the approach of the text's central chapter in order to ensure a more prominent place for a violent incarnation of Juvenalian indignation, which repeatedly crosses over into pure invective. After ample use of the farcical veil, the author now reminds us that for the good of truth and freedom of expression, he cannot help but apply "vile words to vile things" (108), an approach triggered by the "complaint" at the end of Satyre 2: "What evil I endure / Waiting for God the Savior" (37).

In Satyre 3, before giving way entirely to indignation, marked by a reference to Juvenal's Satire VI, the final remnants of a more benevolent laughter concentrate on the clergy's eating, drinking and sexual habits, a commonplace of attacks on churchmen; but this amusing banter proves to be increasingly insufficient to take on a cruel adversary. It is clearly the danger of impending massacres of "heretics" that weighs on the Reformers. The clergy's apparently ridiculous abuses prove to be "deadly

---

[7] As early as in Satyre 1, the Pope's motto underlines this tyranny in capital letters: "IL N'EST QUE DE VIVRE A SON AISE. / QUE CHACUN ME CROYE ET SE TAISE" (22).

mockeries" for the adversaries of the Catholic Church. The threat of being exploited financially and butchered surpasses the preventive powers of honest and curative laughter, which is expressed in an equivocal play on "butchery" (boucherie) and a "laughing mouth" (bouche rit, 45), a paradox that implicitly underlines cynical or exasperated laughter and is reinforced at the end of Satyre 3 in a rhetorical question that confirms the author's resignation: "Mouth, what do you want?" (71). But laughter stops when the massacre begins.

This more somber orientation of the *Satyres chrestiennes* evokes not only the tragic tendencies of Juvenalian satire, but also an Aristotelian precept which claims that the comical hinges on defects and ugliness, provided that neither pain nor harm is caused (*Poetics,* 1449a 35). Aristotle also justifies the use of vulgarity and obscenity, which had greatly disturbed critics such as Ch. Lenient,[8] by stressing the pursuit of authenticity. In this perspective, "ugliness" is underscored in the name of *imitatio,* a key concept of Renaissance letters: "Nous prenons plaisir à contempler les images les plus exactes de choses dont la vue nous est pénible dans la réalité, comme les formes d'animaux les plus méprisés et des cadavres (Ibid, 1448b 10; "We take pleasure in contemplating the most exact images of things which are painful to look at in real life, such as the shapes of the most despised animals and of corpses."). Such "pleasure," however, seems abstract when actual pain and harm enter the picture, as is the case in the "boucherie" of Satyre 3. As Aristotle concluded, whenever the emotional investment becomes overwhelming, laughter disappears. It is interesting to note in this regard that Laurent Joubert, in his *Traité du ris* (1579), came to the same conclusion as Aristotle, stressing the importance of "ugliness and a lack of pity", i.e., of emotional investment, as well as the absence of any substantial evil, danger or calamity" in order to provoke laughter.[9]

Whereas ugliness remains a key ingredient of the *Satyres chrestiennes de la cuisine papale*, the avalanche of shocking images, the brutality of the

---

[8] Ch. Lenient, *La Satire en France ou la littérature militante au XVIe siècle* (Paris, 1866), 211-12.

[9] L. Joubert, *Traité du Ris* (Paris, 1579), 17-18. Although the oldest known edition of the *Traité du Ris* is from 1579, a version seems to have circulated as early as the 1550s. H. Bergson would reiterate those same thoughts some four centuries later; see *Le rire* (Paris, 1940), 3: Signalons maintenant […] l'*insensibilité* qui accompagne d'ordinaire le rire. Il semble que le comique ne puisse produire son ébranlement qu'à la condition de tomber sur une surface d'âme bien calme, bien unie. L'indifférence est son milieu naturel. Le rire n'a pas de plus grand ennemi que l'émotion.

satirical attacks, and the crude outspokenness that dominate the central chapters of the text clearly indicate the author's attempt to expose the dangerous threats behind his powerful enemies' aptly named "predi*caca*tions" (emphasis added) and "parasitations" (64). Together with an increasingly disgusting lower body stratum dominated by one of the text's recurring themes, a foul stench, the *ad hominem* attacks against prominent representatives of Catholic orthodoxy (such as Esprit Rotier, Antoine Cathelan, or Artus Désiré), which cover more than sixty lines at the end of Satyre 3, do not allow any lingering doubt as to the nature of the shock therapy that Theodor of Beza considers the only suitable means to combat evil.

This approach reaches its inevitable heights in Satyres 4, 5, and 6. Instead of trying to make his readers laugh, the author will endeavor henceforth to nauseate them. It is above all the theme of the foul stench that conveys the author's disgust, particularly in Satyre 4. Bad smells emanating from latrines are explicitly linked to the hypocrisy of a clergy hiding behind "false doctrines" and justifying all sorts of deceit and illegalities, culminating in the order to burn the adversaries "by the millions" to preserve one's power and financial might (77). So despicable is the mindset reflected in the clergy's daily behavior that the purification of the soul, which should be the ultimate objective of any religious service, becomes completely subverted. The priests' drunkenness and gluttony lead to vomiting that symbolizes the perversion of Catholic cleansing (74). Such blunt accusations lead directly to the main reproaches of Satyre 5: an uncompromising attack on the clergy's sexual debauchery. The "bread of lies" is actually transformed into the "bread and wine of perversity" (87) during a mass whose hymns are merely supposed to cover the priests' lasciviousness, as they prepare to indulge in the crudest kinds of sexual debauchery in their "beds of fornication" (86). The equivocation "dominus/dormir nuds" and the rather explicit insinuation of an insatiable clergy's quite unexpected oral sexual practices ("true gourmands with strong throats") underscore the author's mounting anger at the discovery of such repugnant and inexcusable behavior hidden behind a hypocrisy that enables "sanctification" to elide with "fornication." Laughter is henceforth associated with vomiting ("Let us go elsewhere to laugh and throw up," 100; with a quote from Juvenal in the margin). The criticism is now directed against the materialism—the sale of Indulgences as a classic example—that dominates the Roman Catholic Church.

It is hardly surprising that in the face of such abuses, the moral vocation of the text leaves very little room for laughter, even of the darker shadings. The author-pedagogue seems determined to continue his lesson without shrinking back from even the most shocking images as long as they are a logical consequence of his critical construct. The hymn *Agnus Dei*, which is meant to prepare the Holy Communion, is audaciously associated with a lower body function devoid of all creative forces. As it is a centerpiece of contemptible Catholic superstitions, at least according to the Protestants, the rite is here reduced to its digestive aspect, which, in turn, implies one of the most daring equivocations in the context of the accusation of "theophagy": "agnus" and "anus" (107-8). Consequently, this revolting image is pursued to its logical conclusion at the end of the chapter. As any food needs to be digested and eliminated, Catholic "paradise" was therefore to be found in the stomach or the outhouse (110-111).

In Satyre 6, this progressive dismantling of the Catholic cult culminates in the exposure of the full extent of the perversion of mass, based on the "fausses doctrines." For some twenty lines marked by anaphora, the monotonous repetition of the term "messe," the poet touches on all facets of the mass, which he sees as conceived precisely to ensure the clergy's domination over its constituents' minds and, more importantly, material wealth (120).[10] This abusive domination is established on the basis of violence wielded over Christianity with Pilatus serving as a model (127).

The accumulation of such threats ends up justifying the link between satire and tragedy and, despite the text's linguistic verve, relegates amusing laughter to the margins, particularly in the central chapters. At first glance the return of more gentle laughter in Satyre 7 might appear surprising, but we will see that it fits not only into a certain narrative logic but also functions on at least two levels. The return of farce is sketched out as early as in line 10 when the sophists are qualified as "vrais disciples de Pathelin" (143), referring to the protagonist of the anonymous *Farce de Maître Pathelin* (ca. 1465). Having painted a frightful picture of the clergy's abuses in Satyres 3 to 6, the author, in a veritable *cry de sottie*, mockingly calls upon the "Docteurs subtils, subtilissimes, / Docteurs illuminatissimes, / Docteurs solennels, seraphiques, / Irrefragables, deificques (irreproachable and godlike)" (146) that sets the tone for the facetious "colloquium" at the center of Satyre 7.

Even stylistically, we witness a return to the more amusing comedy of the sotie: the title of the chapter, "Les devis d'apres disner," ("After-

---

[10] It is noteworthy that the clergy is frequently compared with conjurers or diabolical magicians in this context; see for example Satyre 5, p. 107, where one of their representatives is called "Maistre Gonin," prototype of the illusionist, or Satyre 6, p. 138, where they are chastised for "l'obscur de leur magie."

Dinner Talk") recalls the famous "menuz propos" ("Smalltalk") that are characteristic of farce and sotie and also relate to the incoherence of the *coq-à-l'âne* ("Let's change topics," 157). The interlocutors, in accordance with their ironic names that indicate stereotypes (Nostre Maistre Friquandouille; Frere Thibaud; Messire Nicaise), ridicule themselves through their own words, which makes them appear far less frightening than the anonymous violent theologians from the previous chapters. For the clergymen, this laughter at the people's pious behavior and honest repentance ("mea culpa," 154) remains firmly anchored in the lower body ("peter de rire," idem) and belongs to what Y. Bellenger calls transgressive laughter; it expresses the "jubilation of unpunished transgression."[11]

Not only are the adversaries well aware of the ridiculous nature of their rites and superstitions, they also lose their terrifying and intimidating impact as they are depicted as simpletons. Since their transgressions are precisely not based on convictions, as badly conceived as those might be, but rather on pure self-interest, they become even more contemptible, even criminal. Moreover, they have all the more reason to live in fear themselves, as the lies of some of the most radical Catholic zealots, such as Antoine de Mouchy or Artus Désiré, had been exposed, which enabled the Reformers to intensify their mockery of Catholicism and considerably strengthen their own position ("Nos ennemis, chacun les voit, / Et tout clairement apperçoit / Tout le rebours de nos mensonges." ([The Catholics themselves admit that] "Our enemies, anyone at all can clearly see the truth despite our lies" [158].)

The fear that orthodox Catholicism instilled in the central chapters of the text is thus well diminished, even reversed by such revealing comments wherein the "mocking" is no longer lethal. We recognize here a second variant of the laughter of transgression, "a laughter of liberation from fear and anguish" (Bellenger, 164, following Freud). The violent portrait painted in Satyres 3 to 6 has therefore reached its objective of inciting the reader to take the initiative and fight against the imminent danger. By means of the two types of transgressive laughter featured in the colloquium of Satyre 7, any fear of the brutal enemy has been eliminated, since the latter's moral, ethical, and doctrinal inferiority has been clearly exposed. A more carefree laughter thus becomes possible yet again, as is evident in an almost naïve observation by "Maistre Friquandouille" at the end of the colloquium: "Marris ou non, je veux du ris / Tousjours à l'issue

---

[11] Y. Bellenger, "Le comique comme résultat de la transgression," *Studi di letteratura francese* 10 (1983), 164.

de table" ("Sad or not, I want laughter / Always at the end of the meal"
161). The famous "Complaint of Messire Pierre Liset about the passing of
his Nose," a parody of the classical genre of the *lament*, marks the return
to the buffoonery of the first two Satyres by offering a mock encomium of
the "boozy nose" ("nez beuvatif," 164) of the drunkard Lizet, one of
Theodore of Beza's arch-enemies.

The short poems of Satyre 8 complete this reversal of the initial
situation and therefore demonstrate the effectiveness of the satirical cure
administered by the text. Even the food has become "divinement
delicieux" (169) yet again. The adversaries are given buffoonish
nicknames, such as the "confesseur Hume-brouët" (Suckgruel), a character
from a carnival play, the "chambrier Songe-creux" (valet Visionary) a
famous author and actor of Parisian farces and morality plays, or the
"grand choriste, Pain-perdu" ("chorister French Toast") another character
from farce (170-172). By rediscovering this type of laughter, the satire has
fulfilled its principal function. The remedy of the ills is further
underscored in the last lines of the text that celebrates the death of Pierre
Liset, "the most fearsome beast of all time" (175). Consequently, the
monster of orthodoxy is far from invincible. This triumph is portrayed as
inevitable, like death, and the adversary, in this case Pierre Lizet himself,
unwittingly contributes to it in his boundless ignorance ("sot et ignorant").
Its defeat helps to eliminate the fear of the supposedly all-powerful
orthodoxy and transforms the monster into a laughing-stock. It is this
moral lesson that closes the text.

To conclude these brief remarks, one notices that satire proves quite
useful to elucidate the phenomenon of laughter. The *captatio
benevolentiae* that opens the *Satyres chrestiennes* as well as the comic
relief that closes it showcase amusing variants of laughter, which, at least
at first glance, inform the text's overwhelming farcical and buffoonish
orientation. Despite a few subtle hints (in the preamble) of the storm that is
brewing, such as the Pope's motto or the lists comparing catholic saints
and pagan idols, the raw and violent aspects of laughter remain latent at
best at this moment. Farcical equivocation and other comical elements
assert their dominance in a rather joyful atmosphere. This impression,
however, is quickly corrected by the aggressiveness and severity of the
attacks in the central chapters of the *Satyres chrestiennes*. An oppressive
sadness quickly gains the upper hand over innocent pleasure in this
construct of contradicting emotions emanating from the overarching
notion of "ridicule," which radically reverses the readers' reactions, as L.

Joubert has observed.[12] Even the more bitter and biting variants of laughter, discernible from the very beginning of the text, are rapidly being incorporated into the somber Juvenalian tragic, the only appropriate way to approach the immense abuses and crimes depicted in the central chapters of the text. This bleak situation, which finds additional support in Aristotelian doctrine, justifies Beza's use of crude language and imagery.

If there is laughter in Satyres 3 to 6, it is either of the variant that would be called "libertine" in the following century, of an ironic and cruel nature,[13] or a grim laughter provoked by linguistic verve and its unusual creations ("boucherie/bouche rit"). The emphasis is put on an appreciation of the text's formal esthetics without taking into account its repulsive content.[14] Moreover, we should not neglect the impressive display of humanist erudition that permeates the text, even the most daring passages, and which adds an important layer to the clash of form and content. Such "contrary movements" (Joubert, 87) contribute significantly to the persistent impression of comical mixture that characterizes the text despite the tragic *indignatio* that dominates its main chapters. In addition to their undeniable value as a literary witness of protestant polemics, the *Satyres chrestiennes de la cuisine papale* constitute a precious document for the study of satirical ethics and the esthetics of laughter in one of the most problematic and most complex eras for polemical literature in particular and for satire in general, faced with the increasingly pervasive threat from pure invective and gratuitous vulgarity. It is above all the brilliant use of all the facets of laughter that enables Beza not only to avoid falling prey to this menace but, more importantly, to create a comic and satirical masterpiece that had been neglected far too long by critics. The *Satyres chrestiennes de la cuisine papale* provide an important contribution to the elucidation of the eternal question at the center of this collection: at whom are we laughing?

---

[12] Here is the theoretical basis, according to L. Joubert, *op. cit.*, 87-88, for this radical change in direction: "Car la chose ridicule nous donne *plaisir et tristesse*: plaisir, de ce qu'on la trouve indigne de pitié, et qu'il n'y ha point de dommage, ne mal qu'on estime d'importance. Dont le cœur s'an rejouït, et s'elargit comme an la *vraye joye*. Il y ha aussi de *la tristesse*, pour ce que tout ridicule provient de laideur et messeance: le cœur marry de telle vilainie, comme santant douleur, s'etressit et resserre. Ce deplaisir et fort leger: car nous ne sommes gueres faches de ce qu'avie[n]t aus autres, quand l'occasion et petite. La *joye* que nous avons, sachans qu'il n'y ha dequoy plaindre (sinon d'une fausse apparence) ha plus de force au cœur que n'a la legiere tristesse." (emphasis added)

[13] Such libertine laughter adds another facet to the comic of transgression analyzed by Y Bellenger, art. cit., 169-70.

[14] See Y. Giraud, art. cit., 69: "Ici, tout le comique tient au langage."

Works Cited

Bellenger, Yvonne. "Le comique comme résultat de la transgression," *Studi di letteratura francese* 10 (1983): 161-175.

Bergson, Henri. *Le rire*. Paris: PUF, 1940.

Du Bellay, Joachim. *The Defence and Illustration of the French Language*, bk. 2, ch. 4, p. 71 in *Poetry and Language in 16th-Century France*, transl. L. Willett. Toronto: CRRS, 2003.

Debailly, P. "Juvénal en France au XVIe et au XVII siècle," *Littératures classiques* 24 (1995): 29-47.

—. *La Muse indignée*, vol. 1.Paris: Classiques Garnier, 2012.

Giraud, Y. "Le Comique engagé des *Satyres chrestiennes de la cuisine papale*," *Studi di letteratura francese* 10 (1983): 52-72.

Joubert, L. *Traité du Ris*. Paris: N. Chesneau, 1579.

Lenient, Charles. *La Satire en France ou la littérature militante au XVIe siècle*. Paris: Hachette, 1866

Renner, Bernd. *La Satire dans tous ses états*, éd. B. Renner. Geneva: Droz, 2009: 25-48,

Renner, Bernd and Y. Giraud. "Rire et satire à l'aube des guerres civiles: l'exemple des *Satyres chrestiennes de la cuisine papale*," *The Romanic Review* 101 (2010): 655-671.

INSIDE JOKES AND TRIVIALIZED SPACE: THE CHANCERY OF THE PALAZZO VECCHIO AND THE BATHOS OF MACHIAVELLI'S *FLORENTINE HISTORIES*

PAUL WRIGHT

My project takes as its inspiration the foundational and still unmatched work of Nicolai Rubinstein, Randolph Starn, and Loren Partridge on the Palazzo Vecchio.[1] The Palazzo, also known as the Palazzo della Signoria—home of the Florentine government and chancery, and now the historic town hall of Florence—has always been a civic space marked by the contested values and histories of the Florentine commune and republic. Yet I would emphasize that the Palazzo della Signoria is not only a civic space charged with meaning and power, but has also sometimes been rendered a space of political comedy and even bathos. A literary example of how civic architecture and gallows humor go hand-in-hand is Machiavelli's relatively neglected *Istorie Fiorentine* (*Florentine Histories*), the subject of a book near completion, *The Alloy of Identity: Machiavelli's* Florentine Histories *Reclaimed*. Too often Machiavelli's *Istorie* are read parasitically—always with an eye toward what they tell us of the iconic works like *The Prince* or *The Discourses on Livy*. The premise of my book is to treat the *Histories* as the iconic text, thereby reversing the usual dynamic of interpretation. To this end, one of my chapters explores Machiavelli's text as a civic and political topography of Florence itself, and in particular how Machiavelli represents the Palazzo Vecchio as a site of contestation, deliberation, but also if such a thing exists, civic humanist comedy.

---

[1] See Nicolai Rubinstein, *The Palazzo Vecchio, 1298-1532: Government, Architecture, and Imagery in the Civic Palace of the Florentine Republic*, ed. Denys Hay and J.B. Trapp, *Oxford-Warburg Studies* (Oxford: Clarendon Press, 1995); Randolph Starn and Loren W. Partridge, *Arts of Power: Three Halls of State in Italy, 1300-1600* (Berkeley: Univ. of California Press, 1992).

Before turning to the Palazzo itself, I want to sketch the ways in which civic comedy is manifest in the Florence and the greater Italy that Machiavelli imaginatively reconstructs—a comedy that, to him, is never less than absurd. Wayne Rebhorn has argued that the *Florentine Histories*

> [are] also a pervasively satirical work, and a bitter one to boot. Rather than write an epic about his native city-state, as both Vergil and Livy did about Rome, Machiavelli presents Florence as a comic inversion, an ironic parody of everything for which he celebrated ancient Rome in the *Discorsi*. [...] The *Istorie* thus reveal fully the brilliant satirical streak that runs through all of Machiavelli's works. (Rebhorn, 196)

I would go so far as to say that Machiavelli's achievement as a social satirist lies not only in his caustic *Mandragola*, another Machiavellian comedy centered on the impurity of origins and intentions, but also in the *Istorie*. Indeed, the critical tradition surrounding Machiavelli's least-appreciated work has been generally receptive to such appraisals. The urge to find satire and irony in the *Istorie* can be traced back to the work of Felix Gilbert and Gennaro Sasso.[2] Never lagging far behind that satire, of course, is Machiavelli's essential misanthropy; Sasso found in the *Histories* Machiavelli's deepest, almost primal skepticism and what he called "the anguish of a world without future or hope" (Sasso, cited in Di Maria, 249; translation mine).

Today's finest historian of Florence, John Najemy, identifies that Machiavellian irony as a tactical tool by which history itself is deployed to enable Machiavelli's "self-liberation" (Najemy 574) from the literary fiction of the redemptive prince and the myth-making of the all-too real Medici who had commissioned the *Istorie*. And Salvatore Di Maria has illuminated Machiavelli's use of paradox and the absurd as a coherent Aristotelian project that takes history as a "fatalistic process of inevitability [...] effectively dramatized by a narrative largely emplotted in the tragic mode" (Di Maria 259). All of these insights, coming from quite different critical voices and perspectives on Machiavelli's work, nevertheless have in common the conviction that Machiavellian laughter—or what Maurizio

---

[2] See Felix Gilbert, "Machiavelli's *Istorie Fiorentine*: An Essay in Interpretation," in *History: Choice and Commitment* (Cambridge: Harvard Univ. Press, 1977), 135-53; Gennaro Sasso, *Machiavelli e gli antichi e altri saggi*, 4 vols. (Milan & Naples: R. Ricciardi, 1986-97).

Viroli has evoked as "Niccolò's Smile"[3]— has behind it festering political
and psychic wounds. With Niccolò, we always find that the proverbial
"tears of a clown" rain down like daggers.

But what I would emphasize here, and what most of the critical
tradition has missed in the *Histories*, is the essential *playfulness* with
which Machiavelli deploys those rhetorical weapons. In the final chapter
of the unfinished *Istorie*, it is the infamous and, above all, playful image of
Lorenzo il Magnifico that captures the alloying of character and identity
that Machiavelli saw pervading not merely Florence, but all of Italy. In
precisely the same passages where Machiavelli praises Lorenzo's virtues
and prudence, he acknowledges him to have overindulged "cose veneree"
("things of Venus"), as well as "uomini faceti e mordaci" ("facetious and
caustic men" [*IF* 8. 36]),[4] men Machiavelli would no doubt admit were
rather like himself. Machiavelli's self-awareness of his own facetiousness
is the source of his biting humor, and not merely in the plays. When on 15
March 1526 he writes at length to Guicciardini of Emperor Charles V and
the entire political mess ensuing from the emperor's taking Francis I
hostage, he hilariously addresses his own pretensions to informed analysis.
He ends his analysis simply with an appeal to his friend to look out for the
actress Machiavelli is taken with:

> La Barbera si truova costì: dove voi gli possiate far piacere,
> io ve la raccomando, perché la mi dà molto più da pensare
> che lo inperadore. (Machiavelli, 1996: 348)

> [Our Barbera is there: where you can be of help to her, I
> commend your assistance, since I think much more of her
> than of the Emperor.]

He even depicts Lorenzo as something of a child among his own offspring,
"intra i loro trastulli mescolarsi" ("mixing in their games" [*IF* 8. 36]).
Ultimately, Lorenzo to Machiavelli remains the emblematic mystery at the
heart of a social world whose origins have been engulfed even at the level
of description itself: "[…] si vedeva in lui essere due persone diverse,

---

[3] See Marizio Viroli, *Niccolò's Smile: A Biography of Machiavelli* (New York:
Farrar, Straus, & Giroux, 2000).

[4] For the *Istorie fiorentine*, I have used Niccolò Machiavelli, *Tutte le opere*, ed.
Mario Martelli (Firenze: Sansoni Editore, 1993), 629-844. The format for citations
will be: (*IF* bk. and ch. #). Translations are provided only for extended passages or
those in which clarification is necessary. Translations are my own unless
otherwise noted.

quasi con impossibile coniunzione congiunte" ("[…] one saw in him two different persons, united in a nearly impossible conjunction" [*IF* 8. 36]). This playful and paradoxical depiction of Lorenzo speaks to Machiavelli's deeper conviction that the malleability of character is less a product of choice than of inexplicable alchemy, and that the rules of the Florentine political game admit and encourage admixture, if there are any rules at all.[5] The laughable mess of Florentine political life is not always bemoaned by Machiavelli; in this text it is often positively *celebrated*.

In a social landscape dominated by impurities of motive and identity, one shares Machiavelli's wry smile at the plight of Piero de' Medici, who, when he drew up a list of friends and enemies, "trovò tanta varietà e instabilità negli animi de' cittadini, che molti de' soscritti contro di lui ancora in favore suo si soscrissono" ("found such variety and instability in the minds of citizens, that many listed against him were also listed in favor" [*IF* 7. 13]). This uncertainty motivates the grim causality and gallows humor of the *Histories*, both of which spin along the axis of chance meetings, rumors, and hearsay: "Indugia assai la moltitudine tutta a disporsi al male; ma quando vi è disposta ogni piccolo accidente la muove" ("Slowly enough is the whole multitude disposed to evil; but when so disposed every little accident moves it" [*IF* 6. 24]). To exemplify this, Machiavelli dramatizes the phenomenon beyond the walls of Florence. He imagines in Milan a commiserative meeting of two of Milan's poor: "duoi […] di non molta condizione, ragionando, propinqui a Porta Nuova" ("two … of rather low station, reasoning next to the Porta Nuova" [*IF* 6. 24]), whose bitterness sets off a parodic chain of accidents. In the wake of the mob that forms in earshot of these two working-class complainers, upheavals rock Italy at large and recoil on the Milanese as Francesco Sforza returns to power. What is so strikng is that the two plebes are "ragionando" ("reasoning and discussing"), not merely agitating. The joke lies in how the aggregation of reasoning agents leads to potentially irrational and unintended political consequences, the "accidenti" of civic life and death.

---

[5] This marks a decisive emphasis on admixture that Machiavelli previously found troubling. In *Discorsi* 1. 27, Machiavelli had bemoaned the fact that leaders were for the most part unable to be wholly good or wholly evil. With Lorenzo in the *Istorie*, we see something beyond grudging acceptance of that impurity, even a kind of approving wonder. It is perhaps feasible for ironic readers of Machiavelli to find insincerity in the Lorenzo portrait, but I think insincerity misses the mark. Machiavelli directly entertains the paradox inherent in a world of Lorenzos and deploys him to communicate it, most especially to Clement.

Another of these playful barbs comes at the expense of someone who took the patriotic fervor of Petrarca for "Italia mia" absolutely seriously—the Roman patrician Stefano Porcari (1400-53), a humanist and would-be revolutionary who failed dismally at the political resurrection of classical values in papal Rome. Porcari believed in the prophetic sensibility of poets such as Petrarch, and being that he held himself superior to any other citizen of Rome, especially in the realm of learning and eloquence akin to those of great poets, he deemed himself worthy of the task of realizing the intent of "Italia Mia." However, Machiavelli portrays Stefano as arrested with his followers by agents of Nicholas V at a dinner prematurely celebrating the triumph of their conspiracy to restore republican Rome. Already dressed in robes of state and flush with classicist inspiration, Porcari and his followers are captured and executed by the Pope that very evening. Machiavelli observes how Porcari's considerable learning and eloquence go unmatched by any capacity "in modo cauto governarsi" ("in his cautious way of behaving") and he is parodically exposed "con le parole, con le usanze e con il modo del vivere" ("by his words, habits, and lifestyle" [*IF* 6. 29]). Machiavelli sees Porcari's cabal suffering according to their merits, and while he no doubt admires Stefano's humanist "intention," he sarcastically finds the latter's "judgment" deeply suspect (*IF* 6. 29)[6]—or the opposite of "cautious." That is, his superiority did not provide him with the ability to fully comprehend the situation, and this deficiency was enabled by Porcari's belief in political glory (inspired by poetry) over political pragmatism. The irony is that he was not so "cauto" in his ways, since his "words, habits, and lifestyle" were predictable enough for Nicholas V to suspect his conspiracies; with his own eloquence Porcari provided the victim of his would-be conspiracy with the necessary insight to stop it before it began.

---

[6] Porcari's life in itself is a wonderful example of the alloying of identity Machiavelli alludes to throughout the *Istorie*. Member of a Roman patrician family, Porcari spent time in Florence as Capitano del Popolo from 1427-1428, mediated between anti-papal forces and Eugenius IV in 1434, worked on and off for the Papacy, and was exiled to Bologna in 1448 on suspicion of conspiracy. Whether he was culpable in that case or not, he decided to merit the charge by fomenting the revolt against Nicholas V that led to his execution as described in the *Istorie* 6. 29 [Source: J.R. Hale, ed., *The Thames and Hudson Encyclopaedia of the Italian Renaissance, World of Art* (London: Thames & Hudson, 1981), 264]. See also "Civic Humanism in Practice: The Case of Stefano Porcari and The Christian Tradition," in Martels and Schmidt, *Antiquity Renewed: Late Classical and Early Modern Themes,* Groningen Studies in Cultural Change, vol. 4 (Leuven & Dudley, MA: Peeters, 2003).

This incident alone speaks to the extent that Machiavelli has tried to liberate himself not merely from redemptive princes, but redemptive writers as well. He challenges Italian recuperation as a *telos* based in literary nostalgia for an identity that never was. By satirizing Porcari, Machiavelli also leaves Dante and Petrarca to the hallucinatory domain of letters, to the civic humanist equivalent of Dante's Limbo, where Machiavelli had once half-jokingly consigned his former boss, Piero Soderini, head of the Florentine republic that fell again to Medici tyranny in 1512.[7]

Elsewhere in the *Histories*, Machiavelli figures the hollowness of literary claims to Italian purity in what is for him a jarringly literary metaphor, a portent of Italy's renewed wave of foreign incursions. With the arrival in 1456 of a "turbine" ("whirlwind") driven by forces "either natural or supernatural," Machiavelli prefigures French intervention in Italian affairs, something that would have lasting consequences into Machiavelli's own era. This whirlwind is the most ethereal emblem that Machiavelli has ever allowed himself, and it whips through Italy, putting the lie to insularity and Petrarcan valor both, producing a "romore" ("noise/rumor") as of "il fine del mondo," such that it seemed "la terra, l'acqua e il resto del cielo e del mondo, nello antico caos, mescolandosi insieme, ritornassero" ("the land, the waters, and the rest of heaven and earth would return to the ancient chaos, intermingled" [*IF* 6. 34]). The reliable narrative comfort by which the story of Italy against the barbarians was continually retold, even by Machiavelli in *The Prince*, begins to give way to a realization that in the face of the "turbine," we *are* they. The cosmic joke, Machiavelli makes clear, is on us. The chaotic "turbine" becomes for Machiavelli the only true engine of history, and his *Florentine Histories* emplot themselves not so much as concise tragedies, as Salvatore di Maria has suggested (Di Maria, 259), but rather as a perverse, new *comedia*.   Dante and Stefano Porcari might not have appreciated it, but Ariosto surely would.

Now to turn specifically to the Palazzo Vecchio, we see how the Pazzi conspiracy against the Medici is almost theatrically recounted as a comedy of errors occasioned by a botched assassination attempt in the middle of mass. A key scene (*IF* Bk. 8, chs. 6-7) shows the conspiracy devolving

---

[7] In the infamous epigram which runs: "La notte che morì Pier Soderini, / l'anima andò de l'inferno a la bocca; / gridò Pluton: --Ch'inferno? anima sciocca, / va su nel limbo fra gli altri bambini" ("The night Piero Soderini died, his spirit went to the mouth of hell; Pluto howled: —Why hell? Idiot spirit, go up to limbo with all the other babies" [Machiavelli, 1993: 1005]).

into what can only be read as absurdist, macabre comedy, whose pratfalls include one of the Pazzi wounding himself in the leg. Additionally the scene includes a group of co-conspirators locking themselves in the chancery of the Palazzo Vecchio, in effect cornering themselves as Lorenzo il Magnifico's revenge quickly took shape. That Machiavelli imagines the conspirators ineptly trapping themselves in his own future office in the chancery is itself a remarkable jab at his own political fortunes. That the conspiracy had as its chief casualty the father of Pope Clement VII, Machiavelli's own patron in writing the *Istorie*, raises a number of questions about just how Machiavelli expected his most important reader to take the trivia and the bathos of the account offered here—an account remarkably different from the typically flattering narratives of the conspiracy produced by Angelo Poliziano and others.[8]

If one visits the Palazzo and sees just how small the *scrittoio* is relative to the entire structure, one cannot help but laugh at the ludicrousness of a band of murderous conspirators trapped not in one of the many immense, architecturally staggering *sale*, but in a civil functionary's Spartan office. The ballast of Machiavelli's narrative lies precisely in its trivia, and *telos* seems to be thrown overboard. Maurizio Viroli has written eloquently of the *Istorie* deploying "the rhetorical power of history" as a deliberative complement to the theorizing of the *Discorsi*, as a mode of civil life rather than a programmatic understanding.[9] Machiavelli himself quite ambivalently understood Florence as a "città di parlare avida e che le cose dai successi e non dai consigli giudica" ("city yearning to talk, which judges things by success and not by counsel" [*IF* 8. 22]). "Avida" can be rendered variously, as "eager," "greedy," or "yearning," and to Machiavelli, this city is all of these things, caught in the semantic and ideological charge of a politics and a literary discourse to which it noisily bears witness.

Perhaps it is Florence's unwillingness to be counseled that finally motivates Machiavelli to stop counseling as an expert and start narrating as a witness, but without the safety net provided by the eschatology implicit

---

[8] Angelo Poliziano was the accomplished humanist and poet who benefitted greatly from Medici patronage, although forensics experts and historians now suspect he may have died a victim of poisoning ordered by Piero de' Medici. During his earlier years under the protection of Lorenzo il Magnifico, Poliziano wrote a scathing indictment of the Pazzi and their plot against his Medici patrons. The most accessible English translation can be found in *The Earthly Republic: Italian Humanists on Government and Society* (eds. Benjamin Kohl and Ronald G. Witt) (Philadelphia, PA: Univ. of Pennsylvania Press, 1978), 305-24.
[9] See Viroli, 97-107.

in xenophobia and redemption alike. In other words, where the *The Prince* and even the *Discourses on Livy* encouraged Machiavelli to think about potential saviors of the Florentine polity (either in the form of a redeemer prince or of a reformed republic), by the time of the *Histories* Machiavelli is engaged in an altogether different rhetorical enterprise—namely, an effort to account for the failures of his native city rather than formulas for its success.

What is most important here is Machiavelli's use of the physical space of the Palazzo as a literary infrastructure for his narrative, and how he specifically imagines the Chancery in relation to the rest of the Palazzo as it morphed from a republican space into an iconic Medici stronghold. The potential place of absurdity and comedy in the emerging identity of the Medici regime calls for further analysis. Even today, the Chancery is represented and made to signify modesty relative to the ornate riches of the rest of the Palazzo. I engage the Chancery space as currently archived and "lived" by visitors, and consider the ways in which the Chancery is tamed by what at last is a subordinate gaze that viewers are trained to deploy as they pass it by in favor of other *sale*. That subordinate gaze ultimately directs the viewer toward the ideological 'eye candy' of a structure that has been in large measure reconfigured as a celebration of Medici power.

We might recall here Stephen Greenblatt's now classic formulation of the competing yet complementary impulses of "resonance and wonder" in the experience of any museum or archive. In this theoretical light, the Palazzo Vecchio has certainly been curated with both historical resonance and aesthetic wonder firmly in mind, and yet the Chancery remains a space that has been relatively muted in both dimensions. The space offers up only the bust and the portrait of Machiavelli lingering on as the visual counterparts to the echoes of Niccolò's ironic laughter—a laughter never at the expense of his beloved Florence, but in shared bemusement at its shifting political fortunes.

Works Cited

Di Maria, Salvatore. "Machiavelli's Ironic View of History: The 'Istorie Fiorentine'." *Renaissance Quarterly* 45, no. 2 (1992): 248-70.
Gilbert, Felix. "Machiavelli's *Istorie Fiorentine*: An Essay in Interpretation" in *History: Choice and Commitment*. Cambridge: Harvard Univ. Press, 1977:135-53.

Greenblatt, Stephen. "Resonance and Wonder" in *Learning to Curse: Essays in Early Modern Culture*. 2nd ed. New York and London: Routledge, 2007: 216-46.

Machiavelli, Niccolò. *Lettere a Francesco Vettori e a Francesco Guicciardini, 1513-27*. Giorgio Inglese, ed. 2nd ed. Milan: Rizzoli, 1996.

—. *Tutte le opere*. Mario Martelli, ed. Firenze: Sansoni Editore, 1993.

Najemy, John M. "Machiavelli and the Medici: The Lessons of Florentine History." *Renaissance Quarterly* 35, no. 4 (1982): 551-76.

Poliziano, Angelo. "The Pazzi Conspiracy" in *The Earthly Republic: Italian Humanists on Government and Society*. Benjamin Kohl and Ronald G. Witt, eds. Philadelphia, PA: University of Pennsylvania Press, 1978: 305-324.

Rebhorn, Wayne. *Foxes and Lions: Machiavelli's Confidence Men*. Ithaca: Cornell Univ. Press, 1988.

Rubinstein, Nicolai. *The Palazzo Vecchio, 1298-1532: Government, Architecture, and Imagery in the Civic Palace of the Florentine Republic*. Denys Hay and J.B. Trapp, ed. Oxford-Warburg Studies. Oxford: Clarendon Press, 1995.

Sasso, Gennaro. *Machiavelli e gli antichi e altri saggi*, 4 vols. Milan & Naples: R. Ricciardi, 1986-1997.

Starn, Randolph and Loren W. Partridge. *Arts of Power: Three Halls of State in Italy, 1300-1600*. Berkeley: Univ. of California Press, 1992.

Viroli, Maurizio. *Machiavelli*. Mark Philp, ed. Founders of Modern Political and Social Thought. Oxford & New York: Oxford Univ. Press, 1998.

PARODIES VIA THE NEW TESTAMENT IN *LAZARILLO DE TORMES*

KEVIN S. LARSEN

We do not know for certain who was the author of the first Spanish picaresque novel, *Lazarillo de Tormes* (1554), though there is ample reason to suspect that he was a New Christian, that is, a *converso* or *marrano*, a person of originally Jewish stock now converted to Catholicism.[1] Writing (spitting, even) in the eye of the Inquisitorial whirlwind, he wisely maintained anonymity, since the trenchant irony that pervades the novel could quickly constitute a two-edged sword, rending writer and reader alike (Nepaulsingh). In episode after episode the cleverly constructed, if not completely concealed, critique of contemporary culture cannot but come to the fore. For instance, Lazarillo, the child, or Lázaro, the adult speaking through/as the child, describes his thieving and subsequently "martyred" father in what reads like a parody of Evangelical idiom: "he confessed and denied not the accusations, suffering persecution for the sake of justice … as the Bible tells us, 'blessed are they which are persecuted for righteousness' sake'" (5).[2] The irony of this usage is augmented considerably, given the "Jewishness," the "Old Testament roots," not only of the Sermon on the Mount, from where this passage seems to originate, but of the entire New Testament.[3] More cryptic still are other references to that Christian Scripture which inhabit the novel. It is my purpose to conjure some of the legion of these internal voices. I mean to illustrate how the novelist shows that, while the Old Christian Establishment might pay lip service to the letter of its own

---

[1] On the author's religious background, see: Castro; Deyermond; Márquez Villanueva; Gilman; Lázaro Carreter; McGrady; Guillén; Agulló y Cobo; Ferrer-Chivite; Nepaulsingh; Ricapito; De la Concha; Stone; Aronson-Friedman.

[2] Here and throughout the rest of my text, I'll cite parenthetically from the Markley translation. Cf. Perry

[3] Throughout the rest of my essay, I'll cite parenthetically from *The Jewish Annotated New Testament* (Levine and Brettler, eds.). The verse here in question is certainly Matthew 5:10.

Scripture, in practice it had strayed far from the spirit of the teachings of Jesus and His first followers.

If the author of the *Lazarillo* pillories "bad" Christians, he does not really satirize Christianity. Instead, he uses passages from that Scripture to critique those who falsely or facilely profess its teachings. The result is not so much a *desacralization*, as it is a *resacralization,* which serves to validate the Counter Reformation program of inward renewal and restoration. Moreover, this reimagining of Scripture, grounded in both the Old and the New Testaments, also takes shape within a traditionally Jewish medium, the *midrash*, which is a retelling of Biblical stories as they might have been (Neusner). Under such a rubric, satire resembles more a surgical probe, rather than a cannonade. Behind the comic mask may also lurk a degree of passive aggression, but the author's reliance on Judeo-Christian Scripture indicates a genuine belief therein. Paradoxically, such ironic use of the Bible may actually reaffirm textual, even doctrinal, authority, while proving to be more truly honorific than the slavish devotion or willful ignorance of hypocrites. Social criticism develops into a devastating discourse against the *status quo*, an incisive counter-narrative showing how distant 16th-century Iberian reality is from the prophet Isaiah's paradisiacal prediction. In Spain, the "wolf" does not dwell with the "lamb," the "leopard" does not lie down with the "kid," and "a little child"—not Lazarillo, not anyone—does not lead them to pasture (RSV Isaiah 11: 6-9).

Given the contemporary climate so hostile to vernacular versions of the Bible and Scriptural commentaries, the *Lazarillo*'s comedic exegesis must hide, though in plain sight.[4] The novelist shows himself to be a humanist of the first magnitude: his hermeneutic serves to explicate, rather than to expurgate, Scripture. He is guardedly candid, though not at all tentative in his practice of New Testament criticism, utilizing Holy Writ to illuminate the contemporary human tragi-comedy. Lazarillo's developmental arc may reflect the decadence of his milieu, as he projects a grotesque image of the young Jesus, who "increased in wisdom and in years, and in divine and human favor" (Luke 2:52). Come to maturity, the Nazarene will be similarly misunderstood, rejected, and betrayed. It is significant that the lad suggests that he was "in the stomach of the whale" when he was knocked cold for three days by the priest of Maquema, his second master (32). This situation alludes to the Old Testament story of Jonah (RSV

---

[4] The Inquisition's first printed *Index Librorum Prohibitorum* (1551) formally forbade the Holy Scripture in Castilian, while the *Index* of 1559 outlawed the Bible or Biblical commentaries in any vulgar tongue whatsoever. Incidentally, it was this latter list that decreed against the *Lazarillo*.

1:17-2:10), which is Christianized to typify Jesus' time in the tomb for three days until His resurrection (Matt. 12:40). Like Lazarillo, the New Christians found themselves stuck in the digestive tract of a monster that might spew them out at any time, though not to renewed life, for the Old Christian Establishment often spurned what might otherwise have developed into genuine conversion.

From a boy to a mature *pícaro*, Lazaro heeds his mother's advice that he should associate_with the "worthy" people, those good folk who, he soon learns, are the ones with the goods (5, 67). Despite such "decent" associations, he still must live by his wits and on the margins of society, even in a time of prosperity and "the peak of all good fortune" (68). Even within this dubious frame of reference, Lazarillo, in whatever avatar, may yet prove to be a more worthy Christian than are his ostensible superiors. As was the case with Jesus of Nazareth, who called himself "least in the kingdom of heaven" (Matt. 11:11): those who would condemn him, almost by default, ended up condemning themselves. Additionally, the novelist must have savored the irony that the original proselytes of same Jesus were Jewish New Christians, "children" in the new faith. Jesus' doctrine reverberates throughout this scenario: "Let the little children come to me, and do not stop them for it is to such as these that the kingdom of heaven belongs" (Matt. 19:14). In turn, Lazarillo references his own "childishness," recalling how he inadvertently and innocently betrayed his "stepfather" (7-8; Sieber 2-9). Deftly, the mature writer portrays his childish self against a backdrop of ironic intuition. The unvarnished truth issues, in Jesus' words, "out of the mouths of infants and nursing babies" (Matt. 21:16; RSV Psalm 8:2).

Indeed, the Nazarene invokes in Himself the ultimate model for such infantile expression of the truth to power, as a twelve-year-old teaching the elders of Israel in the Temple (Luke 2:41-52). In like manner, chapter 53 of Isaiah, which Christians traditionally read as foretelling the coming of Jesus the Christ, propels the picaresque paradigm: however ironically, Lazarillo grows up "like a root out of dry ground . . . despised and rejected by men," to become himself "a man of sorrows and acquainted with grief" (RSV vv. 2-3). If Jesus extols childish innocence and exuberance, such a lack of guile could prove disastrous to those yet young in the faith of Christ, given the Holy Office's readiness to provide passage from the kingdom of this world to the next. After all, beginning a century before the *Lazarillo*, from 1449, the Statutes of Purity of Blood held that the "stain" of Semitic origins could never be expunged. Lazarillo quickly realizes that there's nothing funny about his inescapable condition as a *converso*. His first master, who's most certainly of that same ethnic extraction, slams the erstwhile guileless child's head against the stone figure of a bull. Knocked nearly senseless, he "awoke from the naiveté in which as a child [he] had been sleeping," intuiting that he must "sharpen up [his] eye and take stock of [himself]" so as to "consider how to get along in this world" (8; Herrero, "Icons," 3-18).

Granted, certain figures in the novel are more clearly corrupt than the blind man, all the while evincing an aura of sanctity. For instance, the seller of indulgences not only calls on Heaven for a sign, but dictates the terms thereof, suggesting those sign-seekers Jesus denounces (Matt. 12:39, 16:4). He also recalls the attitude of the Inquisitors, who sought concrete proof of the *conversos'* faithfulness, outward manifestations of inward grace, to which they then refused to grant credence. Likewise, the seller of fake papal bulls would have had little or no success were his clients less susceptible themselves, searching, however secretly, for similar portents to buttress their apparently flagging faith. Still, with most characters in the novel we need to be cautious, chary with outright condemnation, realizing that the narrator is no disinterested spectator and may act as something of an inquisitor himself.

For example, the cleric of the second chapter is roundly condemned for his niggardliness, and rightly so, although he is probably just an impoverished parish priest. His young assistant describes him as eating "like a wolf—at someone else's expense" (23), calling to mind Scriptural passages describing "ravenous wolves" which shall afflict the Lord's flock (Matt. 7:15, 10:16; Acts 20:29). Even the blind man figures in this ecclesiastical chorus. Lazarillo himself insinuates that his sightless master embodies better guidance, albeit subversively so, than do those charged with providing such leadership. The blind man's discourse recalls that of St. Peter to a crippled beggar: "I have no silver or gold, but what I have I give you; in the name of Jesus Christ of Nazareth, stand up and walk" (Acts 3:6). Lazarillo recalls his master's saying to him: "I can give you neither gold nor silver, but precepts for living I can teach you" (8; Rico, ed. 23). The guide boy's guide in life is as good as his word. That a naively "visionary" child and a blind man seem to see more clearly than the willfully sightless potentates of society resonates with the Biblical ideal of infantile insight and innocence, not to mention, with Jesus' denunciation of those who ostensibly "see," but refuse to perceive. Teaching in parables, His "precepts for living" were in plain view, so that the humble and sincere could see and understand clearly, while those not so inclined would experience only the surface meaning of the narrative (Matt. 13:13-15; RSV Isaiah 6:9-10).

So also with the parables of *Lazarillo de Tormes*: chapter three, the narration of the young protagonist's stay with the impoverished squire, could be construed in similarly parabolic terms. This master figures as a prime example of his contemporaries' misdirected zeal for outward niceties, particularly given his morbid fixation on honor (though he's as much of a *pícaro* as Lazarillo) and "cleanliness"—probably not so much of personal hygiene as of purity of blood. The dismal, almost funereal, domicile where the squire and his servant live, described in considerable detail, recalls first the almost empty, nearly dilapidated dwelling of the priest. Such a bleak portrayal also summons to mind Jesus' expostulation of Jerusalem: "your house is left to you, desolate" (Matt. 23:38). This sort of imagery also depicts the squire's rootless, effectively vacuous existence, together with that of the *pícaro* and his other masters. Even more ironic is the at least implicit suggestion of another homeless wanderer, Jesus of Nazareth (Matt 8:20). In the Old Christian ethos of contemporary Spain, Jesus himself continues to wander, becoming one more avatar of the "wandering Jew." In like manner, the *conversos* roam as melancholy exiles in their own homeland, strangers in a land that should not be so strange, but is (Yovel).

The parabolic parallels continue. Lazarillo's very name invokes a nexus of potential meanings and associations: two New Testament namesakes for Lázaro are indicated.[5] First, there is the Lazarus that Jesus brought back from the dead (John 11:1-44). In theory, Lazarillo and other *conversos* have been revitalized, reborn via the water of Christian baptism, though as New Christians they enter into a kind of living death. It is a bitter irony for them that the "narrow gate" that Jesus commands his followers to enter, may well lead the New Christians to effective "destruction" (Matt. 7:13-14). The *conversos* are trapped between the old religion and ethnic identity they have attempted to abandon and the new creed and culture so reluctant to receive them. The second Lazarus is described in one of Jesus' parables: a beggar, scorned by the magnates of his time, only to be received after death into the "bosom of Abraham." While in the mortal world, this second Lazarus was afflicted with a loathsome disease, perhaps auguring as to how Lazarillo and his fellow New Christians suffered from an equally incurable malady of body and spirit, one which the sacrament of baptism could neither cure nor palliate, to be remedied only by death. Such pessimism also infuses Lazarillo's testament: the novelist probably expects little lasting benefit from his satire, for the contemporary authorities, like the recently deceased rich man

[5] Relative to the avatars of the Biblical Lazarus in the novel: Deyermond 21, 26-32, 88; Gilman, "Death" 166; Perry 141-146; Wardropper 202-212; Sitler 91-92.

Cover of the 1554 edition of *Lazarillo de Tormes* (Anonymous; Biblioteca de Barcarrota)

and his otherwise oblivious siblings of Jesus's parable, have not only Moses and the prophets of the Old Testament, they also have those of the New (Luke 16:19-31).

A dominant theme of the *Lazarillo* is hunger, whether for temporal sustenance or for more metaphysical honor. The picaresque protagonist can never find any real security; his is always to be a hand-to-mouth existence, for both body and spirit, and prosperity will only be fleeting (68). Bread and wine may pass his lips, but these sacramental entities can never satisfy his spirit. The *converso* may take communion, but his congenitally soiled soul can never truly commune with the Divine. In this regard, the priest's rigorous rationing, his outright denial even, of bread from the chest, takes on added significance. The *pícaro* might for a time pass into a "paradise of bread" (25),[6] but he is only passing through. Just as the sacramental emblem cannot be truly absorbed by his system, neither can the New Christian be readily absorbed into the societal order then current in Iberia. At one point during his service to the priest of Maqueda, Lazarillo claims to be "inspired by the Holy Ghost," so as to barter with the "God-sent angel of a tinker" for a key to the chest where the loaves are kept (24-25). This exchange also recalls Jesus' bestowal of "the keys of the kingdom of heaven" on St. Peter, who has just confessed Him to be the Messiah. This sequence may turn on a flawed, even fallacious, Biblical reading, though one that informs Lazarillo's current condition. Whereas Apostle's "keys" unlock or seal the heavens at his discretion, under the current Iberian ecclesiastical regime, Lazarillo's key, though briefly useful, finally proves futile, for the heavens remain closed to him, as does his master's chest of food (Matt. 16:13-20).

Instead of sharing the "bread of life," as Jesus terms Himself and His Gospel (John 6:35), instead of multiplying their loaves (if not their fishes) and thereby feeding—physically and spiritually—the multitudes in their charge, instead of nourishing refugees from Israel with manna from heaven and/or from earth, as did God through Moses, the ministers of the Gospel hoard the victuals they have been ordained to dispense. The priest carefully counts *a priori* his cache of loaves, even fragments thereof, so as not to lose (or let loose) any of them, this, in ironic contrast to the liberality of Jesus, who feeds 5000 men, plus women and children, with "five loaves and two fish" (Matt. 14:13-21). Granted, when he rejects Satan's temptation to turn stones to bread, Jesus states: "One does not live

---

[6] See, among others: Deyermond 27, 53; Piper 269-271; Perry 141-44; Gilman, "Death" 164; Sieber 17-44; Brancaforte 558-563 *et passim*; Weiner 931-934; Sitler 85-97; De la Concha 261-65; Torrico 419-435.

by bread alone, but by every word that comes from the mouth of God"
(Matt. 4:3-4). But neither category is available to Lazarillo, neither the
"daily bread" (Matt. 6:11) that Jesus taught His followers to pray for, nor
the more spiritual sustenance. The novel provides ample evidence that
neither the spiritual nor the temporal should obviate the other from the
horizon of humanity's needs. In the bread he pilfers, Lazarillo sees the
very "face of God" (26; Ricapito 142-146), illustrating and even
confirming transubstantiation, together with Jesus' admonition that the
faithful must literally ingest His flesh (John. 6:51-58). Additionally, that
this food for body and soul is locked away in the priest's "ark" may recall
the Ark of the Covenant, emblem of the Mosaic faith of the lad's
forefathers. Once this receptacle foreshadowed Israel's Divine Communion,
but now it forbids such exchange to those of the erstwhile chosen lineage.

The narrator maintains an equally tenuous relationship with wine, the
other sacramental entity, a token of the redemptive Blood of Christ which
was originally shared by Jesus and His first followers, though in current
practice is to be taken only by the priest. His young helper at mass has
developed quite a taste for this beverage, though it never really quenches
the thirst in his body or in his soul. Wine becomes for Lazarillo a sort of
pharmakon—that is, a poison, as well as a panacea. Recalling those who
washed the crucified Lord's corpse and prepared it for burial, the grinning
blind man uses wine to wash the cuts and bruises he inflicts on the boy:
"The same thing that made you sick is curing you and giving you back
your health" (12). But such health is only physical and frustratingly
fleeting. For a time at least, Lazarillo attempts to go along to get along.
However, the final lesson he learns (and teaches!) resounds when he runs
his blind master into the column, breaking the old man's head, as he had
once cracked his own (20). Since the Law of Christ's Mercy cannot be
invoked, the Mosaic *lex talionis*, an eye for an eye and a tooth for a tooth,
is reaffirmed. Jesus would emend this antiquated legalistic program,
exhorting His disciples to turn the other cheek (Matt. 5:38). But in 16th-
century Iberia, this utopia was not to be. Rather than follow their purported
Master, the Old Christian Establishment continues to exact physical
retribution. No cheeks are turned, except perhaps for slashing or branding.
In the Inquisitorial economy, "the old wineskins" cannot contain the
Gospel's "new wine," not to mention the New Christians who try to
integrate themselves into it (Matt. 9:17).

Before the abrupt end to their relationship, the sightless seer distills his
young guide's once and future relationship to the fruit of the vine: "you
owe more to wine than to your father: he gave you life only once, and

wine has given you your life a thousand times" (18). Later in life, the *pícaro* will work as a wine peddler (popularly construed as a *converso* occupation), achieving at least for a time a level of material prosperity that as a boy he'd never have imagined. But he is merely a merchant, a middleman. A glaring irony of this stance is that, according to Christian teaching, it can be only Jesus who fills the role as the one true "mediator between God and humankind" (I Timothy 2:5; Hebrews 8:6, 9:15, 12:24), while Lazarillo is once again just pretending, somewhere between an imposter and a place-holder, whose association with the life-giving liquid in question remains tangential. Lázaro may traffic in wine, but his relationship to this surrogate father, as to the Christian God, will always be less than legitimate, and he will never find the satisfaction, security, and salvation that he seeks, Lázaro's ambiguous posture may elicit another contemporary question: a major controversy arising with the Protestant Reformation was Luther's argument that the Roman priesthood interfered with the work of salvation, coming between the individual and his God and even replacing Jesus in His role as intermediary. In this regard, the *pícaro* as priest embodies controversies that remain with us even today. Not only does the novel's protagonist follow in the footsteps of the contemporary clergy, he also calls to mind their counterparts, the scribes and Pharisees against whose dominion Jesus preached (Wills).

Lázaro's economic "good fortune" comes at a high cost, for he must accept the ambiguous conjugal circumstances imposed at the end of the narrative. Having learned just how little worldly "honor" is really worth, he now lives in an apparent *ménage-à-trois*. His associates admonish him concerning such domestic irregularity, but Lázaro will hear none of it, as he finally feels "comfortably" situated. The *pícaro* may be completely venal, pimping his own wife, who—like the wine, the blind man's abbreviated prayers, the fake bulls, and so on—becomes one more commodity for her husband's traffic. Nonetheless, his "tolerance" of her "transgressions" calls to mind the story of an accused adulteress, caught in the very act. When she is brought before Jesus, He offers His verdict: "Let anyone among you who is without sin be the first to throw a stone at her." Once her accusers have dispersed, Jesus does not immediately forgive the woman, but assures her that He doesn't condemn her either (John 8:3-11). For whatever reason(s), neither will Lázaro condemn his spouse. Nor does he actually forgive her: they just reach an accord in which certain matters cease to matter, including his friends' "false" accusations. He thereby manufactures "peace in [his] house" (68). He is determined to "stick with the decent people" (67), though such folk are far from sinless. The novelist follows the Nazarene's example in the condemnation of the hypocrites who would condemn in another the sin that remains in themselves. His picaresque protagonist, like "the decent people" of his association, opts against poverty, whether of spirit or of earthly goods, hoping for a reward in the here and now. As if to emulate the ecclesiastical "exemplars" along his way, he gives lip service to otherworldliness, though his real "treasure" is strictly temporal and eminently corruptible (Matt. 6:18-21).

The Nazarene preaches that "those who hunger and thirst for righteousness [...] will be filled" (Matt. 5:6). At the end of his narrative, Lázaro may for a while be filled with food and drink, though real satisfaction, genuine righteousness, at least according to the Old Christian Establishment, can never be his. The water and the wine he vends are simply not the kind Jesus describes as quelling thirst eternally (John 4:13-14). Moreover, Jesus affirms that "the merciful ... will receive mercy" (Matt. 5:7). Working to establish his domestic accord, the mature Lazaro is "merciful" to his wife, as to their employer, the Archpriest of San Salvador. In like manner, his fellow *conversos* strive for a "separate peace," be it a venal measure of personal acceptance and security or even approval on a grander scale. But in Inquisitorial Spain they can never truly be(come) "children of God," although such beatitude was promised to the "peacemakers" by Jesus Himself (Matt. 5:9).

Along a similar vein, Jesus instructed the faithful: "Ask, and it will be given you" (Luke 11:9). Yet, by hard experience Lazarillo learns early on that he must take care of himself, and that God, or at least His ministers, will probably not provide. Thus, the poignant irony of the *pícaro*'s name, short for Eleazar, which means "my God has helped." Likewise, in apparent accord with Isaiah's prophecy of the ministry of John the Baptist and the Advent of the Messiah, in the *Lazarillo* the "Mount" of Jesus' Sermon is "made low," by many more ironic references than the very few I've examined here. Still, the "valley" the prophet describes, and by extension those at lower points on the social scale, are not elevated. The novelist stands as something of a forerunner himself, with an authorial voice like that of the Baptist, as of "one crying in the wilderness," while signaling the sins of the present "brood of vipers." The *Lazarillo* may not straighten all "the crooked ... ways" of contemporary Spain, nor can the author "smooth" all his nation's "rough ways." But this desperately needed landscaping is at least indicated (Luke 3:4-7; RSV Isaiah 40:3-5; see: Gilman, "Matt. V:10" 257-265).

I am hopeful that at this point it is clear why the author of the *Lazarillo de Tormes* remained anonymous. Had he not kept his head, he could well have lost it, as his fate might easily have paralleled that of the martyred

Baptist. Had the Inquisitors seen through his text, had they comprehended more than the merest fraction of his pervasive satire, the novelist's hermeneutic could have proved disastrous for him. Anonymity notwithstanding, his apparently satiric employment of Biblical imagery and Christian ideology would certainly have brought down on his head the full rigor of Holy Office, much as the blind man slammed the wine jug down on his guide and as the priest clubbed his young helper.

The novel remains a classic example of Counter-Reformation writing, one motivated by a sincere—albeit not necessarily idealistic—desire for ecclesiastical and societal renewal. In this same vein, the picaresque tradition flows out of and alongside of the New Testament and, thereafter, Erasmian tradition of *Laus Stultitiae*: St. Paul contends that the wisdom of the world is foolishness, that believers must accept worldly ignorance to become truly wise.[7] In this light, the Apostle to the Gentiles and even Jesus himself might be seen as *pícaros*, at least in their stance against the *status quo*. Some readers, led "to seek surprises beneath unremarkable surfaces" (Shipley, "Hardworking" 253), will intuit the import of the stories, whether viscerally, intellectually, or spiritually. But the willfully uninitiated, those who are wise in their own eyes, will miss the point. Jesus said to his disciples: "blessed are your eyes, for they see" (Matt. 13:16). The same might be said of you for your patience (like that of Job!) in reading this text. Judge it for yourself, but remember Matthew 7:1-2.

Works Cited

Agulló y Cobo, Mercedes. *A vueltas con el autor del* Lazarillo. Madrid: Calambur, 2010.

Anonymous. *Lazarillo de Tormes*. Ed. Francisco Rico. Madrid: Cátedra, 1998.

—. *The Life of Lazarillo de Tormes*. Trans. J. Gerald Markley. New York: Macmillan, 1985.

Aronson-Friedman, Amy I. "Identifying the *Converso* Voice in *Lazarillo de Tormes*," *Approaches to Teaching* Lazarillo de Tormes *and the Picaresque Tradition*. New York: Modern Language Association, 2008: 36-42.

---

[7] See Lewis relative to "picaresque saints" and other putative oxymorons. Guillén suggests that although in the Lazarillo "the travel motif" was "basically unreligious," later picaresque works would come to identify "with the Pauline view of life as pilgrimage or exile within the confusion…of earthly existence" (98). The same could be said concerning Jesus of Nazareth. Cf. Hanrahan.

Brancaforte, Benito. "La abyección en el *Lazarillo de Tormes*." *Cuadernos Hispanoamericanos* 387 (Sept., 1982): 551-566.

Castro, Américo. *Hacia Cervantes*. Madrid: Taurus, 1957.

De la Concha, Víctor G. "La intención religiosa del *Lazarillo*." *RFE* 55 (1972): 243-277.

Deyermond, A.D. *Lazarillo de Tormes. A Critical Guide*. London: Grant & Cutler/Tamesis, 1973.

Ferrer-Chivite, Manuel. "Sustratos conversos en la creación de Lázaro de Tormes." *NRFH* 33 (1984): 352-379.

Gilman, Stephen. "The Death of Lazarillo de Tormes." *PMLA* 81 (1966): 149-166.

—. "Matthew V:10 in Castilian Jest and Earnest," in *Studia Hispanica in Honorem R. Lapesa*. Madrid: Cátedra-Seminario Menéndez Pidal/Gredos, 1972: I: 257-265.

Guillén. Claudio. *Literature as System*. Princeton: Princeton U P, 1971.

Hanrahan, Thomas. "*Lazarillo de Tormes*: Erasmian Satire or Protestant Reform?" *Hispania* 66 (1983): 333-339.

Herrero, Javier. "The Ending of *Lazarillo*: The Wine against the Water." *MLN* 93 (1978): 313-319.

—. "The Great Icons of the *Lazarillo*: The Bull, the Wine, the Sausage and the Turnip." *Ideologies and Literature* 1 (1978): 3-18.

Iarocci, Michael P. "Alegoría, parodia y teatro en el Lazarillo de Tormes." *RevistaCanadiense de Estudios Hispánicos* 19 (1995): 327-339.

Lázaro Carreter, Fernando. Lazarillo de Tormes *en la picaresca*. Barcelona/Caracas: Ariel, 1972, 1978.

Lewis, R.W.B. *The Picaresque Saint*. Philadelphia/New York: J.B. Lippincott, 1956.

Márquez Villanueva, Francisco. *De la España judeoconversa*. Barcelona: Bellaterra, 2006.

—. "El *Lazarillo* y sus autores." *Revista de Libros* 90 (June, 2004): 32-35.

—. *Espiritualidad y literatura en el siglo XVI*. Madrid/Barcelona: Alfaguara, 1968.

McGrady, Donald. "Social Irony in *Lazarillo de Tormes* and its Implications for Authorship." *Romance Philology* 23 (1970): 557-567.

Nepaulsingh, Colbert I. *Apples of Gold in Filigrees of Silver*. New York/London: Holmes & Meier, 1995.

Neusner, Jacob. *Invitation to Midrash*. Atlanta: Scholars Press, 1998.

Perry, T. Anthony. "Biblical Symbolism in the *Lazarillo de Tormes*." *Studies in Philology* 67 (1970): 139-146.

Preuss, James Samuel. *From Shadow to Promise*. Cambridge, MA: Harvard UP, 1969.

Ricapito, Joseph V. "'Cara de Dios': ensayo de rectificación." *Bulletin of Hispanic Studies* 50 (1973): 142-146.

Rico, Francisco. *La novela picaresca y el punto de vista.* Barcelona: Seix Barral, 1989.

Shipley, George A. "Lazarillo de Tormes Was Not a Hardworking, Clean-Living Water Carrier." *Hispanic Studies in Honor of Alan D. Deyermond.* Madison, WI: Hispanic Seminary, 1986: 247-255.

—. "The Critic as Witness for the Prosecution: Making the Case against Lázaro de Tormes." *PMLA* 97 (1982): 179-194.

—. "Lazarillo and the Cathedral Chaplain: A Conspiratorial Reading of *Lazarillo de Tormes*, Tratado VI." *Symposium* 37 (1983): 216-241.

Sieber, Harry. *Language and Society in* La vida de Lazarillo de Tormes. Baltimore/London: Johns Hopkins UP, 1978.

Sitler, Robert. "The Presence of Jesus Christ in *Lazarillo de Tormes*." *Dactylus* 12 (1993): 85-97.

Stone, Robert S. *Picaresque Continuities.* New Orleans: UP of the South, 1998.

Torrico, Benjamín. "Retorno al 'Paraíso panal': Derecho civil y canónico como claves eucarísticas en el Tratado Segundo de *Lazarillo de Tormes*." *Hispanic Review* 74 (2006): 419-435.

Wardropper, Bruce W. "The Strange Case of Lázaro Gonzales Pérez." *MLN* 92 (1977): 202-212.

Weiner, Jack. "La lucha de Lazarillo de Tormes por el arca," in *Actas del III Congreso Internacional de Hispanistas.* Mexico City: Colegio de México, 1970: 931-934.

Wills, Garry. *Why Priests?* New York: Viking, 2013.

Yovel, Yirmiyahu. *The Other Within.* Princeton: Princeton UP, 2009.

INVECTIVE AND HUMOR IN THE POETRY OF DANTE AND CECCO ANGIOLIERI[1]

NICOLINO APPLAUSO

Medieval invective poetry poses many questions to modern readers. Why does an author ridicule an individual or an entire society with aggressive words articulated in poetry? Is it simply to shock an audience and generate laughter for its own sake? Or does the author use laughter to stir their sense of responsibility toward the wrongdoing of specific individuals and groups? By employing as examples a selected canto from Dante's *Commedia*, and one of the most irreverent sonnets by Cecco Angiolieri, this essay seeks to address these questions through a cultural and literary exploration of poetic invective.

Invective is generally defined as the practice of verbally insulting, attacking and ridiculing an opponent. I relate invective to its etymological and historical significance as it refers to the past participle of the Latin verb *invehi* (to inveigh against) and the noun *invectiva* (vituperation, reproachful speech). The usage of the term *invectiva* is first documented in the fourth century to describe polemical writings (Ricci 406). It is then widely used during the early and late Middle Ages for any kind of denunciatory speech in situations of controversy and dispute.

In general, invectives are launched to demolish the image of an opponent, be it an individual, a group, or a city. In classical antiquity, invective was essentially *ad hominem.* Fashioned in verse, it was chiefly delivered publicly for the purpose of persuading an audience with forensic or deliberative arguments against a named individual or for launching a grievance (Watson 762; Rutherford 6). During the Middle Ages, it was used in a variety of settings and applications: in courts through forensic speeches; at the diplomatic level through epistolography; pedagogically, in centers of learning through the study of rhetoric and theology; and in

---

[1] I would like to thank F. Regina Psaki for her valuable comments, the Oregon Humanities Center for providing me with the Graduate Dissertation Fellowship, which enabled me to complete this study in 2010, and finally my dear wife Jeannette for her encouragement and support.

creative writing through the exchange of poetry. Lawyers, notaries, professors, theologians, and poets launched invectives against different targets during debates and controversies (Rao 113).

The importance of using humor to foster ridicule through hyperbolic and malevolent caricatures is consistently stressed in early rhetorical and grammatical treatises that confirm that humor was the basic component of invective.[2] Scholars have recently examined the connection between the verbal attack of invective and its resulting physical violence in medieval society.[3] Several studies have illustrated numerous episodes such as street fights or even riots caused by slanderous insults, and showed the existence of severe laws created to punish whoever composed or sang invective poetry against citizens or prominent political leaders.[4] Very few studies, however, have explored the dimension of humor in invective poetry and the continuity between "language intended to harm and the same language which is intended to amuse" (Forest-Hill 9). This double-edged value of humor is attested in ancient rhetorical manuals (Cicero, *De Oratore*, II.218-219) and also in the writings of St. Thomas Aquinas, who distinguishes between defamation, which is associated with anger and envy, and mockery, which may provoke both lighthearted and hostile laughter (Forest-Hill 7-9). Aquinas even justifies its usage in the theatre when dramatists employ it for the purpose of both entertaining and instructing their audience.

During the Middle Ages, the practice of invective shows a distinct complexity and authorial resourcefulness in the municipal areas of the northern Italian *comuni* (municipalities) of Florence, Siena, Pisa, Bologna, and Mantua through visual art and literature (Ortalli 25-71; Suitner 179-212). It is especially apparent in literary works of the late thirteenth and early fourteenth centuries, such as Dante's *Divina Commedia* and the sonnets of Cecco Angiolieri.

---

[2] See for example Aristotle's *Poetics* 48b37; Cicero, *De Oratore* II, 216-289; and Quintilian, *Institutio Oratoria* VI.3.

[3] See for example the special issue of *Atalaya* on *L'invective au Moyen Age: France, Espagne, Italie*, and Florence Garambois-Vasquez's *Les invectives de Claudien, Une poétique de la violence*.

[4] See Trevor 114-116 and Suitner 57; 163. In Siena, the law against the practice of singing and reciting invective songs was first promulgated in c. 1260-1270 and subsequently (with the explicit reference to sonnets) in c.1300-1302; see Mecacci 141. See also my article"S'i' fosse foco ardere'il mondo: L'esilio e la politica nella poesia di Cecco Angiolieri"forthcoming in *Letteratura Italiana Antica: Rivista annuale di testi e studi*. XIV (2013).

Dante's *Commedia* is known for the bitterness and contentiousness of its invectives, notably in *Purgatorio VI*, which contains his most violent and blunt assaults against the defaults of his society. This 75-line invective, the longest of the *Commedia*, is set in the *Antepurgatorio* where the souls of those who had neglected their religious obligations and died a violent death await entry into Purgatory proper. The invective begins after the momentous encounter between the poets Sordello and Virgil who, realizing that they both are from Mantua, embrace each other warmly (l. 75). Though the invective is generally considered just what Dante called it, a "digression" (l. 128), it is significant for the forcefulness of its language as it divides into four parts the object of its attacks: Italy, the papacy, the empire, and finally the city of Florence.

This invective displays a wide variety of rhetorical strategies, including irony, metaphor, onomatopoeia, anaphora, and hyperbole. Its rhymes resemble speech, deploying less melodic effect and more emphasis on the harsh and pungent sounds audible already in the opening lines:

> Ahi serva Italia, di dolore ostello,
> nave sanza nocchiere in gran tempesta,
> non donna di province, ma bordello! (ll. 76-78)

> Ah, servile Italy, hostel of grief,
> ship without pilot in great tempest,
> no mistress of provinces, but [a] brothel! [Singleton 59] [5]

The corrosive bitterness of the words "nocchiere" or "bordello" is evident not only at the acoustic level in the arrangements of harsh consonants and vowels, but also in the content. Italy is compared to a slave who collects grief and sorrow, to a boat without a pilot during a storm, and to a disoriented prostitute going from one whorehouse to another.

As a corollary of the art of vituperation, churlish or malevolent laughter comes at the expense of others and has the ethical function of denouncing those who have strayed from the proper path. Such a practice is well-documented by medieval school manuals such as Matthew of Vendôme's *Ars Versificatoria* (c. 1175), Averroes's Middle Commentaries, Herman the German's translation of Averroes' commentary (c.1256), and

---

[5] From here on, all quotations from Dante are from Giorgio Petrocchi's *La commedia secondo l'antica vulgata*. All English translations are by Charles S. Singleton.

William of Moerbeke's translation of Aristotle's *Poetics* (c. 1278).[6] In his treatise "for the advancement of learning," Matthew acknowledges that laughter is a response to poetic attacks, but warns detractors about a type of "loud laughter" that "is barren and fruitless" (25). He advises these detractors that if they pursue it, a sure punishment by arrow and pestilence awaits them (26). Outlining and following his own rhetorical guidelines, Dante offers an invective related to the function of corrective comedy by representing evil actions in order to reprehend vice and encourage its avoidance. The invective launched at the end of the canto is thus grounded in a moral matrix where the harsh, violent attacks serve both the rhetorical means of persuading an audience to condemn specific wrongdoings, and the practical aim of eliciting in readers the response of disdain expressed with a type of laughter tinged with anger.

The choice of specific terms with comic resonance supports this claim. The term "bordello," as numerous early commentators highlight, literally denotes a house of prostitution but also seems to allude, from the context, to a state of confusion (as it still does in modern Italian).[7] This two-fold allusion comes at the expense of the objects of the invective, not only the medieval political and religious institutions of empire and papacy, but also specific historical individuals. These individuals include the emperor Albert I of Austria, "Alberto Tedesco" (97), current members of the clergy, "people who are supposed to be truly pious" (91), and Dante's own contemporary citizens of Italy. All are reproached for their dishonesty, cowardice, and irresponsibility, and blamed for the current "bordello."

The emperor becomes a ridiculous representation of evil for his failure to fulfill his role of designated guide. In Dante's poetic realm, the citizens of several Italian cities such as Rome and Florence literally gnaw at one another even within their very city walls (l. 83). The final lines of the invective portray Florence as a deliriously sick woman "who cannot find repose upon the down / but with her tossing seeks to ease her pain (ll. 149-151)." This bizarre suffering puts her in restless motion and makes her a tragicomic character. She turns from one side to the other, like a broken spinning top. Her motion becomes part of an absurd construct that evokes the playful image of the "gioco de la zara," a game of dice (l. 1), at the opening of the canto. In the particular setting of the bed, a sexual allusion

---

[6] See Alfie 22.

[7] See for example Francesco da Buti who in his commentary (1385-95) defines the term "bordello" as a "ritenimento di meretrici." Singleton also emphasizes the meaning of the term as a "house of prostitution." Modern commentators usually interpret the term as a metonymy for "prostitute." The cited commentaries are available online at the *Dartmouth Dante Project*: http://dante.dartmouth.edu/

also emerges. By choosing the specific setting of the bed, Dante suggests that Florence also acts like a prostitute as she swings from one suitor to another exclusively for her own economic gain. This possible allusion could have elicited a malicious snicker in Dante's target readers especially if we consider its connection with a popular proverb (Mattalia 151) from Dante's time: "Firenze non si muove, se tutta non si dole" ("Florence does not act unless she is all cracked" [Villani 451; my translation]"). The second line of the proverb reinforces Dante's last lines, which further underline Florence as a comic persona who is motivated solely by self-interest, and who takes late action when the crisis has already reached catastrophic proportions.

A similar bond between vituperation and humor is clearly visible in Cecco Angiolieri's most irreverent sonnet, "S'i' fosse foco, ardere' il mondo." Among the substantial corpus of 111 sonnets attributed to Cecco, "S'i' fosse foco" is by far the most renowned and widely anthologized. Cecco, who is commonly associated with the tradition of the "comico-realisti," is highly regarded as a stylistic innovator of comic parody and subversive innuendo. However, he is less commonly associated with the tradition of medieval invective. Nevertheless, his sonnet "S'i' fosse foco" with its implicit impersonation of current political and religious figures, contains aggressive attacks against all of mankind, prominent political and religious leaders, and finally the poet's own parents and compatriots.
An example of the verbal violence of Cecco's poem is immediately visible in the opening sequence of threatening nouns and verbs, which describe the whole world burned by fire, buffeted by wind, drowned by water and finally thrown into a dark abyss:

> S'i' fosse foco, ardere' il mondo;
> s'i' fosse vento, lo tempestarei;
> s'i' fosse acqua, i' l'annegherei;
> s'i' fosse Dio, mandereil en profondo; (ll. 1-4)

> If I were fire, I would burn down the world;
> If I were wind, I would buffet it;
> If I were water, I would drown it;
> If I were God, I would hurl it into the depths;[8]

The reproaches then become more personalized to Christians[9]:

---

[8] Cecco Angiolieri's sonnet is from Antonio Lanza's *Le rime*. The English translation is mine.

s'i' fosse papa, serei allor giocondo,
ché tutti ' cristiani embrigarei;
s'i' fosse 'mperator, sa' che farei?
a tutti mozzarei lo capo a tondo. (ll. 5-8)

If I were Pope, I would then be joyful,
because I would harass all the Christians;
if I were emperor, you know what I would do?
I would chop off everybody's head at once.

The last two tercets take an enigmatic turn. Cecco, now apparently impersonating himself, redirects his attack onto his own parents:

S'i' fosse morte, andarei da mio padre;
s'i' fosse vita, fuggirei da lui:
similemente faria da mi' madre. (ll. 9-11)

If I were Death, I would visit my father;
if I were Life, I would flee from him;
similarly would I do with my mother.

And then against his fellow citizens:

S'i' fosse Cecco com'i' sono e fui,
torrei le donne giovani e leggiadre:
le vecchie e laide lasserei altrui. (ll. 12-14)

If I were Cecco, as I am and have been,
I would snatch the young and lovely women
and leave the old and ugly ones to others.

In these stanzas, which deal with the hypothetical murder of Cecco's father and mother and the rape of the handsomest young women, the setting is most likely the city of Siena. This is confirmed by the fact that the Sienese author discloses his own identity to the readers (l. 12), and creates a visible downshift from the broader cosmic apocalyptic scenario

---

[9] The term "cristiani," in medieval as in modern Italian, often denotes just "people" (as opposed to beasts) (*Dec.* IV. 5, for example). With this term, Cecco could also refer to medieval Europeans all assumed to be under the rule of the pope and emperor. The term then could be translated as "Christians" or, from Cecco's point of view, even as "mankind."

of the early lines to the more constricted environment of his parent's city, thus suggesting that the final tercet of the invective takes place within his own city walls (ll. 13-14). If we consider this possibility, we might be able to interpret this comic shift as an expression of a mischievous transgressiveness against his own compatriots. Furthermore, the fact that the author evokes himself so explicitly suggests that this final attack could be interpreted in biographical terms.

For reasons not clear (there is no archival evidence, only the poet's own intimations[10]), it seems that Cecco had been exiled at one time from his birthplace. If we may theorize about an unsubstantiated reality, the poet may be alluding here to his personal stance toward issues such as banishment and injustice, and could also be projecting (most likely jokingly) the menace of his potential return. The series of hypotheses from the previous stanzas persuasively creates the effect that the last "si" is another hypothesis as well. The ambiguous rhetorical structure of the last three lines may be an emphatic taunt to the reader rather than a mere premise: "I am who I am." If indeed Cecco is referring to his estrangement from Siena and the complicity of his own compatriots, then through a mocking construct he may be conveying the following warning: "If I were who I really am and was (and I am who I say I am), I am coming back to Siena and I will seize all the pretty women, leaving you all with only the old and ugly ones." Within this statement he seems to pose a hidden question: "What would you do about it?" Such being the case, this verse could elicit uneasy laughter among many readers faced with the author's derisive and violent invective and their vulnerability before its implications.

In his influential study *Cultura e stile nei poeti giocosi* (1953), Mario Marti emphasizes that critics of the post-Risorgimento endorsed a reading of Cecco's poetry as autobiographical, underlining the writer's psychological discontent and dissent against his own time (119-129). As a reaction to this excessively biographical interpretation, Marti developed a strict formalistic approach that drew attention to the stylistic elements contained in medieval comic poetry. Despite a few valuable studies that attempted to mediate between the biographical and stylistic readings, the mainstream tendency of more recent critics, such as Raffaella Castagnola and Paolo Orvieto, has been to focus primarily on the stylistic elements of Cecco's poetry, and to evaluate its rhetorical subversion and parody of

---

[10] See the three sonnets "Se Die m'aiuti, a le sante guagnele," "Questo ti manda a dir Cecco, Simone," and "Dante Alighier, s'i' so' buon begolardo."

other poetic styles, such as the *Stilnovo* and courtly poetry.[11] However, what these stylistic interpretations seem to neglect is the bitter accusations that characterize Cecco's invective poetry and its interaction via humor (through allusions and exaggerations) with a specific contemporary audience. The sonnet's rhetorical structure suggests this interaction from its very opening to its close, as the dual aspect of violence, both literal and hypothetical (in the "se...," elided into "s'i"), instills memorable images that are fictional but also concretely provocative and aggressively polemical.

In the second quatrain readers are confronted with destructive acts of aggression and execution evoked by the verbs "embrigarei" (to harass) and "mozzarei lo capo" (to chop off someone's head). The effect of violence is palpable not only in the content but also phonetically in the repetition of the "r" and "z" sounds in these words. If we read the poem aloud, the two verbs create an effect of dissonance within the metrical equilibrium of the sonnet that even a modern ear can recognize. But the hypothetical frame of the "se" and the comic standpoint of the attack are just as important. By Cecco's impersonating the pope and the emperor, the poetic "I" hurls a comic verbal assault against those agents of power, making them perform hideous deeds with no particular motive, and thus turning them into ridiculous objects of the invective as well. As Menotti Stanghellini suggests, the verb "embrigarei" could refer to the practice of excommunication performed by the pope, while the decapitation enforced by the emperor could describe his most common and simple means of execution (110-111). The damnation and decapitation of all "cristiani," endorsed respectively by the hypothetical Cecco-pope and Cecco-emperor, could reflect the poet's own political environment (which was recognizable to and "enjoyed" by the medieval reader).

Like Dante's invectives, Cecco's sonnet seems both to criticize the institutions of papacy and empire generally, and perhaps also to ridicule the excessive ferocity of the popes and monarchs who ruled when Cecco wrote this sonnet (c.1290-1312); e.g., the Popes Boniface VIII (1294-1303) and Clement V (1305-1314); the Emperor Henry VII of Luxembourg. (c.1275-1313) and the French King Philip the Fair (1285-1314) among others. During this time, the papacy and the various secular monarchies and principalities clashed repeatedly against one another. They also experienced serious domestic tensions due to local criticism of

---

[11] See Franco Suitner's groundbreaking study, *La poesia satirica e giocosa nell'età dei comuni*, in which he proposes a comparative and comprehensive reading of Cecco and other comic poets by providing a solid cultural and historical frame, thus employing both the biographical and formalist interpretations (99-100).

their political schemes. For example, as John Watt notes, the influential Colonna family was vehemently opposed to the pontiff because "his pursuit of territorial aggrandizement, necessarily at the expense of even grander families, inevitably aroused their hostility" (159). In 1297, "the Colonna communicated their accusation against Boniface" while "papal legates throughout Italy were preaching a crusade against them" (Ibid. 159-160). King Philip the Fair encountered a similar unpopularity with his legacy of numerous executions (as in the war in Flanders, 1290-1305) and later unpopular persecutions and exterminations, such as the well-known suppressions of the Knights Templar in 1307 (Burman 259).

Far from being an example of a generic literary practice, or a mischievous whirl, or a sketchy reflection of the poet's anger and verbal aggressiveness, "S'i'fosse foco" addresses serious issues from the perspective of a poet engaged with the tensions of his own time. Both the elements of threat and the comic exaggerations contained in his sonnet could be intended as elements carefully constructed to stimulate the audience's response, a response through laughter that ultimately interacts with the author's stance on challenging questions. The interrelation between authors and readers through this ethic is not inert or unilateral but rather a dynamic expression of an encounter with the other.

In short, invective in medieval Italian poetry is both an indictment of an abusive society and a call for action by its citizenry. Dante's invective assails the emperor's irresponsibility, the clergy's dishonesty, the pope's corruption, and his compatriots' selfishness as ethical counter-models and primal causes of the present state of disorder and paralysis. Cecco's sonnet represents the absurd role played by violence in a make-believe world where the emperor, the pope, and even the poet himself play pernicious roles in a world doomed by wrongdoing. Once the audience recognizes its own responsibility in the perpetuation of these injustices, once the morbid laughter has "stuck in its throat," the final stage of awareness between the reader and the author has been reached.

Works Cited

Alfie, Fabian. *Dante's Tenzone with Forese Donati: The Reprehension of Vice*. Toronto: University of Toronto Press, 2012.
Angiolieri, Cecco. *Le rime*. Ed. Antonio Lanza. Rome: Archivio Guido Izzi, 1990.
Aquinas, St. Thomas. *Summa Theologiae*. Trans. Marcus Lefébure, 60 vols. London: Eyre and Spottiswoode, 1975.

Aristotle. *Poetics with the 'Tractatus Coislinianus.' Reconstruction of 'Poetics* II' *and the Fragments of the 'On Poets.'* Trans. Richard Janko. Indianapolis: Hackett, 1987.

Averroes. *Averroes' Middle Commentary on Aristotle's Poetics.* Trans. Charles E. Butterworth. Princeton: Princeton University Press, 1986.

Burman, Edward. *Supremely Abominable Crimes: The Trails of the Knights Templar.* London: Allison & Busby, 1994.

Castagnola, Raffaella. *Cecco Angioleri: Rime.* Milan: Mursia, 1995.

Cicero. *De Oratore.* Ed. H. Rackham. Trans. E.W. Sutton. Vol. 1. London: St. Edmundsbury Press, 1988.

—. *Rhetorica ad Herennium* Trans. Harry Caplan. London: William Heinemann, 1981.

Dante, Alighieri. *La Commedia secondo l'antica vulgata.* Ed. G. Petrocchi. 4 Vols. Milan: Mondadori, 1966-67.

—. *The Divine Comedy.* Trans. Charles S. Singleton. 3 vols. Princeton, N.J.: Princeton University Press, 1970- 1975.

Dussol, Étienne. "Petite introduction à l'invective médiévale." *Invectives: Quand le corps reprend la parole.* Eds. Didier Girard and Jonathan Pollock. Perpignan: Presses Universitaires de Perpignan, 2006. 160-173.

Forest-Hill, Lynn. *Transgressive Language in Medieval English Drama: Sign of Challenge and Change.* Aldershot: Ashgate 2000.

Garambois-Vasquez, Florence. *Les Invectives de Claudien: une poetique de la violence.* Brussels: Editions Latomus, 2007.

Grant, Mary A. *The Ancient Rhetorical Theories of the Laughable: The Greek Rhetoricians and Cicero.* Madison, WI: University of Wisconsin Press, 1924.

Herman the German. "Averrois expositio poeticae." *Aristoteles Latinus.* Ed. L. Minio-Paluello. Vol 33. Brussels: Descée De Brouwer, 1968. 41-74.

Marti, Mario. *Cultura e stile nei poeti giocosi.* Pisa: Nistri-Lischi, 1953.

Mattalia, Daniele. *La Divina Commedia. Purgatorio.* Vol. 2. Milan: Rizzoli, 1975.

Matthew of Vendôme. *The Art of Versification.* Trans. Aubrey E. Galyon. Ames, Iowa: State University Press, 1980.

Mecacci, Enzo. *Condanne penali nella Siena dei Nove: tra normative e prassi. Frammenti di registri del primo Trecento.* Siena: Università degli Studi di Siena, 2000

Ortalli, Gherardo. *La pittura infamante nei secoli XIII-XVI.* Rome: Jouvence, 1979.

Orvieto, Paolo and Lucia Brestolini. *La poesia comico-realistica: dalle origini al Cinquecento.* Rome: Carocci, 2000.

Quintilian. *The Orator's Education.* Ed. and trans. Donald A. Russell. Cambridge, MA: Harvard University Press, 2001.

Rao, Ennio. *Curmudgeons in High Dudgeons (?) : 101 Years of Invectives (1352-1453).* Messina: Edizioni Dr. Antonio Sfameni, 2007.

Ricci, Pier Giorgio. "La tradizione dell'invettiva tra il Medioevo e l'Umanesimo." *Lettere Italiane* 4 (1974): 405-414.

Rutherford, David. *Early Renaissance Invective and the Controversies of Antonio da Rho.* Renaissance Text Series 19. MRTS 301. Tempe, AZ: Renaissance Society of America, 2005.

Stanghellini, Menotti. *Cecco Angiolieri: Sonetti.* Siena: Edizioni il Leccio, 2003.

Suitner, Franco. *La poesia satirica e giocosa nell 'eta dei comuni.* Padua: Antenore, 1983.

Villani, Giovanni. "Cronica di Giovanni Villani." *Croniche di Giovanni, Matteo e Filippo Villani secondo Ie migliori stampe e corredate di note filologiche e storiche: testo di lingua.* Vol. 1. Trieste: Tipografia del Lioyd Austriaco, 1857.

Watson, Lindsay, C. "Invective." *The Oxford Classical Dictionary.* 3rd ed. 2003.

Watt, John. A. "The Papacy." *The New Cambridge Medieval History: c. 1198-c.1300.* Vol. 5. Ed. David Abulafia. New York: Cambridge University Press, 1999. 107-163.

William of Moerbeke. "De arte poetica." *Aristoteles Latinus.* Ed. L. Minio-Paluello. Vol. 33. Brussels: Descée De Brouwer, 1968. 3-37.

V.

LAUGHINGSTOCK

HUMOR AND IDENTITY IN PANCHO GUERRA'S
LOS CUENTOS FAMOSOS DE PEPE MONAGAS
AND IN CHO JUAÁ'S ILLUSTRATIONS

MARÍA-JESÚS VERA CAZORLA

This paper explores the relationship between humour and identity in the works of two well-known Canarian authors, *Los cuentos famosos de Pepe Monagas* by Pancho Guerra and *Humor Isleño* by Eduardo Millares, better known as his own character, Cho Juaá. An analysis of some typical scenes in the stories and of the use of language will show the crucial role that membership in a particular cultural group plays in the interpretation of jokes.

Backgrounds

In the late 1970s, the Commonwealth of Councils of Las Palmas, with the collaboration of San Bartolomé de Tirajana Town Hall and the help of the president of the "Pancho Guerra Association" in Madrid, decided to edit and publish in four volumes the collected works of Francisco Guerra Navarro, known as Pancho Guerra. To illustrate them they engaged a number of famous artists from the Canary Islands such as Felo Monzón, Creagh, Manuel Padrón Noble and Eduardo Millares Sall (also known as Cho Juaá), some of them related to the so-called "Canarian native art movement." This artistic movement sought not only to capture certain aesthetic values of Canarian pre-Hispanic culture, but also aimed at reflecting what they called the essential features of the landscape and the rural life of the islands, undistorted by romantic myths. The painters questioned the myth of the Fortunate Islands[1]; they revealed the hidden

---

[1] According to Marcos Martínez (2002, 23-24), the Canary Islands have experienced from the beginning of their history a process of mystification that few lands in the world have undergone. Four factors have favored this concentration of the mythical and extraordinary in the archipelago: the island, the mountain, the ends of the known world and the climate factor. Martínez (2002, 27) and Bello Jiménez (2005, 71), among other researchers, have stated that classical Greek and Roman authors

image of the Canaries, reevaluating its history and capturing the feel of its unique natural frame. They copied images and symbols from our aboriginal world; they depicted the inhabitants of the cliffs of Las Palmas and the figure of the sharecropper to mirror the world of the lower classes, and they painted the arid landscapes of the southern part of the island. The Canarian art historian Fernando Castro notes that "for the first time in the history of the Canary Islands, there is a need to establish an artistic tradition that opens a process of reflection on the signs of identity of Canarian culture and of Canarians' place in the world; that is, a process that could reflect both our ways and how to interpret our social reality" (Castro Borrego 2012).[2]

Among the illustrations of Pancho Guerra's work, Cho Juaá was both the main character of Eduardo Millares Sall's artistic production and his alter ego. In fact, Millares used this pseudonym to sign his own writings and cartoons. When drawing some of the scenes of the Cuentos, he used a cartoon very similar to his own Cho Juaá to depict Pepe Monagas, with the subsequent consequence that for many Canarians Pepe Monagas and Cho Juaá share the same physical appearance: he is a tall strong man with a belly; he is wearing a white shirt, black trousers, the typical Canarian hat or "cachorra" and a black sash where anyone could see the typical "naife" (knife). It is my belief that both Pancho Guerra and Cho Juaá's (Eduardo Millares') work forged the image of the typical Canarian and helped in the construction of Canarian identity.

Humor and identity

The identity of a person or a group can be expressed in several ways, specifically by taking into account their "nationality, geographical location, ethnicity, gender, social class, occupation, etc." (Swann et al., 140). However, it is generally accepted that identity is "in large part established

---

considered these islands heaven on earth, a blissful paradise where they thought mythical lands such as the Elysian Fields, the Fortunate Isles, the Islands of the Blessed, the Atlantis, the Garden of the Hesperides or the island of Saint Brendan were found. Among these records, Pliny the Elder, who refers to the Fortunate Isles several times in his writings, mentions a Carthaginian general's expedition to West Africa during which he made out a high white mountain (possibly the Teide volcano in Tenerife), also the news that king Juba from Mauritania sent an expedition to the Fortunate Isles and they came back with two huge dogs. The Latin word for dog, *canis,* is sometimes quoted as one of the possible origins of the islands' name (Blanco 1976, 15-17; Abreu 1978, 209-211).

[2] This was an online quotation from a talk by Castro Borrego. The translation is mine.

and maintained through language" (Gumperz 7). From a psycholinguistic perspective, Kachru (1992) argues that social identity is acquired together with the mother tongue and that, along with this social identity, a personal or individual identity is also forged. Sociolinguistic research, in turn, shows that "language can act as a vehicle for conveying important social information about the speaker" and that "certain linguistic features come to be associated with particular local characteristics" (Dyer 101). In other words, phonetic, lexical and syntactic peculiarities frequently lead us to identify the speaker's geographical origin, and humor is perhaps the most revealing.

In *Personality and Sense of Humor*, A. Ziv states: "Cohesion is one of the main characteristics of groups. [...] A cohesive group provides its members with defense from external forces" (32). According to Martineau's model for the social functions of humor, humor not only strengthens ties between the group members and raises their morale, but also contributes to the maintenance of consensus and narrows social distances. Pancho Guerra and his illustrators' work meet these two objectives of the social function of humor mentioned by Martineau. First, it helped to lift the spirits of Canarian citizens during some difficult times in Spanish history, such as post Spanish Civil war, when the existence of a character who faced the financial difficulties of the moment but still wanted to enjoy life was very much needed. Secondly, this type of humor strengthens ties and group cohesion: the Canarian against the mainland Spaniard or the foreigner. No wonder there are so many foreigners and Spaniards in Pancho Guerra's stories and Cho Juaá's cartoons. The group is able not only to understand the joke but also to grasp the background of certain comic situations with their social references or cultural implications.

In the introduction to the 1969 edition of Cho Juaá's *Humor isleño*, J. A. Alemán maintains: "Whoever sees these cartoons has to be able to identify to some degree those antecedents that cannot be embedded in the cartoon. Perhaps this difficulty is what makes some people dislike Cho Juaá's jokes, but Millares cannot be blamed; he gives the precise elements, but the reader is not sufficiently imbued with the necessary atmosphere." Canarian writers and illustrators have a common language and their own vocabulary and expressions, and language serves the dual purpose of identifying the group members and differentiating them from the others. The Canarian variety of Spanish is one of the main sources of humor in these two works as are foreigners' attempts to communicate with their poor command of Spanish.

The humor of Pepe Monagas

In the introduction to the 1961 edition of Cho Juaá's *Humor isleño*, the well-known Canarian poet Pedro Lezcano stated that "humor and tragedy, although distant, inhabit the same world, and that there is a relationship between irony and comedy. […] Great humor rises gracefully and without rancor from misfortune, for laughter is the way in which simple people express their ancestral philosophy of resignation" (Lezcano 1961). Similarly, in the 1969 introduction of *Humor isleño*, José A. Alemán speaks of "quiet fatalism." *Los cuentos famosos de Pepe Monagas* by Pancho Guerra and *Humor isleño* by Cho Juaá are both comic and tragic at the same time; they are comic in their scenes, characters and the language they use, but also tragic and sad in their portrayal of the hunger and misery many people suffered at that time. The stories also reflect the longing of a provincial society that admires and envies the rich foreigners who visit the islands.

Los cuentos famosos de Pepe Monagas, published between the years 1976 and 1978, is a series of short stories normally with no real beginning or end. The protagonist is Pepe Monagas, a 20th-century picaresque character who, in post-Spanish civil war times, does whatever he can to provide for his family. In some stories he undertakes little assignments, usually legal, to get some money. Thus, he is seen painting a house, taking care of little children, training the parrot of a Cathedral canon to sing the aria «Ritorna vincitor» from the opera Aida, selling brooms he had "borrowed" from a nearby stall, guiding tourists or driving a carriage. And although he sometimes works, he is most remembered for his famous aphorism "Todo aquel que trabaja es porque no sirve pa otra cosa" (Guerra 384), that is, "People work only if they're no good for anything else."

His neighbours call him for help or as a mediator, but especially when there is a party. Witty, mischievous, funny, there is a mixture of admiration and greed in his attitude towards the English visitors, the major group of tourists in the islands, whom he really likes much better than Spaniards and considers an endless source of money. In turn, Cho Juaá's cartoon scenes offer insights from everyday life to which the reader has to add the context of what preceded them and what they expect will follow. The vignette is an economical and brief artistic medium which requires from its author a large process of synthesis so that the reader can infer what happened before the depicted scene and understand what could happen later.

There are certain characters and topics that appear in both works repeatedly. The most significant characters are the country bumpkin, the tourist with his money and weird habits, and the mainland Spaniard; the most common topics deal with the hardships of an era. These are the classic types:

1. The country bumpkin

Both Pepe Monagas and Cho Juaá could be considered country bumpkins, even though they live in Las Palmas de Gran Canaria. The way they speak and dress, their habits and hobbies and especially their sense of humor make both characters clear representatives of the romantic concept of being a Canarian. According to Franck González (430), relying on the model outlined by Canarian cartoonist Diego Crosa in 1900, the archetype of the country bumpkin has become the authentic backbone of the islands' graphic humor for roughly one hundred years. Crosa's peasant contrasted with the negative image of the countryman first depicted in the islands in 1784 by Juan de la Cruz (428).

Initially mocked, the country bumpkin soon evolved into the emblem of the "common man", culminating in the fifties and sixties as the mythical symbol of cultural resistance in the hands of Eduardo Millares. The figure of the country bumpkin would become an ideal. Emerging from his portrait as a free man during the Romantic period, he came to embody Canarian identity during years marked by major structural changes in the islands. Pepe Monagas, with his popular wisdom and sense of humor, remains a clear representative of the concept of being a Canarian, while Cho Juaá's image in the sixties as a symbol of cultural resistance started to fade with the arrival of Spanish television, mass tourism and the landing of peninsular labor in the islands (González 430-431).

2. Mainland Spaniards

Closely related to the concept of the genuine Canarian is that of the Other. There are many instances of the presence of the Other in Canarian writings, primarily of the mainland Spaniard and the British, the latter not only as a tourist but also as a permanent resident. When considering otherness, Petersoo proposes a typology of Others based on two dyads: external versus internal and negative versus positive, resulting in four ideal types (120). In general, it could be said that in the Canaries, while the Englishmen are the external positive Other, Spaniards are usually the internal negative Other (depicted in many folk stories and songs with aquiline noses, fricative sounds and pretensions of superiority). A specialist on cultural pluralism, the Greek scholar Anna Triandafyllidou notes the significance of this Other: "it serves to overcome crises because it unites the people in the face of a common enemy; it reminds them of 'who they are' and emphasizes that 'we are different and unique'" (cited in Petersoo 119).

According to Franck González (399), although the presence of Spaniards had been uncommon since the time of the Spanish Conquest, during the 1950s and sixties there began a significant surge of settlement by continental Spanish citizens in the Canary Islands. At that time, three important factors contributed to establishing an identity relationship between the country bumpkin (either in its most archetypal figure as Cho Juaá or any other) and being Canarian, and between the mainland Spaniard and Spain. The first factor was an important migratory flow; the second, the 1964 arrival of Spanish television in the Canaries, an event that institutionalized a strong linguistic acculturation process; and the third, the beginning of the tourist boom.

From the time of his appearance in Cho Juaá's imaginary world in the fifties, the typical image of the mainland Spaniard in Eduardo Millares' work is that of a man with a prominent nose who is always dressed in a jacket and a tie (Gónzalez 398-399). This portrait would be accentuated by the use of terminology eminently from the Iberian plateau. Once again, the mimicking or disparagement of the Other's language serves as a cohesive device. Foreign tourists also appear in some stories of Pepe Monagas and in several of the Cho Juaá vignettes. In his research on graphic humor in the islands from 1808 to 1998, Franck González states that tourism, which began in the last decades of the 19th century, contributed a new character who is generally identified with the British tourist and is known as "mister" or "choni," a popular derivation from the diminutive "Johnny" (445).[3] In fact, foreigners appear in some of Pepe Monagas' stories and in some of Cho Juaá's cartoons. These foreigners are basically the English, although Pancho Guerra distinguishes between English residents in the islands and tourists, both groups united as an endless source of money.

When dealing with the role of the mainland Spaniard in both Pancho Guerra and Cho Juaá's work, language is a vital tool to create humor and to distinguish the native from the outsider. Moreover, both of these authors imitate the sounds and expressions used by visitors when trying to communicate with Canarian people; and Pancho Guerra is especially adept at reproducing the attempts of many Englishmen to speak Spanish: their difficulties in pronouncing the "r" or the "j" sounds, their changing of the gender of certain Spanish words, the verb tenses and forms, and other typical problems. There are four stories with an English character always involved in a funny situation or a joke in *Los cuentos famosos de Pepe Monagas*. Among them are: "When Pepe Monagas Outdid Some *Chones*

---

[3] It is interesting to note that the tourist does not appear in mainland political cartoons until the era of Franco and especially in the last decades of the twentieth century.

Who Were Boasting" and "When Pepe Monagas Made a Tourist Mad." In all of them, their speech when speaking Spanish is transcribed exactly as it sounds.

In the first of these scenarios (Guerra 360-361) Pepe is showing the city of Las Palmas to a group of pseudo-tourists—that is, some sailors who have just landed in the port. Half of them are British and the other half American, but they are all "chones," that is, "Johns," or "foreigners." For hours Pepe has been taking them to different parts of the city when an Englishman comments that the whole population of Las Palmas could fit into a London park, that it isn't true that San Antonio was the church where Columbus prayed before leaving on his trip to America, and so on and so forth. Pepe just keeps quiet, and then an American begins to talk about New York and says in broken Spanish:

> —Nousogtros en Ameggica tenegmos a unos siroujanos especialesss… A oun solgdado delg Pacífico le llevó ouna bala de canión una piegnna entegra. Oun cirougano amegicano le opuso ouna mecánica y ahoga es el mejor cogedor del moundo. ¡Ooooh!

> We Americans have special surgeons. When a cannon bullet took away a Pacific soldier's leg, an American surgeon gave him a mechanical one and now he is the best runner in the world. How about that![4]

The Englishman replies:

> —¡Ouug, señoggg! Eso nou es nagda. En Inglategra oun mégico inglés pouso a oun soldado ingless que él había pegdido aun brazo entegro oun brazo mecágnico. Y él volgvió a hasegrr sus cosas togdas del bragso. Y hoy él es el megorr vioulinisgta del moundo…

> Oh, man! That's nothing. In England an English doctor put a mechanical arm on an English soldier who had lost his arm. And he went on using the arm as if nothing had ever happened. And now he's the best violinist in the world…

Things get more and more heated and neither tourist can agree on whose country is more prodigious than the other, until Pepe chimes in about a

---

[4] All translations are mine.

Canarian boy who was working digging a well when a gunpowder explosion blasted off his chest from his Adam's apple to his guts. So a doctor from the island took the breast from a goat and "grafted" it onto the boy and now he is producing milk without that cow-y, sheep-y froth.

In "When Pepe Monagas Made a Tourist Mad" (Guerra 449-451), Pepe this time is driving a typical Canarian carriages. Although he does not understand a word of what a tourist utters, he takes him to different sights in Las Palmas: San Telmo Park, the Cathedral and the like. The tour over, Pepe takes his fee out of a wad of cash produced by the tourist, but the latter complains because he thinks it is too much. He looks up in the dictionary the word "fee" in Spanish, which is "tarifa," and shouts "¡Tagifa, tagifa!" With the noise a crowd gathers around Pepe and the tourist, and a local policeman arrives and asks what the problem is. Quickly, Pepe tells the policeman that the tourist wants him to take him to Tafira, a village close to Las Palmas, and that due to the heat and the state of his horse he cannot drive him there—all this while the poor tourist keeps shouting "¡Tagifa, tagifa!"

Since for many Canarians foreigners are notorious for their appearance and clothing, this can be seen in some of the cartoons of Cho Juaá's *Humor isleño*. In one cartoon, a local policeman scolds a man in unseemly walking shorts wearing a hat with a flower and carrying a camera: "Don't you know that you can't walk like that on the street?" The confused tourist says "Mi no comprende" and the policeman answers "¡Aah, sorry. You are a foreigner. Go on, go on." In another cartoon, a tall couple in bizarre clothes is walking along the street while a lady dressed in black tells a friend "¡Ay, Saturninita, Carnival is coming soon!" and the other answers: "Carnival? No, my child, don't you see they are tourists?" Aside from their eccentric clothes, tourists sometimes behave in astonishing ways, such as when they get undressed or nearly so on the beach. And so we have another cartoon in which an old Canarian woman complains: "I do not know if he is a Swede or a Dane. All I can tell you is that he was naked."

As in Pancho Guerra's stories, Cho Juaá's cartoons also prove how tourists are an attractive source of income. They seem rich and willing enough to spend the "pound." In a street we find a taxi-driver, a man in black and a foreigner in shorts and a flowered shirt holding a map. The taxi-driver asks the man in black: "Marsialito, how much could I charge this choni to go from the Port to the Cathedral?" and the man answers: "Well, I think twenty 'duros'." The taxi-driver continues: "How do you say that in English?," and the other answers: "Tell him, uan pon" (a phonetic approximation of "one pound"). "And if he wants to go to Tafira [a town near Las Palmas]?" Marcialito answers: "¡Ooh, pon, pon" (pronouncing the word "pound" Canarian style). Finally, the taxi-driver exclaims: "Well, at that rate, if we go to Mogán [the farthest village on the island] this pon, pon, pon, pon, one after the other, is going to sound like a machine gun...ya know, mister?"

It is difficult to translate a comic novel or play, especially when humour lies more in its form than in its meaning; and although it is possible to paraphrase the meaning of a sentence, the vocabulary and the expressions are often lost. For this reason we believe these typically Canarian works are fundamentally untranslatable. Furthermore, many of the words and expressions used in the two books are also, regrettably, disappearing from the current Spanish of the islands. The media, the national education system in the 60s and 70s with teachers from mainland Spain correcting pronunciation and vocabulary, and the lack of prestige related to Canarian Spanish have contributed to this fact. Ironically, these are the very factors that led to the creation of such characters as Pepe Monagas and Cho Juaá.

In conclusion, at a time when many Canarians felt their identity threatened by the arrival of mainland Spaniards and tourists, Pepe Monagas and Cho Juaá became symbols of Canarian culture and identity. Contrary to these outsiders, they represented the shrewd down-to-earth common man. Pancho Guerra and Eduardo Millares Sall (aka Cho Juaá) endowed them with the characteristics that Canarians believed were their own indigenous traits, from an ironic understanding of human nature and their "bananafied" idiosyncrasies to a roguish sense of humor. Physically, they resemble a country bumpkin, and when they speak, both characters use the Canarian variety of Spanish, considered to be "uneducated" and disreputable due to its differences in pronunciation and vocabulary from standard Castilian Spanish. Despite the fact that they could both be considered of "lower class," Canarians soon romanticized these symbols of cultural resistance and identified their features with that of the real Canarian.

A final note: From the time these characters appeared in the 1960s and 1970s many things have changed in the Canary Islands politically, socially and culturally. Since 1982 the archipelago has become one of the Spanish Autonomous Communities and an Outermost Region of the European Union, and Canarian history, culture and variety of Spanish have been widely recognized and studied. Yet the process of acculturation that produced Guerra's and Millares' characters has ultimately contributed to the disappearance of many of the expressions and vocabulary necessary to be able to follow these works. Nowadays, a large number of Canarian people cannot understand much of the language used to recount Pepe Monagas' adventures.

Works Cited

Abreu Padrón, Adolfo. "Historia de las Islas Canarias", in *Natura y cultura de las Islas Canarias*, edited by Pedro Hernández Hernández. La Laguna: Litografía A. Romero, S.A., 1978.

Alemán, José A. "Cho Juaá", in Millares Sall, E. *Humor isleño*. Las Palmas de Gran Canaria: Imprenta Lezcano, 1969.

Bello Jiménez, Víctor M. *Allende las columnas. La presencia cartaginesa en el Atlántico entre los siglos VI y III a.c.* Las Palmas de Gran Canarias; Ediciones Anroart, 2005.

Blanco, Joaquín. *Breve noticia histórica de las Islas Canarias.* Las Palmas de Gran Canaria: Ediciones del Excmo. Cabildo Insular de Gran Canaria, 1976.

Castro Borrego, F. "La pintura canaria en el siglo XX", accessed October 22, 2012, <<http://www.gevic.net/>>

Dyer, Judy. 2007. "Language and identity," in Llamas, Carmen, et al. (eds.). *The Routledge Companion to Sociolinguistics.* London and New York: Routledge, 2007.

González, Franck. *El humor gráfico en Canarias. Apuntes para una historia (1808-1998).* Las Palmas de Gran Canaria: Ediciones del Cabildo de Gran Canaria, 2003.

Guerra, Pancho. *Los cuentos famosos de Pepe Monagas.* Las Palmas de Gran Canaria: Excma. Mancomunidad de Cabildos de Las Palmas-Ayuntamiento de San Bartolomé de Tirajana, 1976.

Gumperz, John J. (ed.) *Language and Social Identity.* Cambridge: Cambridge University Press, 1982.

Kachru, Braj B. *The Other Tongue: English across Cultures.* Urbana & Chicago: University of Illinois Press, 1992.

Lezcano, Pedro. Prologue "Cho Juaá", in Millares Sall, E. *Humor isleño.* Las Palmas de Gran Canaria: Imprenta Lezcano, 1961.

Martineau, W. H. "A Model of the Social Functions of Humor". *The Psychology of Humor.* Eds. J. H. Goldstein and P. E. Mhee. New York: Academic Press, 1972

Martínez Hernández, Marcos. *Las Islas Canarias en la antigüedad clásica: mito, historia e imaginario.* Tenerife and Gran Canaria: Centro de la Cultura Popular Canaria, 2002.

Millares Sall, E. *Humor isleño.* Las Palmas de Gran Canaria: Imprenta Lezcano, 1961 &1969.

Petersoo, P., "Reconsidering Otherness: Constructing Estonian Identity," in *Nations and Nationalism* 13, (2007): 117-133.

Swann et al. 2004. *A Dictionary of Sociolinguistics.* Edinburgh: Edinburgh
    University Press, 2004.
Ziv, A. *Personality and Sense of Humor.* New York: Springer Publishing
    Company, 1984.

PARODIES OF DON JUAN IN THE TALES OF CLARÍN AND GALDÓS

MARÍA MONTOYA

The presence of a Don Juan in the Spanish narrative dates back to the publication in 1880 of *Don Juan Solo*, a novel by José Ortega Munilla, followed in 1895 by "El caballero de la mesa redonda" ("The Knight of the Round Table"), a tale by the Asturian novelist Leopoldo Alas (Clarín), and two novels by Benito Pérez Galdós, *La desheredada* (*The Disinherited Woman,* 1896) and *Misericordia* (*Compassion*, 1897).[1]

As Ignacio Javier López notes in his study of *donjuanismo*, the myth of Don Juan Tenorio that realist writers caricature in the novels of the late 19th century is the one that appears in the romantic portrayals of the *folletín* genre (popular serialized stories), not the one created by Tirso de Molina.[2] "The irony that will characterize the description of Don Juan in the novel,"observes the critic, "arises from the double contrast between reality and appearance, and between mythical model and conventional follower" (López 17).[3] This contrast is particularly evident in Clarín's novelette and in Galdós's *Misericordia*. In both works we find a

---

[1] José Ortega Munilla (1856-1922), father of José Ortega y Gasset, was a journalist and novelist of moderate renown within the realist-naturalist movement of late 19th and early 20th century Spain. Benito Pérez Galdós (1843-1920), arguably Spain's foremost novelist, and Clarín (1852-1901) were among its finest exponents. Actually, the seven parts that make up "The Knight of the Round Table" appeared in 1896, although the first four parts had already come to light in *Revista de Asturias* in 1885.

[2] Don Juan Tenorio, the protagonist of Tirso de Molina's *El burlador de Sevilla o el Convidado de piedra* (*The Stone Guest,* 1630) is not a lover but a cynic, a deceiver, a mocker of all conventional values, spiritual, moral or civil. In this Counter-Reformational drama, Don Juan is eventually dragged to Hell by the stone figure of a man he killed and whose daughter he had deceived into seduction. It is not until José de Zorrilla's wildly popular romantic drama, *Don Juan Tenorio* (1844), that the notorious libertine is saved from perdition by the love of one of his own victims.

[3] All translations in this essay are mine.

discernible parody of the romantic ladies' man, as the interplay between reality and appearances holds the two antiquated *tenorios,* Don Mamerto Anchoriz and Ponte Delgado, up to ridicule.

Don Mamerto Anchoriz, the protagonist of "El caballero de la mesa redonda," is an aging but still attractive Don Juan: "He was tall and burly, fair-skinned and soft, with a delicate little hand and pink nails" (Clarín 381). The portrayal of Clarín's character is based on the ambivalence of his physical description. This technique of contrasts, used to the highest degree by the Romantic writers, acquires here an ironic tinge that insinuates the possibility of an effeminate seducer, although the reputation of Don Mamerto is that of a famous Don Juan. "For half a century," says the narrator, "he had been seducing both married and single women, widows and nuns, marchionesses and trimmers, village girls and dancers" (381). For *el fiscal* (the prosecutor), a regular visitor to the spa in Termas-Altas where Clarín's story is set, the amorous conquests of Don Mamerto are unseemly, since the gentleman who draws the admiration of the hotel guests merely acts like "a dirty old man" (380). These words remind us of the short story by precisely that title, "Un viejo verde," that Clarín wrote in 1893 about the relationship between a beautiful young woman and her older admirer. Carolyn Richmond cites in her first note to "Un viejo verde" the novelist's words on this subject: "Nothing is more disgusting than an old man who's still active 'in the flesh', and nothing is more interesting than an old man who's still active in spirit and mind" (Clarín 124). Indeed, in "El caballero de la mesa redonda," Clarín draws with singular subtlety the figure of a seducer past his prime.

The self-centeredness of Don Mamerto and his lack of generosity or concern for the good of others are the target of the narrator's ironic comments in section IV of the story. "Never in his whole life had he been seen at a funeral, nor visited the sick, nor given alms, nor lent a penny or done a favor for anyone" (382). His vanity as a womanizer is constantly evident, as if he were always "on stage." He primps and fusses with himself, trying to hide the advent of years with cosmetics and spas: "With his fine black and white straw hat, round and narrow-brimmed, he greeted the guests, while the majestic and benevolent smile of his thin pink lips glowed under the tightly curled moustache poised between his thick black shiny sideburns" (381). Nevertheless, Don Mamerto represents for the locals a unique model for his spiritual and physical virtues: "Oh, Anchoriz! A perfect gentleman! And how well-preserved!" (384).[4] Don

---

[4] "His caricature," notes Marta E. Altisent, "is based on the interplay between reality and appearances articulated in three motifs: i) the challenge of the ladies' man to age, or false biological impasse achieved by cosmetics...; ii) the spa, as a

Mamerto's only concern is to get to enjoy perfect health and to appear to be young, which he thinks he can attain by refraining from any type of reading. Illness and literature appear as two inseparable evils, since for him healthy people have no time or need for reading. His tremendous presumption even leads him to think that he can avoid death, as "this is only a word, a threat, a fantastic creation" (385).

In part V, we witness one more "performance" by don Mamerto before his audience, the hotel guests of Termas-Altas. Everyone wants to hear the news that "the flamboyant rooster" brings from the city, listening with rapt attention to the stories about "weddings, dances, love and gambling scandals" (386). The scene, although described very briefly, reminds us of a similar scene when Álvaro Mesía, in *La Regenta*,[5] recounts his love affairs to the dinner guests gathered at the Casino. Don Mamerto, to satisfy his pride in being an irresistible lover, invites *la fiscala* (the prosecutor's wife) to dance, proving to the hotel guests that there is no woman in the world who can resist the sweetness of his charm, not even his enemy's wife. *La fiscala* accepts his invitation, seduced by "that handsome evergreen" (387). This world sustained by shallowness and the desire to be admired is subtly criticized by the narrator, a witness of the events (in the story's introduction he identifies himself as one of the spa's visitors), by emphasizing the absence of values beyond the purely earthly. "With no more than a fine invitation, a gallant gentlemanly look, and some smiles in which health and good lineage served as poetic spirituality, Anchoriz had seduced *la fiscala*" (387). At the end of this section, the narrator recounts the illness of the protagonist, who becomes at this point a "failed Tenorio" (389). The parody works therefore on two fronts: first, the fact of his being a sick old man clashes with the archetype of the romantic, ever young Don Juan; on a second level, the allusions suggested by both the title and the text reinforce the parodic nature of the character, since his chivalry is more feigned than real.

---

metonymic extension of his persona, ... a space for enjoyment and concealment of old age; iii) the gossip, as an ubiquitous choir that celebrates and mocks anyone who doesn't follow conventions" (185).

[5] *La Regenta* (*The Judge's Wife*, 1885), Clarín's masterpiece and arguably the best 19th-century Spanish novel, is a tale of adultery set in Vetusta (identifiable with Oviedo, the capital of the province of Asturias). Doña Ana Ozores, "la Regenta," married to a man far older than herself, falls eventually into the arms of Álvaro Mesías, Vetusta's aging Don Juan.

Section VI introduces the major changes that are going to take place in
the final weeks of the useless libertine: the beginning of his relationship
with *la fiscala* and the abandonment by his admirers as his disease
progresses. Don Mamerto (seducer) and *la fiscala* (seduced woman) have
now reversed with a kind of grotesque resonance the roles they had
previously performed in the dance scene. Don Mamerto begins to feel
attracted by the sweet attention he receives from the lady he at first
disdained: "It was a delight to feel how she would maneuver about with
delicate and efficient movements that seemed like caresses and medicines"
(391). Until the moment of falling sick, Anchoriz was a mere puppet, an
actor devoted to play the role of an irresistible lover who lives an eternal
youth. Subtly, the narrator's detailed enumeration of the objects found on
Don Mamerto's dresser reinforces the theatrical nature of his character:
"dozens of combs, hair brushes, nailbrushes, toothbrushes, syringes; also
dozens, hundreds of cans, bottles, jars, cosmetic bars, triangles of tulle to
set his mustache, soap boxes, mysterious chemical artifacts... and over a
thousand boxes of cheap toiletries, as in an actor's dressing-room" (390).

Stripped of his acting mask, Mamerto begins to become aware of the
farce performed by the people around him, and the hypocrisy that
transpires in "the minutiae of ordinary life": "Not all that glittered was
gold. He realized that for most of the guests, taking care of him was an
entertainment. Many would pretend they were doing something. And not a
few began to lose heart" (391). Still, pride and vanity prevent him from
accepting in others the behavior that he identifies with his own: "They
were doing with him what he had always done with them. However, it was
not the same. For others to do it was wrong" (Ibid.).

In his study of *donjuanismo* and death in the works of Clarín, Douglas
Rogers notes that when the time for truth arrives, both Zorrilla's Don Juan
and   Clarín´s Don Mamerto must face the consequences of their behavior.
The theatrical Don Juan will experience fear and penitence before he is
ultimately redeemed by love, while the novelesque Don Juan will discover
the horror of loneliness (Rogers 334.) The Don Mamerto admired,
applauded and even envied by the hotel guests, is now a lonely and sick
old man. No one comes to visit him, except for *la fiscala*, the "only kind
soul" (393) in the Termas-Altas hotel. The loneliness of the protagonist
gradually deepens with the worsening of his disease: employees and
bathers leave the resort for fear that Anchoriz' ailment is typhoid fever. At
the same time, the empty lounges and the silence that has taken the place
of meetings and card games anticipate the proximity of death: "there was

no other journey but to bring him back to the bedroom again, which
seemed to him like the waiting room to the grave" (Ibid.).

Anchoriz, the seducer of the most beautiful women in the region, is
dying, accompanied by the bony figure of *la fiscala*, who in his delirium
he has mistaken for the specter of death. The last lines of the story reveal
an extremely pathetic scene when Don Mamerto, from his deathbed, sees
la fiscala entering his room, "horrible in her midnight ugliness, brought
there by a spirit of charity [...] or by some prurient curiosity [...] or was it
by some kind of love, ridiculous and romantic" (394)?

***

The character of Frasquito Ponte from Galdós' *Misericordia* embodies
in the same way the figure of the decrepit lover. The first details about Mr.
Ponte reach the reader through the opinions of other characters of the
novel, a technique already used by the writer in *La desheredada*. In her
description of Don Frasquito, Doña Paca, the spendthrift mistress of
Benina, the novel's leading character, claims that "he is a good person, a
gentleman of principles" but also "older than a palm grove" (Galdós 122).
When Benina tells her mistress about Ponte's grinding poverty, Doña Paca
reminds her that in her time "he was a bachelor who lived the good life.
He had a good job, ate in the homes of the rich, and spent his nights at the
Casino" (Ibid.). The features noted so far (gentlemanly conduct, single, old
and fond of worldly pleasures) are similar to those indicated in the figure
of Don Mamerto. Both of them coincide likewise in their excessive desire
for pretending what they are not. Anchoriz wants to appear before society
as the eternal lover; Ponte, on his part, tries to hide at all costs his financial
ruin before the people of his same social class: "Frasquito would rather
starve to death than do something without dignity" (161).

On the other hand, the narrator's portrayal of Don Frasquito elicits in
the reader a certain compassion for this "withered lover" (173) and does
not distance us from his character as it did with Don Mamerto. In
Misericordia, irony is not presented with the same critical eye that we
found in "El caballero..." On the contrary, there is a hefty dollop of
sympathy and even humor in depicting the failed Don Juan. "Don
Frasquito was what is commonly called a kind soul ... He possessed the
unusual privilege of a physical preservation that could compete with that
of the mummies of Egypt, and that neither time nor hardship would alter"
(157).

Vanity, another feature of Don Mamerto, is also apparent in Ponte
Delgado's demeanor. Don Frasquito, the man of "sparse eyelashes,

creased eyelids, long crows' feet" (158), is proud of his curly locks and dainty feet. The emphasis, however, is not on the character's self-centeredness but rather on his absurd and ridiculous personality and his ploys to pass as a fine gentleman: "no one knew like him how to use benzene for cleaning grime, or how to hand-iron creases, stretch shrunken clothing, and mend knee patches" (158), nor could they could figure out how he gave volume to the loops of his long hair. All this highlights the comic side of Ponte, absent in the description of Don Mamerto.

Both the hairstyle of Don Frasquito—"he wore his hair long, not in the romantic style, disheveled and fluffy, but the way that was in style in the 50s" (157)—and his old- fashioned ideas symbolize, according to Luciano García Lorenzo, "the unaltered continuation of attitudes from the times of Isabel II, before the Revolution of 1868 and throughout the period following Restoration" (163).[6] Ponte Delgado's life, in this sense, represents a stage in the political history of Spain:

> His decline did not begin to manifest itself in a notorious
> way until '59; he fought heroically till '68, and in that year,
> marked in the tablet of his destiny with very dark strokes,
> the unhappy lover fell into the depths of poverty, and did not
> rise again. (160)

The extraordinary ability that Ponte has to escape reality and settle in the fantasies he shares with Obdulia, the daughter of Doña Paca, is the main feature of this Galdosian character. The past of the decrepit Don Juan becomes the center of the anecdotes he recounts to the young lady. In these stories he appears as the gentleman who rubs shoulders with the cream of Madrid's society, the romantic follower of Italian opera, the enthusiastic admirer of Gregorio Romero Larrañaga's melodramatic verses[7] and "other bards of those foolish times" (164)—the talk of an "elegant fossil" (165), a set of clichés, the prototype of the romantic hero of the early decades of the 19th century. Don Frasquito not only likes to boast of his former love affairs but also to portray himself as starring in duels with "vigilant husbands or angry brothers" (165). He is the actor

---

[6] Queen Isabel II reigned for twenty-five years (1843-1868) at the end of which the "Glorious Revolution" of September 1868 toppled her from power. After a brief period of republicanism, the Bourbons were restored to the throne when Alfonso, Isabel's son, was proclaimed king of Spain in December 1874.
[7] Gregorio Romero Larrañaga (1814 -1872), a second-rate Romantic novelist, playwright, and poet.

who plays—in home theaters—the lead in the most popular *zarzuelas*[8], or the nostalgic who remembers "that grand party, attended by the Calabrian bandit" (166). The parody of the romantic libertine is also obvious in the ironic tone adopted by the narrator: "Day after day, he would talk about the ups and downs of his social life, which contained all the varieties of naive debauchery, poor elegance and refined nonsense" (165).

The ladies' man who dazzles Obdulia with the stories of his trips to Paris and his visits to the sites that the "great men" knew (168) remains in reality a "poor starving fellow" (156). He survives with the help of Benina, as she knows better than anyone else the gentleman's weak points. García Lorenzo notes in his introduction to the novel the "squirely attitude" (170) of Don Frasquito, as reflected in both his behavior and his language. Thus, the *peseta* he receives from Benina is, in his words, "a loan" (177), even though he knows beforehand that he will not be able to return it.

The friendship that Ponte strikes up with Benina bears some similarity to the relationship between Don Mamerto and *la fiscala*. In both cases, we are faced with two actors playing their role by pretending what they are not, and who feel attracted by women who do not stand out precisely for their vitality or beauty. However, as was the case with the description of the two characters, the humor of the situation reveals itself more strongly in Galdós' novel than in the short story by Clarín:

> The good man expressed his gratitude almost exclusively to Benina, reserving for the lady a polite deference; all his smiles were for Benina, his most ingenious sentences, the tenderness of his languid eyes, like puppy-dog eyes; to so many indiscretions Ponte added calling her two hundred times in the course of the frugal dinner. (218)

Death will also put an end to the career of this truncated Tenorio. Don Frasquito, moved by the desire to impress Doña Paca and her daughter Obdulia, decides to ride around as he used to do in the lush years of his youth. The scene that parodies this romantic vignette concludes with a tragicomic end. Ponte falls off his horse "like a sack half empty" (294) making a fool of himself in the sight of his friends: "and as soon as they put him on his feet he began to shout, red like a turkey, reviling the cart driver who, according to him, was to blame for the accident" (Ibid). The situation is resolved with a paradox since after this blow, "Frasquito Ponte is confronting the middle class, to which he had belonged, by mainly

---

[8] Zarzuelas, Spanish musical plays consisting of spoken dialogue, songs, choruses, and dances, reached the height of their popularity in the late 19th century.

reproaching its ingratitude" (García Lorenzo 304). In the moments before his death, Ponte Delgado, like Don Quixote, opens his eyes to the true reality and not that of his fantasies, to criticize the hypocrisy and selfishness of the social class which he hitherto defended and now rejects for the first time. Yet for Doña Paca and her family, his words amount to the speech of a madman.[9]

In her essay "Romanticism as Hipotext in Realism," Biruté Ciplijauskaité notes that "Romanticism may be present in realistic work as an assimilated technique, as a subject to criticize, or as a caricature to parody both the subject and the technique" (91). In the years that Galdós wrote *Misericordia* and Clarín wrote "El caballero de la mesa redonda," Romanticism represented a set of literary clichés in the work of the realist writer instead of an influence on his style. In the novels and story presented here, parody aims at unmasking those clichés in the figures of two out-of-date *tenorios*.

Works Cited

Altisent, Marta. "El topos del 'viejo verde' en un relato de Clarín." *Bulletin of Hispanic Studies* 75: 183-199. 1998

Ciplijauskaité, Biruté. "El romanticismo como hipotexto en el realismo". In *Realismo y naturalismo en España en la segunda mitad del siglo XIX*, edited by Yvan Lissorgues, 90-97. Barcelona: Anthropos. 1988

Clarín, Leopoldo Alas. "El caballero de la mesa redonda" (1895).   In *Treinta relatos*, edited by Carolyn Richmond, 371-394.   Madrid: Espasa-Calpe. 1983

—. "Un viejo verde." Ibid.

López, Ignacio Javier. *Caballero de novela. Ensayo sobre el donjuanismo en la novela española moderna, 1880-1930*. Barcelona: Puvill. 1986

Mandrell, James. *Don Juan and the Point of Honor*.   University Park, Penn: Pennsylvania State University Press. 1992

Pérez Galdós, Benito. *Misericordia* (1897). Introduction and notes by Luciano García Lorenzo, 11-53 and 61-318. Madrid: Cátedra. 1982

Rogers, Douglass. "Don Juan, *Donjuanismo*, and Death in Clarín". *Symposium* 30: 325-42. 1976

---

[9] The Galdosian novel, *Doña Perfecta* (1876), also features another obsolete suitor in the character of Don Juan Tafetán, who in his youth had been "un Tenorio formidable" (130). See James Mandrell, *Don Juan and the Point of Honor*.

POSTMODERNISM AND HUMOR
IN SINDO SAAVEDRA'S *CUENTO, LUEGO EXISTO*

DOLORES MARTÍN-ARMAS

> *El humor postmoderno renuncia de partida a mostrar en primer plano los aspectos oscuros o desagradables de la realidad. Le interesa lo lúdico, lo brillante, lo festivo, lo espectacular, lo estrafalario, lo llamativo.*
>
> *Postmodern humor refuses offhand to highlight the dark or unpleasant aspects of reality. It stresses the amusing, the intriguing, the festive, the spectacular, the off-beat, the titillating.*
>
> — Alejandro Romero

Sindo Saavedra, who was born in 1948 in Las Palmas (Canary Islands, Spain), and died in 2005 at the age of 57, is an example of a "postmodern" in the broadest sense of the word. Known primarily as a composer, singer and folklorist, he composed an operetta and a musical and is the author of the hymn of the Carnival of Las Palmas. When he died he was about to open his first painting exhibition. As a narrator, *Cuento, luego existo* (*I Am a Storyteller, Therefore I Am*) (2002) is his only published book.

Cuento, luego existo is a collection of 15 short stories with titles that evoke diverse genres and literary productions, musicals and films. For example, they include such pieces as "La metamorfosis de la virgen," "Mary la ladrona" ("Mary the Thief"), "El cartero siempre mata dos veces" ("The Postman Always Kills Twice"), "El contrato de Doryan Gray," and "La vita é bella."

Before opening the book, the first thing one notices is that the cover is completely blank—not a word, not even a title. The name of the publisher is missing. However, the work contains an original jacket cover—a collage with drawings that evoke the comic strips and at the same time represent all the images that one will encounter at the beginning of each story. The artist of the drawings is Antoine. On the back cover are photos of the author and the illustrator and logos of the organizations and businesses that collaborated in the publication of the volume.

The second thing that stands out is the prologue, which is signed by Gabino Diego, a theater and film actor and interpreter of comic roles. After some brief words of thanks, Gabino Diego says that he intends to preface the work in such a way that it will conform entirely with its content. He writes:

> Dear Sindo: I've received the manuscript of your book of short stories and the collages of Antoine. I'm very flattered that you want me to write a prologue, and although it would be easy for me to describe clearly and simply how clever and funny your writing is, I'm not going to do it in the usual way. I prefer to follow your lead and maintain as much as possible your originality, so here comes my prologue. (9)[1]

From here Diego continues with 32 lines of letters and symbols that convey no content whatsoever. In my view this does not capture the totality of the book. After reading the prologue it seems that we will encounter a cryptic text, a hieroglyphic impossible to be deciphered, but that is not the case at all.

Postmodern art and literature criticize the system of categories that order modern society. They reject the definitions and barriers between disciplines (academic and nonacademic), and call into question the difference between reality and fiction. "It [postmodernism] is not simply an attack on the modern vocabulary" says George Ritzer, "it is an attack on a way of ordering the world" (quoted in Romero). The postmodern features in this work by Saavedra are expressed in various ways, among them for example, is his combination of narrative with the collages by Antoine and the musical notations that accompany the songs and verses of the stories "El as es sino" and "El as es sino" (2). (Notice the play on the words "asesino" ["assassin"] and "as... sino" ["ace," "star," or "destiny"].) Although many of the stories contain parodies of literary works and references to Hollywood movies, they are unique in the humor they project

---

[1] This and all other translations in the text are mine.

through the subversion of narrative and generic models and the unconventional use of language.

Madrid

Querido Sindo:

Recibo los textos de tu libro de cuentos y los collages de Antoine. Me halaga el que quieras que te escriba el prólogo y, aunque podría poner en él, de una manera clara y sencilla, todo lo de ingenioso y divertido que tienen tus escritos, no voy a hacerlo de forma convencional: prefiero seguir la línea del libro y, por lo tanto, estar lo más acorde posible con la originalidad de tu obra, así que paso a prologar este último trabajo tuyo:

Un saludo

Gabino Diego

9

Critics seem to agree that humor is a characteristic of postmodernism, but there exist various theories about how it uses humor and the disagreements are palpable. Some scholars call it parody or pastiche, while others say that parody is different from pastiche. For example, Fredric Jameson says that in the context of postmodernity pastiche takes the place of parody:

> Pastiche is, like parody, the imitation of a peculiar and unique, idiosyncratic style, the wearing of a linguistic mask, speech in a dead language. But it is a neutral practice of such mimicry, without any of parody's ulterior motives, amputated of the satiric impulse, devoid of laughter and of any conviction that alongside the abnormal tongue you have momentarily borrowed, some healthy linguistic normality still exists. Pastiche is thus blank parody, a statue with blind eyeballs. (17)

The critic Jorge Ruffinelli alleges that postmodernity celebrates the de-sacralization of the artistic product and its replacement by the consumerism of "mass culture…the commercialization of knowledge and art, the denial of individualism and originality, the conversion of literature into a game without cognitive functions or social commitment, and an emblem of intranscendency" (32). Linda Hutcheon, on the other hand, argues that the irony of postmodernist parody is replete with meaning; that it probes our intrinsic values, our historical traditions and our political systems. In fact, postmodern parody has a wide range of forms and purposes, from the ridiculous and playful to the severe and humorless (*Irony's Edge* 2), and Sindo Saavedra explores them all.

Cue*nto, luego existo* moves away from critical intention in many of the stories, but in others its deconstruction of myths through literary humor involves serious criticism, especially of such values of modern society as virginity, beauty or material acquisition. The sense of parody within every story is apparent because all of them conclude with a literary quotation related to the content of the story. These quotations come from different sources: Pancho Guerra's *Los cuentos de Pepe Monagas*, Dante's *Divine Comedy*, Robert Louis Stevenson's *Treasure Island*, Friedrich Nietzsche's *Thus Spoke Zarathustra; On Narcissism* by Sigmund Freud, Jean Genet's *The Thief's Journal*, and others by Dashiell Hammett, Epicurus, Calderón de la Barca, Lorca, and Victor Hugo. However, the overall transposition of thematic elements and of the characteristics, personality and motivations of the protagonists is so far removed from the original that each of

Saavedra's stories becomes a totally new piece. Perhaps less disengaged from the model are the stories in verse, "El as es sino" and "El as es sino 2," which are actual parodies of *El burlador de Sevilla* and *Don Juan Tenorio*.[2] The other tales should be considered pastiche, and the use of irony as Saavedra's predominant technique serves merely to provoke the reader to laughter. To a certain extent Saavedra's book does reflect the kind of humor that Gille Lipovetsky defines in his book *La era del vacío (The Era of Emptiness)*—a humor that vulgarizes and trivializes whatever it touches, that seeks only the cheap laugh, with unheroic "heroes" who see only the surface of life and couldn't care less (142). Giving examples of the humor in advertising, animation and the comic strips, Lipovetsky insists that today's humor eliminates the negative aspect of earlier satire or caricature, substituting for it an uninhibited adolescent kind of comedy of gratuitous absurdity and zero intellectuality (140).

Despite this blanket condemnation, the use of irony in *Cuento, luego existo* can be classified according to the various types that Hutcheon defines in *Irony's Edge*. Irony as an assault against conventional institutions and attitudes is evident, for instance, in "Mary the Thief." The episode takes place on a television show called "The Hall of Wanted Thieves," where the woman guest is one of the most famous thieves of the moment and is introduced to the audience in this way: "This evening we're going to have the pleasure of getting to know in depth the adventures of a woman who is completely dedicated to her profession—a dangerous and demanding profession wherever it may be—a woman who has devoted her whole life to holding up banks of every kind [...] from neighborhood branches and savings and loan associations to large and powerful financial institutions" (83-84; my translation).

Socially conscious or satirical irony is not very abundant in Saavedra's collection, but it is particularly noticeable in the description of many of his characters, both male and female. Take, for example, this depiction of the 29-year old Catalina Sosa, from "The Metamorphosis of the Virgin":

> Su estatura no era baja sin que por ello fuese alta, aunque la media melena rubia, que se le derramaba, sin gracia maldita, por su reducida espalda, la hacía parecer un poco raquítica y torsicorta. . . . y tenía una dentadura vivaracha, perturbadora y algo saltona, aunque bastante blanca, que le dificultaba cerrar del todo la boca; pero aun siendo bien parecida...

---

[2] *El burlador de Sevilla... (Tirso de Molina); Don Juan Tenorio... (Zorrilla)*

vestía de forma inapropiada para su edad: blusa blanca de volantes y manga larga, falda de tablas a cuadros verdes, negros y rojos, . . . y unas gafas de cristal grueso, que, en conjunto, le daban el aspecto de una vegetariana intelectual del Opus Dei. (13)

She was neither short nor tall, although the blondish mane of hair spilling gracelessly down her small back made her look a bit scrawny and short-waisted. She had a stunning set of teeth, quite white really, but so large and protruding that she could hardly close her mouth; but even with those good looks, she dressed inappropriately for her age: a white ruffled blouse with long sleeves and a pleated skirt with green, black and red checks... and she wore such thick Coke-bottle lenses that she ended up looking like a vegetarian intellectual from Opus Dei.

On the other hand, her boyfriend, Agapito Del Campo,

[e]ra atractivo, fastuoso y sensual, pero bruto e ignorante hasta el enojo y la pena. Llevaba puesto un pantalón tejano, ceñido, del que destacaba un tremendo bulto que disculpaba su ignorancia, y una ajustadísima camiseta marlonbrandianatranvíadeseo que le marcaba hasta el alma. (13)

...attractive, well-dressed and sexy, but so stupid and ignorant he could drive you up a wall. He wore tight Texan jeans that revealed an enormous bulge that compensated for his ignorance, and a clinging Marlon-Brando-Street-Car-Named Desire tee-shirt that showed off everything right down to his soul.

The best example of Saavedra's humor is his use of language—popular slang, expressions drawn from the palette of the collective imagination, ungrammatical, and defiant of any formal linguistic structure (Ruffinelli 40), all of which are prevalent throughout *Cuento, luego existo*.

Predominant in some of the stories are the well-recognized words and expressions of the inhabitants of the Canary Islands. These words in the mouths of the characters or the narrator accentuate the humorous content, especially for Canarians. Like the tales of Pepe Monagas, Saavedra's stories also capture their often crude manner of speaking. For example, in the first story, "Metamorphosis", the protagonist, Agapito del Campo, is a character who is unrefined and uneducated, and these characteristics are reflected in his speech. Here are some examples. Agapito begins:

> "Ante la atrasión sexuá, cucha bien, Catalina, no hay curtura ni arrefinamiento que valga, ¿tú me oíte?" "--Qué burro eres, mi amor, pero qué burro eres…, mi amor." -- "Pos sí, de burro lo tengo tóo, eh; quej'eso lo que ves en mí, ¿no?, que tarde ha sío, pero ma dao de cuenta de que eres una viciosecilla." (15)

> "When it comes to sex, listen, Catalina, culture and refinement ain't worth a damn, you hear? --"Oh, you're such an animal, honey, you're such an animal…" --"You bet I am. And that's what you see in me, right? After all this time I just found out you're a pretty hot babe."

Another of Saavedra's linguistic devices is fabricated words derived from names. For example, in "El Parlamento" the narrator says:

> Le informó, sobreactuando, que sí, que era la Mujer Pirada ¿y qué?, y que era como era, y que tenía ese carácter tan agrio, áspero y avinagrado porque se vio obligada a abandonar el encaje de bolillo y a surcar por los Mares del Sur, ya que a su esposo, el apuesto corsario *Barbaestreisan*, lo había matado la machona filibustera *Barbaestanwick*. (45)

> She informed him, melodramatically, that yes, she was the proverbial Angry Woman, and so what?, that's the way she was, and she had that dour, harsh, vinegary character because she was forced to give up her bobbin lace and surf the Seas of the South since her husband, the dashing pirate Barbastreisand had been killed by that butchy buccaneer Barbastanwick.

Another characteristic of his language is the imitation of dialectal accents, such as the speech of Andalusia and Argentina. The protagonist of "La psicóloga que no dejaba hablar" ("The Psychologist Who Never Let Anyone Else Speak") is an Argentinian psychologist:

"A ver, desíme qué te ocurre, cual es tu caso, que te abruma? ¿Vos sos de aquí? Bueno, si sos de aquí la cosa es diferente, porque sé que hay muchos problemas psicológicos en esta sona del país, que resién ayá, de donde yo vengo, ayí no..." (70); "No te entendí ni un cachito así, ché" (74): ... "Pero qué desís, vos, estee, che" (76).

"Now let's see, tell me what's on your mind, what's your problem, what's upsetting you? Are you from around here? Well, if you're from around here that's a different thing because there are lots of psychological problems in this part of the country, and you know, back there where I come from, there aren't... I couldn't understand a word you said, OK?... But what do you have to say, come on, OK?"

Turning to Andalusians, people labeled with the stereotype of being the most comical in Spain (owing to their peculiar accent), Saavedra gives us a number of examples. Here is one: In the tale "Dentro de un año" ("Within One Year") a fairy has lost her memory and does not know whether the enchantments of her spells will be for good or for evil. She asks a gypsy woman if she thinks she is a good fairy or bad fairy, and the gypsy replies:

"Pos no zé, mi arma, la verdáááá... y ya pa empezá, má bien lo que le veo es cara de bruja, qué quiere que la diga, mire uzté. De *brujabruja*." (160)

"Well, dearie, to tell the truth, I really don't know... So let's see, to begin with, I sort of see you with the face of a witch ... look, what can I say?... a real ugly witch.

Then the fairy touches her with her wand and she turns into a beautiful and elegant princess loaded with jewels:

"Grazia, grazia, oh, mil grazia! Mire uzté que tenía yo una necezidá tan grande de zé princeza, . . . claro, yo, zabe uzté, pues, que eztá tö mu achuchao y ahora pues, a vé, amos... ¿Y no me puede dá también un caztillito y zervidumbre y ezo?" (Ibid.).

"Oh, thank you, thank you, thank you so much. You know, I really needed so badly to be a princess... of course, I ...

well, you know, everything is so messed up these days... so,
let's see...   Maybe you can give me a little castle and
servants and all that stuff?"

Other sources of humor in Saavedra's book are the incisive dialogues
filled with puns and double meanings and the references to popular songs
that make up his pastiches. Saavedra does not cite the entire song; rather
he incorporates phrases that introduce it into the dialogue of the characters
or the narrator's descriptions, thus transforming the popular culture into
humor.

Despite their controversial nature, the tales of Saavedra, steeped in the
humorous heritage of the Canaries, are a unique example of an innovative
and daring form of literature that confirms this genre within the current
Canarian postmodern culture. With the use of pastiche, parody and irony,
the stories erase the boundaries between high and low culture, breaking the
reader's expectations and in the end, eliciting humor and laughter.

Works Cited

Hutcheon, Linda. Irony's *Edge: The Theory and Politics of Irony.* New
    York: Routledge, 1994.
—. "La política de la parodia postmoderna." *Criterio* (Julio 1993): 187-
    203.
Jameson, Fredric. *Postmodernism, or The Cultural Logic of Late
    Capitalism.* Durham: Duke UP, 1991.
Lipovetsky, Gilles. *La era del vacío. Ensayos sobre el individualismo
    contemporáneo*, Barcelona: Anagrama, 1998.
Ritzer, George. *Postmodern Social Theory.* New York: McGraw-Hill,
    1997.
Romero, Alejandro. "Lipovetsky: Una teoría humorística de la sociedad
    postmoderna." Web. 10 Oct. 2012.
    <<http://www.tebeosfera.com/1/Documento/Artículo/Humor/Lipovets
    ky/teoria.htm>>
Ruffinelli, Jorge. "Los 80: ¿Ingreso a la posmodernidad?" *Nuevo Texto
    Crítico* 3.6, (1990): 31-42.
Saavedra, Sindo. *Cuento, luego existo.* Las Palmas de Gran Canaria:
    Saavedra Padrón, Gumersindo Editor, 2002.

«WITH A JEER I REPLIED»: LAUGHTER IN RIMBAUD'S POETRY

MYRIAM KREPPS

"With a jeer I replied..." (Rimbaud, 2005; 331).[1] Humor is a trend in late 19th-century poetry and has often been noted in the work of the bohemian French poet Arthur Rimbaud (cf. Grojnowski's "La poésie..."). However, Rimbaud's tone, often mocking, even chafing, is far from the conventional. For this poet, who composed all of his works in a five-year period before the age of twenty, there is not a single topic that cannot be ridiculed, perverted by the gaze of a sneering teenager.[2] He is the "Infernal Bridegroom" who leaves his Foolish Virgin in tears, wondering why he has to always hide his feelings behind derision: "If he explained his sadness to me, would I understand it any better than his mockery?," asks the Foolish Virgin. "He attacks me and spends hours making me feel shame for everything that ever touched me, and he is shocked if I cry" (Rimbaud 2005; 285).[3] This necessary perversion to achieve his "derangement of all the senses" (Ibid. 371)[4] can be seen in many instances. Not only is it inscribed in the relationship between the bridegroom and his Foolish Virgin, where it can be accepted as the functioning drive of this unusual couple, but it also sneaks up in the first titillations of love,

---

[1] This edition, translated by Wallace Fowlie, is used for all translations of Rimbaud's work herein.

[2] Jean Nicolas Arthur Rimbaud, a prodigy described by Victor Hugo as "an infant Shakespeare", was born in 1854 in Ardennes, France. The fifteen year old Arthur caught the attention of the French symbolist Paul Verlaine, with whom he developed a turbulent and violent relationship that ended five years later in a life of restless adventure and misadventure on three continents. Although Rimbaud died in 1891, shortly after his 37th birthday, the poems of his adolescence, identified with the "decadent" movement that spanned the distance between romanticism and modernism, influenced the later symbolists and surrealists in literature, music and the arts.

[3] Taken from "The Foolish Virgin: The Infernal Bridegroom" *A Season in Hell*.

[4] Letter entitled "Charleville – A G. Izambard – 13 mai 1871."

explored in poems such as "To Music" (49-51), "The First Evening" (27), or "Nina's Replies" (29-35).

Laughter is not produced in Rimbaud's poems by their "actors" (characters described in the poems); rather, the comic effects come from a semantic clash, an unexpected juxtaposition of oftentimes incongruous words.[5] This juxtaposition increases the feeling of confusion, lack of meaning, or nonsense, provoking an external laughter because we readers are not entirely sure we have grasped the whole meaning (if there is one) of Rimbaud's work and life. Laughter in Rimbaud's poems is difficult to grasp fully: a shifting laughter, always on the move, passing from the poems' actors to the reader, always under the poet's close control. Laughter gives the reader a sense of complicity with the author, only to be deceived by the latter, who is always hiding the key to the final solution, a meaning that can only be found in the realm of the laughable.

Laughter in Rimbaud's poems appears especially as an element of instability when it is linked to carnal desire. In these instances it brings two kinds of actors onto the stage: the lothario and the girl in love. The laughter produced by the girl in love makes fun of no one; it appears simply as a pure physical reaction. This instinctive laughter must be punished, harshly at times, because it exposes a sensual unsophistication. Jeering, by contrast with laughter, is always mocking: it implies an uneasiness, a seeking to annihilate all simple pleasures. At whom, or at what, is the jeering directed? Is it laughing at innocence that does not exist, or at the young predator whose senses, like the poetic experience, are irremediably deranged by Rimbaud's anti-poetry? This study goes beyond the simple humoristic elements seen in Rimbaud's poetry. In the poems we have selected, our goal is to understand the different levels and quality of laughter and jeering that can be observed throughout their descriptions.

Aside from the phenomenon of perversion, we note two main traits in Rimbaud's laughter, and therefore two categories of actors: either it appears as *laughing with*, or as *laughing at / making fun of*. In the instances of *laughing with*, laughter is contained within the poem: it belongs to the poem's narration—the actors ("I" / "the lotharios / "him"; "you" / "young girls" / "her", etc.) are described as laughing. *Laughing with* is not asking for the reader's own laughter, because it does not expose an inherently comic situation; indeed, the complicity between the reader and the actors' laughter is quite limited. However, as Henri Bergson points

---

[5] This incongruous clash is pushed to its limits in Denis Arché's illustrated biography, where Rimbaud's text becomes the caption to a fantastical pictorial piece (*Iconographie fantôme d'Arthur Rimbaud*. Paris: Curandera, 1985).

out, in each instance of laughter, there exists a presupposed complicity with an external voyeur because "laughter always implies a kind of secret freemasonry, or even complicity, with other laughers, real or imaginary" (Bergson 1956; 64). Therefore, there must be a voyeur to the scene described in order for laughter to fully take hold of the text and its readers. The voyeur can be external to the text— in that case, the part is played by the reader; we can also find an internal voyeur, an "actor" belonging to the composition of the poem, allowing laughter to show itself inside the text. The internal voyeur triggers the process of *laughing with*, whereas the external voyeur participates in *laughing at*. Witness Rimbaud's poem "À la musique" ("To Music"):

> Le long des gazons verts ricanent les voyous ;
> Et, rendus amoureux par le chant des trombones,
> Très naïfs, et fumant des roses, les pioupious
> Caressent les bébés pour enjôler les bonnes. . .

> Moi, je suis, débraillé comme un étudiant
> Sous les marronniers verts les alertes fillettes:
> Elles le savent bien, et tournent en riant,
> Vers moi, leurs yeux tout pleins de choses indiscrètes.
>
> (ll. 21-28)

> Along the green grass loafers sneer at everyone;
> And, made amorous by the song of the trombones,
> Very naïve, and smoking pinks, young soldiers
> Pat the babies to make up to the nurses...

> Dressed as badly as a student, I follow,
> Under the green chestnut trees, the lively girls:
> They know it, and turn to me, laughing,
> Their eyes full of indiscreet things.

In situations such as this, when one is *laughing with*, laughter often belongs to the girl in love. It can be heard coming from the willing adolescent, the one who is not shy, and allows herself to be seduced by the young lotharios who stare at her. The laughter of the girl in love corresponds to the call of new sensations; it is the anticipation of a pleasure still unknown; it is the ultimate trump-card of the saucy girl who "turns to him, laughing," knowing very well that her seduction has already worked. This is not a display of innocent laughter; yet it is devoid of any meanness. It exposes a joy of the senses, a need for a shared, intimate communication. Laughter is the answer to the pleasure coming from the eyes, undressing and admiring the bodies offered to their gaze, already surrendering. Laughter passes through the poem in small, happy, conceited bursts, establishing the sound bites for the replies between the girl in love and the object of her seduction. It becomes the absent dialogue in their love foreplay, laughter being the direct answer to the young man's greedy gaze. Here, complicity is clearly internal to the poem, established not only among the young men, but also between the narrator, the "student," and the teenage girls and, of course, with us, the readers, since the scene is painted for us. Indeed, the readers can laugh at the affected ease of the "coquettish girls" and at the young men's awkward attempts at seduction.

The laughter of first love that evokes our *laughing with*, can be seen again in "Première Soirée" ("The First Evening"), where the poet ("I") and "she" discover and share their first carnal pleasures. Laughter becomes the concretization of carnal expectation, and also of the pleasure found in the shared moment:

> Je baisai ses fine chevilles.
> Elle eut un doux rire brutal
> Qui s'égrenait en claires trilles,
> Un joli rire de cristal. […]
> La première audace permise,
> Le rire feignait de punir! (ll. 13-16; ll. 27-28)

> I kissed her delicate ankles.
> Abruptly she laughed. It was soft
> And it spread out in clear trills,
> A lovely crystal laughter. […]
> When the first boldness was permitted,
> The laugh pretended to punish!

This laugh is instinctive, sensual, just like the flirtatious girls' laugh in "To the Music." In these instances of *laughing with*, we must point out that only "she" laughs and smiles, a willing prey surrendering to the lusting gaze of the narrator, from whose point of view the poem is written. But her laugh becomes perverted by the lover, whose gaze exposes it to the reader's complicity from which "she" is excluded.

In "Nina's Replies" ("Les réparties di Nina") *laughing with* is also the
lover's promise of seduction. "He" creates a world of desires for her as her
laughter arouses in him a maelstrom of sensations:

> Comme une mousse de champagne,
> Ton rire fou
> Riant à moi, brutal d'ivresse,
> Qui te prendrais. […]
> Riant au vent vif qui te base
> Comme un voleur […]
> Riant surtout ô folle tête,
> A ton amant! (ll. 19-22; 27-28; 31-32)

> Like champagne bubbles
> Your mad laughter
> Laughing at me, who, brutish with drink
> Would catch you (…)
> Laughing at the crisp wind kising you
> Like a thief (…)
> Laughing especially, oh madcap
> At your lover!

Laughing with is not present yet, but the promise of a possible shared
pleasure to be taken outdoors (exposed to all eyes) is expressed by the
anticipation of her laughter. However, this anticipated laugh does not
materialize for the lovers, since following "His" drawn out longing and
exhortation: "Ce sera beau. Tu viendras, n'est-ce pas même..." ("You will
come, won't you? It will be so beautiful..."), the poem closes on his
mistress's single reply. "Et mon bureau?" ("And what about my office?"),
she asks (l. 108), totally insensitive to her lover's words.

This final reply brings on laughter from the readers; they are not
laughing with, but rather, they *are laughing at* Nina and her lack of poetic
sensibility; they *laugh at* the lover's disappointment. Of course, the
readers are also laughing *with* Rimbaud who created a reader's expectation
by the plural used in the title of the poem: "Nina's Replies." The readers
could have surmised that Nina would not accept this sensual, bucolic
invitation because the choice of the word "replies" ("réparties" in the
original text) is closer to "retorts" than to "response" or "answer"; and it
foretells a clash. By using a plural that is not demonstrated in his text,
Rimbaud allows his readers to imagine many scenes following the same
pattern of situations, where the lover's sexual desire is turned down over
and over again by his mistress's need for material comfort. Nina's final

line brings on the death of lyrical poetry, pushing forward everyday materialism, creating a poetic form made of the grit and shabbiness of daily life. The ending of this poem is made incongruous, somewhat grotesque, even obscene because of the clash brought on by placing the lyrical poem in a context of hyper-naturalism This is the very poetic clash that forces the readers to laugh—the true response to Nina's laughter, the only response that can be heard.

The type of humor contained in this final retort functions in a very similar way to the type of humor described by Alain Vaillant in his study of Charles Baudelaire's *Flowers of Evil* (64). In "Nina's Replies" laughter appears to be at a transitional point: at first the reader responds to the instinctual and sensual laughter because desire is not yet transformed into eyes that call in and imprison their prey. However, her laughter morphs into a need to ridicule. At this turning point, Nina represents the refusal to be seduced; she is Venus denying herself to Man, the end of lyrical poetry. The answer finally takes shape and aims to pervert any amorous expectation, sending back a corrupted sound image: laughter becomes a jeer. Again in the words of Bergson, "[. . .] society holds suspended over each individual member, if not the threat of correction, at all events the prospect of a snubbing [. . .]. Such must be the function of laughter. Always rather humiliating for the one against whom it is directed, laughter is really and truly a kind of social 'ragging'"(146).

In Rimbaud's poems, the humiliating function of laughter is directed against a Venus not true to her name, but brought on stage by the poet, exposed to the readers' mocking gaze. The poems "Venus Anadyomene" (*Poésies* 24) and "My Little Lovers" (Ibid. 76) act as grating, cunning, tarnished responses to the simple, fresh tone of "The First Evening" or the lyrical parts of "Nina's Replies." In both cases the poem presents a "correction" to the reader's expectation contained in its title. "Venus Anadyomene" makes fun of Venus, the desirable Woman. It presents the perfect antithesis to the Eternal Woman's beauty and youth, and the over-naturalistic effect of its obscene detail reminds us of Nina's materialistic concerns. It is also a sly reminder of the second part of yet another poem,"Sun and Flesh" (12), when the poet cries out: "I believe in you! I believe in you! Divine mother, / Aphrodite of the sea!" (ll. 1-2); and "Flesh, Marble, Flower, Venus, I believe in you!" (l. 4). Then, in the last lines, he declares his revulsion and disgust toward "CLARA VENUS":

– Et l'Idole où tu mis tant de virginité,
Où tu divinisas notre argile, la Femme,
Afin que l'Homme pût éclairer sa pauvre âme

Et monter lentement, dans un immense amour,
De la prison terrestre à la beauté du jour,
La Femme ne sait même plus être Courtisane !
– C'est une bonne farce ! et le monde ricane
Au nom doux et sacré de la grande Vénus !
("Soleil et chair," ll. 12-19)

– And the Idol in whom you placed such virginity,
In whom you made our clay divine, Woman,
So that Man might illuminate his poor soul
And slowly rise, in boundless love,
From the prison of earth to the beauty of day,
Woman no longer knows even how to be a Courtesan!
– It's a good joke! And the world jeers
At the sweet and sacred name of great Venus!

This great Venus at whom the world is openly laughing, this Woman who does not know how to be a courtesan any longer, who does not know anymore how to seduce or inspire desire is, of course, the anti-Venus described in "Venus Anadyomene". The very title mirrors and negates the "Aphrodite of the sea!" of "Sun and Flesh" as her name, "CLARA VENUS," tattooed onto her revolting flesh, mordantly recalls the light once brought on by male desire: "So that Man might *illuminate* his poor soul / And slowly rise, in boundless love" (my italics). Keeping the last two lines of "Sun and Flesh, II" in mind, "And the world jeers / At the sweet and sacred name of great Venus!" we can now laugh without any restraints at the description of the "Venus Anadyomene," and its grotesque portrait of the anti-Woman.

She too is undressed by the poet's gaze, like all his "little lover girls" with "their white necks embroidered with stray locks" and "The divine back below the curve of the shoulders" ("To Music," l. 30, 32), but in this poem the text presents a parody of the voracious gaze brought on by each appetizing detail. Instead of desire, now only disgust is felt, the detail to be seen "with a magnifying glass" ("Venus Anadyomene," l. 11), useful only in the anticipation of the final revolting fact, the ulcerated anus. This last detail is the most grotesque of them all, and is so by design. It is, indeed, an instance of the "absolutely comic" as described by Charles Baudelaire in his essay on "The Essence of Laughter": "From now on I shall refer to the grotesque as the 'absolutely comic,' to distinguish it from the common-or-garden comic, which I shall define as the 'significantly comic.' [. . .] The absolutely comic [. . .], being much closer to nature, has a *unity* which must be grasped by intuition. There is one acid test of the grotesque, that is, the immediacy of the laughter it provokes" (121-122).

The hilarity triggered by the grotesque element included inside the frame of a classic sonnet, *that* is a sublime perversion, the mark of a Poet who refuses to be limited by beauty. The grotesque does not *murder* Poetry since this *is* a poem, and a Venus *is* presented to the reader.[6] However, in "Venus Anadyomene", the lyrical pretense is reduced exclusively to the title. In its four stanzas only hyper-naturalism can be found, triggering an ironic laughter. The sonnet is satisfied with presenting nothing but a vulgar poetic portrait; and that is exactly why it is so amusing. It is an instrument entirely dedicated to shocking humor embodied in the single act of revolting perversion, catching the voyeur red-handed, that peeping-Tom watching a bathing anti-Venus. It uses the same shocking humor seen in the famous anti-blazon (rather than counter-blazon because of the obvious obscene choice) "Sonnet to an Asshole" published in the *Album called "Zutique"* (Rimbaud 2005; 145).[7]

"My Little Lovers" ("Mes petites amoureuses") follows the same pattern: the message of the poem, "O my little lovers, / How I hate you!" (ll. 25-26), is in complete opposition to the reader's expectation created by the title. On top of the thematic shock established between the title and the poem's content, the reader must face another shock, a semantic shock, since the comprehension of the poem is corrupted by the use of obscure or meaningless words (borrowed from slang or regional dialects), strengthening the incongruity of a tone both prosaic and vulgar, and filling up the text with a crassness that ends up hiding even more its love message. Therefore, laughter derives from the nature of the chosen language (slang, regional, vulgar, etc.), a choice that makes the poem almost incomprehensible. The only certainty left comes from the conflict between the gentle title and the violent hatred and disgust inspired by the

---

[6] Cf. Grojnowski's section "Où gît la poésie: les expériences parodiques" (*Aux commencements du rire moderne: L'esprit fumiste*. Paris: Librairie José Corti, 1997 [169]) on the collective discourse of a literary death sentence and execution, constituting a koinos topos and a condition for poetic rejuvenation.

[7] "Sonnet du Trou du Cul" de l'*Album zutique*. The *Album called "Zutique"* is one of the three literary journals published along the official *Parnasse* from 1866 to 1876. Its goal was to provide a burlesque response to the Elevated Language consecrated by the *Parnasse*. Cros, Nouveau, Verlaine, Rimbaud were amongst the profane contributors, choosing deliberately to adopt a decisively vulgar, even obscene tone (cf. Grojnowski's *Aux commencements du rire moderne* 170).

"love" objects described by the poet—objects of counter-desire. Yet this is *not* a nonsensical poem; rather it is a poem of perversion of senses (sight, taste, smell, etc.) and meanings. The poem opens up comically with a lyrical parody of affection written in gibberish slang, and continues on to a description of the debased love relationship between the narrator and his former girlfriends (mistresses, whores?). The cacophony created by the almost meaningless sounds (unfortunately lost in translation!) strengthens the laughable aspect of the text. Indeed, it presents the reader with an ode to ugliness and hatred, where not only the loving girls, but also the poetic language used to praise them, are corrupted. Here too, bodies are described: breasts, backs, hips are strung along like horrifying rosary beads. The lover's disgust makes the bodies he describes obscene, but also triggers our laughter, forcing us to wonder and ask the mind-boggling question: what inspired love (since he is writing about his "Little Lovers")? This poem presents the victory of incongruity and the grotesque, of cynicism and irony, because the poet, actually, is laughing at himself. "My Little Lovers" is in fact a sublimation of internal laughter and self-ridicule disguised under the appearance of a Villon-style bawdy ballad: "Et c'est pourtant pour ces éclanches/ Que j'ai rimé !/ Je voudrai vous casser les hanches / D'avoir aimé !" (ll.37-40) ("And yet it is for these mutton shoulders/ That I have made rhymes!/ I would like to break your hips/ For having loved!").

Finally, the response to the girl in love's laughter can be found in "H," a prose poem, where lyricism gives in entirely to an elliptical super-naturalism. In spite of the numerous interpretations offered to clarify its meaning, the incongruity (a riddle) and vulgarity (a sexual act made even more sordid by the murky description) of the text give it a high level of humor that can only trigger an ironic jeer from its readers. However, this time, the readers laugh at themselves because they were fooled into looking for the solution, the key, of a grotesque enigma. In this instance, the clash is not happening between the different registers (lyricism / materialism), but between the different degrees of clarity and murkiness that compose this text. Indeed, how are we to look for Hortense when we cannot understand the description that would allow us to find her? The poem laughs at us, the readers, because it set a trap in which we got caught..., since we are still looking for the meaning, a truth to hold, and that will elude us forever. All in all, the grotesque, laughing lustily at both "new loves" and "old lying loves," allows Rimbaud to achieve the ultimate nose snub to his readers, his last words finally claiming knowledge for only himself: "I shall be free *to possess truth in one body and soul*" ("Farewell" 305), and leaving his readers still aimlessly searching...and laughing.

Works Cited

Arché, Denis. *Iconographie fantôme d'Arthur Rimbaud*. Paris: Curandera, 1985.

Baudelaire, Charles. "De l'essence du rire." *Œuvres complètes*. Préface, présentation et notes de Marcel A. Ruff. Paris: Seuil, 1968: 370-378.

—. "The Essence of Laughter and More Especially of the Comic in Plastic Arts." Translated by Gerard Hopkins. *The Essence of Laughter, and Other Essays, Journals, and Letters*. Edited and Introduced by Peter Quennell. New York: Meridian Books, 1956: 107-130.

Bergson, Henri. *Œuvres*. Textes annotés par André Robinet. Paris: PU de France, 1970.

—. "Laughter." *Comedy*. And George Meredith, "An Essay on Comedy." Garden City, NY: Doubleday Anchor Books, 1956.

Grojnowski, Daniel. *Aux commencements du rire moderne: L'esprit fumiste*. Paris:Librairie José Corti, 1997.

—. "La poésie drôle: deux ou trois choses que je sais d'elle." *Poésie et Comique. Humoresques 13* (2001): 71-84.

Louette, Jean-François et Michel Viegnes. *Poésie et Comique. Humoresques 13*. Montpellier & Paris: Humoresques, 2001.

Parisot, Henri. *Le Rire des poètes. Anthologie de la poésie humoristique*. Illustrations par Marx Ernst. Paris: Pierre Belfond, 1969.

Rimbaud, Arthur. *Poésies. Une saison en enfer. Illuminations*. Ed. Louis Forestier. Paris: Gallimard, 1984.

—. *Complete Works, Selected Letters. A Bilingual Edition*. Translated with an Introduction and Notes by Wallace Fowlie. Updated, Revised, and with a Foreword by Seth Whidden. Chicago & London: The U of Chicago P, 2005.

Vaillant, Alain. "*Les Fleurs du mal*, chef-d'œuvre comique du XIXe siècle." *Poésie et Comique. Humoresques 13* (2001): 53-69.

VI.

SUBTLE, SEDITIOUS AND SURREAL

THE SANITY OF THE INSANE: HUMOR AND "HUMORISMO" IN THE WORLD OF RAMÓN GÓMEZ DE LA SERNA

ANA LEÓN TÁVORA

To talk about humor during the European *avant-garde* verges on the unorthodox, considering that this was a period of human history during which everything surrounding reality was full of tension, chaos, destruction, and death. To talk about *avant-garde*, in effect, is to talk about the horrors of the two World Wars. In like manner, most of the artists connected to any *avant-garde* activity were refugees or exiles, people who in most cases did not agree with the horrors of the war and decided to flee to neutral zones. Switzerland, for example, became the meeting point of numerous artists of the epoch, who reunited in the famous Cabaret Voltaire. This hot-spot for intellectuals, founded in 1916 in Zurich by Hugo Ball and his wife, Emmy Hennings, drew the attention of most of the renowned intellectuals exiled in the capital city, which also became the founding place of one of the most important and humoristic *avant-garde* movements, Dada (Cf.Tomkins' *The World...*).[1] In the middle of fervent political and social turmoil, and despite the instability that World War I had caused, humor became the most useful weapon with which to survive the crisis.

Ramón Gómez de la Serna was an innovative artist born in Spain in 1888. He really did not belong to any of the *avant-garde* movements or

---

[1] Calvin Tomkins focuses on humor as an essential element for artists like Duchamp, unlike his Cubist or Futurist colleagues who assumed their artistic roles in a too serious way. As he explains, "Duchamp believed wholeheartedly in the need for humor, but he was not convinced of the need for art." At the same time Duchamp himself declared: "By using humor, though, you can be excused from engaging in very serious considerations. It is an escape, I suppose" (10-14). To Tomkins, this was one of the reasons why Duchamp was excluded from the Puteaux Cubist group after exhibiting his *Nude Descending a Staircase*, apparently contradicting both the Futurist and the Cubist principles of dynamism and the use of objects, in Tomkins' words: "Humor was not permissible in the revolutionary climate of early Cubism" (15).

"isms," and, in fact, he founded his own stream, called "ramonismo," although his works are deeply influenced by all the other artistic styles and he even wrote about them. Like many other authors of that period, Ramón, as he preferred to be called, was surprised by the outbreak of the Spanish Civil War, and in the same manner that some European artists fled to Zurich, he decided to escape to Argentina, where he died in 1963. Ramón was the provocative exponent of the *avant-garde* in Spain, and he even transformed the "Café Pombo," a popular café in Madrid, into the Spanish version of Cabaret Voltaire. At Pombo, he organized "tertulias," or intellectual gatherings, at which he introduced and exchanged the artistic principles that would begin a new artistic era. Ramón was also one of only three foreign members of the Académie Française de l'Humour, together with Charles Chaplin and Pitigrilli.

The humor of the *avant-garde* is a dour kind of humor—a black, acrid and sometimes melancholic form of humor, which probably relates better to the notion of "humor" as explained by Hippocrates' ancient theory. Greek Hippocrates of Cos II, (460-370 BC) based his theory of the four human temperaments on the existence and balance of certain body fluids in the human body, called "humors": blood, yellow bile, black bile, and phlegm. Depending on the balance of these four humors in the human body, the temperament of a given person could be: "sanguineous," if the amount of blood was higher than the other three fluids; "choleric," if there was more yellow bile; "phlegmatic," if phlegm was found in a higher proportion; and finally, if the amount of black bile was stronger, "melancholic." Although obsolete and more poetic than scientific, this theory of human temperaments could explain the humor that developed after the events of World War I.[2]

In this sense, the particular humor of the *avant-garde* would be the humor produced by black bile: a dour response to an awful event. It is the hysterical and nonsensical laugh that is a reaction to a horrendous genocide, a reaction that carries with it ironic tones. For example, the reaction to the war was expressed in adapting a military term, "*avant garde*," to refer to the different artistic manifestations taking place, together with connotations of moving forward, being transgressive and leaving the past behind. Humor in this era is the aseptic drug used to heal the injuries of the war, and to this extent, it also becomes the surgeon that

---

[2] Cf. David Kersey and Mary Bates, *Please Understand Me. An Essay on Temperament Styles* (Del Mar, California: Promethean Books, 1978).

will remove the gangrenous limbs of the old and corrupted "corpse" of Art in order to create from zero or to start anew.

It is very common to find different artistic manifestos of the epoch including references to necrotic limbs, social destruction, or words such as "bitterness" or "aseptic." In 1909, for example, Filippo Marinetti proclaimed in his Futurist manifesto: "we want to deliver Italy from its fetid gangrene of professors, archaeologists, tourist guides and antiquaries." And although Futurism had a much more violent and bellicose tone than Dada, Tristan Tzara proclaimed in his "Dada Manifesto," in 1918: "I destroy the drawers of the brain, and those of social organisation to so demoralisation everywhere, and throw heaven's hand into hell, hell's eyes into heaven" (Tzara 8).

Georges Ribemont-Dessaignes, on the other hand, started his cruel and bloody drama *L'Empereur de Chine* (*The Emperor of China*) at a time when he had to inform many families that their loved ones had died in the war. In a similar tone, in 1921 he wrote his infamous "To the Public," in which the audience is impersonated in a decomposing human body that needs to be "disinfected with vitriol," and he adds in the last line: "we are warning you: we are murderers of your little newborns" (Dickerman 357).

Suicide was also a common reaction to the world situation and a frequent and very accepted end for many Dada artists. Jacques Vaché, close friend of the founder of Surrealism, André Breton, committed suicide by taking an overdose of opium. In one of his letters to Breton, Vaché talks about the term "umour" as opposed to "humor," or more specifically, "good humor." In his letter, he comments on his participation as a soldier in the war and on a picture that appeared in the papers of the time, in which the troops are portrayed dancing in celebration—which gives way to the newspapers making reference to the good humor of the soldiers. Vaché, on the contrary, states in his letter: "We don't act like that because we are in good humour we are in good humour because otherwise we would go to pieces" (Dickerman 357-358). But suicide, like any other acts of evident aggression and violence at this time, must be understood as an attempt to redefine reality, and by extension, to insert a drastic change in the arts. It is a moment of radical change and the search for new ways of expression (Conover 204).

In the field of visual arts, for example, there is experimentation with new shapes and perspectives, as in Cubism, or even a search for new lands of expression, like the subconscious in Surrealism. In the field of literature, there is a certain group of writers that looks for the destruction of language and experiments with new relationships between the signifier and the signified, form and content. Hugo Ball, one of the main leaders of the Dada movement in Zurich, defended the "assault on language as a social order," proclaiming that artists should "return to the innermost alchemy of the word [. . .] give up writing secondhand: that is, accepting words (to say nothing of sentences) that are not newly invented for our own uses" (qtd in Dickerman 28-29). The attack on language and the defense of art for art's sake—or, in the previous case, of the use of language for language's sake—is an attack on pre-established social structures, as well as an attempt to rebuild society starting from the basis: linguistic communication.

Following this premise, Gertrude Stein, the American writer established in Paris, admitted to be doing in literature what Picasso was doing in painting, and she explained that up to the moment when Cubism started, "composition had consisted of a central idea, to which everything else was an accompaniment and separate but was not an end in itself" (Dubnick 18).[3] Most Cubist artists will definitely insist that all the parts of the artistic piece are equally important, which is a way toward decentralization. James Joyce, notorious for his experimentations with literary techniques and with language, on the other hand, dedicated the last years of his life to the composition of *Finnegans Wake*, which he started in 1922—the year of the march of Mussolini over Rome and of the proclamation of the Republic of Ireland—and finished in Paris in 1939, which marked the beginning of World War II. Joyce's last work has been classified as a big joke by many, impossible to understand by others, and by the author himself, as something with which "to keep the critics busy for three hundred years" (Ellmann 703). When asked by many astonished readers whether he intended to reach a deeper meaning in it, he answered that the book simply was "meant to make you laugh" Ibid.)[4] As a matter of fact, the search for new means of expression is usually carried out with a humorous attitude, rather than with a solemn one, as if to mock the gravity of the crucial historical events taking place.

Humor and progress go hand-in-hand at this time: making fun of traditions, laughing at clichés, mimicking the past, and smiling at the future. The absurd starts to overcome reason: many artists believed that the

---

[3] Tomkins also recalls Jean Metzinger, the Cubist painter, insisting upon the importance of all parts of the composition: "that all the parts of his work shall tally with each other logically and justify each other down to the smallest detail" (21).

[4] Ellmann recalls the different moments when Joyce was asked about the meaning of his last composition, during which not only did he describe *Finnegans Wake* as a huge humorous work but also himself as "an Irish clown, a great joker at the universe" (703).

logics of society led to the war; thus, chaos and irrationality became a way to embrace a new order and re-establish peace. Playing, the absurd, and imagination itself, were essential in creating new realities. Exaggeration and eccentricity also played an important role in public speeches that became in themselves another part of the creative artistic piece, and gave way to the later artistic concept of public "happenings." In 1916, Hugo Ball, dressed as a cook and wearing "lobster claw" oven mitts, read his infamous poem "Karawane," in what he described as a "cubist costume" (Dickerman 28). Marinetti's performances in public were rather obnoxious and shocking (Sarmiento 6),[5] while Dada lectures usually consisted of intense provocative discourses or of powerful displays of eccentricity, in which Dadaists themselves often described the entire movement as a joke or a "big hoax" (Dickerman 353-355).[6] Marcel Duchamp created the "ready-mades," a collection of pieces whose main intention was to destitute the traditional aesthetic quality of Art, to laugh at the past, and to invert the classical artistic values. Mariano Brull played with the sonority of words in his first "jitanjáforas."[7] Several years later, Surrealist artists popularized the game called "exquisite corpse" or "cadavre exquis" (Read 138-148).[8]

This mixture of absurdity, melancholy, disappointment, and rebellion, is what defines this new kind of humor that in Spain Ramón baptized as "Humorismo." Werner Beinhauer in *El humorismo en el español hablado* (1973), quotes Sigmund Freud's own definition of "humorismo" as "a clash between two totally different worlds of representation" (my

---

[5] Sarmiento recalls Marinetti's words in his 1916 essay *La declamazione dinamica e sinottica* in which the founder of Italian Futurism explains that a poem is not exclusively made of words, but it must go beyond the page and be accompanied by different instruments, (not only musical instruments but also tools, like hammers, honks, etc). The poet, at the same time, should run, improvise, draw pictures on different blackboards, and to sum up, call the attention of the audience and make his poem alive in his performance.

[6] In the Erste Internationale Dada-Messe or First International Dada Meeting in Berlin, 1920, there was a slogan at the entrance reading "Dada is the world's biggest hoax." Tristan Tzara often addressed his audience by proclaiming words such as: "I'm an idiot, I'm a joker, I'm a fake . . . I'm like all of you."

[7] The word "jitanjáfora" was coined by the Mexican writer Alfonso Reyes after reading Brull's poem, in which the word appears in the third line: "alveolea jitanjáfora."

[8] "Exquisite corpse" was an intellectual game by which several players wrote or drew something on a sheet of paper, folded it and passed it on; the next player had to add his own "creation" without being able to see the previous piece. The result was meant to be an incoherent piece of writing or a dismembered painted figure.

translation) or a mixture of what, logically, cannot be associated (21). This definition of "humorismo," not surprisingly, coincides with Ramón's own explanation of the term in his work "Ismos," where he also mentions the necessity of restoring the power of insanity, or in his own words: "the restoration of madness over sanity" (Gómez de la Serna 1957; 1067). Ramón himself, following the example of his artistic comrades, provided his public lectures with the touch of irrationality, absurdity, and comicality typical of Dada or of its later manifestation, Surrealism. For example, he read a lecture while riding an elephant at *Le Cirque d'hiver*; while in *El Circo Americano* in Madrid he read another speech—written on a roll of toilet paper—on top of a trapeze, as attested by his son, Gaspar Gómez de la Serna. His book *Gollerías* (1946), at the same time, collected a series of his own illustrations accompanied by philosophical elucidations and whose name, "Gollerías," represented a parody of the legendary Spanish master painter Francisco de Goya. Ramón's illustrations were tainted by a touch of implicit morbidity and melancholy, added to their explicit comical tone.[9] In several public appearances, Ramón wore a monocle without a glass, through which he pretended to offer a different perspective of the world, like the reflection of reality on the bottles that he portrayed in *Gollerías*.

Ramón's "Ismos" offers a collection of different movements of the epoch, which were known as "isms," like Surrealism and Cubism. In this book, Ramón takes the opportunity to include other artistic tendencies of his own invention that, according to the author, are representative of modern trends, among them "klaxonismo ("hornblowingism"), "negrismo" and "jazzbandismo," representing the cult of modernity and progress, or in the last two examples, the American influence. Although he mentions important names such as Picasso or Apollinaire in his essay, his writing reaches its peak when the author develops a detailed explanation of "Humorismo," which he considers a totally different stylistic tendency, a lifestyle rather than a mere literary mode or genre.

Although Ramón opens the subject by stating that it is impossible to define "Humorismo," he offers an extensive explanation of what it is and what it is not, relating it to the person who produces it, the humorist. In the midst of this explanation, he asserts that "Humorismo" is first and foremost related to absurdity, irrationality and insanity, and serves as a

---

[9] See also Cardona. To the author, Ramón's "gollerías" represent the creation of an inverted order of values, "an order opposed to logical, common-sense, thinking; and in this strange reversal—humorous in its strangeness—we see man's place in the world re-evaluated and even displaced by things" (84).

means of restoring precisely the opposite, sanity. Thus, Ramón writes different axioms in which the logic seems to be evident, even though the sentences are totally contradictory: for example:

> Humorismo's high level of understanding is based on the fact that it accepts that things could exist in a different way, and not be what they are and be what they are not [...] It is the middle ground between losing your mind with craziness or becoming mediocre with sanity. ("Ismos," 1065-1067; my translation)

In these maxims, the main point is the necessity to turn to insanity—an unconventional way of thinking—and to mix heterogeneous concepts in order to find an order in the midst of chaos. What reason tells us to be logical and organized ended up causing confusion, chaos, and death. Therefore, the opposite of reason, what others call insanity, will put an end to the social commotion that affects these post-war times.

Tragedy and comedy are united in "Humorismo" in such a way that both tragic and comic in the end are taken as tragic, the moment prior to death being one of the most effective occasions to demonstrate "Humorismo." To other authors, however, insanity was precisely a mechanism of self-defense, as in the case of Jean Arp who avoided joining the German army by faking a state of mental insanity.[10] But the use of "insanity" is closely related to a return to innocence, to a primeval state, which was later adopted by many artists who, like children preoccupied with play, tend to ignore the impositions of an overly restrictive society (Dickerman 29).[11] Under this principle, Ramón explains that Humorismo

---

[10] It seems that Jean (Hans) Arp had a very complicated situation due to his mixed nationality since his father was French and his mother was German. Arp decided to move to neutral Switzerland but, upon his arrival, he was notified by the German consul that the Reich considered him a German citizen and, as such, subject of deportation to join the German army. In Zurich, he was forced to fill out a questionnaire which started with a question about his date of birth. Arp filled all the questions with the same answer: 16/9/1887, removed all his clothes, and very solemnly, handed the form to a horrified official, who just asked him to dress up and leave. Apparently, Arp was never bothered again after this "act of insanity."

[11] Hugo Ball called this return to innocence, past memories, and lack of logic, "primeval memory," which he described as "borders on the infantile, on dementia, on paranoia [...] The primeval strata, untouched and unreached by logic and by the social apparatus, emerge in the unconsciously infantile and in madness, when the barriers are down" (Dickerman 28-29). As Pegrum explains, the Dadaist attack on reason is not an attack on human reason in general, but an attack on laws,

will embrace the following: the grotesque, sarcasm, the fool, the pathetic, and the "epicburlesque.". However, it must be differentiated from the joke, the pun, the leg-pull, the satire, the mock, and the irony, all of which, according to Ramón, are offensive, artificial, and only try to imitate "Humorismo" in vain. Therefore, if "Humorismo" is related to the attempt to create a new era as well as a new concept of Art, it will also be related to the ideal of a new language that is capable of creating new universes. This, as a matter of fact, becomes the basis for the composition of Ramón's most popular creation, the "greguería."

Ramón defines "greguería" as the mathematical sum of humor and metaphor: "humorismo + metáfora = greguería." However, the mechanisms in the composition of a "greguería" can vary. In some cases it will consist of a metaphor, in some others of a pun, but there is an element that will always be present in a "greguería": "Humorismo."

"Humorismo" in this sense is expressed as a comical point of view that involves wit, a certain naïveté, and the perception of the world through a new lens. María del Carmen Serrano Vázquez contends that we have to understand "greguería" as the expression of a different reality and of Ramón's rejection of conventional language (Serrano Vázquez 15). The humorist, according to Serrano Vázquez, witnesses the imperfections of mankind and tries to apprehend the most beautiful aspects in life in an attempt similar to a romantic or a tragic act of skepticism. But unlike the romantic, the humorist will adopt an optimistic attitude.

Many authors have tried to classify different "greguerías" by following different criteria. Serrano Vázquez develops a deep study of Ramón's short compositions according to the varied linguistic resources that take place in all of them. Other authors prefer to obey a thematic division and some others, like Víctor García de la Concha, insist on the phonic character and the element of parody that rule most of Ramón's colorful creations (Cf. pp. 221-226). Despite Ramón's independent trajectory with regard to contemporary European movements and the unique features that inform his whole literary creation, it is probably in these short "greguerías" where he captures most accurately the artistic spirit that unified artists of many languages and nations in reacting against their depressing times.

---

restrictions, the "Enlightenment," citing as a perfect example Tzara's 1918 "Dada Manifesto," which, according to the author, "employs the formulas of reason and logic, only to turn them on their heads in a parodic game [...] *Ir*-rationality, *il*-logicality, and *non*-sense are favored Dada techniques [...] as can a ludic tone which is intrinsically opposed to Enlightenment gravity" (73).

As the perfect representative of the characteristic humor of the *avant-garde,* the "greguerías" will sometimes illustrate the touch of primitivism that is mostly typical of Dada with its return to childhood, and above all a refusal to grow up and abandon innocence: "Son molestas las medicinas en cuyo prospecto nos llaman 'adultos'" ("Those medicines whose directions call us 'adults' are really annoying"), or : "Cuando anuncian por el altavoz que se ha perdido un niño, siempre pienso que ese niño soy yo" ("When they announce through the loudspeaker that a child is lost, I always think that I am that child").[12] On the other hand, there also exists the sudden strike of "black bile" or melancholy in these "greguerías," as Ramón turns more philosophical and attacks certain aspects of society or humanity: "In between the train rails, suicidal flowers grow", or "The hanged man expects the rope to snap, but ropes are so evil that they never snap on those occasions". Most of them, however, offer a hopeful and colorful metaphor of an otherwise grey reality, as in: "El beso es hambre de inmortalidad" ("A kiss is hunger for immortality") and in: "El arcoiris es la cinta que se pone la naturaleza después de haberse lavado la cabeza" ("The rainbow is the bow that nature wears after washing her hair").

In any case, one of the most constant patterns in all his "greguerías", as in most of Ramón's humoristic works, is the mixture of the tragic and the comic and the condensation of two opposed or disassociated worlds in a false logical reasoning, either by anachronism or by a paradoxical statement. Sometimes this occurs by means of the association of either the meaning or the sound of different words, as in the infamous examples: "Era tan moral que perseguía las conjunciones copulativas" ("He was such a moralist that he prosecuted copulative conjunctions"), or : "Los orfeones son grandes huérfanos"("Orpheons [choral societies] are merely big orphans"). In this last example: "El Dante iba todos los sábados a la peluquería para que le recortasen la corona de laurel" ("Dante went every Saturday to the barber shop to get his laurel wreath trimmed"), obviously plays with the comic effect caused by Ramón's sharp observation together with the obviously anachronistic situation.

The "Humorismo" that invades Ramón's "greguerías," as seen in the previous examples, helps Ramón's unique compositions go beyond the limiting role of becoming mere jokes. They are not simple epigrams, either. The "greguerías," like the monocle that Ramón used in a symbolic way, provide a different perspective on reality and strive to re-establish the

---

[12] These and all subsequent examples are taken from Ramón Gómez de la Serna, *Greguerías. Selección 1910-1960,* 8th ed. (Madrid: Espasa Calpe, S.A., 1972). All the translations are mine.

order of things, with the intention of returning to innocence and childhood. Ramón's "Humorismo," therefore, becomes the author's personal weapon with which to attack the sanity of a society that has chosen to devour itself. It is through absurdity, innocence, and a different lens that the artist can react against a nonsensical rationality, and an apparently logical order that towards the end of World War I had proven to be more destructive and chaotic than madness itself.

Works Cited

Beinhauer, Werner. *El humorismo en el español hablado.* Madrid: Editorial Gredos, 1973.
Brull,Mariano. "Leyenda," *Una antología de poesía cubana*, ed. Diego García Elío. México D.F.: Oasis, 1984.
Cardona, Rodolfo. *Ramón. A Study of García de la Serna and his Works.*New York: Eliseo Torres and Sons, 1957.
Conover, Roger et al. eds. and transl. *4 Dada Suicides. Selected Texts of Arthur Cravan, Jacques Rigaut, Julien Torma and Jacques Vaché.* London: Atlas Press, 1995.
Dickerman, Leah et al. *Dada: Zurich, Berlin, Hanover, Cologne, New York, Paris.* Washington D.C.: National Gallery of Art, in association with D.A.P./ Distributed Art Publishers, Inc., 2006.
Dubnick, Randa. *The Structure of Obscurity: Gertrude Stein, Language, and Cubism.* Chicago: University of Illinois Press, 1984.
Ellmann, Richard. *James Joyce.* New York: Oxford University Press, 1982.
García de la Concha, Victor. "Época Contemporánea. 1914-1939," vol. 7, *Historia y Crítica de la Literatura Española*, ed. Francisco Rico, 8 vols. Barcelona: Editorial Crítica, S.A., 1984, 221-226
Gómez de la Serna,Gaspar. *Ramón; obra y vida.* Madrid: Taurus, 1963.
Gómez de la Serna, Ramón. "Ismos," *Ramón Gómez de la Serna. Obras completas*, vol. 2 (Barcelona: Editorial AHR, 1957)
—. *Gollerías*, vol. 1. (illustrated by the autor). Barcelona: Braguera. 1963
—. *Greguerías. Selección 1910-1960*, 8th ed. Madrid: Espasa Calpe, S.A., 1972.
—. "Las cinco razones de Ramón Gómez de la Serna," *El águila ediciones. Literatura por venir*, 15 October 2008 <<http://elaguilaediciones.wordpress.com/2007/07/22/ramon-gomez-de-la-serna-la-mano-del-orador/>>
Kersey, David and Mary Bates. *Please Understand Me. An Essay on Temperament Styles.* Del Mar, California: Promethean Books, 1978.

Marinetti, Filippo. *Critical Writings*, ed. Günter Berghaus, transl. Doug Thompson. New York: Farrar, Strauss, and Girox, 2006.

Pegrum, Mark A. *Challenging Modernity. Dada between Modern and Postmodern*. New York and Oxford: Berghahn Books, 2000.

Read, Herbert Edward. *Surrealism*. New York: Praeger, 1971.

Sarmiento, José Antonio. *La poesía fonética. Futurismo/dadá*. Madrid: Libertarias/Prodhufi, S.A., 1989.

Serrano Vázquez, María del Carmen. *El humor en las greguerías de Ramón: recursos lingüísticos*. Valladolid: Secretariado de Publicaciones, Universidad, D.L., 1991

Tomkins, Calvin, *The World of Marcel Duchamp*. New York: Time Incorporated, 1966.

Tzara, Tristan, *Seven Dada Manifestos and Lampisteries*, transl. Barbara Wright, illustrations by Francis Picabia (London: John Calder. Publishers) Ltd., 1977)

MILAN KUNDERA AND SEVERO SARDUY: ON THE MATTER OF KITSCH

ROLANDO PEREZ

I would venture to guess that most readers of contemporary literature know of Milan Kundera—that is, even if they haven't actually read him. His most popular novel, *The Unbearable Lightness of Being*, was made into a film, and his work is often taught in undergraduate courses. On the other hand, I would also guess that most people have neither read nor heard of the Cuban writer, Severo Sarduy. An author of essays on art and literature, of poetry, plays, and novels, Sarduy never enjoyed the same notoriety as other Latin American writers of the Boom generation like García Márquez and Vargas Llosa. The reason for this, I believe, is the kind of work Sarduy wrote: difficult and "experimental," destined to reach a very particular, scholarly audience.

At the level of the writing itself, it would be quite difficult to find two writers that have less in common with each other than Kundera and Sarduy. Yet in their own personal lives they shared similar experiences. For instance, they were both in their own ways victims of Soviet communism, and both became exiled writers living and writing in Paris, for much the same reason. While Kundera turned to Rabelais and Diderot, Sarduy turned to post-structuralist French philosophy and criticism. Interestingly, they were both influenced by extra-literary forms of expression: Kundera by classical music, and Sarduy by painting and architecture. And lastly, but most significantly, they were both concerned with the question of kitsch. On the face of it at least, the viewpoints they each arrived at are as different (and as reversible) as comedy is from tragedy—and therein resides their combined contribution to the notion of kitsch. It is the aim of this essay, then, to bring to light those differences in order to underscore the tragic, the humorous, and the serio-comic dimension of kitsch represented in these two writers.

Milan Kundera and the Germanic tradition

The etymology of the word "kitsch" is as problematic and as uncertain as are the concepts the word is supposed to signify. Of German origin, probably related to the word *kitschen* ("to smear"), it is traditionally associated with 19th-century Romantic imagery of the over-ornate, "sentimental," mass produced type, aimed at a growing middle class consumer market in Munich. That the word should have originated in 19th-century Germany should come as no surprise to anyone who is even slightly familiar with the German philosophy of the time. This was the age of Kant's *Critique of Judgment*, the age of Nietzsche's *Beyond Good and Evil*, of Marx's *Communist Manifesto*, and Hegel's *Phenomenology of Spirit*. It was the age of great philosophical systems, an age in which Reason played a major role in the philosophical conversation—even as it was put into question by philosophers like Nietzsche; and it was the epoch in which modernity (conceived in political and economic terms) finally came into its own. It was the epoch of advanced capitalism, of mass production, and the birth of a new political animal, the middle class consumer against whom all of the philosophers of the time railed. Unfortunately the intellectual richness of this epoch would give rise in the twentieth century to the worst kinds of dictatorships the world has ever known. This is the world that Kundera was born into, and the world which the earliest theorizers of kitsch came from; as for example, the Austrian novelist, Hermann Broch (*The Sleepwalkers*), German philosopher, Theodor Adorno (*Aesthetic Theory*), and the American art critic, Clement Greenberg, whose numerous essays on art were instrumental in defining the avant-garde and abstract expressionism for a very long time.

Herman Broch, whose multi-volume novel, *The Sleepwalkers*, Kundera considered one of the greatest novels of the 20th century for giving expression to the "melancholy awareness of a history drawing to a close in circumstances that are profoundly hostile to the evolution of art..." (Kundera 1988; 67), was also the author of the canonical essay, "Notes on the Problem of Kitsch." There, Broch dismissed what he called the Russian Marxist interpretation of kitsch as the bourgeois degraded art of capitalism, and instead located kitsch as a product of nineteenth century Western European Romanticism (53). Kitsch, he said "owes its existence to the specific structure of Romanticism (i.e., to the process by which the mundane is raised to the level of the eternal)" (Ibid. 62). In fact, Romanticism "is the mother of kitsch," of lofty, overflowing expressions of sentimentality—to the point where it is sometimes difficult to tell the difference between the parent and the child (Ibid; e.g., Wagner, Berlioz, etc).

Broch was no doubt thinking of the kind of Romanticism that inspired young men in love to take their own lives after reading Goethe's *The Sorrows of Young Werther*, where the hero of the novella, a victim of unrequited love, throws himself off a bridge. But kitsch, says Broch, is consumed precisely because there is a subject to consume it, to enjoy it, to give it life. Broch calls this subject the *kitschmensch* or *kitsch-man*. If the emotions generated by kitsch are stereotyped and counterfeit emotions, so be it; the artifice of beauty is what engages the kitsch-subject. And of this connection between kitsch and beauty, Theodor Adorno writes: "In art there is nothing ugly *per se*. All that is ugly has its function in some specific work of art. What is more, all that is ugly can discard its ugliness, once it is free of the attitude of culinary hedonism" (70).

This is precisely what kitsch, with its pretensions to aesthetic beauty, aims to eliminate from the field of art: any expression that does not in some way correspond to the beautiful image that is to function cathartically. This doubtlessly is what Adorno means by "the attitude of culinary hedonism," a position of whitewashing sentimentality (e.g. the souvenir print of a Swiss cow in a green pasture, which evokes feelings in us of Swiss peace and contentment). "In this connection," writes Adorno, "the phenomenon of kitsch or sugary trash is the beautiful minus its ugly counterpart" (Ibid. 71): the Swiss nuclear power station that was digitally excised from the picture of the cow in the putative pastoral field.   In summary, for the Marxian-Kantian Adorno, kitsch is capitalist art. Oppressive and manipulative vis-à-vis its appeal to the emotions, it withdraws rational *judgment* from the proletarian class.

On the other hand, for Clement Greenberg, the American art critic, kitsch was the result of a move away from the medieval conception of form to that of content—a move that began in the late Renaissance with the cult of the "lonely artist" in the personality of Rembrandt (118-119).[1] High art, in contrast, bears its name because it appeals to an educated, trained audience who is able to appreciate formal innovations, and not to the "common man" or the plebeian for whom art is solely allegorical (120). According to Greenberg, then, even if one could educate the masses

---

[1] Consider for a moment the way in which van Gogh has become an icon of the suffering, misunderstood, Romantic artist who cut his ear out of passionate love for a common prostitute. This and not the formal characteristics of his work, is what sells van Gogh tee-shirts, calendars, and posters.

to appreciate Picasso, the common person would ultimately give in to his/her natural inclinations and return to the stereotyped images that he or she has always, un-problematically enjoyed (121).

This, in addition to the foregoing, viz. Broch and Adorno, is what constitutes the Western nightmare of kitsch for Kundera. That is, human stupidity, and the modern State's exploitation of its subsequent sentimentalism. To that end, Kundera declared in his *Jerusalem Address* that "kitsch" was art aimed to please the lowest common denominator by simply re-confirming their "received ideas" or unexamined opinions (2000 163). "Kitsch," says Kundera, "is the translation of received ideas into the language of beauty and feeling" (Ibid), and by extension the withdrawal of reason. Moreover, "as the mass media come to embrace and to infiltrate more and more of our life, kitsch becomes our everyday aesthetic and moral code," writes Kundera (Ibid. 163-164). In place of a personal set of values it posits a manufactured "morality" to be shared by all.[2] But this is only the aspect of kitsch that has to do with its dissemination; with the way in which kitsch is put into effect. Its reception, however, is predicated on something other—the sentimentalism discussed by Broch. In part VI of *The Unbearable Lightness of Being*, entitled, *The Grand March*, Kundera argues that kitsch works by tapping into "basic images people have engraved in their memories: the ungrateful daughter, the neglected father, children running on the grass..." etc., (251);[3] in essence, the very same images for which Hallmark cards are famous. Kundera continues: "Kitsch causes two tears to flow in quick succession. The first tear says: How nice to see children running on the grass! The second tear says: How nice to be moved, together with all mankind, by children running on the grass! It is the second tear that makes kitsch kitsch" (Ibid.).

In a sense, kitsch is the Christian "com-passion" that Nietzsche sought to remove from his ethics; the "false" belief, as he put it, that one could share one's "passion" or feelings with someone else. In Kundera's case, kitsch is the right arm of all totalitarian regimes. He writes:

---

[2] Understood in this way, kitsch morality guarantees its survival by the axiomatic addition of the meta rule which makes it impossible for the individual to question the imposed moral code, or to "break ranks" with it without suffering the accusation of "betrayal," as Kundera points out (2000; 123). Think of the Bush administration's use of patriotism (a kitsch subject) to curb all oppositions to the war on Iraq, and to justify State surveillance on its citizens.

[3] That people spend as much as they do on cards to express their innermost feelings only attests to the undeniable concordance between their sentiments and the mechanical, stereotyped representation of their emotions.

The brotherhood of man on earth will be possible only on a base of kitsch. [...] And no one knows this better than politicians. Whenever a camera is in the offing, they immediately run to the nearest child, lift it in the air, kiss it on the cheek. Kitsch is the aesthetic ideal of all politicians and all political parties and movements [...] When I say 'totalitarian,' what I mean is that everything that infringes on kitsch must be banished for life: every display of individualism...every doubt...all irony... and the mother who abandons her family or the man who prefers men to women, thereby calling into question the holy decree. (Ibid. 251)[4]

"Be fruitful and multiply," states Kundera (252). Emotions, and not reason, are the sustenance of kitsch—the log that feeds the fire. That is why, he contends: "In the realm of kitsch, the dictatorship of the heart reigns supreme" (250); why Sabina, as the voice of Kundera in *The Unbearable Lightness of Being*, cries out: "My enemy is kitsch, not Communism!" (254). Unfortunately, however, one cannot separate one from the other. Communism came into existence through images and not because people, the oppressed proletariat, read Marx's *Das Kapital*. Similarly religion, despite the Lutheran Reformation (the first movement ever aimed at eradicating kitsch from everyday life) has survived not through Thomist and Augustinian theological arguments, but instead through the images we are all familiar with: the Cecil B. DeMille's Moses parting of the Red Sea, Christ walking on water, and statuettes of the pope at the Vatican souvenir shoppe, etc. "If Christ had not been crucified, he would not have had a hundred disciples in Europe," writes Henri Michaux in *A Barbarian in Asia*. "His *Passion* is what excited people" (Michaux 120); in other words, the operatic spectacle of his suffering. Yet Kundera concedes that "none among us is superman enough to escape kitsch completely. No matter how we scorn it, kitsch is an integral part of the human condition" (Ibid. 256). Interestingly, and contrary to Kundera criticism, for the Czech writer lightness is not a virtue, but rather its opposite—the "void" of meaninglessness (2000; 136). This brings us to

---

[4] Bear in mind early twentieth century Soviet posters of the idealized peasant laborer either holding a hoe or sitting astride a tractor; Hitler's love for kitsch imitations of Greco-Roman sculptures and architecture; Mao's young pioneers doing their flag dance; and all the appeals to the *volkisch* spirit *über alles* in whatever guise.

our next author, because for Sarduy, the lightness, not of Kunderian "Being" but of becoming, the lightness of carnivalesque laughter, albeit often ironic, is what constitutes the *joyful wisdom* of kitsch.

Severo Sarduy and the Cuban tradition of "choteo"

Sarduy's notion of kitsch can best be understood through his use of what is called in Cuba, "choteo." A term that is as slippery in its etymology as is "kitsch," *choteo* is more easily understood through its employment than its effects. More devastating than irony or parody, which at least begin by respectfully citing the source and then transforming it for its own ends, *choteo* doesn't take the source or anything else seriously. According to early twentieth Cuban critic Jorge Mañach, *choteo* was everything that was wrong with postcolonial Cuba. If you asked anyone on the street, he said, to define *choteo*, they would all agree that it consists in making fun of everything. In his 1940 essay "Indagación del choteo" ("Investigation into Choteo"), Mañach charged that choteo appealed to the basest and lowest common denominator of Cuban society. Jocular, mocking, and scatological, *choteo* reduced, leveled, and lowered everything with which it came into contact. More importantly, in connection with Sarduy's use of it, it holds absolutely nothing sacred. The sacred, in all actuality, may just be its favorite subject of attack. Anarchic in nature, dismissive of class and social distinctions, it laughs at all traditions by making light of them. And everything is carnival because the belief in authenticity and originality has disappeared in a world where fiction and artifice predominates. Everything, as in kitsch, is a simulation—a disguise. And hence, the importance that Sarduy assigns to the concept of cross-dressing in all its forms.

De donde son los cantantes (*From Cuba with a Song*), Sarduy's novel about Cuba's tri-cultural history, European, African, and Asian, is in all reality a parody of the idea of ontological origins and nationhood. In fact, Sarduy wanted his English translator, Suzzane Jill Levine, to entitle it "From Cuba with Love" as a tribute to the 1963 James Bond movie, *From Russia with Love*. A novel about the Cuba of *representation*—the postcard Cuba of the 1950s—*De donde son los cantantes* elides any claim to the essentialism of "Cuban-ness." Two of its protagonists, transvestite showgirls, Auxilio and Socorro (or MERCY and HELP), perform every night at the Shanghai Theater in Havana. Occasionally Auxilio and Socorro—or "las Floridas" (1993; 97) ("the Flower Girls"), as they are alternately called—hunger for some meaning to their lives and for some fullness to their identities: "--¡Metafísicas estamos y es que no comemos!⁵ ¡Vámonos al Self-Service!" (1993, 96) ("My, we're metaphysical, we must be hungry! Let's go to the Self-Service!"), they say, (Sarduy 1994; 15) and march off in an attempt to escape Kundera's "feared" lightness, which only they themselves can assuage. So off they go:

> Apretándose el vientre van, en puntillas, escurriéndose entre carapachos de autos oxidados—los cabellos sedosos fluyen entre las latas--, dando traspiés, saltando sobre ruedas de bicicletas achatadas y sin rayos, sobre manubrios, cláxones musgosos, faros rellenos de papeles, círculos de aluminio con barras rojas. Deidades amarillas. (Ibid. 1993, 96)

> [...] on tiptoes, pressing their tummies, slipping among the shells of rusty cars—their silky hair flows among the tin scraps—stumbling, jumping over flattened spokeless bicycle wheels, over handlebars, moss-covered horns, headlights stuffed with paper, aluminum circles with red bars. Yellow deities. (Ibid. 1994)

Auxilio and Socorro wander through a world of neon signs, street vendors, mass-transit movement, and spokeless bicycle wheels left on city sidewalks, like two hysterics out of Pedro Almodóvar's 1988 *Women on the Verge of a Nervous Breakdown* (Cf. Varderi 1996 137-171).⁶ And after a Cuban-Felliniesque⁷ journey through the night, MERCY/Auxilio

---

⁵ This line is Sarduy's re/citation of a poetic dialogue between Babieca and Rocinante in *Don Quijote*, where the Cid's horse, Babieca says to Don Quijote's horse, Rocinante: "Metafísico estáis" and Rocinante responds "Es que no como." Cervantes' joke, of course, is that instead of saying: "My, you look consumptive," or "Tísico estáis," the horse confuses the word "tísico" with metafísico or metaphysical, and Rocinante who has not understood the mistake, "correctly" answers by saying: "That's because I don't eat."

⁶ The sally of Auxilio and Socorro after they have put on their makeup recalls the sally and transvestism of Don Quixote. Don Quixote's makeshift medieval knight garb is as kitsch in its "sentimentalism" as that of Auxilio's and Socorro's, whose mannerisms betray their desire to be "ideal women."

⁷ The Felliniesque world is the circus and the medieval carnival described by Bakhtin where a "clown" is chosen to play the king. "The clown was first disguised as a king but once his reign had come to an end his costume was changed, 'travestied,' to turn him once more into a clown," writes Bakhtin (1968 197).

and HELP/Socorro finally arrive at the Self-Service where we are told:
"Tanto los manjares como los platos que los contienen están hechos de
material plástico" (Ibid. 1993; 99) ("The delicacies, like the plates which
contain them, are made of plastic" [Ibid. 1994; 419]). The circus world is
permeated by kitsch. As such, numerous are the references, as in a James
Bond movie, to brand name products: *Romeo y Julieta* cigars, *Coca-Cola*,
Kleenex tissues, and Auxilio's and Socorro's *Max Factor* eyeliner.

The fourth and final section of the novel, "The Entry of Christ into
Havana" ("La entrada de Cristo en La Habana) parodies James Ensor's
painting *The Entry of Christ into Brussels* but more significantly Castro's
1959 march into Havana as a savior. Christ, of course, no less than anyone
else is the subject of kitsch's *choteo*. An object of consumption like any
other fetishized object of capitalism, "He" is voraciously consumed like
candy by the masses:

> Su nombre en todas las vitrinas. Se Lo comían en caramelos
> de menta. Estaban disfrazados de él, con coronitas de
> espinas (blancos de cascarilla) y florecitas de sangre. ¡Todo
> era tan bonito! (Ibid. 1993; 224)

> His name was in all the shop windows. They ate Him in
> mint candies. They dressed up like Him, wearing little
> crowns of thorns (their faces white with rice powder) and
> small blood flowers. It was all so pretty. (Ibid. 1994; 143)

And as they carry the wooden Christ to Havana, his body, consumed
by his fans, deteriorates into nothingness. People from everywhere come
to touch him, to worship him; and consequently they wear down "la
madera de los pies" (Ibid. 1993; 213), "the wood of His feet with kisses"
(1994; 131). By the time he arrives in Havana, "Christ" has pretty much
disintegrated: "He saw himself crumble," writes Sarduy.

> Se vio desmoronar. Cayó en pedazos, con un quejido.
> Madero al agua. La pelada, la leprosa, Su cabeza partida en
> dos. El hueco vacío de los ojos, los labios blancos y
> perforados, la nariz en el hueso, las orejas tupidas por dos
> coágulos negros. (Ibid. 1993; 232)

> He fell into pieces, with a moan. Wood falling in water. His
> bald, leprous head split in two. The empty holes of the eyes,

the white, perforated lips, the nose in its bone, the ears
plugged with two black clots. (Ibid. 1994; 152)

The entry of Christ into Havana is also the entry of Christ into death. The
procession that has carried the crumbling Christ to the capital arrives in
the middle of a snowfall that covers everything in white. Sarduy's Christ
dies in the snow,[8] a victim of kitsch, as Luther had feared.

If the sacred has been emptied out, this has primarily come about, as
Augustine feared, through images—the great procession of simulacra, or
"The Grand March," as Kundera calls it. "The snow that covers Havana at
the end of the last story in *De donde son los cantantes* (1993; 1967) [*From
Cuba with a Song*] anticipates the Tibetan snow that closes *Cobra*
(1995;1972) and opens *Maitreya* (1995; 1978). Whiteness is death,
absence, the empty page," writes González Echevarría (1993; 212). The
snow that covers Lhasa in *Maitreya* can be read as a symbolic marker of
the Chinese communist revolution of 1949. And in effect, in October 1950
the Chinese Red Army invaded Tibet with 40,000 troops, destroying
temples and homes and killing over 4,000 Tibetans who opposed them.
"But Buddhism will continue to live in the reincarnation of the fourth
Buddha," declares the Lama, prophesying the invasion (1995 *Maitreya*
158). "I will be reborn," he proclaims: "[R]enaceré. Me encontrarán en el
agua, con los ojos cerrados. Seré el Instructor. Un arcoíris de anchas
franjas me rodeará los pies. (*Maitreya* 1999 589)—"You will find me in
the water, with my eyes closed. I will be the Instructor. A rainbow of wide
stripes will encircle my feet" (Ibid. 158).
    Indeed, in India the late master's prophecy comes true. A group of
traveling Tibetan monks one day comes across the person whom they
believe to be the fourth Buddha foretold by their master. Sarduy describes
two sisters washing a little boy in a fluorescent plastic washbasin when
suddenly the monks enter. Sarduy writes: "[E]n una gran palangana de
plástico...bañaban a un niño que apretaba los ojos para que no le cayera
jabón." (Ibid. 1999; 595)—"In a large plastic basin...they were bathing a
little boy who squeezed his eyes shut so that soap wouldn't get in" (Ibid.
164). The child deity does not close his eyes in meditation, but, as Sarduy
irreverently tells us, to avoid getting soap in his eyes. But the monks—like
Don Quixote who mistook the barber's basin for Mambrino's

---

[8] In a world of artifice that trumps the ideals of verisimilitude, the climatic
impossibility of snow in Cuba is as possible as snow falling inside a shakable glass
ball.

helmet--interpret the "plastic basin" as the prophesied container of holy water, and the little boy's closing of his eyes, as a sign that he is in fact Maitreya, the One whose coming has been foretold. And so, "we witness the superimposition of the Cuban culture or specifically, the *choteo* onto Oriental philosophy" (Kushigian 76).

It is not just the Orient that suffers the slings and arrows of Sarduy's *choteo*--so does the West as the perpetrator of much of the kitsch. The cultures of the ancient and the modern world, of East and West, meet in Sarduy's texts as consumer objects. Hence the difference between Tibetan monks and S&M practitioners is negligible. Since everything is a surface, everything appears on the same plane. Buddhist monks seated at the feet of a statue of Buddha share their space with a movie poster of Marlon Brando's *The Wild One*. And why not when we live in a society that venerates movie stars like deities? The religious fetish and the media fetish are one; both erotically charged and destined for the same place—Sarduy's "empty center" of consumption.

The options, then, are clear: Rage against kitsch, raise the flag of nationhood, continue to invoke the existentialist categories of authenticity and betrayal, promote a purity that is untenable and perhaps even undesirable, and defend the Grand Narratives of Western Civilization. Or put on a disguise: dress up as a knight like Don Quixote, a Wall Street Executive, or as Auxilio and Socorro, if that is your bent, and go out into the street as a Carmen Miranda "look alike" with the fruit hat on your head. The first option, quite understandably is—ironically so—sentimental, and aims to underscore the tragedy of a world made light by commercial garbage and the State machinery of "manufactured consent," to borrow Chomsky's term; the second option, comic and affirming, is the sadder of the two, because in affirming the carnival of kitsch, it ends up accepting, as in all carnival, the comic sadness of the human condition.

Works Cited

Adorno, T. W. *Aesthetic Theory*. Trans. C. Lenhardt. Eds. Gretel Adorno and Rolf Tiedmann. London: Routledge & Kegan Paul, 1984.
Bahktin, M. M. *Rabelais and his World*. Trans. Helen Iswolsky. Cambridge: MIT P 1968.
Broch, Hermann. "Notes on the Problem of Kitsch." *Kitsch: The World of Bad Taste*. Ed. Gillo Dorfles. Trans. From Italian. Studio Vista Limited, London. NY: Universe Books, 1969. 49-75.

González Echevarría, Roberto. *Celestina's Brood: Continuities of the Baroque in Spanish and Latin American Literatures*. Durham: Duke UP, 1993.

Greenberg, Clement. "The Avant-garde and Kitsch." *Kitsch: The World of Bad Taste*. Ed. Gillo Dorfles. Trans. From Italian. Studio Vista Limited, London. New York: Universe Books, 1969. 116-126.

Kundera, Milan. *The Unbearable Lightness of Being*. Trans. Michael Henry Heim. New York: Harper & Row Publishes, 1984.

—. *The Art of the Novel*. Trans. Linda Ashes. NY: Harper Perennial, 1988.

Kushigian, Julia. *Orientalism in the Hispanic Literary Tradition: In Dialogue with Borges, Paz, and Sarduy*. Albuquerque: U of New Mexico P, 1991.

Michaux, Henri. *A Barbarian in Asia*. Trans. Sylvia Beach. New York: New Directions, 1949.

Sarduy, Severo. *De donde son los cantantes*. Ed. Intro. Roberto González Echevarría. Madrid: Ediciones Cátedra, 1993.

—. *From Cuba with a Song*. Trans. Suzanne Jill Levine. Los Angeles: Sun & Moon Press, 1994.

—. *Cobra* and *Maitreya*. Trans. Suzanne Jill Levine. Intro. James McCourt. Normal, IL: Dalkey Archive Press, 1995.

—. *Obra completa*. Vol. II. Ed. Gustavo Guerrero and François Wahl. Paris: Ediciones Unesco, 1999.

Varderi, Alejandro. *Severo Sarduy y Pedro Almodóvar: del barroco al kitsch en la narrativa y el cine posmodernos*. Madrid: Editorial Pliegos, 1996.

NARRATORIAL IRONY AND TEXTUAL PARODY

PATRICIA HAN

The use of narratorial irony is in no short supply in nineteenth-century French literary texts. Major writers such as Balzac, Baudelaire, Flaubert, and Stendhal exploited the role of the narrator to offer commentary on the social and cultural landscapes of their times. Their narrators' ironic attitudes towards the characters whose stories they relate reflect the literary and artistic rejection of a society increasingly dominated by the bourgeoisie. The insatiable bourgeois appetite for works of questionable literary merit aroused the antipathy of the literary elite, for it precipitated a constant stream of derivative work by marginally talented writers. The fact that those writers enjoyed financial success only further exasperated those who held to a vision of pure art unsullied by commercial gain.

The innumerable literary works published during the nineteenth century provided any number of potential targets of parody, and parody itself became a widely-practiced and appreciated literary form. While all parody is necessarily self-parody in the sense that it cannot take itself seriously, a self-referential parodic text creates a dynamic and dialogic self-parody unseen in the great nineteenth-century writers. It was two lesser-known writers, Jules Laforgue and Isidore Ducasse, writing under the pseudonym of the Comte de Lautréamont, who produced some of the most innovative self-parodies by assigning a new role to the ironic narrator. No longer conduits for social commentary, Laforgue's and Lautréamont's narrators turn their irony inwards, not only towards the text itself but towards their own narrating acts, thereby producing both narratorial and textual self-parodies.

Laforgue's *Moralités légendaires*, a collection of six tales, were published in a volume for the first time in November, 1887, three months after his death. Lautréamont's *Les Chants de Maldoror* (*The Songs of Maldoror*), although published in 1869, were censored and not available for sale in 1874, four years after his death. In both works, but particularly in "Le Miracle des Roses," the second of the *Moralités*, and in the "Chant Sixième" of *Les Chants*, the narrator's use of diegetic irony to create a parodic text is doubled by a metadiegetic irony to create a self-parodic text.[1] Diegetic irony, which bears on the narrative, is necessary to parody. Metadiegetic irony, which concerns the narration, is not; a parody can be read as such without the component of narratorial self-irony.[2]

Irony and parody have in common the pragmatic function of conveying mockery, but there are important differences between the two. Irony can be perceived at the levels of sentence or short discourse; parody must occupy an extended discursive space, most often that of an entire work. Thus, whereas the targets of irony are unrestricted, those of parody must be broad: literary parodies target other works, genres, or conventions. Finally, although the effects of irony are frequently humorous, humor is not one of its essential features. Parody, on the other hand, always incorporates humor, and it is irony that furnishes the primary mechanism through which the humor in parody is communicated.[3]

Indeed, it is irony that enables the reader to identify a parodic intent. Irony must signal its presence in order to ensure successful communication, and the manners in which it does so are virtually limitless. Any technique that creates incongruity or produces an unreadable result, such as exaggeration and repetition, the use of unusual punctuation, neologisms, or specialized vocabulary, and the juxtaposition of different registers of language, can be coopted to serve an ironic, and potentially parodic, purpose. All of these tactics are present in both the Laforgue and Lautréamont texts. A self-parodic intent, however, requires irony at the metadiegetic level. The narrator must ironize his own narrating of the text in order to produce metadiegetic parody. Such narratorial metacommentary often appears in parenthetical remarks, or through observations made by a first-person narrator. Narratorial intrusions effectively split the narrating voice into an ostensible omniscient observer who relates the story and a first-person narrator who comments upon his relation of that story. The only necessary

---

[1] Gérard Genette uses metadiegetic to refer to a second-degree narrative, a story-in-the-story. However, since "diegetic" refers to the narrative—the *énoncé*—"metadiegetic" should rightly refer to the act of narration—the *énonciation*—since in both parody and irony it involves commentary upon the narrative. Genette himself acknowledges that his designation runs counter to the normal use of the prefix *meta-*. Genette, *Narrative Discourse*, 228.
[2] For a fuller discussion of this metafictional quality of parody, see Margaret Rose's *Parody: ancient, modern*.
[3] For an opposing view, see Linda Hutcheon, *A Theory of Parody*, chapters 2 and 3. Following Iouri Tynianov, she rejects the comic as a defining feature of parody. Tynianov offers as his justification for excluding the comic the fact that a comedy can be parodied to produce a tragedy (Tynianov, "Destruction, Parodie," 76). However, in the absence of humor, parody will pass unrecognized.

condition of metadiegetic parody is ironic narratorial intrusion into the narrative, whether or not the meta-commentary is presented in the first person, as Laforgue's text reveals.

By its very title, "Le Miracle des Roses" distinguishes itself from the five other tales that comprise Laforgue's collection. While the titles of the other stories, designating well-known characters such as Hamlet or Salomé, announce their relationships to the parodied texts, or what Genette terms "hypotextes," the target text of this story is not immediately evident (*Palimpsestes* 13). The legend after which it is named is the same one that provided the inspiration for Liszt's oratorio "The Legend of St. Elisabeth," which Laforgue heard performed in Berlin (Laforgue v.1, 870).[4] According to this legend, Elisabeth, the wife of a count, regularly provides food to the poor, against the orders of her husband. He finds her one day carrying something in her apron and, suspicious, asks her what is in it. She responds that she has been gathering roses, and indeed, when she opens her apron, the food has miraculously turned into roses.

Based upon this relatively minor legend, Laforgue's version transforms Saint Elisabeth into the wealthy but sickly Ruth, who brings not life, but death, to those who fall in love with her. It is filled with clichéd Romantic depictions, Decadent themes and figures, apostrophes that ridicule lyrical poetry, and references to the *opéra-comique*, Shakespeare, and Balzac, to name but a few targets of the narrator's irony. While the Liszt oratorio and this particular miracle story surely inspired Laforgue's parody, the oratorio is not, in fact, the true *hypotexte*. The characterization of the story as "légendaire," the extended description of the Corpus Christi Day parade, the ironic attribution of the bizarre events in the narrative to "He who reigns in Heaven (v.2, 402)"[5] and the formulaic response to the occurrence of a miracle, the final word of the story, "Alléluia!," suggest that it is not one specific work but the entire genre of hagiography that forms the primary *hypotexte*.[6]

"Le Miracle des Roses" is divided into three parts, the first of which is a mise-en-scène to the story that follows in the next two. In this first section, the narrator shares his fond memories of a small spa town and

[4] The concert is indicated in Laforgue's notebook entry for April 4, 1883.
[5] All translations are mine.
[6] In *Parody and Decadence*, Michele Hannoosh identifies the oratorio as the major *hypotexte*, noting the proliferation of both flowers and musical references throughout the story. See her fine analysis in chapter 4. Both Hannoosh and Daniel Grojnowski also identify the Corpus Christi day procession in Flaubert's *Un coeur simple* as a *hypotexte*. Grojnowski, *Jules Laforgue et l'«originalité»*, 210-212.

almost immediately asserts his presence as a first-person observer. As he remembers a popular waltz playing in the Casino, he describes himself, in parentheses: "(moi navré dans les coins, comme on pense)" ("[me, in a corner, forlorn, of course]") (402). A second intrusion again appears in a parenthetical remark that seems to indicate the narrator's desire to convey his emotions to us: "(Cette valse, oh! si je pouvais vous en inoculer d'un mot le sentiment avant de vous laisser entrer en cette histoire! (Ibid) "[7] In fact, however, this interruption allows the narrator to signal his firm control over both the story and the reader's access to that story.

Neither of these intrusions reflects on the narratorial act; both are typical examples of diegetic irony that use exaggeration and punctuation to ridicule the overwrought and emotional Romantic narrator. The narrator transforms an earlier expression of his fondness for the town, "Oh, little village, little village of my heart" into "O petite ville, vous avez été mes seules amours, mais en voilà assez." ("... you were my only loves, but enough of that") (Ibid). While the terse "mais en voilà assez" that ends the panegyric may merely signify the narrator's repudiation of his love for the town, the apostrophe and the reprisal of "petite ville" in the first half of the sentence intimate that the referent of "mais en voilà assez" is the narrator's own narrative and turns the diegetic irony into an ironic commentary on the narration itself.

As the story of Ruth unfolds in the second section of the work, the *je* (the narrating first-person voice) is conspicuously absent, appearing only twice in the form of the first-person plural. Despite the illusion of a narrative devoid of narratorial commentary, the indications of metadiegetic irony are inescapable. The narrator pronounces the tale to be "une seconde édition plus esthétique du Miracle des Roses!" and emphasizes "Oui, le légendaire Miracle des Roses (405)!" The proclamation of the story's legendary nature is immediately recanted; the complete deflation of the dramatic presentation devalues from the outset the very story that the narrator will be telling.

Its heroine is a "typical creature too young to be taken from the affection of her loved ones and from the dilettantism of her friends" (Ibid.), a description in which the words *typique* and *dilettantisme* reinforce the undoing of the narrative. The epithet *typique* recurs two more times, marking both Ruth's status as a parody of a heroine and an ironic distance between the story being told and its telling. The narrator makes explicit

---

[7] "This waltz, oh! If only I could, in one word, inoculate you with/inoculate you against its sentiment before letting you into this story!" The French *inoculer* does not differentiate the two connotations: figuratively, it can mean both to instill or convey, as well as to protect against. The ambiguity is surely intentional.

this metadiegetic irony in the third description of Ruth as "the unfortunate and typical heroine that I have taken on" (410). His acknowledgment of his choice to narrate a tale unworthy of being narrated, given its lack of legendary status and its stereotypical heroine, bears on the narration and in essence mocks his creation of the narrative.

The narrator's seeming compassion for his dying young heroine turns his self-mockery into self-parody, as Ruth is taken not only from the affection of her family but from the dilettantism of her friends. The expression is repeated in her characterization as an "idéale agonisante, trop tôt enlevée" ["an ideal dying person, taken away too soon"] au dilettantisme de ses amis" (406). With this second reference to dilettantism, and the unintelligibility created by the concept of an ideal dying woman, the narrator suggests that what Ruth's friends will rue upon her death is not the person but the model of the perfect heroine that she provides. The irony is two-pronged. On the narrative level, it targets the Decadent writers whose marked preference for artifice demonstrates their perception of life as a mere source of art. On the narratorial level, it is impossible to avoid identifying the narrator as one of these dilettantes, since he, too, makes Ruth his heroine.[8] Despite the absence of the *je* and of any parenthetical remarks, the narrator adroitly ironizes his own narration and creates a doubled text, both parody and self-parody.

As the culminating point of the story approaches, the narrator offers a commentary on the scene he has just described. Ruth, hallucinating that the ground is covered with the blood of the suicides she has caused, has fainted. A young girl carrying a basket of rose petals scatters them all around her chair. At this moment, instead of the "miracle" that the reader has been led to expect, what takes place is a complete sabotage of the narrative. The narrator pauses to observe that "[i]l y a dans la vie des minutes absolument déchirantes, déchirantes pour toutes les classes de la société. Celle-ci n'en fut pas, mais il en est, et l'exception ne saurait que confirmer la règle" ("In life, there are moments that are absolutely heartrending, heartrending for all of society. This wasn't one of them, but those moments do exist, and the exception just proves the rule.") (v. 2, 410-411). The comic anti-climax effected by the narrator's ironizing of the narratorial act inflects the entire text in the direction of its true target:

---

[8] Richard Hibbitt argues that for Laforgue, dilettantism expressed a complex esthetic principle that coincided with his turn towards a more ironic mode of writing. Hibbitt, "Dilettantism and Irony: Jules Laforgue and C.M. Wieland." In fact, Laforgue more than once referred to himself as a dilettante in his letters. See those to Mme. Mültzer (Laforgue, vol. 1, 753, 762-763) and to Gustave Kahn (vol. 1, 800).

itself. By confiding that his story lacks a moment of any import, the narrator proffers to the reader an invitation to take part in generating a self-parodic text.

Lautréamont's narrator does not extend an invitation as much as oblige the reader to collaborate in the self-parody. The role of the narrator is more complex in Lautréamont's work, for at different points in the text he presents himself as an omniscient narrator, a participatory *je*, and the godless and depraved Maldoror himself. The very insistent and intrusive *je* draws attention to the narration and forces the reader to acknowledge the fictitious nature of the narrative. Furthermore, the *je* explicitly identifies himself as both the narrator of the work and the writer of the text that the narrator is relating. This conflation of the *énoncé* and the *énonciation* announces the metafictional nature of the parody even more emphatically than in "Le Miracle des Roses."

As was the case with Laforgue's narrator, Lautréamont's *je* devalues the narrative by conspicuously highlighting its unoriginal or typical characteristics as pure convention. Unlike the preceding five *chants*, the "Chant Sixième" takes the form of a novel, for only the novel has the capacity to create real beings:

> Désormais, les ficelles du roman remueront les trois personnages nommés plus haut: il leur sera ainsi communiqué une puissance moins abstraite. La vitalité se répandra magnifiquement dans le torrent de leur appareil circulatoire, et vous verrez comme vous serez étonné vous-même de rencontrer, là où d'abord vous n'aviez cru voir que des entités vagues...des êtres doués d'une énergique vie. [...] (Ducasse, *Les chants de Maldoror*, 219)

> Henceforth, the novel's strings will move the three above-named characters: in this way, a less abstract power will be conferred upon them. Vitality will spread magnificently through their circulatory system, and you will see how astonished you are to encounter beings endowed with an energetic life when you thought that all you saw was vague entities.

While the comical exaggeration of the power of the novel to create flesh and blood takes aim at the realist novel, the fact that the *je* is writing precisely such a novel redirects the irony to target the text and its narrator.

The narrator's interjections reveal his tactics to be simply the routine stock-in-trade of the novelist. As Mervyn, Maldoror's soon-to-be victim, walks home, the reader anticipates the imminent arrival of the predator. The narrator poses a series of four rhetorical questions, a common indicator of irony, designed to heighten the tension. These questions are immediately followed by a parenthetical remark:

> (Ce serait bien peu connaître sa profession d'écrivain à sensation, que de ne pas, au moins, mettre en avant, les restrictives interrogations après lesquelles arrive immédiatement la phrase que je suis sur le point de terminer). (225)

> (It would really show a lack of understanding of one's profession as a sensationalist writer to not, at least, draw the reader's attention to the restrictive interrogations following which comes the sentence that I am about to finish writing.)

The narrator's self-inclusion in the category of sensationalist writers divests the story of any uniqueness, and his metadiegetic commentary demystifies the process of literary invention. After another transparent ploy to dramatize the scene, the narrator once again interrupts his narrative to remark:

> Mais, nous ne sommes point encore arrivés à cette partie de notre récit, et je me vois dans l'obligation de fermer ma bouche, parce que je ne puis pas tout dire à la fois: chaque truc à effet paraîtra dans son lieu, lorsque la trame de cette fiction n'y verra point d'inconvénient. (241)

> But, we haven't yet reached that part of our story, and I see that I'm forced to keep my mouth shut, because I can't relate everything at once: every literary trick in the book will appear in due time, when the storyline of this fiction sees no reason not to use it.

The narrator calls attention not only to the fiction but to his own ironic use of a standard tactic to create suspense. The metadiegetic irony undoes his own narrative, and at the same time his use of the first-person plural renders the reader an accomplice to the text's self-destruction.

The praise for the novel's capacity for realism serves to justify the *je*'s declaration of his intention: "Today I am going to fabricate a little 30-page novel" (221). This play between reality and fiction is, to be sure, itself a fiction, an intentional slippage between the moments of narrative and narration. At every turn, the narrator erodes the foundations of his narrative by underscoring the fact that he is engaged in the writing of a fictional tale. In fact, he repeatedly refers to the physical act of writing. He lays out the preparatory actions he will take before composing the story: "Je vais d'abord me moucher, parce que j'en ai besoin; et ensuite, puissamment aidé par ma main, je reprendrai le porte-plume" ("First, I am going to wipe my nose, because I need to; next, aided powerfully by my hand, I will pick up the pen again.")[9] (Ibid, 223). The nonsensical detail "puissament aidé par ma main" focuses our attention on the hand and the pen that produce the story.

The narrator sets the scene for Maldoror's first encounter with Mervyn in a dark and foreboding street, a place that "my pen (this true friend who serves as my accomplice) has just rendered mysterious" (224). This description of the pen, following the appearance of the hand in a superfluous clause, creates an inversion that purports to transfer the power of narration to a writing implement. However, the narrator's seeming willingness to play a secondary role only reveals his greater control over the narration, for he demonstrates his consciousness of distance as the major criterion that must be in place before self-parody can exist. As the narrator-writer details each step of the writing process and the temporal distance between the moments of narration and narrative evaporates, the reader has no choice but to accept full complicity in the production of the elaborate artifice that both narrator and reader must pretend to believe.

In addition to the mockery aimed at his narrative, Lautréamont's *je* ironizes his own writing style, the final stage in the complete invalidation of the narrative. Despite an amply demonstrated penchant for overly long and impenetrable sentences, the *je* characterizes the 175 pages that form the first five *chants* as "the quick sketch of clear and precise generalization" (221) of his work. The tongue-in-cheek humor devolves into outright farce when, in the midst of a description of his style, an ellipsis is followed by: "je ne sais plus ce que j'avais l'intention de dire, car je ne me rappelle pas le commencement de la phrase" ("I no longer know what I wanted to say, for I don't remember the beginning of the sentence") (223). The narrator once again signals his self-irony and obliges the reader to ironize both with him and against him.

The *je*'s extreme consciousness of the writing act and his persistence in demonstrating that consciousness bring about the impossibility of accepting the narrative as presented. Although Lautréamont's *je* invades his narrative

---

[9] The *porte-plume* is the shaft of a calligraphy pen.

more patently than Laforgue's, in both works the narrator's use of conventional literary devices to ironize his telling of the story renders transparent the process of writing and completely undermines the narrative that the narration is ostensibly producing. For these narrators, the act of narrating transforms the texts into parodies of their own textual creations.

The theatrical dimension in each text neatly stages this metafictional parody. Mervyn's meeting with Maldoror on the Pont du Carrousel is twice described as a "spectacle"; it offers a "unique scene that no novelist will ever reproduce!" (245). The narrator of "Le Miracle des Roses" explicitly describes the Hôtel de France as the "théâtre" where Ruth will "entrer en scène" (Laforgue v.2, 405). The presentation of critical moments as theater permits the distance necessary for metadiegetic commentary by an ironic observer; rather than keeping the production hidden from view, the narrators draw back the curtain so that the reader can see the inner mechanisms at work. The narratorial self-awareness of the act of composing a fictional tale necessarily deconstructs the narrative, but paradoxically constructs a new, self-parodic text.

Curiously, the authors of these two unusually self-conscious self-parodies share similar backgrounds. Both were born in Montevideo to French parents who had emigrated from Tarbes, in the Pyrenees, during the great wave of French immigration to Montevideo under the July Monarchy.[10] Both were sent back to Tarbes for schooling, Laforgue at the age of six, and Ducasse at the age of thirteen, before they moved to Paris, where they died at young ages. Laforgue was twenty-five when he wrote the first tales in the *Moralités* and died in 1887, just a few days after his twenty-eighth birthday. Although little is known about the composition of *Les Chants de Maldoror*, the "Chant premier" was first published in 1868, two years before Ducasse's death at the age of twenty-four.

The youthfulness of two writers endowed with a prodigious and exquisite sense of the comic may, in part, explain the appeal of a genre that relies on humor. Laforgue and Lautréamont take full advantage of the nature of self-parody to give free rein to the imagination and to demonstrate a thorough irreverence for literary conventions and traditions. That their exploitation of the genre could set them apart and bring the literary success that they sought could not have been lost on them. In a

---

[10] The July Monarchy refers to the reign of Louis Philippe (1830-1848), a turbulent period during which a liberal constitutional monarchy originally weighted toward the wealthy bourgeoisie culminated in uprisings from the republicans on the left, the legitimists on the right, economic crises, and eventually its displacement by the Second Republic in February of 1848.

manner reminiscent of Baudelaire's description of his *Petits poèmes en prose*, Laforgue writes to Gustave Kahn that the *Moralités* are stories "which are not like Villiers' or Maupassant's" (v. 2, 737).[11] Lautréamont's *je* boldly proclaims that "the end of the 19th century will have its poet. [...] He was born on American shores, at the mouth of the Plata River" (Ducasse 78).

While the fusion of fictional narrator and real author is hardly surprising, the reference to Montevideo is striking. In fact, while both Ducasse and Laforgue accepted their new lives in France, neither renounced his Uruguayan heritage.[12] Although Laforgue never references his heritage in his works, his letters attest a permanent connection to Montevideo and a nostalgia for his early childhood there. In an 1882 letter to Charles Henry, he relives the difficulty of the transition and expresses a desire to return to Montevideo:

> Depuis que j'ai traversé l'Atlantique (6 ans, couchant sur la mer) je n'avais eu d'aussi noires crises de spleen. Si j'avais de l'argent et pas de famille, je planterais l'Europe là (v. 1, 757).

> I hadn't suffered such dark bouts of spleen since I crossed the Atlantic—6 years old, sleeping on the ocean. If I had money and no family, I would now just dump Europe.

In 1886, he writes to Gustave Kahn that, once in Paris, they will no longer need to communicate through letters, "unless we return, you to Gomorrah, I to Montevideo" (v 2, 869).[13]

The very division of the narrating voice into two personae, a *je* and an *il*, required by self-parody may have drawn two writers whose backgrounds gave them a dual identity. The sense of displacement or

---

[11]In an 1861 letter to Arsène Houssaye, Baudelaire says of the prose poems: "je me pique qu'il y a là *quelque chose de nouveau*" ("I like to think that there's something new here.") (Baudelaire, *Correspondance générale*, 33-34).

[12] Jacques-André Duprey believes that the overwhelmingly French culture of Montevideo would have made for a smooth adjustment (Duprey, "Laforgue et Lautréamont, deux manières de vivre leur binationalité," 342). José Pedro Diaz, on the other hand, notes "l'intensité du changement de situation" for Ducasse (Diaz, "Lautréamont, le Montevidéen," 103).

[13] Letters to sister Marie (vol. 2, 796) and to his brother Emile (vol. 2, 823) offer further evidence of the enduring impression that Montevideo left on Laforgue.

isolation caused by their return to France may also have found an outlet in the exteriorization of the *je* required by self-irony. Writing texts in which the *je* observes from an external vantage point may have resonated with these authors, who not only experienced a significant displacement but seem to have led rather solitary lives. The fact that precious little is known about Ducasse's life following his return to France, and in particular about his life once he arrived in Paris, itself suggests a solitary existence. There is no mention of Lautréamont among the writers of his time, and his death in Paris went unnoticed. Laforgue, on the other hand, boasted a broad circle of friends and acquaintances among the literary and artistic elite. Yet these relationships did little to alleviate his experience of isolation while carrying out his functions as reader to the Empress Augusta in Germany. Laforgue's physical absence from Paris left him feeling desperately lonely and disconnected from a literary scene upon which he wanted to make his mark. The sheer volume of letters he wrote during his time in Germany suggests an isolation that is confirmed by his constant pleas for news of the current literary picture in Paris and his repeated references to exile. To Gustave Kahn, who was carrying out his military service in Tunisia, he writes that he is "every bit as exiled as you" (689). To Charles Henry, he complains that he feels "seriously exiled," or "rudement exilé" (726).

As Ursula Franklin observes, "isolation and alienation, whose ultimate degree is exile, characterized irony from the outset" (4). If irony translates a sense of exile, its presence in self-parody only multiplies the degrees of self-separation for those who practice it. Self-parody was certainly not the exclusive domain of these authors, but the inventiveness and humor that infuse their works set them apart, even in a century gorged with literary talent. Beneath the disingenuous irreverence and gleeful lampooning of literary genres and conventions lies a prescient *remise en question* of the relationship between narrator, reader and text that predates by several decades the first theoretical articulations of this relationship by the Russian Formalists and that continues to be debated to this day.[14] Both Lautréamont and Laforgue fully realized the latter's oft-cited desire, "faire de l'original à tout prix" ("to be original, above all else") (Laforgue, v.1, 821)[15] through a literary innovativeness that the foregoing discussion has attempted to illuminate.

---

[14] Tynianov's article was originally published in 1919.
[15] Letter to Marie Laforgue.

Works Cited

Baudelaire, Charles. *Correspondance générale*, vol. 6. Edited by Jacques Crépet and Claude Pichois. Paris: Conard, 1953.

Bouché, Claude. *Lautréamont: du lieu commun à la parodie*. Paris: Larousse, 1974.

Compère, Daniel. "Parodie et autoparodie dans l'oeuvre de Jules Verne." In *Poétiques de la parodie et du pastiche de 1850 à nos jours*, edited by Catherine Dousteyssier-Khoze and Floriane Place-Verghnes, 83-94. NewYork: Peter Lang, 2006.

Diaz, José Pedro. "Lautréamont, le Montevidéen." In *Lautréamont et Laforgue dans leur siècle*, edited by Daniel Lefort and Jean-Jacques Lefrère, 101-111. Paris: AAPPFID, 1994.

Ducasse, Isidore. *Les Chants de Maldoror*. In *Lautréamont, Germain Nouveau Oeuvres complètes*. Paris: Gallimard, 1970.

Duprey, Jacques-André. "Laforgue et Lautréamont, deux manières de vivre leur binationalité." In *Lautréamont et Laforgue dans leur siècle*, edited by Daniel Lefort and Jean-Jacques Lefrère, 335-344. Paris: AAPPFID, 1994.

Franklin, Ursula. *Exiles and Ironists*. New York: Peter Lang, 1988.

Genette, Gérard. *Palimpsestes*. Paris: Seuil, 1982.

—. *Narrative Discourse*. Translated by Jane E. Lewin. Ithaca: Cornell University Press, 1980.

Grojnowski, Daniel. "L'Ironie laforguienne dans les *Moralités légendaires*." In *Lautréamont et Laforgue dans leur siècle*, edited by Daniel Lefort and Jean-Jacques Lefrère. Paris: AAPPFID, 1994: 203-211.

—. *Jules Laforgue et l'«originalité»*. Neuchâtel: A la Baconnière, 1988.

Guillot-Muñoz, Gervasio and Alvaro. *Lautréamont et Laforgue*. Paris and Montevideo: Agencia General de Librería y Publicaciones, 1925.

Hannoosh, Michele. *Parody and Decadence*. Columbus: Ohio State University Press, 1989.

Hibbitt, Richard. "Dilettantism and Irony: Jules Laforgue and C.M. Wieland." *Forum for Modern Language Studies* 43, no. 3 (2007): 290-300.

Hutcheon, Linda. *A Theory of Parody*. New York: Methuen, 1985.

Laflèche, Guy. "L'Hispanisme des *Chants de Maldoror*."In *La Littérature Maldoror:Actes du Septième Colloque international sur Lautréamont*, edited by Paul Aron, Jean-Pierre Bertrand and Pascal Durand, 65-74. Tusson: Du Lérot, 2005.

Laforgue, Jules. *Oeuvres complètes*, tome II. Lausanne: L'Age d'Homme, 1995.

Lefort, Daniel and Jean-Jacques Lefrère, eds. *Lautréamont et Laforgue dans leur siècle*. Paris: AAPPFID, 1994.

Rose, Margaret. *Parody: Ancient, Modern and Post-modern*. Cambridge: Cambridge University Press, 1993.

—. *Parody/Meta-fiction*. London: Croom Helm, 1979.

Sangsue, Daniel. *La Parodie*. Paris: Hachette, 1994.

Thut, Martin. *Le Simulacre de l'énonciation: stratégies persuasives dans "Les Chants de Maldoror" de Lautréamont*. Bern: Peter Lang, 1989.

Tynianov, Iouri. "Destruction, Parodie." *Change* 2 (1969): 67-76.

THE LUDIC UTOPIAS OF GERARDO DIEGO'S ULTRAIST POETRY[1]

JUDITH STALLINGS-WARD

Laughter is a serious matter for Gerardo Diego, the most prolific writer of *ultraísmo*,[2] Spain's first avant-garde movement in poetry, and also winner of his country's national prize for literature in 1925. In his address to a conference on children's music held in Buenos Aires in 1928, Diego affirms the vital role laughter plays in the poet's vocation:

> Curiosos de todo, riámonos puerilmente ante las eternas maravillas de la vida. [. . .] Hay que jugar, jugar profundamente, se entiende, con todos los motivos de la naturaleza. [. . .] Juguemos a hacer arte como el niño juega a hacer vida. (Música 43)

> Let us be curious about everything and laugh like children beholding the eternal miracles of life. [...] Let us play, play to the depths of our souls with all the elements of nature. [...] Let us make art the way children play at making life.[3]

The many ludic utopias created by Diego in his ultraist verse bear out the above enjoinder. The poems in *Manual de espumas* (1924), the central

---

[1] This essay is dedicated to Zenia Sacks DaSilva in whose ludic utopia was once joyfully celebrated the miracle of humor.

[2] Ultraism is Spain's first avant-garde movement in poetry. It embraces the aesthetic platform of creationism, a school of poetry founded by the Chilean Vicente Huidobro, which it applies with two other techniques—dehumanization and purification. The former strives to empty the poem of profuse emotional expression and reference to the poetic "I" (although humor and contained sentiment are admitted, while the latter involves the stripping away of all non-essential elements in favor of pure form (the poem's imagery). Ultraism was a literary movement—although short-lived—whose social concerns, expressed in boisterous public meetings, transcend those of an aesthetic school.

[3] All translations are mine.

work of ultraism, are studded with humorous images ranging from curious hybrid entities and visual puns (ambiguous images that deceive the eye), to lyrical abstractions—all existing in topsy-turvy worlds where cosmic order has been reconfigured. The present essay will examine Diego's play with form—whether nature's form or the form of the artist's medium--and show how the poet applies compositional strategies borrowed from Ramón Gómez de la Serna (1888-1963), creator of the *greguería*,[4] and Juan Gris (1887-1927), the theorist of the cubist school of painting, to create his ludic utopias. The *greguería*´s humor stems from its hybrid composition blending the opposing realms of the mechanical and the natural, as in: "La palmera ancla la tierra al cielo" ("The palm tree anchors the earth to the sky"), "El piano tiene esqueleto de pescado" ("The piano has the skeleton of a fish"), or "Se apagan las sonrisas como las luces" ("Smiles turn off like lights") (Torre 526).

Humor abounds in the paintings of Juan Gris, who began his career as a humor magazine artist. While still studying in Madrid he contributed to *Madrid cómico*, and after moving to Paris in 1906, his drawings were published in *Le Rire* (*Laughter*), the most successful of all the humor magazines published in France during the "Belle Époque". One rather infamous example is figure 1: "View of the Bay" (1921), where Gris exploits the tension between interiority and exteriority: a cloud floating at the corner of his bricolage composition contains the French words "le pet" ("the fart").

Diego's dedications of poems in *Manual de espumas* provide reliable indices to the roots of his ultraist humor. The book's second poem "Mirador" is written to Gómez de la Serna, while the work's longest poem "Canción fluvial" ("River Song") pays homage to Juan Gris. The importance of these two artists for Diego is also patent in the book's opening poem "Primavera" ("Spring"), whose imagery bears resemblance to the *greguería*, while its composition recalls Gris's cubist painting.[5]

---

[4] *Greguerías* are the prose images of *ramonismo*, a literary school preceding ultraism and founded by Gómez de la Serna. The *greguería* combines baroque "conceptismo", or wit, and the vanguard's imaginative play with form. (See Durán 226.) Its comical effect arises from the incongruous mixture of disparate categories. For a discussion of humor, see Bousoño vol. II, chapters XVIII-XX.

[5] The influence of cubism in Diego's poetry came about through a meeting in Paris in the summer of 1922 in the home of Vicente Huidobro, where Diego met and befriended the Spanish painter. The contact proved beneficial for, as a result of this meeting, Diego wrote and two years later published *Manual de espumas*. Indeed in reference to *Manual de espumas*, Diego affirms: "In these poems I want to make a

Indeed "Primavera" may be read as a kind of epigraph to *Manual* that establishes the work's humorous tone, introduces its meta-artistic themes, and deploys the technical strategies of ultraism's poetics.

Figure 1.

"Primavera" refers to a creationist spring, a season of artistic renewal manifest in the poem's non-natural imagery. At the heart of the poem is a creationist sun-tree emblem derived from a construction crane, which the swallows appropriate as their nesting site and place of song. Toward the end of the poem, a white-gloved hand, a synecdoche for the poet, appears in the sky holding doves.

---

poetic transposition of what cubism was at that time." ("En esos poemas quiero hacer una transposición poética de lo que entonces era el cubismo"). (Alonso 248).

PRIMAVERA

Ayer   Mañana
Los días niños cantan en mi ventana
Las casas son todas de papel
y van y vienen las golondrinas
(5)   doblando y desdoblando esquinas

Violadores de rosas
Gozadores perpetuos del marfil de las cosas
Ya tenéis aquí el nido
que en la más bella grúa se os ha construido

(10)   Y desde él cantaréis todos
en las manos del viento

                          Mi vida es un limón
                          pero no es amarilla mi canción
                          Limones y planetas
(15)   en las ramas del sol
                          Cuántas veces cobijasteis
                          la sombra verde de mi amor
                          la sombra verde de mi amor

La primavera nace
(20)   y en su cuerpo de luz la lluvia pace

El arco iris brota de la cárcel

Y sobre los tejados
mi mano blanca es un hotel
para palomas de mi cielo infiel

"Yesterday … Tomorrow/ the infant days sing at my window" (lines 1-2). The words "ayer" and "mañana" are separated by a wide stretch of white space (line 1), with the word "ventana" ("window") centered directly underneath, like a title beneath a painting (line 2). With this typographical arrangement, the poet establishes an analogy between page and canvas whereby his use of words is compared to the painter's use of brushstrokes. The word "ventana" lends depth to the two-dimensional flat space establishing yet a third meaning. This ironic treatment echoes the visual puns of Juan Gris, which are seen, for example, in figure 2: "Table Overlooking the Ocean" (1925) and figure 3: "The Violin Before the Open Window" (1926).

Figure 2.

Yet the poet does more than transpose Gris's visual pun from canvas to poem; he stretches the limits of his own medium to infuse the blank space with a temporal dimension. The words "ayer" and "mañana", framing the white space on either side, impose the chronological order of a series. The "gap in between" is thus read as the unnamed present moment, "hoy" ("today"), which exists between and connects the past and the future. The multi-dimensional void derived from the poet's play with multiple meanings (blank page-empty canvas; window-new day) does not provoke *horror vacui*; it serves instead as the perfect resonator for the speaker's sense of youthful optimism conveyed by the double image of "días niños" ("infant days")[6] that sing in the window (line 2). The double image,

---

[6] It is instructive to compare this double image with a similar one used by the *modernista* poet José Martí—"días azules" ("blue days"). Martí uses the symbolic

frequently used in ultraism, omits the "as" or "like" to collapse the metaphor and convey the immediacy of a double virtuality. The poem's window provides a view onto the spring of artistic creation. Rather than placing the emphasis on the speaker's emotion, it focuses on the material of substances and the repetition of forms, tinting the verse with a playful tone inspired by the plastic lyricism of Gris's paintings (See figure 4: "The Three Masks" (1923).

Figure 3.

In "Primavera", this new lyricism of form is expressed in the whimsical origami imagery of paper houses and swallows that fold and unfold their corners (lines 3-5). The swallows, we are told, who perpetually savor the ivory-coat of all things, are notorious violators of roses (lines 6-7). With their menacing treatment of the rose and their self-serving materialism, the swallows not only fly in the face of romanticism's

value of the color blue to suggest a sense of optimism and youthfulness associated with the days of which he speaks. Diego, on the other hand, prefers concrete imagery over suggestive symbols; for that reason he uses a double image to achieve immediacy, or iconicity. See Gullón 38.

symbols and intense emotion; they also articulate ultraism's preference for concrete imagery and humorous tone.

Figure 4.

A construction crane that provides a "most beautiful" ("más bello") nesting place for the swallows (lines 8-9) recalls the *greguería* of Gómez de la Serna. This surprising hybrid entity is the centerpiece of the poem's delightful humor. The tiny birds wittingly appropriate the giant mechanical prosthesis as their pre-fabricated nest and inspiration for public song: "Y desde él cantaréis todos / en las manos del viento"("and from there too will all your voices rise in song, carried by the hands of the wind") (lines 10-11). The lyrics to the song describe a man-made sun tree crafted by techniques borrowed from Juan Gris.[7] The poet extracts the roundness belonging to both lemons and planets (line 14) and adds the color yellow (line 13), belonging only to the lemons, to re-configure a new image--the sun.[8] The sun has rays resembling branches from the lemon tree (line 15).

---

[7] Diego´s use of cubist strategies to make the sun tree fulfills the creationist injunction issued by Vicente Huidobro in the poem "Horizon Carré" to 'make a poem the way nature makes a tree'.
[8] Diego discusses Gris's aesthetic theory as set forth in a conference held at the Sorbonne in 1924 as a transposition of nature's order in which the painter shuffles the properties and qualities of objects and subsequently re-configures them to arrive at new forms. ("Devoción" 172).

The branches, in turn, suggest that the sun is a lemon held by the branches of the tree. A harmonious resonance ensues from the interplay between the repetition and the variation of the qualities of the images. The refrain "Cuántas veces cobijasteis / la sombra verde de mi amor" ("How many times you were sheltered in the green shade of my love") (line 16) is attached as a coda closing the song with a feeling of imaginative and nurturing vitality.

The cubist strategies Diego applies in the visual imagery have also been applied to a song, drawing yet another analogy between cubism and music; in both, the compositional structures of harmony, counterpoint, repetition, and variation come into play. Diego, who was an accomplished pianist and music critic, uses these strategies of musical composition in his poems as well: "A large part of my poetry is created using music as a compositional guideline, not exactly melody (verbal sonority); the important thing is structure ..." (Pérez 31). Thus, the ultraist poem shares a compositional affinity with music as well as with cubist painting and with the *greguería*. For the poet, the spiritual value of poetry is similar to that of music. For the painter, the spiritual value of painting is equal to that of poetry, since he refers to its plastic lyricism.

The sun-tree heralds the birth of a creationist spring amidst hybrid weather that fuses opposite categories of sunshine and rain: "La primavera nace y en su cuerpo de luz la lluvia pace" ("Spring is born and from its body of light the rain is fed.") (lines 19-20). With its blend of hybrid weather, nature seems to imitate art, undercutting the mimetic theory of art. This creative flux augurs hope for tomorrow, as indicated by the placement of the sun tree in the right-hand column beneath the word "mañana" (line 1) and the appearance of the rainbow over the jail: "El arco iris brota de la cárcel" (line 21).

The poem's closing image, the hand in the sky, is a synecdoche for the artist and supports Huidobro's conception of the poet as a "pequeño Dios" ("little God"), expressed in his poem "Arte poética." Yet the doves held by the hand and the backdrop of the uncertain sky are important qualifiers that show that this artist-god is dependent on a superior entity for divine inspiration. The dove is an index to the spiritual inspiration imparted by creative flux and divine power, while the whiteness of both gloved hand and dove connotes the spiritual value of purification that is imparted in the artist's work.[9] Within this incongruous ludic frame lies a utopia in which

---

[9] Huidobro's poem "Altazor" (1919) points to another significant difference in meaning of this imagery. The poetic "I" yearns for eternity as an escape from pain: "I want eternity like a hand-held dove. . .What have you done with my voice laden

objects sensible and insensible are melded, where the artist is at one and perfection lies in the striving.

"Primavera" is followed by a poem dedicated to Gómez de la Serna and entitled "Mirador" A *mirador* is a glass encased balcony that offers a vantage point for viewing one's surroundings; but it also refers to a prodigious and incisive observer of his surroundings such as Gómez de la Serna. The *mirador* exemplifies a way of viewing life and art that eschews display of excessive emotion and focuses instead on surprise, humor, and wonder. Life is a series of non-sequiturs, and coherence is the exception, not the gauge.

The poem begins: "De balcón a balcón / los violines de ciego / tienden sus arcos de pasión (lines 1-3). The "mirador" (here, the "observer") evades the cliché of blind violinists strolling from balcony to balcony (from house to house) lifting their passionate bows to play. For here it is the instruments, rather than the musician, that raise their bows (lines 1-3) and the music is played by invisible hands. A song is born, born of itself as a mélange of passing thoughts follows: "Es algo irremediable / cortar con las tijeras estas calles" (lines 4-5). Inevitably these streets—these ingrained life-frames—shall be cut up into scissor-pieces. But is the poem really speaking of streets and scissors? Or is this a metapoetic reference to its own undercutting of narrative links, as evidenced in the series of disconnected images? The flashes of awareness continue, half-coherent, non-sequential: "Las cartas nacidas de mi regazo / aprenden a volar algo mejor" ("the letters born of my bosom learn to soar to new heights") (lines 6-7).

The poem's central image is a *greguería* of seminal metapoetic value. It appears in the middle of the poem: "Y tú, manso tranvía / gusano de mis lágrimas / que hilas mi llanto en tus entrañas / Condúceme a tu establo / y sácame del pozo en que te hablo" ("And you, humble streetcar, slithering worm formed of my tears, weaving my wails into your innards, take me to your source, lift me out of this well from which I beseech you.") (lines 14-16). "Mirador" now weaves toward an idyllic prophecy: "Yo te prometo que esta primavera / tu vara florezca en todos los tejados / tejados olvidados / en los que ya no pastan los ganados / y a los que nunca sube el

---

with birds in the afternoon / The voice that pains me like blood? (Canto II)" The speaker in "Primavera", by contrast, holds doves in his hand and lays claim to the infinite as "mi cielo infiel" ("my volatile heaven") (line 24). Where the creationist poet is filled with yearning and laments the loss of creative force, the ultraist eschews heterodoxical emotion and maintains possession of the creative force.

surtidor" (lines19-23), promising that in spring "your staff will burst into flower over all the roofs / forgotten roofs / where cattle no longer graze / and the waters of the fount are still." Hope now abounds. There will be renewal, even where death seemed to hold dominion, and lifelessness will return to life. Clearly, because the poem is dedicated to Gómez de la Serna, these lines refer to the artistic innovation of his greguerías, but its outreach is also universal. In the end, the speaker's outlook is filled with humor and equanimity as he whimsies: "Dejemos al Señor / que arranque las estrellas / y durmámonos / sin consultar con ellas" ("Let God pull out the stars, if he will / and let us go to sleep / without consulting them.") (lines 24-27). Such is the utopia that emerges, not one of order and complacence, but a helter-skelter of imperfection, disarray, and from it the vitality of transformation.

Figure 5.

In "Aldea" ("Village"), Diego parodies the idealized and nostalgic view of rural life while also poking fun at the myth of Arcadia, the home of Pan, god of shepherds and flocks. The poem's temporal stasis and spatial disorder create a total inverisimilitude, which is set in sharp relief against the poem's brilliantly perfected vignette format. Diego's detemporalization of the poem finds its inspiration and counterpoint in Gris's deliberate flattening of perspective, while his inverted geography reflects cubism's tendency to reconfigure normal compositional order. Both tendencies are exemplified in figure 5: "The Teacups" (1914).

ALDEA

Del campanario va a volar el día
pero las nubes mías no han vuelto todavía

Ni han regresado los corderos
de su viaje a la luna sin pacer los luceros

(5)   Aplicando el oído sobre el césped
                                       en vez del tren o el grillo
                                       se oye una pieza de organillo

Y el pastor no sabe
que en su cabaña está la noche
(10)   y que el molino es el motor del baile

                                       Las vacas del establo
                                       quieren lamer el sol
                                       plato del día
                                       que sirven los pintores de fantasía

(15)   Es la hora del cigarro y de la jaula
        Sin mirar el reloj pernocta el gallo
        y las estrellas tristes contemplan al caballo

The main body of the poem, which contains the narration, is placed flush left, while musical and visual motifs are set to the right, outside of the main narrative, like interludes in the main action. There is perfect balance between the number of couplets and tercets. This formal virtuosity offers itself as a counterweight to the poem's free reign with nonsense and its forays into the absurd.

In "Aldea," life does not flow with the rhythm of the seasons, nor does the landscape reflect pastoral harmony. The future is imprisoned by a static present. Although the belltower has tolled the arrival of dusk (line 1), night has been locked in a shepherd's cabin, preventing the normal passing of the day. Both spatial and temporal laws governing cosmic order are inoperable. The shepherd tends his flocks in an upside-down world:

clouds have not yet returned home to the speaker, and sheep have not yet returned from grazing in their celestial fields (2-4).

The tercet placed to the right and outside the main body of the poem (lines 5-7) offers a comical *intermezzo* using Arcadia as a foil. In Arcadia the sound of pan pipes, or *zampoña*, floats through the air as Pan blows through the reeds; in "Aldea," the sound of the *organillo*, or hurdy-gurdy, is piped through the grass-covered earth: "Aplicando el oído sobre el césped / en vez del tren o el grillo / se oye una pieza de organillo" ("If you apply your ear to the grass / instead of the roar of a train or a cricket's chirp / you can hear a hurdy-gurdy playing." (Ibid.). The main narration continues (to the left, line 8) with a declarative statement that the shepherd does not know that the night is lodged in his cabin and that his mill is the motor of the universal dance. Since ignorance of nonsense does not amount to a lack of information, humor results from the tension between the declarative statement and the non-information it contains. A second interlude (introduced in lines 11-12 and continued to the right in line 13, outside the main body of the poem), is a pun on *hors d'oeuvre*—the culinary version of the literary interlude. The double image "sol / plato del día" ("sun / the daily special") is based on a formal similarity—the round shape of both the sun and plate, as well as a conceptual similarity; both are renewed daily, since the sun rises and the menu changes each morning. The placement of the words "plato del día" above the longer line "que sirven los pintores de fantasía" ("that the painters of fantasy serve") is iconic of the waiter's laden tray. The reference to painting reminds the reader that the double image is a transposition of the cubist painter's visual pun.

Line 15 floats between two couplets, linking them and lending structural harmony and counterpoint to the typographical format. The first half of the compound sentence "es la hora del cigarro" ("it's time for a cigar") refers to the conclusion of the meal, while the second sentence "es la hora del jaula" ("it's time for the cage") refers to the animals' bedtime. The rooster, unmindful of the clock, stays up all night, disoriented by the night's failure to arrive. And the reader can hardly blame him. In "Aldea" time as we know it has no meaning. The closing image of the stars sadly regarding the horse replicates the inverted order where sheep graze in celestial pastures. In the end, we don't know whether the stars are looking down or up at the horse … or if it is even a horse ...

Diego's poem "Novela" is a parody of an altogether different theme—the detective story which, as Jorge Luis Borges, a former collaborator in ultraism affirms, is never without a beginning, a plot, and a dénouement.

Although the poem presents a detailed and ordered narration of events, in the end little action occurs, with the exception of the passing of time.

The poet emphasizes the dynamic nature of his subject by beginning in *medias res*: "El auto que pasaba se llevó los sollozos" (line 1): A car that was driving by made off with the sobs, while the garden fence simply folded it arms and let it all happen. The police are already at the scene of the crime: "He aquí los tres policías / a investigar el rapto / buscando huellas de la huida / por las teclas del piano" ("Look. Three policeman have come to investigate the theft, looking for clues among the keys of the piano") (lines 7-10). Diego has inserted a clue for us as to the nature of the crime. The reader familiar with his poetry will know that, in his poem "Nocturno," piano keys are a metaphor for the stars, associated with the night. We suspect, then, that the crime being investigated is the theft of daylight: "Son las cinco de la tarde..." It is five p.m. and with spring awaiting its turn nearby to arrive, the moon rushes over to bathe hidden lovers in its light. We now see the police reconstructing the crime by retracing the events leading up to nightfall, when nature and the city take on a sinister appearance. Mysterious and ominous shadows wait in balconies and corners like hit-men spying on their assigned targets. The arrival of night is like the arrival of a Mafia boss "cuando se vio saltar de un coche / del brazo traidor / la inesperada noche" ("when without warning nightfall is seen jumping out of the perpetrator's car") (26-28).

The poet creates a sense of conspiracy among the shadows, as if they were plotting the death of daylight. The clock is a witness to the crime, even though a temporary glitch in its movement set the roosters off on their wakeup calls. "Henos aquí ante el ladrón" ("Here, here, we've found the thief!") (36). The drama reaches its climax when "entre el llorar de las cortinas / la luna estalla de pasión" (37): amidst the weeping curtains, the moon bursts forth with passion. Immediately thereafter the dénouement ensues as the quiet and peace of night are restored to nature and to the city. Diego makes fun of the night's stillness, just as he toys with the fall of night. "Y en el lugar del suceso / el farol asustado contempla el árbol preso" (41-42). The street light is paralyzed with fright and the tree stands petrified, as if it had been arrested. The comic interchange is complete in its very incongruity, its very unlikelihood.

In conclusion, we have visited the humorous and incongruous worlds of four ultraist poems and experienced the hybrid imagery of the *greguería* and the imaginatively reconfigured environment in which that imagery thrives. We laugh first in reaction to the surprising half- mechanical half-natural images that enter in the poet´s work through the influence of

Gómez de la Serna. And we laugh again in response to the subversion of traditional notions of art, inspired by the cubism of Juan Gris. The poet´s deconstruction of the illusion of spatial perspective and temporal perspective undercuts the notion of art as a reflection of the natural world. And its simultaneous embrace of the ordinary and the absurd creates a new utopia in which space and time conform to the individual frame, in which all life is liberated from the constraints of cosmic laws and its inhabitants live in a state of ultra conscience, allowing unexpected and magical experiences to unfold. In these roots lie the keys to Gerardo Diego's unique, and ingenious, humor.

Works Cited

Alonso, Dámaso. *Poetas españoles contemporáneos*. 3rd ed. Madrid: Gredos, 1969.

Bousoño, Carlos. *Teoría de la expresión poética*. 2 vols. Madrid: Gredos, 1985.

Cano Ballesta, Juan. *Literatura y Tecnología*. Madrid: Orígenes, 1981.

Diego, Gerardo. "Devoción y meditación de Juan Gris." *Revista de occidente* 17 (1927): 160-180.

—. *Manual de espumas. Versos humanos*. Madrid: Cátedra, 1986.

—. "Música infantil". *Conferencias y discursos*. Buenos Aires: Club español, 1928: 43-59.

Durán, Manuel. "Notas sobre García Lorca, la vanguardia, Ramón Gómez de la Serna y las greguerías." *Cuadernos Hispanoamericanos* 433-436 (1986): 221-229.

Gómez de la Serna, Ramón. *Greguerías. Selección 1910-1960*. Madrid: Espasa-Calpe, 1960.

Gullón, Ricardo. "Simbolismo y modernismo." *El simbolismo*. Ed. José Olivio Jiménez. Madrid: Taurus, 1979: 21-44.

Kahnweiler, Daniel-Henry. *Juan Gris: His Life and Works*. New York: Harry N. Abrams, 1969.

Marinetti, Filippo. *Marinetti: Selected Writings*. Ed. R. W. Flint. New York: Farrar, Straus and Giroux, 1972.

Pérez, J. Bernardo. "Fases de la poesía creacionista de Gerardo Diego". Valencia: *Albatros Hispanófila*, 1989.

Torre, Guillermo de. *Historia de las literaturas de vanguardia*. Madrid: Guadarrama, 1965.

VII.

I LAUGH ONLY WHEN IT HURTS

AFTER THE CURTAIN:
DARK HUMOR IN NEW ROMANIAN DRAMA

SAVIANA STĂNESCU

Alex Drace-Francis, professor at the School of Slavonic and East-European Studies, writes in his essay "Sex, Lies and Stereotypes: Romania in British Literature Since 1945":

> On the scholarly level, interest in Romania is apparently extremely healthy. On the everyday level, the presentation of Romania in Britain is considerably less consistent. The launch of a new Romanian helicopter may make the news if it is named after Count Dracula; of ten articles treating Romanian politics published in 1996, five featured the former tennis player Ilie Năstase; all three articles on the Romanian economic situation in 1998 concerned the sale of former President Ceausescu's possessions in order to raise funds. Orphanages, gypsies, drug-trafficking and murders all get a mention. If the Romanian football team's participation in the 1998 World Cup made any impression, it was perhaps caused less by their (purely fortunate) victory over England than their players' propensity to anoint their faces with a magic potion made up of holy water, basil, olive oil and honey (accompanied by the sign of the cross three times) or even their superstitious-strategic dyeing of their hair blonde in the midst of the tournament… Romania is portrayed synecdochically as a helpless, victimized woman, equally let down by the sympathetic but uncommitted West and the brutal, abusive man that is the communist state.

What, then, is the role of Romanian writers and scholars? Are we not responsible for offering a more complex and nuanced portrait of that allegorical "victimized woman" Romania, so that Romanian hi/stories can be read, seen and understood beyond stereotypes, labels, compassion and sex appeal? And how can we proceed to have more impact in the Western world now, when the dichotomy West-East is gradually fading away as countries that were part of the former-Soviet block have joined the European Union and NATO? Now, when we all are, more or less, global foreigners traveling from one place to another, in the real world and cyberspace? Now, when we have internet, and *google*, and *facebook*, and *myspace*, and blogs, and so many other instant means of communication. This paper is an attempt to offer an answer that places dark humor at the center of the new Romanian playwrights' artistic endeavors to examine the Eastern European post-communist society and its redefining relationship with the West.

It is a truth universally acknowledged that one of the most effective dramatic tools used by writers with a social consciousness to achieve lasting impact is humor. Bleak humor has often been a worthy device for making people laugh while "swallowing" bitter comments on the everyday reality. Playwright George Bernard Shaw (1856-1950) is credited with saying: "If you are going to tell people the truth, you'd better make them laugh. Otherwise, they'll kill you." The quote is sometimes attributed to W. C. Fields, Charlie Chaplin, and Oscar Wilde. It might possibly derive from Shaw's statement in *John Bull's Other Island*: "My way of joking is to tell the truth. It's the funniest joke in the world" (50). The variants are many, but the idea of humor-coating social and political commentaries is especially relevant for many Romanian artists.

Romanian playwriting has a long tradition in a tragicomic absurdist style. Tragicomedy and biting irony were the dramatic tools of Ion Luca Caragiale, who wrote incisive and insightful satires on society and lifestyle in late 19th-century Romania. Caragiale is still considered "our national dramatist," an expression contested by the new generations of indie Romanian theatre makers who actively fight the mainstream's need for centralized hierarchies, one of the die-hard "dinosaurs" inherited from the totalitarian regime of Nicolae Ceaușescu. However, at the other extreme, at the opposite pole of the nationalistic, WE is an attitude to be found in many "small" cultures with a strong paternalistic tradition: the desire to impress the Big Daddy. In Eastern Europe, after 1989, the "Big Daddy" could openly be the capitalist "daddy," the West. New York, London, Berlin, Paris are some of the new father-figures expected to fulfill most Romanians' tragicomic need for approval. Swinging between self-victimization and self-confidence, between love and hate for The Almighty West, many East European playwrights mock Hollywood, West

End and Broadway for their industrialism and entertainment values while secretly dreaming of that kind of commercial success.

In the spring of 1990, in the aftermath of the Romanian revolution, British playwright Caryl Churchill ran a ten-day research workshop in Bucharest that led to her play *Mad Forest*—a fast and brilliant response to our recent history and a perspective from outside on a major socio-political event. However, one could wonder where are the Romanian plays written in the early 1990s to explore, question, analyze, dramatize the historical tornado of December, 1989. One possible explanation for the lack of immediate response of the native Romanian playwrights is the fact that they were too busy with dramatic living to be able to focus on dramatic writing. Distance in time or space is often necessary for such soul-searching identity-reshaping undertakings.

Playwrights like Teodor Mazilu, Iosif Naghiu, or Dumitru Solomon who wrote non-propagandistic plays in communist Romania drew their inspiration from the theatre of the absurd of Samuel Beckett and Eugène Ionesco, as well as from the classic Romanian playwright Ion Luca Caragiale. The same absurdist vein nourished Matei Vișniec, who emerged in the late 1980s and had to flee Bucharest for Paris after his play *Horses in the Window* was censored. He became the most prolific Romanian dramatist of the 1990s and his plays are still produced very often in Romania and France. Although poetic, surreal, and absurdist elements are still to be found in plays written after the fall of communism, there is an overall tendency to *address* reality rather than *escape* from it.

At the same time, the Western European theatre scene of the early and mid-1990s witnessed the appearance of a new wave of British, German, and Scandinavian playwrights who shared a dark, desperate, depressive, yet humorous view of humanity at the crossroad between millennia. All of them provoked controversy and shock but grew to become very popular among young theatergoers and progressive audiences. Eventually they became icons of the so-called Generation X or E-generation: the generation of internet, ecstasy, fast food, fast connection, and fast love. They shared certain undertones from the historical avant-garde, Brecht, Artaud, Shakespeare, and the theatre of the absurd, employing a heightened, confrontational, graphic, violent, uncompromising, visceral dramatic style, imbued with extremely bleak humor and a social conscience. In the UK, their work has been referred to as "The New Brutalism," "Sperm and Blood," or "In-Yer-Face Theatre."

Through their summer international residencies and workshops led by representative members of their community of artists from various countries, the Royal Court's aesthetic has arguably represented a major influence for the new Eastern European dramatists. One of the first Romanian playwrights to participate in the Royal Court Theatre residency program was Alina Nelega, who was subsequently inspired to create a new initiative called Dramafest in the late 1990s, in which writers were paired with directors and encouraged to write for theatre in process-focused workshops. The new Romanian writing began to reach the theatres through productions by young directors who felt the need to discover fresh perspectives in dramatic texts. The cutting-edge Cristian Teodor Popescu memorably staged Andrea Vălean's play *When I Want to Whistle, I Whistle*, while Radu Afrim, a provocative idiosyncratic artist offered innovative productions of my own *Final Countdown* (under the title *Black Milk)* and *INFANTA*. In 2000 my dark comedy, *The Inflatable Apocalypse*, won the UNITER (the Romanian Theatre Guild's) Award's Best Play of the Year.

The border between millennia found Romanian theatre in a state of European effervescence. Young artists were more and more present in workshops and festivals in the UK, Germany, Austria, France, Spain, and even in the countries of the Balkans. In the summer of 2001, both Andrea Vălean and I were selected to participate to the Royal Court Theatre's summer residency. After her return to Bucharest, together with her directing colleagues, Andrea Vălean founded *dramAcum (dramaNow)*, one of the leading indie organizations for promoting young writers. Kate Loewald, the producing artistic director of *The Play Company*, was impressed by the energy and self-deprecating humor of the new Romanian writing and produced five short Romanian plays (including Ion's and Georgescu's) at the 59E59 Theatre in New York in the fall of 2006, under the title *"Romania. Kiss Me."* Jason Zinoman writes about one of the plays in The New York Times:

> "Red Bull," a cagey Romanian drama by Vera Ion about two bored young people who find common cause, could have been written by any number of American purveyors of suburban angst. In this tautly organized work, He (John Boyd) and She (Julie Jesneck) narrate their own lives in alternating monologues that detail the grueling and mundane process of making a living. He works three jobs; she works four. And there is a deep, melancholy irony when she says, "I feel so free I could do anything," right before she steals a car while drunk on vodka.

The critic notices the irony and dark humor in Vera Ion's play, a good sign that the message and style of the new Romanian drama can come across well for American audiences. Meanwhile, Cărbunariu's play, *Kebab,* a bleak *in-yer-face* tragicomedy about sex traffic and juvenile prostitution, opened at the Royal Court Theatre in the fall of 2007. In April 2007, gallows humor saved the day again, as my play *Waxing West* opened at La MaMa Theatre in New York.

The anthology *roMANIA AFTER 2000,* edited by myself and the late CUNY professor Daniel Gerould, is the first professional anthology of new Romanian drama published in the United States. Alienation, dark humor, generational gaps, dysfunctional families, strenuous adjustments to the consumerist society in post-communist Romania, dislocation, exile, immigration, and fascination with the Western world are a few of the topics that unite the five plays included in the anthology as they draw a map of dramatic living and dramatic writing in an emerging democracy.

Cărbunariu's *Stop the Tempo* tells a story of anarchy and rebellion: three twenty-something guys in Bucharest, alienated by the chaotic invasion of the consumerist society, are trying to find an outlet for their despair, lack of love, and feelings of helplessness. They come up with a "terrorist" plan that fills them with excitement and reveals hidden passions, frustrations, and desires. It is a strong play that gives a poignant glimpse into the psychology of young Romanians, struggling in search of identity and truth, particularly in the monologue, spoken by a certain Paula, about working in advertising in the newly emerged consumerist society. This is a powerful example of bleak humor combined with irony that addresses issues of identity and alienation while delving into tragicomedy:

> PAULA: Three years ago I got a job in an advertising agency, sorry…consultancy. So I've been a creative director, brand manager, executive creative artistic director assistant senior manager group chief executive artistic creative director WHATEVER… In the end I chose copywriting. That's what I really liked doing. It was perfect. The money kept pouring in, the contracts kept coming, and two months ago I quit. One morning, our boss comes in and tells us: "We're promoting a new product, a wonder laxative, it's going to be an all channel TV ad and the brief goes like this: 'We take a mother… generous, voluptuous, motherly, almost hysterically zealous, *but* friendly, and she's serving this incredible laxative for breakfast to the

entire family. Cut to them all singing, smiling and jumping around'"'... I couldn't take it anymore.

Vera Ion's *Vitamins* has the same alienated youth at the center of the drama. It explores generational gaps through the daily life of a dysfunctional family living in a media-dominated and money-obsessed world. In both plays, an individual's personal life is shattered by the socio-political changes triggered by the post-communist society. The generation of the parents seems unable to adjust to the new world while their children blame them for the compromising attitudes during the totalitarian regime.

Stefan Peca's *Romania 21* is a musical parody on similar issues: the negotiation between the old values of living under a dictatorship and the new values of the capitalist lifestyle. A political point of view is attempted in depicting this "transition period," but self-irony and mockery undermine a realistic take on the matter. The result is a hilarious and juicy farce-with-songs that captures the atmosphere of corruption and confusion in post-1989 Romania:

PECA (*animatedly*): Good evening, ladies and gentlemen. I hope you've had a good night so far because it's going to get better and better. My name is Peca and I am the author of the play you're about to see—ROMANIA 21. My real name is Ştefan Peca but my playwright pseudonym is just...Peca. You know, like Kafka...in a way. (*Beat*) OK, now that I made that clear I'm just gonna cut straight to the point here. The show is about my country, and my country is all about simple people, like you and me. People you want to write about and see on a stage. (*Beat*) Trust me, I grew up over there and a lot of exciting shit is going on in Romania. Even right as we speak. (*Beat*). In spite of that, Romanians are really simple to understand and many times poor. Anyway, the thing is that usually Romania is a misunderstood concept. In your minds it equals Dracula, vampires, incest, communism, Russia, third world countries. But I can tell you it's more than that. (*Beat*). Much more than that. (*Beat*). A whole lot more. (*Pause for thinking.*) I won't enumerate right now, but please take my word for it.

In *Romania. Kiss Me!*, Georgescu expresses the same cynicism and disappointment with his country, using gallows humor in a specific dramatic situation. Scoffing at the classic Aristotelian unities of time, location, and action, he places his characters in a train that is supposed to take them out of their homeland. Stylistically, Georgescu surprises audiences through the use of a chorus that conveys noises, smells and screams, and wraps the plot in a vibrant, colorful environmental package.

In my play *Waxing West (a hairy-tale in four seasons)*, a Romanian cosmetologist arrives in the United States as the mail-ordered soon-to-be bride of Charlie, an American computer engineer. As she seeks to adjust to her new life in the land of dreams, dictator Nicolae Ceauşescu and his wife Elena return as vampires to haunt her and make her life miserable. This comic, yet socio-politically oriented, drama journeys between New York and Romania, between past and present, between the American Dream and a reality far closer to an American nightmare. The chorus is in this case composed of voices from the past that won't allow the heroine to move on and start a new life. It is as if Romania is still there, under her skin, ready to show its hidden head:

> **DANIELA** (*to the audience*): "Don't laugh at other people's dreams or nightmares"—I read this in 'Introduction to Chinese Wisdom'. It's not a stolen book. I found it in the trash, on our street. I had to take it home! This is how I learned that I was born in the year of the Horse…One can find so many great things in the garbage here, in New York.
> **CEAUSESCU:** Shut up, horse!
> **DANIELA:** It's like they wait for us there, in the rubbish, feeling sad, lonely and rejected…
> **ELENA:** On! On! Move on, pig!
> **CEAUSESCU:** Horse. She's a horse.
> **ELENA:** Whatever.
> **CEAUSESCU:** We shouldn't have taken her here. Everybody left their pets at the door.
> **ELENA:** She's not a pet. She's a servant.
> **CEAUSESCU:** She's our horse. Our dog. Our rat. Our darling little guinea pig. And our cook, of course.
> **ELENA:** Our cleaning girl.
> **CEAUSESCU:** Your waxing lady.
> **ELENA:** I've got so hairy now that I'm dead. Why does hair grow on dead people? Look: everybody is so hairy around here.
> **CEAUSESCU:** Let's not ruin our mood for the sake of hair!
> (*They take two glasses of red wine and drink with relish.*)
> **ELENA:** To … forever!
> **CEAUSESCU:** To… Draculand!
> **ELENA:** You mean Disneyland.

CEAUSESCU: Not at all. We'll have our own park! They're building Draculand in Transylvania, near Sighisoara.

The Past doesn't seem to allow Daniela to move on happily in her new American life. In a bizarre, inexplicable way, she feels somehow responsible for the death of the Ceauşescus—who were executed during the popular uprising in December 1989—and struggles to find her center and be in charge of her life in the "land of all the possibilities." Waxing the unwanted hair on people's bodies is for her an idealistic and humorous fight against Death and an affirmation of Life and Beauty, but the reality of her situation slips in: she doesn't have a work permit that would allow her to work legally in the USA. She is an illegal alien, who depends on her marriage to Charlie. The age-old conventions of boy-meets-girl are subverted here into a strangely funny parable of dislocation and anomie. The play ends with a surreal recitatif that blends images of the fall of dictator Ceauşescu in 1989 with the fall of the Twin Towers in 2001. Individuals' lives are always affected by unexpected collective traumas. No longer torn between New York and Bucharest, finally connected with Charlie on a deeper level, Daniela is painfully braided into the bad-hair-roots of the American Dream.

In conclusion, the playwrights in *roMANIA AFTER 2000* convey the drama of being Romanian today with vitality, force, humor, and a refusal to look at life through rose-colored glasses. They want to "zoom" around and describe the grim reality of everyday life; they want to be artist-citizens who respond to the immediate history and are ready to laugh loudly, shouting their worries and stories. Let's listen to them. And laugh of course—that deep laughter of understanding and appreciation.

Works Cited

Drace-Francis, Alex. "Towards a natural history of East European travel writing." In W. Bracewell and A. Drace-Francis, eds. *Under Eastern Eyes: A Comparative Introduction to East European Travel Writing in Europe.* Budapest - New York, Central European University Press, 2008.

—. "Paradoxes of occidentalism: on travel and travel writing in Ceauşescu's Romania" In A. Hammond, ed. *The Balkans and the West: Constructing the European Other, 1945-2003.* Aldershot, Ashgate, 2004.

Gerould, Daniel and Saviana Stanescu. *roMANIA After 2000: Five New Romanian Plays.* Martin E. Segal Theatre Center Publ., New York, 2007.

Menta, Ed. *The Magic World behind the Curtain: Andrei Serban in the American Theatre.* Peter Lang Publishing Inc., 1995, 1997.

Saunders, Graham. *"Love me or kill me": Sarah Kane and the theatre of extremes.* Manchester University Press, 2002.

Shaw, George Bernard. *John Bull's Other Island.* Fairfield (Iowa): 1st World Publishing, 2004.

Sierz, Aleks. *In-Yer-Face Theatre: British Drama Today.* London: Faber & Faber, 2001.

Stanescu, Saviana. *The New York Plays.* Introduction by John Clinton Eisner. Southgate (California): NoPassport Press, 2011.

GALICIAN "RETRANCA" GONE GREEN: HUMOR ON THE PRESTIGE OIL SPILL

ISABEL CASTRO-VÁZQUEZ

When our emerald coast turned black in November of 2002, Galician humor turned green; that is, ecological. Even though it may seem paradoxical to relate a serious catastrophe like the Prestige oil spill with humor, which tends to be associated with comedy, it is actually the most accurate combination of strategies with which to expose the contradictions evidenced by the events.[1] In fact, there is no paradox at all when we consider an important differentiation between the humorous and the comic. Comedy is related to laughter, whereas humor reveals drama by unveiling two perspectives; in this case, the official version of the government and actual events as they unfolded for the people who live by and of the sea.

To better understand Galician popular humor, known as *retranca*, we can refer to definitions and studies with varied approaches—philosophical, anthropological, post-modern, linguistic,[2] cultural and sociological—all of them pertinent for gaining a better knowledge of Galicia, the European traditions of which it is part, and the oppressive conditions it has endured. As early as 1963, Celestino Fernández de la Vega in his study *O segredo do humor* (*The Secret Behind Humor*) acknowledges the existence of *retranca,* an autochthonous, subtle, popular humor, a unique kind of "irony" or "sarcasm" that is apparent even to non-Galicians (166). More recently, the anthropologist Marcial Gondar Portassany describes this traditional popular mode of speech and conduct as an innate ability to respond evasively, cautiously, ambiguously—a weapon with which to fend off and mystify the intruder (46-47). For Burhard Baltrusch it is a form of outward and also inward protection, a refuge from what one finds difficult to comprehend and accept (121).

---

[1] For information on the events that led to the Prestige oil spill see Catalán Deus, De Toro, García, Gómez and Ordaz, Lobato, Paz and Vázquez as well as Rei-Doval.

[2] See especially Alice Piccardi, 2004.

In 2012, John Rutherford, Oxford Professor and translator of *Don Quixote* into English, inspired by De la Vega's work, wrote *The Power of the Smile: Humour in Spanish Culture*, in which he elaborates on the concept of *retranca*:

> In the Galician language Galician irony is called *retranca*, a word that also refers to a double bar used to secure windows and doors of traditional houses in the closed position and to various kinds of brakes on carts. *Retranca* originated as the defensive weapon of a poor, weak, rural, peripheral people oppressed for centuries by the power of the centre, the imperial power of Madrid. [...] *Retranca* originated as a way of keeping the door shut, of stopping the cart. Cunning is weak people's best defensive weapon, often their only one, and *retranca* originated as a cunning way of resisting those powerful intruders, the Castilian authorities, of avoiding the perils of what seem to be the only three possible responses to their invasive enquiries: refusing to answer—and being condemned for insubordination; answering and telling the truth—and revealing some punishable wrongdoing; answering and telling a lie—and being condemned for perjury. (36-37)

In this ample explanation Rutherford makes the colonial conditions explicit as they relate to place: center vs. periphery. With it comes class oppression and discursive repression in the writing of the official "History". Aware of this, Manuel Rivas, writer, cofounder of Green Peace Spain and one of the leaders of the movement *Nunca máis* (Never Again),[3] praises the ability to express horror with humor, arguing that "for humor to be effective, to allow life to sabotage the implacable machinery of History, language must be conscious of the drama; it has to smell Hell and breathe the sulfurous air of the ogre" (2002: 123). The bellicose tone emphasizes his awareness of humor's potential to counter the official discourse represented by the capitalized "History." Such inequality in the power struggle is represented in Galician traditional jokes, as Rivas reveals when he goes on to ask himself: "'What do we laugh at and why?' In Galician popular humor there is an abundant repertoire of jokes on priests. Blessed be the people that laughed at the ones who ruled and not the ones who were hungry!" (1999: 242).

---

[3] A popular organization created to protest against the causes that lead to the Prestige oil spill.

This approach to humor in a way coincides with that of Simon Critchley who, following Freud's defense of jokes that rebel against authority or the certainty of our knowledge, and elaborating on the incongruity theory developed by Kant, Schopenhauer and Kierkegaard, comments that jokes are meaningful and paradoxical social practices. On the one hand, they show a clear connection with the social structure and on the other, they play with the incongruence within it. Therefore, Critchley argues that "Humor both reveals the situation, and indicates how that situation might be changed" (16). These philosophical explanations, although generic, clarify Rivas's admiration for the ability to express horror with humor; for humor evidences reality even if only on a discursive level, and in holding it up to ridicule, leads to its transformation. This type of expression is in itself a revolution both in content and in the form of the message.

Retranca's birth in popular culture and a rural environment under repression has tainted it with shades of ignorance. In a presentation entitled "A retranca: ironía e metáfora na identidade cultural de Galicia" given in 2006, Xosé Luis Barreiro Rivas, Professor of Sociology at the University of Santiago de Compostela defined *retranca* as a way of speaking with ambiguity that allows for keeping up a conversation when uninformed on the topic. Barreiro relates it to a rural, dispersed society, arguing that as the rural world disappears and the urban one takes over with its education, political socialization, media and globalization, *retranca* progressively disappears; it is a sign of social modernization. Rutherford too notes that from reactive *retranca*, proactive *retranca* developed in less oppressive times with a more aesthetic and less defensive role (42).

I would argue, nevertheless, that in the contemporary global world, where the potential for oppression is still high, this form of humor is still useful. Proof of this is its current use by contemporary Galician writers and intellectuals like Suso de Toro and Antón Reixa (Baltrusch 1998) or Manuel Rivas (Castro Vazquez 2007), as well as by youth in the popular culture of T-shirt sayings like those of <www.caramuxo.com> or <www.reizentolo.com>. *Retranca* maintains an intrinsic essence that makes it readily identifiable and remains part of popular culture, transforming and adapting to current issues and needs. This was evident during the Prestige oil spill.

Clearly, the drive to increase rates of profit was one of the key factors in the oil spill of the Prestige. Ignacio Ramonet and Ramón Chao spoke of liberal globalization that ignores cultural and political plurality, and they warn about the process of privatization of everything related to life and nature. Gondar discussed capitalist economy as a pathogen (2003; 33) and Carlos Taibo argued that the so called "accident" of the Prestige was a consequence of neoliberal globalization. The response was widespread popular protest imbued with autochthonous *retranca* to face the incongruence of the official discourse. There was a myriad of artistic manifestations that included poetry (Bermúdez), short films (Santana), music (*Marea de música*), comic strips in numerous newspapers and collected in books (Catalán, Gómez), pictures (Lobato, Paz, Stein), countless slogans and even manifestos that were read at various demonstrations and performances. I would like to pay closer attention to three of these texts: a performance accompanied by a poetic discourse, a scientific article, and a journalistic text.

On December 28 (Día dos Santos Inocentes, or Fools Day), 2002, there was a public gathering of protest at the Orzan beach in La Coruña where crosses and candles were set to create the image of a cemetery for the funeral of the Sea. The whole happening was very *retranqueiro* in itself, expressing horror with humor. Inspired by the prehistoric inhabitants of the castros,[4] contemporary Galicians resorted to a pantheistic performance and prayed to the Sea. It was the actor Manuel Lourenzo who read a manifesto, a prayer to the Lord Sea, written by Manuel Rivas. Here are a few of its lines:

> Aquí estamos, Señor do Mar, no teu día. / O día dos inocentes, / Entoando este Réquiem no Réxime do *Todo Vai Ben*: / Nadando na ambulancia, / de caspa caída, / entre a espalda e a parede, / no medio das hostilidades / […] / "*Donde los hilitos como de plastilina / se solidifican al alcanzar la verticalidad*" / Líbranos, Señor do Mar, dos *hilitos* que tecen a mentira, / da plastilina dos caraduras / e da verticalidade impasible dos parvos superdotados. / […] / Líbranos, Señor, / das pestes da cobiza e da rapacidade, / dos buques nada fantasmas que acarretan a usura, / dos delincuentes ceibos que cotizan coa tolemia das vacas, / dos fabricantes de odio que trafican coas armas, / dos señoritos da merda / e dos enterradores do mar. (Rivas 2002; 290-291)

---

[4] Briefly, castros were prehistoric Celtic settlements in the northwest of Spain, mainly Galicia. They were so abundant that "castro" became a common last name, such as that of Fidel Castro's grandparents who were native to Galicia.

Here we are, Lord of the Sea, on your day. / Fools day, / Singing this Requiem under the Regime of All is Well: / Swimming in an ambulance[5], / between our backs and a hard place[6], / amidst the blows[7] [...] / Where the "little threads kind of like play dough/ solidify when they hit the seabed" [8]/ Free us, Our Lord, Lord of the Sea, from the little threads that weave the lie, / from the play dough of the shameless / and from the impassable "vertical position" of the over-privileged who act so stupidly / [...] / Free us, Our Lord, / from the plagues of envy and rapacity, / from the not so ghostly ships that carry usury, / from delinquents who are free and trading with the madness of the cows, / from the creators of hate that traffic with arms, / from the rotten "gentlefolk" / and the assassins of the sea.

The last two lines of this Requiem allude to two ecological catastrophes that had taken place shortly before in Galicia (the Mad Cow disease and the massive oil spill from the Prestige), implying that they were caused by valuing profit more than natural, animal and human life. Such disregard contrasts with the reverence for the Sea so manifest throughout the prayer and with the appreciation for popular malapropisms which, instead of being presented as errors springing from ignorance, bring to mind the original saying in an even more insightful, dramatic, humorous way; they are the *retranca* at play.

Quoting the authorities (highlighted in italics) also became a repeated form of *retranca* when time after time actual events contradicted the official discourse. It snidely insinuates the lack of connection between the Galician authorities, who merely mouth what is coming from Madrid, and the people who are suffering the consequences of their bad decisions. Those words, (in this case the statement that the fuel would solidify at the

---

[5] This is a malapropism of the popular saying "swimming in abundance," meaning being in the lap of luxury.

[6] Malapropism for the popular saying "between a rock and a hard place"

[7] Malapropism for "amidst hostilities" playing with the combination of the words *hostilidad* and *hostia* (blow).

[8] These were the official words of a politician who appeared repeatedly in the news at the time of the Prestige oil spill. They were meant to assure that the fuel leaking out of the sunken ship at the bottom of the sea would solidify before coming back to the surface. The leaks were called "little threads, like play dough" in order to minimize the tons of leaking fuel, and the language was intended to be sophisticated and elegant. The result was a pretentious, meaningless statement that Galicians quote till today. (That politician is the current president of Spain.)

bottom of the sea) when contrasted with the actual reality of the sea and the beach in which they are reading this Requiem, spur the *retranca*. Such reality also puts into question one of the most repeated quotes of the Spanish president at that time: "All is Well".

Not only writers and journalists, but also intellectuals in all areas, like Ricardo Beiras, Professor of Ecology at Vigo University, resorted to it:

> Os xestores da crise tiñan outro papel reservado para a ciencia: o de fornecer unha respectable envoltura académica a accións trabucadas e suposicións sen fundamento, como a teórica solidificación do fuel no fondo, cando non a arbitrariedades, como a expulsión dos voluntarios das praias en nome do dano ecolóxico, dicindo que moitos voluntarios equivalen a unha escavadora, sen esquecer o esperpéntico *affaire* dos barcos da Generalitat refugados pola posible invasión do mexillón zebra, unha especie de auga doce, como sen dúbida sabía pola súa condición de biólogo quen empregou tan cativo argumento. (Beiras 23)

> Those dealing with the crisis had another role reserved for science: that of furnishing a respectable academic cover for wrong actions and baseless assumptions, such as the theoretical solidification of the fuel on the bottom, and even arbitrary actions, such as expelling people who voluntarily offered to clean the beaches, under the pretext that the ecological damage they could cause would be equivalent to that of a bulldozer; and let's not forget the outlandish affair of the ships sent by the Catalonian government that were rejected because of the possible invasion of the zebra mussel, a non-salt water species, which the person who used such small argument certainly knew, being a biologist.

Although the article discusses the Prestige oil spill of 2002 from an ecological, economic and social perspective, *retranca* permeates its scientific discourse as an unavoidable cultural form of expression particularly appropriate to the paradoxical events that surrounded it. For example, Beiras comments: "The population of commercial crustaceans […] has not diminished, but some specimens do have a hint of fuel in their taste" (18). Actually, in light of the tons of oil leaked, the choice of subtle words like "a hint of" mimics the official discourse while alluding *retranqueiramente* to the massive problem. The contrast between the government's official position and the actual reality even requires redefinition as Beiras refers to "a new concept of accident: the accident that lasts 140 hours" (21).

Another Galician intellectual deeply involved in reporting the events from the beginning was Suso de Toro, whose journalistic discourse also resorted to *retranca* and Galician mythology:

> Galicia ten días. Ás veces está envolta en algo como néboa, ou fume de petróleo, entón os reis que marcharon e os santos peregrinos arriban en barcas de pedra. Esteamos atentos, un deses días chega: este sábado un mariñeiro dunha vila da Costa da Morte guindou ao mar unha pedra de cinco quilos e a pedra aboiou. (De Toro 15)

> Galicia has its days. Sometimes it is covered by something like fog, or oil smoke; then the departed ancient kings and the pilgrim saints arrive in boats made of stone. Let's watch out, for one of those days is coming: last Saturday a seafarer from a village in a *Costa da Morte* threw a ten pound stone into the and the stone floated.

Legends from popular culture provide the basis for a parallel between the floating of mythic stone boats, in which saints like Saint James, Saint Andrew or The Virgin of the Boat are said to have arrived in Galicia, and the reality of stones floating in the sea filled with fuel, thus denouncing the ecological as well as the cultural tarnish. As Rivas stated: "the sea is at once a natural and a cultural heritage" (2004).[9] Therefore, when natural fog can be confused or interchangeable with smoke from burning fuel, it is obvious that something deeply damaging is affecting not only our environment but also our perception, our culture, and our humanity.

These were some of the voices that rose in protest, infused with *retranca*. Galicia's autoethnographic humor served as a powerful arm to protest, to cope with a challenging reality and to re-exist during the distressing times of the oil spill; that is, it helped to defend ecology in the broadest sense of the word. It also managed to change the government that ruled at that time.

---

[9] This appeared in an online Galician newspaper that has disappeared under the current government

Works Cited

Baltrusch, Burghard. "Teoría e práctica sincrónica da *retranca* a partir do refraneiro e da literatura galega vangardista." *Anuario de Estudos Literarios Galegos* (1998): 117-140.

Barreiro Rivas, Xosé Luis. "A retranca: ironía e metáfora na identidade cultural de Galicia." *Conferencia do Encontro de Culturas*. June 2006.

—. "Barreiro Rivas valora a desaparción da retranca como signo de modernidade." *O Xornal*. 11 June 2006. <<http://www.xornal.com/article.php3?sid=20060611102843>>

Beiras, Ricardo. "A catástrofe do Prestige: Unha oportunidade para a transformación da sociedade galega." *Grial,* 157 (1) 2003:15-26.

Bermúdez, Silvia. "Poetry on the World Wide Web: The www.Redesescarlatas.Org and the Weaving of a 'New' Public Sphere in 21st Century Galicia." *Journal of Spanish Cultural Studies* 7 (2) 2006: 123-33.

Castro-Vázquez, Isabel. *Reexistencia: A obra de Manuel Rivas*. Vigo: Xerais, 2007.

Catalán Deus, Gustavo. *Desprestige: El ocaso del PP ante la mayor catastrofe ambiental en España*. Madrid: La esfera de los libros, 2003.

Critchley, Simon. *On Humor*. London and New York: Routledge, 2002.

De la Vega, Celestino F. *O segredo do humor*. Vigo: Galaxia, 1983.

De Toro, Suso. *Nunca máis Galiza á intemperie*. Vigo: Xerais, 2003.

García Pérez, J.D. 2003. "Early socio-political and environmental consequences of the *Prestige* oil spill in Galicia." *Disasters*, 27 (3): 207-223.

Gómez, Luis and Pablo Ordaz. *Crónica negra del Prestige*. Madrid: Ediciones El País, 2003.

Gondar Portassany, Marcial. "Da marea negra á saúde mental contextos sociopolíticos do enfermar" in *¿U-lo Prestige? Entre a ecoloxía e a globalización*. Sada, A Coruña: Ediciós do Castro, 2005: 31-64.

—. *Crítica da razón galega: Entre o nós mesmos e o nos-outros*. Vigo: A nosa terra, 2003.

Lobato, Xurxo. *No país do Nunca Máis*. Vigo: Galaxia, 2003.

Marea de música [Grabación sonora]: Homenaxe dos músicos galegos aos afectados pola marea negra do Prestige: vintecatro cancións exclusivas e inéditas. Santiago de Compostela: Plataforma Cidadá Nunca Máis, 2003. 1CD-Rom

Paz, Xavier e Alba Vázquez Carpentier, eds. *Nunca Máis: A voz da cidadanía*. Ourense: Difusora de Letras Artes e Ideas, 2003.

Pérez Oliva, Milagros. "Manuel Rivas: El guardián de la memoria." *El País.es*. 05 november, 2006. <<http://www.elpais.com/articulo/portada/guardian/memoria/elpepuso ceps/20061105elpepspor_1/Tes>>

Piccardi, Alice. 'A *retranca* como acto lingüístico' *Cadernos de lingua*, 26: 99-108, 2004.

Ramonet, Ignacio and Ramón Chao. *Abécédaire partiel e partial de la mondialisation*. Paris: Plon, 2003.

Rei-Doval, Gabriel. "Realpolitik, Galician style: the aftermath of the Prestige Disaster". *Planet*, 163: 6-14. 2004

Rivas Barrós, Manuel. "'A ecoloxía das linguas', Manuel Rivas na presentación de Linguamon-Casa de Les Llengües." *Vieiros Barcelona*. 6 september, 2006. <<http://www.vieiros.com/nova/52334/a-ecoloxia-das-linguas-manuel-rivas-na-presentacion-de-linguamon-casa-de-les-llengues>>

—. "Prestige: Renacer en el naufragio". *O Xornal*. 5 february, 2004. <<http://www.xornal.com/article.php3?sid+20040205143343>>

—. *Muller no Baño*. Vigo: Xerais, 2002.

—. *Galicia, Galicia*. Vigo: Xerais, 1999.

Rutherford, John. *The Power of the Smile: Humour in Spanish Culture*. London: Francis Boutle Publishers, 2012.

Santana, Andrés. *Hay motivo!*. España: Cameo Media, 2004. (Video documental)

Stein, Norman. *Report Book Galicia Prestige: Real Views by Norman Stein*. Barcelona: Editorial Norman Stein S.L., 2003.

Taibo, Carlos. "Unha metáfora da globalización miserenta" *¿U-lo Prestige? Entre a ecoloxía e a globalización*. Sada, A Coruña: Ediciós do Castro, 2003.

WHAT'S SO FUNNY ABOUT WARTIME EXILE?

CHRISTINE ANN EVANS

Some 30,000 French men and women sought refuge in the United States during World War II and quickly built up a network of cultural and political organizations, notably in New York City. The École Libre des Hautes Études opened to students officially in 1942, hosting displaced French intellectuals, offering a wide range of courses and academic degrees and serving as a gathering place for Francophones. The diverging political views held by the French were given voice by a number of political organizations and their periodicals. Until November 1942, when Germany invaded "la France libre," the still significant number of Vichy supporters gathered around that consulate,[1] while other organizations claimed to speak for their anti-Vichy countrymen, among them France Forever (many of whose members, but not all, were Gaullists) and le Comité français de la libération nationale (which neither endorsed nor disavowed de Gaulle).

Central to this French community reconstituted in the United States were publishing houses established to assure Francophone writers a public when avenues in France closed to them after 1940. Éditions de la Maison française and Brentano's published the most important names in New York's exile community, among them the novelists Jules Romains, André Maurois, Saint-Exupéry and the poet Saint-Jean Perse. While many of the works brought out by these houses during the war were, understandably, memoirs and commentary on France's defeat in 1940—Jacques Maritain's *A travers le désastre* and André Maurois's *Tragédie en France*, to name two—the whole gamut of French literary production was represented, from the masterpiece to the potboiler, from the frivolous to the high-minded and anguished, written by *académiciens* as well as those now forgotten. These publishing endeavors constituted a political statement: the

---

[1] Raoul Aglion, *Roosevelt and de Gaulle: Allies in Conflict: A Personal Memoir* (New York: Free Press, 1988). Aglion, de Gaulle's representative in New York City, estimates this group as a significant majority in 1942.

tradition of French *belles lettres* would continue to exist in exile even while emigration, censorship and material shortages restricted it in France.

While "exile literature" most often evokes pieces that treat loss of homeland in a tragic, or at least serious vein, of interest for this paper are novels and commentary that treat the French *émigré* experience in a comic or "spring" mode (to borrow terminology from Northrop Frye's anatomy), where obstructions and difficulties are overcome and lead to an evolved situation or social grouping. The very fact that comic treatments could arise in a community that has experienced defeat and expatriation and, what is more, be seen as an appropriate response to this situation, is the focus of this study. Sociologists term such figures as those treated in this study, variously, "stranger," "exile," "immigrant" or "refugee." "Crisis," from milder to more severe, attends this condition, and the questions of whether one chose to go, and whether there is a possibility of return, partly define the level of crisis experienced.

The figure of the exile can clearly invite tragic treatments. Against any argument of the "interest" and "literary evocativeness" of the figure of the exile, Edward Said insists upon "the crippling sorrow of estrangement" (173), the spiritual starvation that necessarily follows from the loss of "the nourishment of tradition, family and geography" (174). Likewise, the sociologist Aron Gurwitsch demands acknowledgement of the irremediable nature of the exile's loss and bristles against any study that emphasizes "accommodation" and mastery of "recipes": "I will never accept that for man the important thing is a well-oiled operation, that it is all a matter of making a smooth functioning possible via *adjustment*" (Gurwitsch 71).

However, as the polemical tone of these pronouncements makes clear, there are those who treat exile in a more "comic" mode. For Alfred Schuetz, himself an exile, the exile is the ultimate Cartesian, or skeptic; as a stranger in a strange land, every convention is a puzzle to be solved, "not a shelter but a field of adventure, not a matter of course but a questionable topic of investigation" (506). The exile is best situated to view the "approached" culture free of the press of ingrained and unconscious assumptions—"[He has learned] that man may lose his status, his rules of guidance, and even his history and that the normal way of life is always far less guaranteed than it seems" (507). Enzo Traverso positively celebrates the figure of the exile, arguing that for the category of individuals, if not for the specific individual, what is gained largely compensates for what is lost (8). Rather than victims they are beneficiaries of adverse circumstances that both liberate them and endow them with a gift they would not otherwise have possessed, an "epistemological privilege" (11).

The works I will discuss chart a delicate course between the comic and the tragic: they espouse a comic stance while keeping a wary eye on the specter of tragedy. Two different contemporary texts will serve as the focus of this study, Michel Georges-Michel's *Nulle part dans le monde: Il est grand d'être à Miami* (*Nowhere in the World: It's Great to Be in Miami*) and Jules Romains's *Salsette découvre l'Amérique* (*Salsette Discovers America*). The author of the first was a prolific writer of the 1930s and 1940s who is better remembered now for organizing exhibits of the works of Picasso, Matisse and other artists than for his novels. The second is the *académicien* best known for his serial novel depicting pre- and post-World War I French society, *Les Hommes de bonne volonté* (*Men of Good Will*). Both were considerable figures in the French artistic and literary worlds, both fêted and appreciated in France and the United States, both reduced to the status of refugee by the war. For their main characters, these two novelists plot an arc similar to their own: newly-arrived "innocents" who "enact" the comic through their readings and misreadings of the new culture.

What complicates the formula in the case of these two works is the fact that the "innocent" eye is in fact very sophisticated and cultivated. David Adams, the hero of Michel Georges-Michel's novel, is a worldly writer of note who has left behind in Paris an elegant apartment decorated with tasteful antiques and works by Velasquez and Picasso, a secure place within the publishing intelligentsia, and friends and acquaintances among the elite of Europe—in short, a man with a biography very similar to that of his creator. Albert Salsette, the eponymous main character of *Salsette découvre l'Amérique*, is an equally erudite and well-traveled French university professor. The author of this book appears as one of its characters, Salsette's friend, "Romains," so that Jules Romains is likewise inscribed within this novel. These two main characters navigate their translations into a new culture differently: David Adams fails spectacularly at a "well-oiled adjustment" to his new circumstances, while Salsette reveals the "epistemological privilege" attributed to luckier exiles. Both, however, are similar in retaining as an essential bedrock their French identity and the particular virtues associated with that by their authors.

David Adams's misadventures all derive from the fact that he requested a "visitor's" visa in the American embassy in Paris, rather than an immigrant visa, because of the "offense" to France that a request for an immigrant visa might imply. Once he arrives in the United States, he finds it almost impossible to change his immigration status, despite heroic efforts. This error typifies his difficulties—what passes for a virtue in his homeland (patriotism and loyalty) transmogrify into a blunder in the medium of exile. He spends days in the waiting room of the local immigration office trying to correct this initial misstep, encountering first-hand the catch-22s placed in the path of émigrés—the vagaries of different types of visa and the barriers to getting them; the circuitous routes into the country for those hoping for a visa (seeking first visas for Cuba, Haiti, Venezuela, Guadeloupe as propitious places from which EVENTUALLY to apply for a visa for the United States); the bureaucrats functioning as Cerebrus-like gatekeepers; ever-changing immigration laws.

David Adams takes the virtue of French rationality to lunatic ends. He refuses to leave the United States in order to apply for a visa to the United States from another country, the established route to getting a valid visa, opining logically that it makes no sense to leave a country where one wishes to remain in the uncertain hope of returning to it. Unfortunately, logic has no part in immigration procedure. The qualities of forthrightness and honesty that he showed during a preliminary hearing also prove a bane rather than a blessing. During an interrogation by officials, he immediately falls into difficulties as he tries to convince them that he had expressed himself badly during his first interview:

> —Alors, tout ce que vous avez répondu lors du premier intérrogatoire, ce n'était pas vrai? […]
> —C'était une série d'erreurs, dues à ma mauvaise compréhension de l'Anglais.
>
> David commença à haleter. […]
>
> —Vous avez dit clairement que vous aviez quitté la France pour fuir la guerre.
> —J'ai voulu dire que j'ai saisi l'opportunité de la guerre pour venir ici, ce que j'avais l'intention de faire depuis longtemps. (Georges Michel, 108-109)
>
> —So, everything you said at the first hearing was untrue? [...]
> —It was a series of errors due to my faulty understanding of English.
>
> David began to breathe heavily. [...]

—You clearly stated that you had left France to escape the war.
—I meant to say that I took the opportunity that the war gave me to come here, something I had intended for a long time.[2]

Representatives of the American bureaucracy can reduce this self-possessed cosmopolitan to a perspiring and stammering defendant. As one official remarks after another unsuccessful interview, "'Décidément cet homme me surprend chaque jour. [...] Je pensais d'abord qu'il voulait nous tromper: il est bien plus honnête que nous ne le croyions. [...] Ou bien, il parle trop,' conclut-t-il." ("'This man surprises me every day, certainly. [...] I thought at first that he wanted to deceive us: he's much more honest than we thought. [...] Or else he talks too much', he concluded" [195]).

In comic mode David plays out the inability to translate his gifts and knowledge into anything like passable currency in a new setting. David is invited to the home of Mrs. Littleblum, the head of the Graceful Ladies charity, a Hadassah-like organization set up to help Jewish refugees. When she lets him know that part of that afternoon's entertainment will include listening to an Arthur Rubenstein piano recital—on the radio—David refers to his past acquaintance with the pianist:

—Quoi, vous l'avez connu, lui aussi, comme la Princesse de Hohenloë?
—Je pense bien! J'ai assisté à ses débuts chez Astruc et écrit une des premières critiques à sa gloire. [...] Je l'ai revu à un dîner chez l'Infante Eulalie, après lequel il m'a emmené à travers l'Espagne, dans la nuit, jusqu'à Pampelune, où il devait jouer le lendemain. Puis, à Paris, où tous les deux avons déjeuné à l'Escargot: c'est un fin gourmet et un amateur de cigares comme le fut Edouard VII.
—Que vous avez connu, bien entendu.
—J'ai eu cet honneur. Il m'a reçu deux fois en particulier.

Mrs. Littleblum regarda David de travers. (207-208)

—What, you knew him, too, as well as the Princess de Hohenloë?

---

[2] All translations are mine.

—I certainly did. I witnessed his beginnings at Astruc and
wrote one of the first critiques praising him. [...] I saw him
again at a dinner at the home of the Infante Eulalie, after
which he drove me across Spain, during the night, as far as
Pamplona, where he was going to play the next day. Then,
in Paris, where we both lunched at l'Escargot. He's a
discriminating gourmet and a connoisseur of cigars, as was
Edward II.
—Whom you knew, of course'.
—I've had that honor. He received me in a private two times.

Mrs. Littleblum scowled at David.

David's cosmopolitan profile and his intimacy with the celebrated do
not add to his luster in this new milieu; instead, they invite skepticism,
distrust and even annoyance. Any casual reference to his past social
successes only alienates those who consider him now a charity case.

As a product of the Third Republic, and as a French Jew, a beneficiary
of its policy of *laïcité*, or secularism, David espouses the tenets of
assimilation and separation between church and state. These convictions
put him at odds with the charitable organizations established to aid Jewish
refugees, many of whom are overseen by religious groups. At a visit to a
synagogue one Sabbath, David finds it impossible not to warn against the
dangers of sectarianism.

—Mais assimilez-vous sans particularisme. Soyez juifs,
restez-le, c'est un devoir humain et une gloire divine. Mais
chez vous, dans vos temples. Pas dans la rue. [...]
—Voyez le beau prophète qui ne parle pas même yiddish!
—Jérémie, Ezéchiel, Saint Paul, parlaient-ils cette langue?
Et Moïse, et Jésus-Christ?
—C'est vous qui parlez une langue qui n'est pas la nôtre,
qui est ennemie de la nôtre'— s'écria l'homme à la voix de
fausset. Et ramassant un petit caillou qu'il lança contre la
tribune: —Je te lapide symboliquement!
—Lapidons-le!— s'écria une jeune fille. (152-154)

—Assimilate, without particularism; be Jewish, it's a human
duty and a divine glory, but at home, in your temples. Not
in the street. [...]
—Look at the great prophet who doesn't even speak
Yiddish.

—Jeremiah, Ezekiel, Saint Paul, did they speak that language? Or Moses? Or Jesus Christ'?
—It's you who speak a language that isn't ours, that is an enemy to ours— cried the man with the falsetto. And picking up a small stone he threw it at the podium. —I stone you symbolically!
—Let's stone him!, cried a young girl.

In a sectarian milieu, his secularism makes him suspect, and here, the symbolic scapegoat of the group. This particular French republican virtue undoes rather than recommends him.

David serves a kind of negative apprenticeship, increasingly aware that his former connections, cultivation and stubbornly-rooted Third Republic virtues are unhonored currency in this new environment. Proving unable to adapt throughout most of the novel, David is an example of Said's exile, rudderless once deprived of the nourishment of "tradition, family and geography." Like Antaeus, he loses his strength once removed from French soil. His is a sad decline, albeit in the ambit of a comic novel; he runs out of money and is slowly sapped of his optimism and verve, inducing compassion-fatigue in those who once helped him. This former Parisian *boulevardier* is eventually reduced to skipping haircuts and shaves to save 50 cents, paying court to an elderly woman with no personal charms in hopes of being fed a bowl of soup or a tuna fish sandwich, and at his lowest point, crying openly in the streets about his hopeless situation.

His breakdown in the street should, logically, be the denouement of our hero's story. He has reached the end of his resources, resilience, support networks and legal options. But this being a comic novel, a savior miraculously appears in the form of a "man with a wooden pipe" in Washington, someone who is able to cut through bureaucratic barriers and assure David a visa. David's salvation comes not through the logic of cause and effect, but through the suspension of these rules, through the grace of a *deus ex machina*. What is more, on the very day he learns he has been granted a visa, a job offer falls into his lap: he signs a contract to write for a Francophone press in the United States. All this good luck in one day constitutes an embarrassment of riches, which only emphasizes the comic intervention of the *deus ex machina*.

While the reader is invited to laugh at the hero's haplessness and at the comic portraits of the various representatives of American and émigré society he encounters, this novel never loses from sight the fate of other, less fortunate émigrés depicted in the novel and known to us from the historical record, who experienced exile in the tragic mode. David encounters émigrés who keep to darkened rooms and languish in chronic depressions, others who rot in a pestilent Mexican swampland waiting out the five years necessary to apply for a visa into the United States.

Professor Albert Salsette finds the road much easier when he arrives in the United States: his visa is in perfect order; he has a job waiting for him in a small New England town for the next academic year; and in the person of the narrator has a close friend ("Romains") who can introduce him to America and draw him out about his impressions. He experiences America as idyll. Rather than surly immigration officials, the first American to greet Salsette is a "colored" customs agent who, on learning he is a professor and writer, asks him for an autograph. This auspicious beginning suggests what will follow, as valleys are raised and mountains leveled for the main character.

While the narrator, "Romains," serves to "instruct" Salsette on America, as the novel proceeds, Salsette himself comes to offer the most important analysis. It is thanks to him, rather than his guide, that an image of America takes form, as the narrator's preface acknowledges:

> Les traits en sont fort incertains; elle est pleine de gaucheries et d'erreurs de proportions. Elle manque de relief. Elle n'a aucune profondeur. Vraiment, c'est presque aussi naif qu'un portrait dessiné par un enfant. [...] Mais tout de même, c'est à sa façon une image de l'Amérique (Romains 11).

> Its outlines are quite uncertain; it's full of awkwardness and mistakes of proportion. It lacks contrast. It has no depth. Really, it's almost as naïve as a portrait drawn by a child. [...] All the same, it is in its way an image of America.

This passage, despite the negative constructions and privatives, prepares us for a startlingly original view of the United States.

Several chapters are devoted to American food and women (the only subjects to merit two chapters each), aspects of American culture that fascinated a good number of French émigré writers. Increasingly, the duty of "explanation" shift from the expert ("Romains") to the innocent, whose view comes to bear more and more the weight of analysis in the novel.

After some mediocre meals shared together, Salsette and "Romains" have a much happier experience at the country home of a wealthy New Yorker from an old family. The food and drink are, as could be expected, much more to Salsette's liking and serve as the focus of much of the evening's conversation. Both the narrator and the host, W. H. B., draw him out and press him on his impressions of American wines (from both California and New York), vegetables, lunches, in short, all of his impressions so far of American cuisine. His "innocent" but incisive views help bring into clarity their own, until then perhaps more intuited than expressed in critical, discursive language. His appreciation of a white wine, which he guesses to be from Alsace but is in fact from California, ends the dinner in an approval of things American which carries great weight in the book. In the narrator's chapter-closing words, "Et c'est ainsi que le vin américain reçut un hommage qui, à mon sens, avait son prix" ("And thus it was that the American wine received praise that, to my way of thinking, was worth having") (184).

American womanhood also fascinates Salsette. He is struck by the number of beautiful young women whom he sees as he and the narrator walk down Fifth Avenue one day. He notices their clothes, which fit so well despite the fact that his friend informs them they were all bought "off the rack"; the fact that they use makeup so skillfully; the undergarments that undergird and engineer all this attractiveness and that in France would be available only to wealthy women; the distance that seems to separate them from their European ancestors—they do not look like Germans, Italians, Frenchwomen, but seem to constitute their own subgroup. Some of the things that most strike Salsette reflect an economic reality: a well-nourished population as well as relatively inexpensive "luxury" items available to a wider public, as his guide makes clear.

But in a later chapter, Salsette's analysis goes further. He notes a certain lack of "romanticism" in young American women, a fact attested to by the absence of any news stories about unhappy love affairs and crimes of passion. Americans, he concludes, prefer romantic comedies and happy endings to tragedy. And it is exactly this "tragique" that he notes as lacking in American society. In avoiding the concept of the irreplaceable in romantic relationships, one avoids tragedy, but in the process the beloved becomes a replaceable commodity. "Romains" pushes Salsette to a level of wide-ranging, speculative analysis that he himself, though more expert on American society, could not have ventured. Salsette himself recognizes this:

—Vous me faites rire!—s'écriat-t-il. —Je viens juste de débarquer. [...] Je ne connais rien de rien. [...] Et vous attendez de moi que je résolve des questions auxquelles, au bout de vingt ans, un pénétrant observateur serait peut-être embarassé de répondre!

—You make me laugh!—he cried out. —I have just
disembarked. [...] I know absolutely nothing. [...] And you
expect me to resolve questions to which a perceptive
observer would be at a loss to respond at the end of twenty
years'!") (184).

Clearly, the apprentice has become the master here. If Salsette is still
learning about America, he is also, and more importantly, helping those
who already know it to see it in clearer outline. He manifests the
"epistemological privilege" that Schuetz and Traverso claim for the
stranger as well as the particularly French gifts of discernment and
analysis. Despite their defeat, Salsette proves that the French are still those
who, in Simone Weil's (ironic) formulation, "think for the universe"
(146).

The conundrum raised in the beginning of this paper remains: what is
the significance of the fact that exile, for this population of writers, invites
a comic treatment, or at least does not preclude it? Schuetz laid out the
principle that the level of trauma experienced by an exile depends partially
on whether or not the exile had chosen or was forced to leave the
homeland and whether or not eventual return to it was possible. What
distinguishes the situation of the French from that of exiles from Germany
or Italy, for example, is the fact that the capitulation of their legitimate
government (the Third Republic), rather than its policies, had forced them
to emigrate. Unlike many German émigrés, whose homeland was forever
tainted for them by Fascism and Holocaust (Thomas Mann and Herbert
Marcuse, for example), most French had no qualms about going back to a
liberated France after the war. So, by this criterion the degree of trauma
for most French refugees was not as great as that for some other refugee
groups.

Furthermore, "France" as a coherent historical construct was able to
survive the defeat. The French were aware that the events of June, 1940,
posed a challenge to the French historical narrative. Did the French
Republic's rout at the hands of a fascist state invalidate the narrative of
continual progress? Was it cataclysmic, with deep causes, traceable to
ideological, moral and even spiritual failings on the part of the French
Republic and its underpinnings, as some argued? Or was the defeat the
result of limited causes, for example military blunders or the failings of
only a narrow stratum of the population?

Georges-Michel and Romains clearly espoused the second view. These
comic treatments of exile fit into a larger narrative of French history that

traces an arc of inevitable progress despite temporary setbacks. In both of the works discussed here, the initial trials of the heroes give way to vindication and success. In *Il est grand d'être à Miami*, (*It's great to be in Miami*) there is the assurance that a calm, competent agency is at work in the halls of Washington (the man with a wooden pipe), one which has the power to transform the situation of the unfortunate—and one that will bring the United States into the war in 1941.

In the figure of Albert Salsette, we see the persistence of a French mind and intellect that continue to "think for the universe." His gifts of analysis, expression and discrimination prove him to be a worthy product of a collective that had provided the world with the major thinkers of the Enlightenment and had spread the concept of instrumental reason. His success in his temporary home argues for the survival of these gifts as well as France's continued ability to disseminate them to the rest of the world.

Works Cited

Azéma, Jean-Pierre and Michel Winock. *La troisième République (1870-1940).* Paris: Calmann-Lévy, 1976.

Georges-Michel, Michel. *Nulle Part dans le monde: Il est grand d'être à Miami.* New York: Editions de la Maison française, 1941.

Gurwitsch, Aron. In *Philosophers in Exile: The Correspondence of Alfred Schuetz and Aron Gurwitsch, 1939-1959.* Ed. Grathoff, Richard. Tr. J. Claude Evans. Bloomington: Indiana University Press, 1989.

Romains, Jules. *Salsette découvre l'Amérique.* New York: Editions de la Maison française, 1942.

Said, Edward W. "Reflections on Exile." In *Reflections on Exile and Other Essays.* Cambridge, MA: Harvard University Press, 2000: 173-186.

Schuetz, Alfred. "The Stranger." *American Journal of Sociology* 49 (1944): 499-507.

Traverso, Enzo. *La Pensée dispersée: Figures de l'exil judéo-allemand.* Paris: Lignes: Scheer, 2004.

Weil, Simone. *L'Enracinement: Prélude à une déclaration des devoirs envers l'être humain.* Paris: Gallimard, 1949.

White, Hayden. "Marx: The Philosophical Defense of History in the Metonymical Mode." *Metahistory: The Historical Imagination in Nineteenth-Century Europe.* Baltimore: Johns Hopkins University Press, 1973: 281-330.

VIII.

WHAT´S SO FUNNY
ABOUT MODERN TIMES?

THREE SHADES OF LAUGHTER:
THE COMIC ART OF MENDOZA,
SORRENTINO AND GARIBAY

ZENIA SACKS DASILVA

A funny thing happened today on the way to the library. Well, it wasn't really on the way to the library, and it wasn't today. But somehow people get themselves ready to laugh when they hear that "A funny thing happened on the way to...," and then you can talk about anything you please—even about three very serious contemporary writers, Eduardo Mendoza, Fernando Sorrentino and Ricardo Garibay (a Catalan, an Argentine and a Mexican)—and the anticipation keeps growing that sooner or later you *will* say something funny. So before your expectations crash, let me tell you quickly why I think Eduardo Mendoza's novel, *Sin Noticias de Gurb (No Word from Gurb)* is one of the most amusing social commentaries of recent vintage and exactly how its author gets it to work.[1] First, the story line.

Gurb is an extraterrestrial—no physical body, just pure intelligence— who alights in a spaceship with his commander in the vicinity of Barcelona, and promptly disappears. Days go by, noted tersely in the log

---

[1] Eduardo Mendoza Garriga, arguably Spain's premier contemporary humorist, novelist, stage and screenplay writer, was born in Barcelona in 1943. A prolific writer of many tones and themes, he is able to inject into even his most serious works an element of humor from satiric to picaresque to the brim of the absurd. His most recognized novels include *La ciudad de los prodigios* (*City of Marvels*, 1986), which treats with a certain historicity the urban evolution of Barcelona; a series of intriguing parodies of detective fiction, among them *El misterio de la cripta embrujada* (The Mystery of the Bewitched Crypt); the wildly comical and introspective science-fiction *Sin noticias de Gurb* (*No Word from Gurb*, 1990) and *El último trayecto de Horacio Dos* (*The Last Journey of Horatio Dos*, 2001); and the recent *El asombroso viaje de Pomponio Flato* (*The Amazing Trip of Pomponio Flato,* 2008) *and El enredo de la bolsa y la vida* (*The Tangled Case of the Stock Market and Life*, 2012).

of his perturbed commandant, who finally decides to go out in search of him. Now, in order to avoid attracting attention, our interplanetary voyager decides to materialize in human form, starting out as the Conde-Duque de Olivares and passing through many such transformations as Gary Cooper (sheriff's badge, holsters, harmonica and all), Pope Pius XII, Admiral Yamamoto, José Ortega y Gasset, the tabloid badboy Paquirrín, and the Duke and Duchess of Kent. But no sooner does his quest begin when he stumbles on—and into—some of the quotidian difficulties of life in Barcelona. He falls into endless potholes, is smothered by traffic, both auto and pedestrian, is overcome by the visible pollution of the air and water, is mugged at every turn of the corner, accosted by con-men and teenage marauders, confounded by the spasmodic telephone service, and abashed by the extremes of wealth and poverty, the inequities of criminal and social justice, and the inefficacy, if not corruption, of its zealous administrators. Everything is so different here from his home in outer space, he notes—the human body itself, with its strange, uncomfortable mechanisms, the language that uses words instead of mathematical equations—everything except, of course, the two passions they hold in common—soccer, and the Catholic Church—and the need to brush one's teeth and don one's pajamas before going to bed at night. And yet he seems to fall in love with it all—with the *churros* he ingests in massive quantities, with the enticement of the feminine figure, with the liquors that lead to a blissful nirvana. He is entranced by the "autochthonous fauna" he encounters, and a very odd lot of people they are. He wants to be part of them, and he wants them to like him. Still he must find Gurb and return to his land in the outer ether. . . Does he? Well, at last. . . I won't tell you the rest, only that it is a very funny thing, and that it did not happen on the way to the library.

Obviously, the premise of *Gurb* in itself is intrinsically funny, and the episodic intensity never subsides. But there is more than comic invention in the humor of Mendoza. What creates the momentum is the composite of changing rhythms that move with the spin of a roulette ball, bounding from rim to rim, yet held to tempo by the metronome of the journal entries—day, hour, and minute, minute, hour, day. It is a humor of repetition in crescendo, as the events replicate themselves before the ultimate, unexpected turn. Here is a very short segment:

8 AM   I materialize in a place called Diagonal – Paseo de Gloria. Am run over by Bus #17, Barcelona-Vall d'Hebron. Have to recover my head, which rolled off after the

collision. Operation difficult due to large number of vehicles.
8:01 AM Run over by an Opel Corsa.
8:02 Run over by a delivery van.
8:03 Run over by a taxi.
8:04 Recover head and wash it in a public fountain. Take the opportunity to analyze the composition of the water: hydrogen, oxygen and a quantity of feces. (5-16) [2]

The device of the serial buildup, so recurrent throughout *Gurb,* adds a rhythmic consistency to the implacable framework that underlies the tale. We wait for it. We know it is coming—in every shape, form and adventure, even in the total irrelevancies of the atmospheric weather reports that are sprinkled all about—and with each compounded sequence, the comic effect increases. But this is only part of Mendoza's formula.

As with all good humorists, Mendoza's primary ingredient is surprise—the unanticipated conclusion, the anomalous character, the incongruous response. To this he adds an elastic imagery that stretches from mildly hyperbolic to "over the top." His focus is mobile, his phrasing clipped, his style matter-of-fact, his pacing relentless. There is seldom a splurge of dialogue, never a change of perspective. Yet from it emerges a social reality devised through a lens that moves with an air of mischief from gentle distension to the surreal and grotesque. Take our extraterrestrial´s multitudinous transformations into personages of all ilk, past and present. Take the moment when finding himself without money to pay a restaurant check, he mentally instructs the bank´s computers to transfer billions of pesetas into his account—or when his super-intelligence enables him to predict with ease the winning number of the national lottery. Yes, our visitor is a much-endowed non-person, and Mendoza paints him lovingly, but not without pathos. In one sense he is an innocent, nonplused by our inadequacies both as individuals and as a social form. In another, he is a sophisticate, bemused by our blundering, but feeling himself yet the misfit, almost jealous of our imperfections. He wants to be accepted; he longs for some kind of friendship; and he lusts for the pleasure of a woman—all this, while enjoying to boot a wealth come quickly and without too much to-do.

At whom, then, is Mendoza laughing, and what is the color of his humor? Surely he is laughing at himself, at us all, who muddle through a life that comes with no instructions, and whose time is measured in the

---

[2] All translations are mine.

briefest of moments, a pittance of our extraterrestrial's thousands of years, and counting. It is a sly laughter, in some ways like that of a Cervantes, who can smile at the vagaries of our existence and its inevitable conclusion, and still find a level of acceptance. It is a wry laughter, in some ways like that of a Gomez de la Serna,[3] who blends the material world with the realm of fantasy and daubs it with greys, golds, and an occasional turgid mauve. In all, there is no malice in Mendoza's *Sin noticias de Gurb*, just a wince at the pains of living, and the shrug of one who has not given up. And we laugh along with him, knowing he has caught us *in flagranti* ... though somehow we feel that everything will be all right if we can only make it to the other side. But when? How?

As chance would have it, Barcelona is also the site of Mendoza's novel *La ciudad de los prodigios* (*The City of Miracles*, 1986), a picaresque tale whose protagonists—both the city itself and its panoply of nonentities and rogues—are set in the framework of four decades, from the World's Fair of 1888 to that of 1929. Its primary figure is a slick-witted young runaway who rises from petty thief to professional thug, to ruthless mob leader, illicit arms dealer, financial wizard and the richest man in Spain. Its story line zigzags forward and back, with an impudent disregard for present, future and past, straddling social strata, criss-crossing fiction and fact.

It can be palpably real or brazenly fantastic, shaded with irony or awash in brash colors. And its humor can be subtle, insinuating, laced with a skeptical smile—as when the mothers of the soldiers on a train bound for war camp out on the railroad tracks, and some pious ladies who are handing out crucifixes urge the engineer to run them all down... It can leap into an ultra-world, as when the long-adored saint Eulalia discovers that she has been demoted to a side chapel for being counterfeit, in fact, for not having existed at all. Chagrined beyond repair, she asks the statues of Saint Lucia and Our Lord of Lepanto to cover her absence, steps down from her stone pedestal and marches off to protest at the City Hall. And its humor can be broad, campy, preface to a guffaw—as when the mayor, thwarted by Madrid in his plan to rebuild his entire city in Biblical

---

[3] Ramón Gómez de la Serna (1891-1963) was a unique figure of Spain´s literary vanguard of the early 20th century. Although unclassifiable within any specific movement, his short stories, his intensely dramatic theatre verging on the surreal, and his "greguerías", which he described as "humor + metaphor", were notably influential on his own and succeeding generations of poets and artists, in Spain and beyond. See the articles in this collection: "The Ludic Utopias of Gerardo Diego's Ultraist Poetry" and "The Sanity of the Insane: Humor and 'Humorismo' in the World of Ramón Gómez de la Serna."

configurations, determines that he and his whole Council, for the honor of
Cataluña, must challenge their Castilian counterparts to a duel. He hurls to
the floor his gray kid glove, over which he has kept vigil all night before
the altar of Saint Lucia, and his assemblymen, overcome with enthusiasm,
follow suit hurling their own hats, dickies, shoes or whatever they have at
hand in a great show of support and admiration—and with not the slightest
intention of ever following through. And so takes shape the city of
marvels, erratic and multi-visaged, traced by the pen of a son who sees all
its failings, and still is in love.

Let me touch lightly on one more of Mendoza's novels, *El misterio de
la cripta embrujada* (*The Mystery of the Bewitched Crypt*). In this tongue-
in-cheek parody of a typecast whodunit, the protagonist-sleuth, actually a
resident of an insane asylum, describes his own entrance in the world with
these tender reminiscences:

> When I was born, my mother happened to be madly, and of
> course hopelessly, in love with Clark Gable. Well, in the
> middle of my baptismal ceremony she suddenly decided that
> my name would have to be "Gonewiththewind," which
> infuriated the officiating clergyman. The argument turned
> into a free-for-all brawl and my godmother, who needed
> both arms to beat up on her husband ... left me floating in
> the baptismal font, in whose holy waters I nearly, nearly
> drowned. (76) (My translation)

"Gonewiththewind" *is* an odd name, he admits, but that's all right, because
nobody ever calls him by his real name, only by an assortment of
nicknames like "meathead," "vermin" and other derivatives that display
the unfailing inventiveness of the current Spanish idiom. And so the novel
proceeds, with a slate of characters each more unlikely than the other, a
language as suave as that of an army barracks, and a denouement as
involved as a Rube Goldberg contraption. In short, even though
Mendoza's work is not always comic, there is an unmistakable humor that
animates its course. Incisive, yet forgiving, it plucks out the marrow
without crushing a bone.

Crossing the Great Pond of the Atlantic and moving a bit to the South,
we come to the Argentine Fernando Sorrentino, a humorist quite apart
from Mendoza, an artist of multiple shades who paints his tales with a

thinner, harder brush, prickly on the edges. [4] He splashes no broad sweeps of society, although the single beings he posits can spin off into legions. And therein lies the cast of his vision—the absurdities that arise from the foibles of individuals, the complacencies, the vanities, the inborn hostilities, the inevitable stupidities. Yes, there is a bristle in his brush that strips away the veneer, and where the pigment is thickest, probes with a scalpel-tip the wound that lies beneath. And still, Sorrentino's novelettes and stories are really very funny, subtle-funny, cynical-funny, grotesque-absurd-whimsical funny, even in an unguarded moment, tender-wistful-self-questioning-funny. These are a few of his tales.

Sanitarios Centenarios is the very amusing history of the Spettanza Bathroom Fixture Company and its rise to iconic glory in the firmament of bathtubs, toilets and bidets. It is also the story of Hernando Genovese, an aspiring young writer whom fate has detoured as a hireling of the Persuasive Conviction Advertising Agency—prime mover of the corporation's success—and who weaves his sardonic way through the morass of banality that is the family Spettanza, and the mass of chicanery that is his own adoptive craft. The characters are many and fully-fleshed, each a living, human, breathing cartoon: the Spettanzas, untutored, good-humored, loud, proud, and brash; Hernando, uneasy, supercilious, yet "go with the flow"; his boss, seductive, manipulative, all "go for the cash." And so they do, with no bounds to their successes and no curbs to their campaign. The world is caught up in their jingles, their television skits and their movie scenarios. Social clichés are set ablaze with the lust for these new status symbols. And the clamor grows as their centennial approaches. Not even the death of the patriarch can quell their celebration as his funeral is held in one corner of the vast, festive stage from which the dancing continues and the beauteous Miss Toilet Bowl majestically reigns.

In short, Sorrentino's *Sanitarios centenarios* is an uproarious and brilliantly contrived piece. It is real; it is fanciful. It engages us with uncommon characters and traps us in unexpected turns. But that is not its sum. For under the cover of laughter—from the dialogue that veers from

---

[4] The short story writer Fernando Sorrentino, born in Buenos Aires in 1942, spans the literary gamut of humor with more than 30 works of fantasy and the everyday, children's books, screenplays and food for the sophisticate. Although his stories appear in many collections of Latin American humor, they are especially known abroad, where they have been translated to date into at least 13 foreign languages: English, Italian, German, French, Finnish. Hungarian, Polish, Bulgarian, Chinese, Vietnamese and Tamil. His other works include series of personal interviews with Jorge Luis Borges and Adolfo Bioy Casares.

commonplace to seditious, from the portraits that move from gentle to snide—a bitter-sweet, raspy-voiced, brown-grey image appears. The fact is that Sorrentino's laughter, in this tale and in many of his others, is a laughter of discomfort, of people who really don't like each other; who turn their frustrations in upon themselves or spew their hostility onto others—not usually in violent eruption, but with a subtle, unspoken urge for revenge. His perspective is not broadly social, although society weighs unequivocally on each of his beings. It is the individual whom he targets more than the whole. And we laugh because we share his discomfort, and it feels good to know that somebody is "getting even" for us.

Despite their consistent undercoat of shade and of tone, there is a notable diversity within Sorrentino's stories. Some are of undeniable social thrust, like "Ars Poetica"—the narrative of an extraordinarily ungifted young poet whose father's money and strategic deployments convert him into a literary lion, "crowned with ivy and eternal laurel." There are those like "Mi amigo Lucas" whose Kafkaesque figures traverse an oxygen-less surface, flailing their arms to be sure they're alive. Lucas, for one, is a man so mild, so timorous, that he crosses the street whenever someone approaches; a man ignored by his colleagues, passed over by his employer; and so effaced by his wife and his son that he is not given a key to his very own home. And nevertheless... nevertheless... whenever he boards a trolley or a bus, Lucas becomes a very different person. There is no maneuver known to mankind or yet to be discovered that he does not employ to discomfort the driver and every one of the passengers around him. So deft is he at these slow, mini-tortures that when he descends from the conveyance and walks toward his house, he is flushed with the fever of success, victorious at last. But the joy soon subsides as he waits on his doorstep ... till his wife concludes her assignation with his employer inside.

There are stories of petty piques that turn to murderous desire, like "In Self-Defense," and "The Fetid Tale of Antulin." And there are those almost childlike fantasies, like the fable of "Piccirilli"—a man whom the narrator finds living on his bookshelf, a figure the size of an index finger, dressed like Dumas' hero D'Artagnan—and "There's a Man in the Habit of Hitting Me on the Head with an Umbrella," the tale of an obsessive little nuisance who in the end becomes essential to the narrator's existence. Curiously, Sorrentino's protagonists are frequently writers; more often than not, males on the defensive; and almost invariably "me, I, yo." How many of them, we wonder, are Sorrentino himself? And at whom is he laughing?

The last of our three authors is the late Ricardo Garibay, story-teller, novelist, screenplay writer, and journalist, a social observer and a satirist of dark, slashing tones.[5] His venue is Mexico; his subject, the spectrum of its people; his technique, a hyper-realism so keenly astute that we find our own flesh invaded, our privacy exposed. And he does it with the scantiest of "stage sets"; his narrative, the spoken word. In his *Diálogos mexicanos*, for example, it is seldom a savory that he offers; at the most, a lick of bitter-sweet. But his sketches are funny because we can hear ourselves talking, and wonder where Garibay was hiding the day he listened in.

Take the story called "Acapulco," a brief encounter between two couples vacationing with their children on the beach, and trying to convince themselves, and each other, that their lives are exactly what they want them to be. Or read "Una muchacha problema," in which a modern young woman tries to buck the stereotypes of her society, only to find that the "problem" everyone else perceives is nothing more than herself... Is it just the irony of these moments that makes us chuckle? Or is it because these people are just like us, and their words, which we too have spoken, seem so ludicrous in the black and white of print? Other times, many times, in fact, Garibay's thrust is political, and he brutalizes his caricatures with deliberate overkill. He draws smug party bosses and the flunkies who jump to their call; police who see only rule books, not the meaning of law; elected officials who take turns in office, trusting in no one, themselves unworthy of trust... and he lets them speak in a language that is real, to the last vulgar phrase, to the last contortion of speech. But the portraits he paints have no fine pencil lines; only layers of pigment on a tautly held sheet. Garibay casts their images in blotches of unequivocal colors, dripping them, spilling them right from the can. He denudes his figures of dimension, deprives them of shades, and mocks them with the despair of a Larra,[6] sobbing as he laughs... Then why do we find them

---

[5] Ricardo Garibay (1923-1999) one of the most astute observers of contemporary Mexican society, was the author of five novels, diverse works for theatre and screen, and of hundreds of newspaper articles, short stories and satirical vignettes. Aside from *Diálogos mexicanos*, his major works include the novels *La casa que arde de noche* and *Par de reyes*.

[6] Mariano José de Larra (1808-1837) was born during the turbulent time of the Napoleonic invasion of Spain and spent the early years of his life in France, where his father had taken refuge after rendering medical services to the enemy regiments. Returning to Spain in 1817, after the restoration of the Spanish monarchy, he enjoyed a remarkable career as a journalist and satirist, and his essays remain among the most incisive, yet broadly humorous portraits of a depleted society mired in glories past. Deeply affected by the repressive monarchy

funny? Perhaps because there is something so familiar within the grotesque that we have learned to accept it as a matter of course. We take the reprehensible and live with it because it's too hard to reject. It's so much easier, isn't it, to smile than to stand up and protest?

We have taken only a sampling of three unique humorists—Eduardo Mendoza, Fernando Sorrentino, and Ricardo Garibay—of their vantage points, visions, and the palettes of their art. We have measured the decibels of their laughter, the contours of their smile. We have seen them subtle, witty, irreverent, snide, brutal, sometimes vicious, or with the fancy of a child. And each time we chuckle, or chortle, or laugh with them aloud, do we know at whom we're laughing? Do we even know why?

Now would you like to hear a funny thing that happened on the way to the publishers?

Works Cited

Garibay. Ricardo. "Acapulco" and "Una chica problema." *Diálogos mexicanos*. Mexico, D.F.: Joaquín Mortiz, 1979.
Mendoza, Eduardo. *Sin noticias de Gurb*. Barcelona: Seix Barral, 1991.
—. *La ciudad de los prodigios*. Barcelona: Seix Barral, 1986.
—. *El misterio de la cripta embrujada*. Barcelona: Seix Barral, 1979.
Sorrentino, Fernando. "Mi amigo Lucas." *Hispanoamérica en 50 cuentos y autores*. Buenos Aires: Ediciones Latinprens, 1973.
—. *Sanitarios centenarios*. Buenos Aires: Editorial Sudamericana, 2000.
—. "Ars Poetica." *El mejor de los mundos posibles*. Buenos Aires: Plus Ultra, 1976.
—. *En defensa propia*. Colección Narradores argentinos contemporaneos. Buenos Aires: Editorial de Belgrano, 1982.

---

of Ferdinand VII and by an unfortunate love affair, he took his life by gunshot at the age of 28.

COMMONPLACES OF LANGUAGE: HORNS AND DEATH IN ACHILLE CAMPANILE

GREGORY PELL

Achille Campanile (1899–1977) is famous for his "battute" (one-liners)[1]. But his one-liners are not necessarily the result of brilliant comedic artifice; no, they come to us through a keen ability of observation and recording. The mechanisms of Campanile's humor in his short, quippy phrases are the sorts of events that one would witness daily—daily absurdities that Umberto Eco describes as "già messi in circolazione dalla letteratura o dal costume quotidiano" ("already circulated by literature and by everyday customs") (271 My translation).

Let us take, for example, an excerpt from one of Campanile's ultra-brief texts ("Presentazione") found in *Tragedie in due battute* (literally "Tragedies in two [punch-]lines," but which I would render as "Two-line Tragedies"), which is really an excerpt from the linguistic interactions found in life itself:

> Interlocutor 1: Permette? Sono Ettore Fragola. E Lei?
> Interlocutor 2: Io no.
>
> Interlocutor 1: If I may. I am Ettore Fragola. And you, sir?
> Interlocutor 2: I am not. (Campanile 56).

The very structures of common parlance offer raw material to Campanile—and to his readers, if only they would realize how fragile language, and therefore existence, can be. In *Two-line Tragedies*, he demonstrates most nakedly his approach, even to novels and plays: if a context is presented properly, any language has the potential for hilarity. Delmo Maestri points out with some satisfaction Campanile's comicity that focuses more on situation and wordplay than on character; that in fact

---

[1] See Achille Campanile, *Tragedie in due battute* (*Two-line Tragedies*), Milano, Rizzoli, 1978. This English title and all other English translations found herein are mine.

Campanile is laughing at NO ONE: "His character advances without any interior complexity; he lacks psychological, moral and ideological stratification; he is flat and repetitive in his behavior, reduced to the motions of a puppet" (87). There is no self-reflexive, philosophical debate about existence as we see in the "umorismo" of Pirandello. Campanile's is comedy for comedy's sake.

Though regarded as a minor writer, now and in his own time, Campanile was considered the Italian Ionesco and also part of the linguistic avant-garde movement. Walter Pedullà (128) reminds us of this fact, and of how in being part of the avant-garde, Campanile was concerned with getting beyond the hegemonic limitations of language itself; besides being absurd, this sort of language is also false ("bugiarda"). Pedullà also remarks how Campanile was happy to live in an absurd world and did not distress over the futility of changing it (123). While *The Naive Wife and the Sick Husband* (1942) discusses the disconnect betwen rhetoric and reality, Campanile's novel, *Poor Piero* (1959), satirizes the inefficacy of proverbial and fixed language in the face of the one event for which we must all be armed with the proper repertoire of words: death.

Perhaps Campanile chooses the absurdist, comic approach, rather than a more Pirandellian existential 'umorismo' when treating death, because there is nothing philosophical about death[2]; it just is. But, what is funny—absurdly funny—is how society attempts to protect itself from death's inevitability and console itself through the convention of trite statements and ready expressions. Therefore, while the comedy of *The Naive Wife* reveals the general confusion of language that can make any context humorous—from the banal to the painful—the comedy of *Piero* poses that what is inscrutable about life is not death, but our own inadequacy to confront death rhetorically, at least without being insincere and unoriginal. We have nothing but borrowed, recycled phrases to offer about even the most singular people when they pass away. In this sense, Campanile forces

---

[2] Michele Mari, in the introduction to *Il povero Piero* (p. iii), notes how un-Pirandellian Campanile is: "Un uomo, in 'L'uomo dal fiore in bocca' è condannato a morire: questa sua situazione lo spinge a indagare nel mistero della vita e a tentare di penetrarne l'essenza." ("A man, in [Pirandello's one-act dialogue] 'The Man with the Flower in His Mouth' is condemned to die: his situation pushes him to investigate life's mystery and to attempt penetrating his true essence.") However, the rhetorical displays that one hears/pronounces at a funeral, in the epitaphs, funeral orations, etc., serve only to show how little we do penetrate that existence; rather, how we stop at the superficial, verbal level of pre-fabricated speech that only stays in the generic, almost infantile and insincere, stages.

us to laugh at ourselves, for we accept the conventions of language and seldom deconstruct it, as if it were fixed, as if it were sacred.

The Naive Wife, narrated by a thief who claims to have witnessed the events through a keyhole, treats the motif of horns, metaphorical and literal, after two protuberances have sprung up on Professor Rune's forehead. Although Rune is bright enough not to reject outright any hypothesis on the origin of his *corneous* growth, all of the others, even the inevitably innocent, chaste wife, Adele, believe that there is only one explanation: that Adele has placed those horns on his head through her infidelity. In an effort to keep his horns a secret—lest society judge him a cuckold *a priori*—Rune falls into a series of misadventures. Among them is a near riot on a train caused by passengers fleeing Rune, whom they mistake for the devil, and Rune's stint in an insane asylum that concludes with his absurd duel with the devil himself: like two bulls, they lock horns as if in a *corrida* without a matador.

Clearly, the motif of *corna*, horns, and their symbolic shame for the cuckold is nothing new in the Italian tradition. As early as the Middle Ages in Italy, the effigy of horns (*cornia bestiarium*) was nailed above doorways of houses inhabited by men whose wives were unfaithful. The folkloric tradition had instilled this into Campanile's society for over 700 years. So, of course, when Rune grows these horns, the society around him prejudges everything in the worst possible sense. In the end, we realize that Adele was innocent after all, albeit the ingenuous victim of an extended metaphor: the commonplace of horns that stand for adultery has allowed society to prejudge the situation and thereby corroborate a perception that supersedes Adele's reality. Additionally, Piero has almost murdered his own lawyer out of a sense of honor, for it was he who had made the unsuccesful advances upon Adele. Despite her rebuffing the lawyer after he forcefully kisses her, the guileless Adele believes that she has committed adultery. Her confirmation? Her husband's *physical* horns.

In *The Naive Wife*, Campanile appears to be laughing at socio-linguistic constructs inherited through tradition whereby the abstract merges with the literal, as seen in the incongruous, absurdly random connection that we have made rhetorically between an illicit tryst and a bestial protuberance on the forehead. Oddly, though his novel revolves around marital issues, Campanile does not write a novel on the nature of love and betrayal; rather, on the relationship of phenomena, objects and behavior with the very medium of words that supposedly represent them. It is as if after living in a society obsessed with the concept of getting horns (*le corna*), Campanile realized how utterly arbitrary this notion is.

Beyond any symbolic meaning of infidelity, the horns themselves are truly whimsical. Recall that when Rune gets the horns, most people think that it is a logical consequence of his wife's cheating—even his wife believes this, despite her chastity. Yet, if we remove the metaphorical context, as the narrator suggests, we realize that our very linguistic system has predisposed his characters to this absurdity: "apart from any metaphor, it would have been just as absurd to have chosen a tale or a trunk" (38).

The disconnect between phenomenon and language is so great that at one point the surgeon who was supposed to remove Rune's horns is confused about his patient's absence. Since Rune is not there for the appointment, the accompanying doorman offers his opinion: rather than separating the horns from his head, Rune knows the correct remedy to his problems is to separate himself from his wife. As a scientist, the surgeon assumes that there is no medical connection between Rune's malady and his wife's actions, and queries: "Ah, so it's not because of his horns that he wants to separate?" (108) When the doorman retorts that Rune wants to separate because of his metaphorical horns and not his real ones, the surgeon exclaims: "That's rich! He'll tolerate real horns but not imaginary ones" (idem), and in one line he reveals that Campanile's characters, in Bergsonian fashion, have modelled phenomena and objects on their ideas and not vice-versa (Ferroni 38).

The Devil himself makes an appearance very late in the novel when word finally gets to him that someone has been passing as the Devil. The Devil "goes up" to investigate and has an encounter with Rune, with whom, as mentioned above, he will engage in a horn-locking contest. The deferred appearance of the real Devil reminds us that even as the characters model Rune's horns on their preconceived folkloric view of infidelity, they have arbitarily excluded any other symbolic interpretation, such as the horns of the devil who represents a more universal view of sin, illicit comportment and immorality. In fact, in Italian we say: "Speak of the devil, and his horns appears." Yet, here we spoke of horns without even considering the devil until he leaves us no choice, appearing infelicitiously and almost purposefully in the story—as if he had felt the need to remind the characters, and the readers, of the obvious connection. Campanile has subverted that expression and revealed how language does not represent a reality; rather it presents even the most false realities that are corroborated by a majority, however ill-informed that majority may be. Until now, all had presumed Rune's protuberances to be the physical manifestations of his wife's infidelity. Yet no one had concluded that the horns might have been proof of professor Rune's identity as the Devil himself. Perhaps in Campanile's contemporary culture the dishonor of being a cuckold greatly outweighed the fear of the devil or of the sin incarnated in his person. By allowing the Devil to appear so late in the novel, Campanile may have been highlighting the horns of infidelity as being the equivalent to the notion of 'a fate worse than death'.

Olga, Adele's sister-in-law, notes that Adele's fatal error has been to confound a metaphor with reality (81). But Adele counters by saying: "What do I know? I hear again and again: get the horns, get the horns; and I believe it my fault" (idem.). Adele comes syllogistically to a reverse conclusion: since infidelity brings a man horns, and Rune has horns, it follows that she must have been unfaithful. This perception is corroborated by the unanimous view of the society around her to the point that her reality is effectively changed. Through the combination of her ingenuousness and society's historic-linguistic beliefs, one truth has been exchanged for another. Though Adele was never unfaithful, Rune's horns are an irrefutable manifestation of her betrayal, for that is the only way in which folk culture could interpret such a corneous protuberance.

Hence, the hegemony of language: when facile rhetorical constructions are repeated enough, people will see the first example of its physical manifestation as inherent and irrefutable proof. This is especially dangerous in a society that would make a man a murderer of his wife or her lover rather than simply allow him to divorce her (as we have seen in such films as Pietro Germi's 1961 *Divorzio all'italiana*, and in real life). In one scene, Rune, thinking of defending his honor, handles a revolver and asks his lawyer what sentence he might risk by killing his wife's lover. His lawyer appears less concerned about a potential murder than about whether Rune has a permit to carry the weapon (109).

On first glance, it seems as if the novel, *The Naive Wife*, were a mere conduit for easy jokes, such as: "What could a doctor know about horns; in your shoes I would go to a veterinarian" (49). The presence of the rare verb "cornificare" ('to cuckold') seems forced, as if to say that Campanile created a 200-page context just so that its insertion would seem natural. He sets up situations in which a comment that would normally NOT be funny——"watch out for the chandelier" (60)— becomes one of the funniest lines in the novel when directed at Rune who, with his horns, has gained extra height; with the unwieldy horns, even negotiating household furnishing and décor becomes fraught with tragicomic potential. Likewise, in *Poor Piero*, Campanile does not miss a chance for an easy, formulaic one-liner. For example, consider the moment when Piero's father-in-law addresses one of four men pushing a coffin on a cart: "Can you satisfy a curiosity: who is the deceased?" (174), to which the other replies: "The one in the coffin." (idem.) However, on further inspection, we realize that in both novels, Campanile laughs at the disconnect between words and objects; metaphor and reality. He attempts to dissolve the most basic commonplaces, as in the early exchange, in *Poor Piero*, involving the timid, ceremonious doctor who asks whether the moment is opportune to enter the patient's room: "Disturbo?," queries the doctor, to which Piero replies matter-of-factly: "Gastrico" (16). The *battuta* relies on the following: the word "disturbo" can be the singular, masculine noun meaning "ache" or "disturbance"; or it can be the first-person conjugation of "disturbare" for which Campanile's use here, with a question mark, can mean simultaneously "Am I disturbing you?" and "Have you any pain?" Clearly, the patient presumes the latter meaning.

Cuckolds are funny; but death is not. However, when told by a witty writer like Campanile, the story of *Poor Piero* transforms the topic into a hilarious comedy. At the death of Piero, his immediate family attempts to respect his bizarre and inexplicable last request: that they give word of his death only after the rites of his funeral have been celebrated. (Perhaps Piero knew that all of the rhetoric and ceremony on the part of the mourners would have been nothing but the typical formulaic, pre-programmed words and actions of a society of puppets to language.) The equivocations abound as each one attempts discretion by resorting to seemingly innocuous periphrasis, which only leads to a series of greater misunderstandings. Though initially Piero's corpse is tossed about, carried off and hidden in closets and powder rooms, in the end it proves difficult to hide his death, and his living room soon becomes full of grieving relatives and friends. Thus begin the customary rituals, traditional gestures, and innocent hypocrisies associated with the ceremonies of death. There are the conventional condolences, the negotiations with the funeral directors, the floral arrangments, the obituary announcements, and letters from friends and loved-ones full of phrases ready-made for the occasion. This is compounded by erroneous reports of the death of Piero's friend and by Piero's own unanticipated revival, followed by the venting of his anger at the fact that his loved ones disregarded his dying request. As the novel alternates laughter and tears in its characters' cavortings, a series of adventures crescendos with surprises and misinterpretations.

In *Piero*, Campanile does not overlook the commercial aspect of death. In the metalinguistic deconstruction of obituaries, epitaphs, telegrams, head stones, and the circumstantial dialogues that surround death, we imagine that the *death business* is profitable for all and that the commonplaces of funerary expressions lack such sincerity that even anonymous third parties can seemlessly interject themselves. Just such a situation presents itself in the novel. At one point, two people by the name of Mr. and Mrs. Nicoloni, who had no prior personal connection with the deceased, Piero, and who just happened to be passing by the typographer's office, overhear Piero's obituary announcement. So moved are they by Piero's obituary announcement that they feel profound esteem for the deceased. In fact, their esteem is so profound that they offer to sponsor a few lines in his death announcement, though perhaps with an ulterior commercial motive as it concludes with: "THE DILIGENT AND UPRIGHT NICOLONIS / PRODUCERS OF THE RENOWNED NICOLONI AND CO. SALAMIS" (177). Another example is the advertisement for the funeral home: "Impeccable service, maximum precision" (65). "Which means," one character imagines, "that they don't send to the other world a living person instead of a deceased one" (idem). Campanile even examines convention and rhetoric in the tombstone carver, whose wife reprimands him for being too jovial in his place of business while customers—in this case, Piero's next of kin—are present: "So, I ought never be cheerful. I must be sad if we have no clients, because there is no work; and I must also be sad when we have them. And the more clients there are, the sadder I must be, while, logically, it ought to be the opposite" (143).

Of course, the most obvious comment on the stale, exaggerated, rhetoric that surrounds funerary ritual is the inflated, insincere panegyric found in epitaphs. Many otherwise average, even sinful, people are raised to near-saint status at their funerals, the grieving attendees choosing disingenuously to focus on only the good in the deceased. Though people might not normally think of a man as "ever-faithful' or "loving," they might not question the hyperbolic use of the prefix "ever-" that precedes "faithful." For when a death has just occurred, it would be impolite to scrutinize the degree of faithfulness of the deceased. So attendees of a funeral either say nothing or nod their heads, lest they contradict the pronouncement and open themselves up to a rebuke for having the audacity and the pettiness to question the character of a man who has just completed the ultimate voyage. Such a case where prefabricated, boilerplate expressions come to be associated with death is found while Piero's in-laws read off the wording for the tombstone to the marble worker: "Incorruptible citizen, indefatigable worker, exemplary spouse and father" (158-159), to which another carver queries: "Oh, he was also a father" (159)? "Yes," replies Piero's brother-in-law, "to an ever-faithful, loving son." Hearing that the son was "ever-faithful and ever-loving," the worker queries with a tone of sympathy: "His son is deceased, too?" Clearly, the son is alive and well, but language has placed him among the

368   Commonplaces of Language: Horns and Death in Achille Campanile

dead. This reflects society's experience with these insincere expressions that place human beings in a dichotomy of immoral behavior: only non-living people are irreproachable; any living person is, by default, the opposite. On this dichotomy Piero's wife replies to the worker's conclusion: "What does that mean? Can't he be alive AND ever-faithful and loving" (idem.)?

We witness further instances of rhetorical commonplaces associated with death when, for example, even as Piero's friends mourn him at his house, signor Giamboni announces erroneously that Piero's friend, Paolo Demagisti, has also passed away. He reports this because when he asked an acquaintance about Paolo, the latter replied: "He has ended his suffering...now he's better off than we are" (215). Demagisti, we later learn, had just had a bad tooth extracted. But before this fact is elucidated, the abovementioned expression, usually pronounced euphemistically about the dead, set in motion a whole series of events, the most humorous of which is the question of etiquette among the mourners. At one point, Piero's brother-in-law, Luigi, sees a visitor standing to one side in tears. As if he were asking the man at a wedding whether he is present for the bride or the groom, Luigi says: "Excuse me, are you crying for Piero or for Demagisti" (204)?

The conventions of language and etiquette have set up a situation in which genuine tears and grief must be categorized. At one point, Piero's widow, Teresa, exclaims that with all due respect for other people's grief, in her house there will be tears only for Piero and not for Demagisti (206). One visitor who values etiquette over authentic emotion opts not to cry at all, so as not to appear suspect (idem.). Another who prefers to honor Teresa's convention, inadvertently demonstrates a cold, inhuman lack of compassion, saying that—quite frankly—he could not care less about Demagisti's death (207). Finally, as if death had gradients or degrees even in its absoluteness, there is a discussion of corporeal warmth, as in 'the body is still warm'. However, here the term takes back its literal meaning in an absurd dialogue, when a member of Piero's family is insulted that one might grieve for Paolo when Piero's body is still warm (metaphorically). Seeing only the literal aspect, one visitor remarks: "I understand, but Paolo's is a bit warmer" (210).

In *Poor Piero*, Campanile exaggerates the absurdity of convention when the unthinkable happens: Piero returns to life. The circumstances are unprecedented for the ready-made language of Campanile's society, and suddenly the inclusion of the prefix "ex" to the words "defunct" and "widow" render them comedic. Moreover, what does one say, after all, to a man who has just revived? A certain signor Palaez, for example, offers to Piero his "most sincere wishes for a most happy resurrection" (218). Even more amusing is how the ex-widow implores the ex-defunct to feign death so as not to cause her weak-hearted brother-in-law, Pantaleo, to have a heart attack. Pantaleo's wife, Elisabetta, says to Piero: "Don't tell Pantaleo that you've come back to life. He would die" (256). To this, the newly revived Piero reacts: "Please. You want me to play dead so that he won't die." In the end, Piero does die—a second, definitive time. It seems that he had to die in order to allow society to return to its easy, albeit insincere and pre-programmed, rhetorical responses to life and death. He must, for this society could not see the irony and inanity of its own words.

In conclusion, I refer to an example of Campanile's ability to point out how routinized and platitudinous language can become—even how factually illogical it can be on the subject of death's inevitability. To illustrate this, Campanile allows a question to be posed by Piero's father-in-law, Marcantonio, as a reaction to the former's first death: "Impossible. Who could have ever imagined such a thing" (41)? To this the narrator responds quite sarcastically: "What would be unimaginable is someone not dying at all, I believe" (41).

Works Cited

Bergson, Henri. *Il riso. Saggio sul significato del comico.* Milano: BUR (Rizzoli), 1961.

Campanile, Achille. *Il povero Piero* (*Poor Piero*). Introduzione di Michele Mari. Milano: BUR (Rizzoli), 2002.

—. *La moglie ingenua e il marito malato* (*The Naive Wife and the Sick Husband*). Milano: Rizzoli Editore, 1984.

—. *Tradegie in due battute.* Milano: Rizzoli Editore, 1978.

Eco, Umberto. "Ma cosa è questo Campanile?" *Sugli specchi e altri saggi.* Milano: Bompiani, 1985: 271-279.

Ferroni, Giulio. *Il comico nelle teorie contemporanee.* Roma: Bulzoni, 1974.

Maestri, Delmo. "Achille Campanile: ritratto di umorista." *Critica letteraria* (Vol. 1, 2003): 79 – 96.

Pedullà, Walter. *Le armi del comico. Narratori italiani del Novecento.* Milano: Mondadori, 2001.

THE GROTESQUE AND VERISIMILITUDE IN DARIO FO'S THEATRE

MARCO VALLERIANI

The grotesque and verisimilitude are intrinsically linked; indeed, one can hardly reflect on or discuss one of the concepts without referring to the other, either to establish or to deny a connection between them. They have in every sense an indissoluble logical connection and this very bond, once on a stage, induces the audience to laugh. In the introduction to *The Grotesque–A study in meanings*, Frances Barasch notes that "In the course of five centuries, the word 'grotesque' has acquired a wide variety of meanings, many of which are still in use" (9). And Goeffrey Galt Harpham, in *On the Grotesque–Strategies of Contradiction in Art and Literature*, underlines that "The word designates a condition of being just out of focus, just beyond the reach of language. It accommodates the things left over when the categories of language are exhausted; it is a defence against silence when other words have failed" (3-4). That is the reason why every time we come to the word "grotesque", its true meaning is hard to grasp: it is in constant evolution. Barasch continues: "At the core of [its] meaning [. . .] is a negation of classical harmony and form, but this negation is applied to a variety of literary matters, and the word 'grotesque' takes on new meanings and connotations with each application" (10).

If we analyse the word 'grotesque' as an adjective in the Italian language, we see that it denotes something bizarre and unusual, capable of inducing hilarity. We laugh because we realise that what we contemplate is out of the ordinary, a surprise for our senses and reasoning. Actually, what is 'ordinary'? It is what our senses perceive in our daily life; it is our everyday experience. In this regard, Gino Gori, in his writings on the grotesque, sets out the principle that the grotesque and verisimilitude are completely antithetical, that one annihilates the other. "The grotesque is that form of art that denies, through philosophical knowledge or ingenious intuition, verisimilitude, laws of nature, fortuitousness; only obeying the unique law of the freedom of the spirit" (62).[1] It is easy to understand that if the grotesque is to be authentic, it has to ignore the 'Laws of Nature'. But what happens when we draw the grotesque close to something that only resembles, but in fact differs from, the ordinary? What happens if we insert the grotesque into a context that merely borders on reality, namely, verisimilitude?

Dario Fo's theatre takes what induces hilarity in everyday life (i.e., the grotesque), wraps it within performing situations that display a plausible alternative reality, and the mixture is ready to explode into loud laughter. Even though the binding connection between the grotesque and verisimilitude is strong and fundamentally important, nonetheless it is possible to appreciate different aspects and to divide them into parts, from the apparently logical to the illogical, from the absurd to the grotesque, from unreality to farce, which is a parody of reality. In short, laughter does not always bear the same meaning.

Before going into the specifics of Dario Fo's theatre, we should address a fundamental question: Why do we laugh? First, laughter has a double psychological component. On the one hand, the object of laughter must not involve feelings on our part: "We do not laugh at the ones we love" (Gori 59). On the other hand, laughter must run counter to our logical reasoning, revealing something that defies logic: "The grotesque creates an irrational anxiety or depression because the world has moved out of its natural order and reason, and the perceiver can no longer find a hold on it" (Barasch 148). For these reasons not everyone laughs at the same things, and laughter is not always an expression of pleasant amusement, as we tend to believe intuitively. On the contrary, laughter can also express and reveal an inner nervous tension of our spirit that cannot be controlled. These components—our psyche, logic and inner nervous tension—make laughter an eminently, and exclusively, human activity. In effect, laughter is the result of a cultural process.

In the course of two decades—mainly, from the end of the 1950s to the end of the 70s—Fo's production developed and became more and more mature. During those years the concept of *culture* itself and of *cultural policy making* became a central issue at a political level as well. But "What does 'culture' mean? Who produces 'culture' and for whom? Bourgeois culture or 'popular' culture, or 'alternative' culture, or 'revolutionary' culture, or 'proletarian' culture? The debate, vague, largely spontaneous and often theoretically unprepared, became central in the

---

[1] All translations are mine unless otherwise stated.

issue of the 'theatre' as well as in the issue of cultural production in general" (Binni 39-40). In Italy, that debate often lead to heated arguments between Croce's vision, on one side, and Gramsci's,[2] on the other, and the concepts of culture seemed to be of at least three types: Tylor's, that defines culture as the whole of the activities and intellectual and manual products of human beings-in-society; a second type, more specifically American, that narrows the concept to values or models that guide individual-social behavior; and a third, that links culture to the universe of signs or symbols of communication" (Cited in Cirese 122). Dario Fo seems to belong to this third trend. Responding in an interview, he replied: "Cos'è la cultura? È una visione diversa del mondo, è il modo di parlare, è quello che ti proponi di fare arrivare, non a te solo ma a tutti gli altri" ("What is culture? It is a different vision of the world; it is the way you talk, it is what you intend to convey, not only to yourself but to everybody") (Binni 4).

The effect of the grotesque in performance arises, then, from the contrast between reality itself (which does not and cannot become compatible with that *new vision of the world*) and the theatrical scene (by contrast immersed completely in that *new vision*). From this point of view, reality itself takes on ridiculous connotations and becomes grotesque to the extent that it makes people laugh. The result is not a normal, light-hearted laughter, but a laughter filled with consequences because it is induced by a grotesque reality. In fact, according to Fo, who gradually distanced himself from the variety shows that we recall from his early days,[3] the grotesque is precisely the real world, everyday life, the struggle between the oppressors and the oppressed, between the captains of industry and the workers. The grotesque is part of this struggle, but Fo's representation of reality is not at all a naturalistic one. Instead, from the point of view of that aforementioned *new vision*, it transfers reality to the stage, and the reality on stage appears to be, and in fact is, a truthful representation for those who share the same vision and perspective as Dario Fo. On the other hand, for those who do not share that vision, the reality depicted on stage is so

---

[2] Benedetto Croce (1866–1952) was an Italian philosopher and literary critic. Antonio Gramsci (1891–1937) was an Italian political theorist and politician, a founder of the Italian Communist Party. His work had a great impact on Italian communism.

[3] In the early years of Fo's career, the themes of challenge to the establishment, protest against despicable aspects of Italian society and Roman Catholicism were merely the tapestry for diverse performances (theatre as well as radio and television) whose true objective was primarily laughter.

far removed from what they consider to be objective reality as to be perceived as the height of grotesque.

The method applied here is spontaneous and yet well-rehearsed: if reality, with all its negatives, were to be performed on stage as it is, the audience would feel merely irritation, a displeasure that would vanish once outside the theatre. That was not what Dario Fo wanted. By transferring and transforming a grotesque reality onto the stage, by making the grotesque border on a potential and indeed possible reality—that is, verisimilitude—it is possible to induce a laughter that gives rise to anger, an anger able to last beyond the performance and ideally able to generate the energy to overthrow the established order of oppressor/oppressed, masters/workers, power-base/people. In this way it is possible to reconcile reality to that *new vision of the world*. Fo himself expressed this concept in a rather vivid way during a debate following the performance of *Morte accidentale di un anarchico* (*Accidental Death of an Anarchist*) in Novi Ligure in 1971:

> Now, the fact that this spectacle might have within it an entire grotesque 'game' is not accidental. We do not want to let the people who come here feel free to leave with just a momentary wave of indignation. We want that rage to stay inside of them, to remain inside and not vent itself, but to become productive, to allow the moment in which we find ourselves to become reflective, so that we might bring it with us to the struggle. (Fo, *Compagni*, 189)

At this point, our initial question should be reformulated and instead of asking ourselves why we laugh, we should ask: 'What makes us laugh'? On this issue, Fo has no doubts, and in his *Manuale minimo dell'attore* (*The Tricks of the Trade*) he gives us an eloquent demonstration in the paragraph devoted to *Tre mimi ciechi* (*Three Blind Mimes*)[4]—an account of a workshop with students of drama and performing arts. With the help of three mimes who perform the same movements, one after the other—

---

[4] Cf. Fo, *Manuale*, 130-131. The manual is basically the account of several workshops that Dario Fo conducted throughout his career: "This publication, in large part, owes a debt to Franca (yet again). It was she who commissioned our collaborators to record—for years and years—every single one of my ramblings [...] even the most unhinged and raving ones, during internships, lectures, seminars, conferences and workshops. And she even took care of transcribing, and having beautifully typed, kilometers of interviews . . . and even of placing them in open site on my work table and even on my pillow before I would retire to sleep" (Fo, *Manuale*, 4).

i.e., an identical scene—and with the complicity of the audience, Fo progressively builds up a different narrative background for each mime: three different situations. The miming objective itself is equal for all: three mimes create and repeat a scene where they look unsuccessfully for a way out through imaginary walls and doors in a sequence of emotions from initial desperation, to temporary hope and to final delusion/ disillusion when they find themselves "completamente accasciati" ("utterly disheartened") (Fo, *Manuale*, 130).

The performing action does not express anything in particular, it is only the situation which gives an independent subtext to the action, a narrative strength able to guide the audience towards laughter. In fact, the first two scenes of the three (a quarrel at a bar and a love affair) run smoothly, enjoyed by the audience with smiles and applause. When a third scene is performed—one of "impellenza tragica" ("tragic desperation")— laughter not only overcomes everyone; it actually explodes: "scoppia un boato" (Ibid., 132). Fo comments: "Well, it is clear that the situation determines the absolute value of the miming action; it changes the meaning of gestures from pathetic to tragic, from subtly humorous to grotesque and obscene. Three identical performances, three theatrical results completely different" (Ibid. 132-133). In this way, Fo shows that the connection with the audience—who become an accomplice under his direction—is fundamental for the performance to be successful.

In the writing and construction of his plays Fo adopts techniques that his wife, Franca Rame, describes as in constant relation with the audience (Fo, *Compagni*, 49), and developed through an improvisation not left to chance but thoroughly planned on and off the stage. Moreover, even unforeseen 'accidents' are an integral part of this construction. What Fo calls the "scienza teatrale dell'incidente" ("theatrical science of the accident") transforms the improvisation into a very effective tool of that silent pact between audience, scene and stage, a pact able to render the verisimilitude (or rather the narrative background of the performing action) psychologically true and acceptable, even though paradoxical and grotesque (Fo, *Manuale*, 98). And the more difficult the 'accident' is to foresee, the more the verisimilitude on stage appears real. Action on stage is always and constantly played to paradoxical extremes and with a non-logical logic, but in spite of that, the audience is able to accept it because of that silent pact.

People who go to see Dario Fo's plays go to the theatre precisely in the expectation of seeing this alternative and plausible world recounted to them, because deep in their hearts they experience it as possible and rational. Dario Fo is able to get his audience to willingly suspend belief, to accept a "possible world" akin to that of opera with its notorious lack of realism (Barasch 145). This is exactly what happens during Fo's *mise-en-scène* as he masters to perfection those psychological mechanisms so inextricably connected with paradox as well as with the narrative techniques we find in farce. In an interview with *la Repubblica* in 2002, he explains that between reality and paradox there is a geometric relation:

> Paradox needs an analysis of the reality, and then it needs a multiple progression, a development with extreme rhythms, outside the usual space. If we imagine reality as drawn on a horizontal plane, paradox is the 'elevation,' of which the ordinary is just a projection: you tip it over, you turn the scene, you look at it upside down, you emphasise what in the scene is secondary and make the main character or situation out of it. (Odifreddi, *la Repubblica* 17 April 2002).

Farce shows the same progression, an actual almost frantic, almost obsessive reiteration of the same comic ploy that leads to the overt contrast between logical expectations related to the *character* involved or to the *main situation* and the farcical incident. And indeed, this was the starting point of Fo's performing career, "short monologues about 'heroes' of bookish history, situations that are grotesquely tipped over: poor Cain— ugly and flat-footed, clumsy and derided by people because of his 'handicap' (poor 'little dwarf')—who is pushed to fratricide, and amusing stories about Julius Caesar, Samson and Delilah, and so on" (Binni 17-18).

As we have noted, Fo's acting career began in variety shows, where laughter is sought through sketches, often intense and extreme, that deride the most common topics of a broadly acknowledged popular culture. Things changed radically in later years when Fo, though firmly anchored in the comic genre, which he deemed more versatile than other theatrical forms, decided to exploit more refined and complex expressive modes. "Within the comic register, I have more freedom to play. I can allow myself to make you laugh and make you feel embarrassed for laughing" (Fo and Allegri 124). This is exactly the technique that has been described so far: Fo engages his audience with an implicit, mutual and silent pact, but at the same time he has no qualms about making this pact explicit and expressing it openly, as he does in the 'Prologue' to *Lu Santo Jullàre Françesco* (*Francis the Holy Jester*): "There is no written source of the text I am going to perform; I have allowed myself the recklessness of reconstructing it through evidence and chronicles of the time. I do not give you an account of that, you have to trust me!" (Fo, *Lu Santo*, 9). On the other hand, he seizes every possible opportunity to provoke his detractors with huge doses of irony. It is especially the case, for instance, when he refers to his sources as he does in *Manuale minimo dell'attore*, where the following note opens the bibliography: "You will find texts with their original title in German or in English. I did it just to impress you" (360).

Fo secures the attention of the audience because he explains unfailingly all his more obscure references, those hooks to publicly acknowledged pieces of information as well as to lesser-known facts. In doing so, he uses prologues and a form of stage-directions delivered in front of the audience (his signature performing style) every time he needs to reinstate that pact between stage and audience. This is the technique seen in *Mistero Buffo (A Comic Mystery)*: following an explanatory prologue, the play itself includes additional explanations in the passages from one scene to another.

As in the examples of *Tre mimi ciechi*, Fo sets the background, the situation in which he develops the action of the play. In *Mistero Buffo*, he creates settings very specific to that moment of *theatrical reality*. He can easily wrap his audience in emblematic situations and bring to life exemplary characters, timeless and adaptable to every age in history, which he can alter and modify according to circumstances. Therefore, for instance, the Middle Ages in *Mistero Buffo* is just a pretext; it is a way of expressing things that would normally be impossible to articulate outside this para-medieval universe. Fo does not need a scientifically accurate Middle Ages, which would add nothing at all to the performance and would in fact burden it with pedantic details; he needs his Middle Ages to be believable, particularly from the point of view of the audience. Therefore, he needs a pseudo-scientific Middle Ages—indeed, verisimilitude. Thus we return to the main point of this discourse, namely that the grotesque and verisimilitude reciprocally support each other and that they are instrumental in expressing the political aims that Fo wishes to pursue in his plays.

In conclusion, I shall offer two examples of 'grotesque' that I would define as *naturalistic*, and two examples of 'objectively grotesque' reality. The first type is linked to the body, with implications of social and political monstrosity and loathing. The second type describes a social and political reality that is grotesque in the sense that the characters involved arouse our indignation and appear to be execrable to the point of being grotesque, even if their bodies are not. Take, for example, the episode of *Moralità del cieco e dello storpio (The Morality Play of the Blind Man and the Cripple*) found in *Mistero Buffo*. In this episode, two human beings with severe physical limitations decide to help each other:

> Guarda che ci starei fino (perfino) a caricarti sulle mie spalle tutto intero, salvo (meno) le ruote e il carrettino! Ci trasformeremmo in una creatura sola da due che siamo… e avremmo soddisfazione entrambi. Io andrei in giro con i tuoi occhi di te e tu con le mie gambe di me» (Fo, *Mistero* 45).

> [Y]ou can be sure that I'd happily take you up on my shoulders, all of you, apart from the wheels and your little trolley of course! We two could then become one… which would make us both happy. I would be able to get around with the assistance of your eyes, and you could get around with the aid of my legs. (Emery, *Comic Mysteries,* 28)

With the cripple on the shoulders of the blind man we have a newly born creature that is overtly grotesque. But the real grotesqueness that fills us with contempt is found in the situation, paradoxical, yet psychologically understandable, and therefore acceptable and real. The situation described is that this creature is chased and pursued by Christ who in the end heals both, but as a result, the cripple immediately starts to despair because he knows that the miracle will be his damnation. Able to walk, he will no longer be free. He will have to work under a master in order to earn his living—a paradox played on a reversal of logic where a miracle is damnation, a curse. The most wicked part of human nature, the one that always wants to gain an advantage, even from the worst situations, is satirised in order to deplore at a social and political level the immutable order of the economic relationship between masters and peasants in the Middle Ages, as well as between masters and workers in Italy of the post-economic miracle of the 1960s.

Another example of the *naturalistically* grotesque comes from the comedy *Il papa e la strega* (*The Pope and the Witch*), where a pope with two heads appears on stage. The morphologically grotesque effect is immediate, but it also represents a dual Church, the kind of Church that Fo criticises harshly—a Church that indeed acts and responds to two different opposite heads, like the Roman deity Janus, and that cannot choose between the meekness and pauperism of the Gospel and the aggressive and ruthless violence of the power base that the Church endorses instead of obstructing.

Il papa e la strega offers us yet another example of the same ambiguity and dualism, but this time of a highly political nature. The Pope is accused of duplicitous behaviour, and when the nun presses him with questions on the topic of Christian poverty, he replies:

> Dove volete arrivare? Ah, siete furba voi!! Sotto, sotto state tacciandomi addirittura di doppiezza e ipocrisia. (Fo, *Il papa*, 52).

> What are you implying? Oh, but you are a sly one, indeed!! After all is said and done, you are actually accusing me of duplicitousness and hypocrisy."

The theme of the grotesque is played entirely against the backdrop of Italian politics, where the accusation of *doppiezza* was typically directed against the parliamentary Left—especially the Communist Party—that on one hand appeared to accept the rules of a liberal democracy, but on the other never gave up the idea of carrying out the Socialist revolution. Here are two realities, both grotesque, paradoxical, and incompatible: one cannot be on the side of the poor and at the same time share the rule of the power base, just as one cannot carry out the revolution without taking up arms and taking to the streets.

A final example is that of Pope Boniface VIII from *Mistero Buffo*, who for Fo epitomises power. In the following extract from *Mistero Buffo*, when Christ kicks him away from the cross, the Pope rages:

> Cristo! Una pedata a me?! Bonifacio! Il Principe! Ah, bene... canaglia... malnato... Oh se lo sapesse tuo padre... disgraziato! Capo degli asini! Senti non ho paura a dirtelo che mi fa piacere vederti inchiodato: che oggi giusto mi voglio ubriacare, voglio togliermi il piacere di ballare... ballare! Andare a puttane!!! Perché sono Bonifacio, io... Principe, sono! Mantellone, cappello, bastone, anelli... tutti! Guarda come luccicano... canaglia... Bonifacio, sono! (Fo, *Mistero* 127)

> Christ! Kicking me?! Me, Boniface! The Prince! Ah, right! You piece of rabble...! Ne'er-do-well...! I tell you, if your father gets word of this... You wretch! You mother of all asses! Listen, I don't mind telling you that it will give me immense pleasure to see you nailed up; and today I'm going to get myself drunk! I am going dancing...dancing! And whoring!!! Because I, I Boniface... I am a prince! Cloak,

> mitre, staff, rings… and everything! Look how they
> glisten… Rabble! I, I am Boniface!

And here is the core of Dario Fo's theatrical experience. With Fo's powerful personification of papal power, of a pope so full of arrogance that he grotesquely wants to replace the Christ in his Passion, the spectator has no difficulty in acknowledging this character as verisimilar, even though he is not a faithful representation of the historic Pope.

The performing strength of Dario Fo lies precisely in this recurrent deployment of grotesque and surreal, yet verisimilar, situations; in the constant reversal of perspective between reality and paradox; in that pact with an audience that willingly relinquishes scepticism and simply accepts what it sees, even when logic would suggest otherwise. In Fo's words, it is the strength of a "great, authentic comic, who wants to penetrate reality and, if necessary, fights injustice with injustice, an injustice that overflows any limit, snatching, doing all he can to get by, clashing with any sense of order, and in doing so is really saying that the world needs a different order, needs a certain madness with a human touch" (Fo, *Totò*, 53-54).

Works Cited

Barasch, Frances K. *The grotesque – A Study in Meanings*. The Hague, Paris: Mouton, 1971.

Binni, Lanfranco. *Dario Fo*. Firenze: La nuova Italia (Il Castoro 123 Series), 1976.

Cirese, Alberto M. *Intellettuali, folklore, istinto di classe*. Torino: Einaudi, 1976.

Fo, Dario. *Compagni senza censura: teatro politico di Dario Fo*. vol 1. Milano: Mazzotta, 1971.

—. *Compagni senza censura:teatro politico di Dario Fo*. vol 2. Milano: Mazzotta,1973.

—. *Il Papa e la strega*. Copione per il suggeritore, Armando Senarica, con correzioni manoscritte durante le prove e gli spettacoli de "Il papa e la strega", Versione precedente a quella destinata alla Casa Editrice Einaudi, 1989 <www.francarame.it>.

—. *Lu santo jullàre Françesco*, Franca Rame (ed.). Torino: Einaudi, 1999

—. *Manuale minimo dell'attore*. Torino: Einaudi, 1987.

—. *Mistero Buffo. Giullarata popolare*. Verona: Bertani Editore, 1977.

—. *Mistero Buffo – Comic Mysteries*, Emery E. (trans.), Hood S (ed.), London, Methuen Paperback, 1988

—. *Totò: manuale dell'attor comico*, Torino, Enna: Aleph, 1995.

Fo, Dario and Luigi Allegri. *Dario Fo, dialogo provocatorio sul comico, il tragico, la follia e la ragione con Luigi Allegri.* Roma, Bari: Laterza,1990.

Gori, Gino. *Il grottesco e altri studi teatrali*, Ed. Giovanelli, P. D. Roma: Bulzoni, 1978.

Harpham, Geoffrey G. *On the Grotesque – Strategies of contradiction in art and literature.* Princeton, Guildford: Princeton U P, 1982.

Odifreddi, Piergiorgio. "Come la geometria è entrata nei miei misteri buffi." *La Repubblica*, 17 April 2002.

CONTRIBUTORS

Nicolino Applauso, who received his PhD in 2010, is currently a Visiting Assistant Professor of Italian at Susquehanna University. He specializes in thirteenth- and fourteenth-century Italian literature with emphasis on political invective and comic poetry during wartime and the ethical weight of such humor in the works of Rustico Filippi, Cecco Angiolieri, and Dante Alighieri. He is currently working on a book titled *Curses and Laughter in Medieval Italy: Dante and the Ethics of Humor in Political Invective Poetry,* an article on Cecco Angiolieri and his exile (forthcoming in *Letteratura Italiana Antica),* and a study on the political reception of Dante during Berlusconi's *Seconda Repubblica* (forthcoming in *Mediaevalia).*

Isabel Castro-Vázquez Ph. D. is Associate Professor of Contemporary Spanish Literature and Cultural Studies at Towson University, Maryland. Her research interests in Galicia and ecocriticism permeate her most recent papers. Dr. Castro-Vázquez wrote the first comprehensive study on the writings of Manuel Rivas (*Reexistencia*, Xeráis, 2008) as well as essays such as "Rosalía de Castro y Emilia Pardo Bazán *En salvaxe compaña*: Un acercamiento ecofeminista a la literatura rivasiana" in *Voces de Galicia,* "De 'Las medias rojas' a Medusa: La mujer silenciada de los siglos XIX a XXI" in *La literature de Emilia Pardo Bazán* or "Entrevista a Manuel Rivas: Memoria, nación y globalización" in Hofstra Hispanic Review.

Zenia Sacks DaSilva is a Professor of Spanish at Hofstra University where she specializes in Cervantes, humor in Hispanic literature, and advanced language studies. She is the author of many textbooks (with Harper and Row, HarperCollins and Macmillan). She has also edited and contributed essays to three scholarly volumes: *The Hispanic Connection: Spanish and Spanish American Literature in the Arts of the World* (Praeger, 2004), *Don Quixote: The First 400 Years* (Lima, Peru: Universidad de San Marcos, 2009) and now, *At Whom Are We Laughing?: Humor in Romance Language Literatures* (with Gregory M. Pell). She is currently co-editing a volume entitled "The Decade of the Thirties: The Reality and the Promise" to be published shortly by Cambridge Scholars.

Jessica Milner Davis is an honorary research associate in Letters, Art and Media, University of Sydney, and convenes the Australasian Humour Studies Network (http://www.sydney.edu.au/humourstudies). She took her doctorate at the University of New South Wales (Sydney), later serving as Deputy Chancellor. A life member of Clare Hall, she has held visiting appointments at the Universities of Cambridge (2011) and Bologna (2012). She was 2001 President of the International Society for Humor Studies, and is an editorial board member of *HUMOR: International Journal for Humor Research* and the *Sage Encyclopedia of Humor Studies*. She researches cross-cultural humour and history and theory of comedy. Her first book, *Farce* (1978), was republished (updated) in 2003 and *Understanding Humor in Japan* won the 2008 American Association for Therapeutic Humor humour research book prize. With Jocelyn Chey, she is co-editor of *Humour in Chinese life and Letters* (2011 and 2013).

Christine Evans is Professor of Comparative Literature at Lesley University in Cambridge, MA. She holds an M.A and Ph.D. from Harvard University and a B.A. from Stanford University. She has written and published on Simone Weil and Simone de Beauvoir and, through them, more widely on French literature of the 1920s, 1930s and 1940s. Her work addresses the historical narratives competing for dominance in France after the 1940 defeat, the one defending a Third Republic narrative and the other attempting to dismantle it. Her interest in exile literature was sparked by her work on Weil, who spent four months in New York in 1942, making contact with the exile community already established there.

Manuel S. Galofaro, a native of Madrid, Spain, studied English Philology at the Universidad Complutense de Madrid. After he graduated with a Baccalaureate's Degree, he moved to the US where he completed an Associate's Degree in Computer Information Systems and a Doctorate in Hispanic Languages and Literature. He is presently teaching Spanish language at Hofstra University and Suffolk County Community College, and combines his teaching activities with academic research, particularly in the field of Golden Age Spanish Literature. He is now working on a critical edition of two 'capa y espada' (cloak and dagger) comedies by Pedro Calderón de la Barca.

Steven Gonzagowski received an MA in Comparative Literature from Dartmouth College in 2005. He is currently completing his Ph.D. in Comparative Literature at Rutgers, New Brunswick, with a dissertation on *Imagined Heroes: Imperial Masculinity and Portuguese Nation-Building*.

He is the author of an article, "Restelo Redux: Heroic Masculinity and the Return of the Repressed Empire in As Naus" in the forthcoming (Fall 2013, Palgrave Macmillian) collection, *Sexing the Lusotropics*.

Patricia Han is Assistant Professor of French at Roanoke College. She received her M.A. and Ph.D. in French from Columbia University, where she wrote her dissertation on verbal irony in Baudelaire's *Petits poèmes en prose*. Her present research focuses on the pragmatics of non-standard language use in literature and music by dominant and marginalized social groups. Currently, she is working on an article that examines the conflicting representations of women and women writers by the 19th-century French author Théophile Gautier.

E. Bruce Hayes is an Associate Professor of French at the University of Kansas. His recent publications include *Rabelais's Radical Farce: Late Medieval Comic Theater and Its Function in Rabelais* (Aldershot, UK: Ashgate, 2010) and articles on French Renaissance writers such as François Rabelais and Marguerite de Navarre. He is currently working on a book which examines the uses of humor to condone or incite violence during the French Wars of Religion.

Myriam Krepps, originally from Toulouse, France, is Associate Professor of French at the Pittsburg State University (Kansas), where in 2012 she was recognized for her excellence in teaching. Dr. Krepps' teaching emphasizes French language, culture and cuisine, and poetry from the second half of the 19th century. Her presentations and publications focus on critical approaches to teaching Rimbaud's poetry, French identity in literature, stylistics of the poetic text (including visual elements), and pedagogical approaches to enhancing reading through writing strategies.

Kevin S. Larsen received the Ph.D.in Romance Languages and Literatures from Harvard University in 1983 with a thesis on Gabriel Miró and literary naturalism (directed by Francisco Márquez Villanueva). Since 1998, he has served as professor of Spanish and Religious Studies at the University of Wyoming. He also heads the Department of Modern and Classical Languages of that institution. He has written or edited six books, as well as some eighty articles and book chapters on topics ranging from the Iberian Middle Ages to the mid twentieth century, which have been published in diverse professional journals and collections. Since 2008, he has served as president of the Instituto Ometeca, dedicated since its beginnings in 1987, to the study of the interface between the sciences and the humanities, principally in the Hispanic tradition.

Ana León Távora is Assistant Professor in the Department of Modern Languages at Salem College. She has also taught at Wake Forest University, UNC Chapel Hill, and at her *alma mater,* the Universidad de Sevilla. Her research interests include European modernism and postmodernism, avant-garde artistic representations and experimental writing, James Joyce, and contemporary art and literature. She is the author of several publications on comparative Spanish-English literature. She recently co-edited and co-translated the bilingual art catalogue *Cuban Artists' Books and Prints. Libros y grabados de artistas cubanos: 1985-2008* (J. La Verne Print Communications, 2009) and is a co-author of the book *Dictatorships in the Hispanic World: Transatlantic and Transnational Perspectives* (Rowman & Littlefield Publishers, 2013).

Dolores Martín Armas was born in the Canary Islands, Spain. After receiving a Bachelor's degree in Hispanic Philology she moved to the United States where she earned a Master's degree in Spanish from Michigan State University and a Ph.D. at the University of Colorado at Boulder. Having served as Assistant Professor at the State University of New York in Potsdam, she is currently a Lecturer at Clemson University in South Carolina. Her scholarly interests include feminism and gender representations in contemporary Spanish language novels, humor in literature, and immigration in the cinema and literature of Spain. Her recent book entitled *El amor lesbiano como sustituto del amor materno en cuatro novelas españolas*: *Julia, El amor es un juego solitario, Efectos secundarios y Beatriz y los cuerpos celestes* is awaiting publication.

Maria Montoya, Ph.D., City University of New York, Graduate Center, is Professor of Spanish and Associate Chair of the Department of Modern Languages at St. Joseph's College, New York. She teaches Spanish language and Hispanic literature courses, in addition to contemporary Spanish cinema and culture. Her research interests include the Spanish avant-garde novel of the early twentieth century, and representations of war in Spanish essays and prose fiction. She has recently coedited *Hijas Olvidadas: Two Contemporary Plays by Hispanic Women Writers* (2009), and has published on writers such as Francisco Ayala, Juan Goytisolo, and Benjamín Jarnés.

RoseAnna Mueller, Ph.D. Comparative Literature, teaches Spanish and Latin American Studies in the department of Humanities, History and Social Sciences at Columbia College Chicago. Her articles and chapters appear in many volumes and journals including *Latin American Women Characters, The Hispanic Connection:Spanish and Latin American Literature in the Arts of the World, Hispania, Letras Femeninas, Revista Espaço Academico, Hispanet, The Journal of the Center for Puerto Rican Studies,* and *The Feminist Encyclopedia of Spanish Literature.* Her book, *Teresa de la Parra: A Literary Life,* Cambridge Scholars Publishing, 2012, is the first comprehensive study of the Venezuelan author for English-speaking readers and focuses on de la Parra as a model of Latin American women writers whose influence is being rediscovered and reevaluated.

Stefano Mula is Associate Professor and Chair of the Italian Department, and the Director of the Comparative Literature Program and of the Linguistics Program at Middlebury College, Vermont. His research interests are medieval narrative, in particular Cistercian *exempla*, hagiography, and Arthurian literature. His recent publications include: "Looking for an Author: Alberic of Trois Fontaines and the Chronicon Clarevallense," *Cîteaux. Commentarii Cistercienses* 60 (2009): 5-25; "Herbert de Torrès et l'autoreprésentation de l'ordre cistercien dans les recueils d'exempla," *La Tonnerre des exemples. Exempla et médiation culturelle dans l'Occident.* M.A. Polo de Beaulieu, P. Collomb, and J. Berlioz, eds. (Rennes, 2010), 187-199; "Geography and the Early Cistercian *Exempla* Collections," *Cistercian Studies Quarterly* 46.1 (2011): 27-43.

Gisela Norat is a Professor of Spanish at Agnes Scott College, a liberal arts college for women in Atlanta, Georgia, where she teaches Latina and Latin American women's literature in the Spanish department. She is author of *Marginalities: Diamela Eltit and the Subversion of Mainstream Literature in Chile* and a number of scholarly articles on Latin American and U.S Latina fiction written by women. Her latest research and publications focus on issues of motherhood.

John Parkin is Emeritus Professor of French at Bristol University where he taught from 1972 to 2011, his specialist courses concerning Renaissance literature and French humour. Having published three books on Rabelais and one on humour in Marguerite de Navarre's *Heptaméron*, he is also the author of *Humour Theorists of the 20th Century* (Mellen, 1997) and co-editor of both *French Humour* (Rodopi, 1999) and *Laughter* *and Power* (Lang, 2006). Married and with two grown-up daughters, he now lives in retirement in Bristol.

Gregory M. Pell, co-editor of this volume, is an associate professor of Italian at Hofstra University where he focuses primarily on cinema and poetry. His critical articles examine such poets as Dante, Paolo Ruffilli, Mario Luzi, Davide Rondoni, Tommaso Lisa, and Mario Tobino. On the subject of cinema he has published pieces on such filmmakers as Mihaileanu, Kore-Eda, Sergio Rubini, Vicenzo Marra, Mohsen Melliti and Matteo Garrone. His latest research deals with the non-human animal in Montale (within the context of post-human studies), and with the novelists Vitaliano Trevisan and Angelo Cannavacciuolo. Additionally, he is working on a monograph on the poetics of Davide Rondoni, Seamus Heaney and Jorie Graham.

Rolando Pérez, Associate Professor at the CUNY Graduate Centre in NewYork, specializes in the area of 20th-century Latin American literature, with emphasis on the relationship between literature and art and between philosophy and literature. In this regard, he has written on Severo Sarduy as well as on thePeruvian poet, César Vallejo, and his on-going projects involve the reading of literature vis-à-vis the philosophies of Nietzsche, Deleuze, Guattari, Baudrillard, Badiou, Levinas and others. His most recent book, entitled *Severo Sarduy and the Neo-Baroque Image of Thought in the Visual Arts*, was published by Purdue UP in 2012 and selections from his creative writing have appeared in *The Norton Anthology of Latino Literature* (2011). Forthcoming is an anthology of essays co-edited with Prof. Nuria Morgado (CSI-CUNY) that bears the title, *Sin fronteras: encuentros entre literatura, filosofía, y artes visuals.*

Lisa Perfetti is Professor of French and English, and Associate Dean of the Faculty at Whitman College. Her primary areas of research are humor and gender in the medieval period and the cultural history of emotion. Her publications include *Women and Laughter in Medieval Comic Literature* (University of Michigan, 2003) and an edited volume, The *Representation of Women's Emotions in Medieval and Early Modern Culture* (University Press of Florida, 2005). She has also contributed articles on "Laughter" and "Women in the Audience" to *Women and Gender in Medieval Europe: An Encyclopedia* (Routledge 2006) and has published essays in several other collections and journals, including *Exemplaria* and *Speculum.*

Bernd Renner is Professor of Modern Languages and Literatures at Brooklyn College, where he held the Bernard H. Stern Chair in Humor Studies (2007-9), and of French at the CUNY Graduate Center. He is the author of *"Difficile est saturam non scribere": L'Herméneutique de la Satire rabelaisienne, Études rabelaisiennes* XLV, Geneva, Droz, 2007, and the editor of *La Satire dans tous ses États: Le "meslange satyricque" à la Renaissance française*, Geneva, Droz, 2009. A member of the *Société d'Histoire littéraire de la France*, he has authored numerous articles on early modern literature and culture and is currently working on a monograph on the formation of modern satire in the Renaissance, an edition of the 1549 apocryphal *Fifth Book of Pantagruel*, and a collective volume on the novels of François Béroalde de Verville.

Paul Schulten is emeritus Associate Professor in Ancient History at the Faculty of History, Erasmus University, Rotterdam. He is currently visiting Researcher at Central Michigan University. His research is divided between Ancient Humor and World War I. His latest book, the *Epos of Gallipoli*, was published in 2009.

Paul Seaver's interest in Hispanic humor began in graduate school when he did research on ribald humor in the *Libro de Buen Amor*. Subsequently, he did his dissertation on the 20th-century Spanish author Enrique Jardiel Poncela. In 1995, he held the First International Conference on Hispanic Humor in Philadelphia and another meeting there in 1997 that included the Portuguese-speaking world. As an outgrowth of the latter conference, he founded the International Society for Luso-Hispanic Humor Studies, an inter- and multidisciplinary organization whose purpose is to promote the study and diffusion of research on Luso-Hispanic humor. He served as President of that society from its founding until 2012 when he assumed the position of Executive Secretary. He has written and spoken extensively on Peninsular and Latin American authors and has been an invited speaker on Hispanic humor in both Spain and the United States. Happily retired, he has recently focused his attention on Colonial Spanish Literature.

Yun Shao, who was born in China, studied Spanish and English language and literature at Beijing University between 1988 and 1993. She continued her graduate studies in the United States, first at the University of Wisconsin-Madison and then at Princeton University, before receiving her Ph.D. in Spanish. She is currently an associate professor in the Department of Modern Languages at Clarion University of Pennsylvania. Speaking Chinese, English, and Spanish, she has a wide range of interests in research and scholarship, particularly in cross-cultural and interdisciplinary studies. Her publications include a monograph and several articles on early modern Spanish writers and playwrights such as Cervantes, Calderón, Zayas and others.

Judith Stallings-Ward holds a Ph.D. from Yale University, an M.A. from Middlebury College, and a B.A. from the University of Texas at Austin. She has published on the anarchism of Gandhi and Durruti, the inter-art relations in the avant-garde poetry of Gerardo Diego, and several articles on Cervantes's *Don Quixote*. She is currently working on a book about Gerardo Diego's poetry and its literary adaptations of the neoclassical works of the composer Manuel de Falla and the cubist strategies of the painter Juan Gris. She is an associate professor of Spanish at Norwich University.

Saviana Stanescu is a Romanian-born award-winning playwright whose recent productions include *Aliens With Extraordinary Skills* (Women's Project, NYC; Sacramento, California; Cincinnati, Oklahoma City, Mexico City; published by Samuel French), *Waxing West* (La MaMa Theatre, 2007 NY Innovative Theatre Award for Outstanding Full-length Script), *For a Barbarian Woman* (Fordham/EST), *Polanski Polanski* (HERE, PS122), and *Ants* at New Jersey Repertory. She holds an MA in Performance Studies (Fulbright), an MFA in Dramatic Writing, both from NYU, Tisch School of the Arts, and an ABD in Theatre Studies with the National University for Theatre&Film, Bucharest, Romania. Saviana is Assistant Professor of Playwriting & Theatre Studies at Ithaca College. is the founder of *Immigrants Artists and Scholars in New York.*

Robert S. Stone is an Associate Professor in the Languages and Cultures Department of the United States Naval Academy in Annapolis, Maryland. He is the author of a book and several articles on the depiction of marginalized figures in Spanish works of literature and art. A native of San Antonio who has studied in England and taught secondary school in both Spain and Pakistan, he holds a Ph.D. in comparative literature from the University of Texas (Austin), a Master's in ESL education from Long Island University (Brooklyn) and a B.A. from Columbia College in New York. He is currently completing a series of articles on the *moriscos* in *Don Quixote*; one of these is to appear in the spring 2013 edition of the journal *Cervantes*.

Marco Valleriani is a Visiting Tutor within the Department of Theatre and Performance at Goldsmiths, University of London. He has specialized in theatre, cinema, and other mass media and their political implications within modern society. He holds a PhD from Royal Holloway, University of London with a thesis on *Religious Themes, Storytelling in Christian Art, and Anticlerical Strands in Dario Fo's Mistero Buffo*. Marco's research interests address the reciprocal contamination between theatre and visual arts, in particular the relationship between traditional iconography and gesture; and the theatre of/for the masses within the theatre policy of the Italian Fascist regime. Forthcoming publications include the chapter: "La Scrittura 'sul pubblico': The Fo-Rame Method" (Legenda); and the article "Teatro delle masse e teatro delle élite: Tatiana Pavlova alla regia."

María Jesús Vera Cazorla is an assistant professor of English and Applied Linguistics at the University of Las Palmas de Gran Canaria (Canary Islands, Spain). Ph.D. in the history of modern language teaching in Gran Canaria, she has published numerous articles on topics related to humor studies and the history of education, along with three books: *La ración de gramática de la Catedral de Canarias* (2003), *La enseñanza de las lenguas extranjeras en la isla de Gran Canaria en el siglo XIX* (2005) and *la Real Sociedad Económica de Amigos del País de Gran Canaria y la enseñanza de las primeras letras en el siglo XIX* (2010).

Paul Wright took his Ph.D. in Comparative Literature at Princeton University, where he specialized in the development of political consciousness in Renaissance humanist thought. In addition to teaching at Princeton, he has also been a Visiting Professor at Osaka University in Japan, then a post-doctoral fellow at Villanova University. He is now Associate Professor of English at Cabrini College near Philadelphia. Dr. Wright has taught, presented, and published on the political philosophy of Niccolò Machiavelli, John Milton, Jacob Burckhardt, and Jürgen Habermas—as well as media studies subjects ranging from world cinema to American television. He is currently completing a book entitled, *The Alloy of Identity: Machiavelli's "Florentine Histories" Reclaimed*. Dr. Wright is also at work on a new project about the psychology and politics of cultural immigration in the early modern world.